Cambridge studies in medi

CW01648448

Edited by WALTER ULLM
Professor of Medieval History in t

Third series, vol. 16

THE LAW OF TREASON AND TREASON TRIALS IN LATER MEDIEVAL FRANCE

CAMBRIDGE STUDIES IN
MEDIEVAL LIFE AND THOUGHT

THIRD SERIES

1 *The King's Hall within the University of Cambridge in the Later Middle Ages.* ALAN B. COBBAN

2 *Monarchy and Community.* A. J. BLACK

3 *The Church and the Two Nations in Medieval Ireland.* J. A. WATT

4 *The Spanish Church and the Papacy in the Thirteenth Century.* PETER LINEHAN

5 *Law and Society in the Visigothic Kingdom.* P. D. KING

6 *Durham Priory: 1400–1450.* R. B. DOBSON

7 *The Political Thought of William of Ockham.* A. S. MCGRADE

8 *The Just War in the Middle Ages.* FREDERICK H. RUSSELL

9 *The Two Italies: Economic Relations between the Norman Kingdom of Sicily and the Northern Communes.* DAVID ABULAFIA

10 *The Church and Politics in Fourteenth-Century England: The Career of Adam Orleton c. 1275–1345.* ROY MARTIN HAINES

11 *The Staffords, Earls of Stafford and Dukes of Buckingham, 1394–1521.* CAROLE RAWCLIFFE

12 *Universities, Academics and the Great Schism.* R. N. SWANSON

13 *The Diplomas of King Aethelred 'the Unready' 978–1016: A Study in their Use as Historical Evidence.* SIMON KEYNES

14 *Robert Winchelsey and the Crown 1294–1313: A Study in the Defence of Ecclesiastical Liberty.* JEFFREY H. DENTON

15 *From the Circle of Alcuin to the School of Auxerre. Logic, Theology and Philosophy in the Early Middle Ages.* JOHN MARENBON

THE LAW OF TREASON AND TREASON TRIALS IN LATER MEDIEVAL FRANCE

S. H. CUTTLER

Research Fellow, Department of German
McGill University

CAMBRIDGE UNIVERSITY PRESS

CAMBRIDGE

LONDON NEW YORK NEW ROCHELLE

MELBOURNE SYDNEY

PUBLISHED BY THE PRESS SYNDICATE OF THE UNIVERSITY OF CAMBRIDGE
The Pitt Building, Trumpington Street, Cambridge, United Kingdom

CAMBRIDGE UNIVERSITY PRESS
The Edinburgh Building, Cambridge CB2 2RU, UK
40 West 20th Street, New York NY 10011–4211, USA
477 Williamstown Road, Port Melbourne, VIC 3207, Australia
Ruiz de Alarcón 13, 28014 Madrid, Spain
Dock House, The Waterfront, Cape Town 8001, South Africa

http://www.cambridge.org

First published 1981
First paperback edition 2003

A catalogue record for this book is available from the British Library

Library of Congress catalogue card number: 81-3880

ISBN 0 521 23968 0 hardback
ISBN 0 521 52643 4 paperback

CONTENTS

Preface page vii
Abbreviations ix
Introduction 1
1 THE CONCEPT OF TREASON IN LATER MEDIEVAL FRANCE: LEGISTS, 'COUTUMIERS' AND TREATISE-WRITERS 4
2 THE CRIMES OF TREASON 28
3 JURISDICTION 55
4 PROCEDURE AND THE TRIAL OF PEERS 85
5 PUNISHMENT, FORFEITURE AND PARDON 116
6 TREASON AND THE CROWN 1328–1356 142
7 TREASON AND THE CROWN 1356–1380 163
8 TREASON AND THE CROWN 1380–1422 181
9 TREASON AND THE CROWN 1422–1461 195
10 TREASON AND THE CROWN 1461–1494 213
Conclusion 238
Bibliography 245
Index 263

To my parents, without whom none of this
could have been possible, and to my sister

PREFACE

This book is a revised version of my 1978 Oxford D.Phil. dissertation. Neither the thesis nor the book could have been brought to fruition without the generous financial support over many years of the Canada Council, the Quebec Ministry of Education and the Woodrow Wilson Foundation; nor without the invaluable moral support of the Joshua Lipschitz Society. For the privilege of pursuing my studies in Oxford I owe an especial debt of gratitude to the Warden and Fellows of New College.

The librarians and staff of the Bodleian Library, always of unfailing assistance, made my researches there a pleasure. I received much help, too, from the staffs of the British Library, the Bibliothèque Nationale de France and the Archives Nationales de France. If not for Mlle M. Langlois, M. H. Martin and Mme J. Metman of the latter institution, I should have wasted much more time than I did in working my way through the registers of the Parlement of Paris and the royal chancery. Unnamed for obvious reasons but not unappreciated is the *président de la salle* at the Archives Nationales who bent a few rules and allowed me to work in the stacks. I should also like to thank J. P. Brooke-Little, Richmond Herald, for kindly giving me permission to consult Arundel MS 48 at the College of Arms.

It is a pleasure finally to record my gratitude to the many scholars and teachers who have all contributed in some way to this book: C. C. Bayley, R. Vogel, R. Klibansky, M. P. Maxwell and especially P. V. Tomaszuk of McGill University; Ph. Contamine of the Université de Paris X (Nanterre); the late W. F. Church of Brown University; P. S. Lewis of All Souls College, who supervised an earlier and much shorter version of this work; M. H. Keen of Balliol College; and M. G. A. Vale of St John's College, who examined me for both the B.Phil. (M.Phil.) and D.Phil. degrees, and whose incisive criticism helped me avoid many errors.

Two scholars above all others have had a most profound influence on me. C. T. Allmand of the University of Liverpool, who together with Dr Vale examined my thesis, has taken a keen interest in my studies ever since we first met in Paris at the Archives Nationales in the summer of 1977. I have greatly appreciated his generous advice, his many kindnesses and his friendship. But the person to whom I owe my greatest debt of gratitude is my former supervisor, C. A. J. Armstrong, now Emeritus Fellow of Hertford College. Although in his characteristic modesty he would deny it, I have benefited much more than I can ever repay from his unrivalled knowledge of later medieval English, French and Burgundian history, his unerring guidance in all matters of scholarship, and his warm friendship. Enlivened by his trenchant wit, our weekly Monday meetings in his rooms at Hertford are my fondest memories of Oxford.

I must thank Professor Ullmann, whose suggestions for revision were invaluable, for including my book in this series. P. M. Daly, chairman of the German Department at McGill University, deserves a special word of thanks for allowing me to take a three-month leave of absence in the winter of 1980 so that I could return to Oxford to finish this book. I am also deeply grateful to George Katkov, Emeritus Fellow of St Antony's College, who most hospitably allowed me to stay in his home during that time.

Many of my friends have read parts of this book in its earlier form, when I was preparing it as a thesis; while others, by perceptive questioning, forced me to clarify my thoughts. Thanks are due to Dr H. Cotton of the Hebrew University of Jerusalem; Dr A. Eisen of Columbia University; Dr M. Gersovitz of Princeton University; R. Herman; Dr S. Herr of Harvard University; B. R. Hoffman; Dr A. Kadish of the Hebrew University; A. Kage; Dr D. S. Katz of Tel-Aviv University; S. P. Koch; L. Ponton; A. Paltiel; N. Ramsay; R. Silverstein; P. Singer; and D. Wasserstein. C. A. Bernheim of the BBC, E. Borod and M.-F. Hill have contributed to this book more than they know.

Lastly, I would like to thank the staff of Cambridge University Press for their professional help in seeing this book through the Press.

ABBREVIATIONS

A.N.	Archives Nationales de France
Anselme, *Histoire généalogique*	Anselme de Sainte-Marie (le Père). *Histoire généalogique et chronologique de la maison royale de France*, continued by M. du Fourny. 9 vols. Paris, 1726–33
B.E.C.	*Bibliothèque de l'Ecole des Chartes*
B.I.H.R.	*Bulletin of the Institute of Historical Research*
B.N.	Bibliothèque Nationale de France
C.D.I.	Collection de documents inédits sur l'histoire de France
E.H.R.	*English Historical Review*
Froissart, *Chroniques*	Froissart, Jean. *Chroniques*, ed. S. Luce *et al.* (Société de l'histoire de France). 15 vols. published. Paris, 1869–1975
Guérin, *Arch. hist. Poitou*	*Recueil des documents concernant le Poitou contenus dans les registres de la chancellerie de France*, ed. P. Guérin (vols. XI, XIII, XVII, XIX, XXI, XXIV, XXVI, XXIX, XXXII, XXXVIII, XLI, XLIV, L, LVI of *Archives historiques du Poitou*)
Lettres de Louis XI	*Lettres de Louis XI*, ed. E. Charavay, J. Vaesen and B. de Mandrot (Société de l'histoire de France). 11 vols. Paris, 1883–1909
l.p.	*livre parisis*
l.t.	*livre tournois*
M.A.	*Le moyen âge*
Mém. soc. hist. de Paris et de l'Ile de France	*Mémoires de la société de l'histoire de Paris et de l'Ile de France*
ms. fr.	manuscrit français
n.a. fr.	nouvelle acquisition française
Ordonnances	*Ordonnances des roys de France de la troisième race*. 21 vols. Paris, 1723–1849
p.j.	*pièce justificative*
Recueil, ed. Secousse	*Recueil de pièces servant de preuves aux mémoires sur les troubles excités en France par Charles II, dit le Mauvais, roi de Navarre et comte d'Evreux*, ed. Secousse. Paris, 1755

Abbreviations

Recueil général des anciennes lois	*Recueil général des anciennes lois françaises*, ed. Isambert, Jourdain and Decrusy. 29 vols. Paris, 1822–33
R.H.	*Revue historique*
R.H.D.F.E.	*Revue historique de droit français et étranger*
s.d.	*sou denier*
S.H.F.	Société de l'histoire de France
s.p.	*sou parisis*
s.t.	*sou tournois*
T.R.H.S.	*Transactions of the Royal Historical Society*

INTRODUCTION

Unlike murder, rape, assault, theft or arson, treason is not easy to define, for it is conceived in abstract political terms. 'Treason', wrote Maitland, 'is a crime which has a vague circumference and more than one centre.'[1] In later medieval France, although specific decrees identified specific offences as treasonable, there was never any precise delimitation of the crime, and what definition there was could be extended by construction. Treason was not just betrayal; it was an injury against public authority as represented by the person of the king and as symbolized by the crown. A felony yet more than a felony, treason was the political crime *par excellence*.

It is clear from even the most superficial reading that treason played a significant rôle in the history of later medieval France. The cases of Bernard Saisset, bishop of Pamiers, in 1301; Godefroi d'Harcourt in the 1340s; Jean de Montfort, duke of Brittany, in 1378; Jean de Montagu in 1409; Jean, duke of Alençon, in 1458; Louis de Luxembourg, count of Saint-Pol, in 1475; and Jacques d'Armagnac, duke of Nemours, in 1476–7 come readily to mind as examples. But it is not so much the treasons as the prosecution of them that will be of concern to us.

Some work, such as R. Guillot's exemplary monograph on the trial of Jacques Coeur in 1451–3, has been done on specific cases.[2] At least one study, Mme Sylvie Troubert's *doctorat de troisième cycle* on the trial of Jacques d'Armagnac, is in progress. Much else, however, remains to be done in other individual cases. More regrettably, there has not been any attempt, large or small, at synthesis, nothing comparable to J. G. Bellamy's comprehensive study on England, to

[1] Quoted in J. G. Bellamy, *The Law of Treason in England in the Later Middle Ages* (Cambridge, 1970), p. 1.

[2] R. Guillot, *Le procès de Jacques Coeur* (Paris, 1975); and see the items in the bibliography under the names Beaucourt, Delayant, Déprez, Fédou, Lanhers, Mandrot, Merlet, Mirot, Rigault and Samaran.

which he has recently added a monograph on the Tudor law of treason, and nothing like J. R. Lander's article on attainder and forfeiture.[3] My aim here is to present just such a synthesis, a balanced account not only of the theoretical framework and legal complexities of the law of treason in later medieval France, but also of the extent and political context of the enforcement of that law. An essay of this kind, of interest in its own right, might also reasonably be expected to shed some light on a larger issue, the interplay of law and politics, authority and power, in fourteenth- and fifteenth-century France.

Any discussion of the law of treason must commence with the contemporary perception of the crime. From the writings of the jurists and the treatise-writers, and from the *coutumiers*, it is possible to trace the principal features of the later medieval French concept of treason. Important in this regard were the evolving notions of sovereignty, obedience and the just war; and one cannot emphasize too strongly the influence of Roman law. Indeed, the reception of Roman law in general meant that the Roman law of treason, essentially the *leges Quisquis* and *Julia maiestatis*, became the basic written authority for the French law of treason. Thus when Louis de Luxembourg, count of Saint-Pol and constable of France, was provisionally condemned to death for manifest treason by the Parlement of Paris on 16 December 1475, *trahison*, the French word etymologically closest to the English 'treason', did not appear in the *dictum*; Saint-Pol, it was declared, was 'crimineux de crime de lese majeste'.[4]

The relationship of law and politics is evinced in one respect by the administration of justice: political authority derives from the maintenance of both public order and private rights; and the exercise of jurisdiction is an exercise in power. In a society in which a single authority exists, the competence of a tribunal is a strictly legal matter; but in a society of conflicting authorities jurisdictional entitlement becomes more of a political issue than a legal one. In later medieval France, because the crown had to contend with the pretensions of seigneurs, towns and above all the church, and because treason was a crime that struck at the heart of royal authority, the

[3] Bellamy, *The Tudor Law of Treason: an Introduction* (London, Toronto and Buffalo, 1979); J. R. Lander, 'Attainder and Forfeiture 1453–1509', *Historical Journal*, IV (1961), 120–51.
[4] B.N., ms. fr. 3869, fols. 37r–38r.

kings and their officers were doubly determined to have sole cognizance of such cases. Political realities, however, often made it difficult for the crown to press to the limit, in opposition to the church, its claims to jurisdiction.

Because of the often vague nature of treason, the decision to prosecute a particular person at a particular time could be a political one. The prosecution itself, in which there could be a great deal of flexibility in matters of jurisdiction, procedure and punishment, could also be determined by political considerations. The most political aspects of all were forfeiture on the one hand, and pardon with full or partial restitution on the other, for the threat of the former and the prospect of the latter could be used as a means of political control. The spoils of forfeitures, furthermore, could be used quite extensively for the purposes of political patronage.

In the course of this study we shall have occasion to examine in detail the several matters that have been alluded to above: the concept of treason; the scope of treasonable crimes; jurisdiction; procedure; punishment; forfeiture; and pardon. We shall also be examining the incidence of prosecution from Philippe VI to Charles VIII for what this might be able to tell us about the policies and characters of the individual kings. As a whole this study of the law of treason and treason trials in later medieval France should contribute to our understanding of the French monarchy's efforts to protect, extend and enforce its authority.

Chapter 1

THE CONCEPT OF TREASON IN LATER MEDIEVAL FRANCE: LEGISTS, *COUTUMIERS* AND TREATISE-WRITERS

I

The concept of treason in later medieval France was a hybrid one. In customary law, for example, the fundamental aspect was that of treachery. In his *Coutumes de Beauvaisis*, written *c.* 1283, Philippe de Beaumanoir proffered a definition of treason that illustrated the vicious nature of that crime. 'Treason', he wrote, 'is when one does not give any indication of hatred but does indeed hate mortally so that, by this hatred, one kills or has someone killed, or assaults someone or has someone assaulted so that he whom one hates by treason is beaten unconscious.' There was no murder without treason, Beaumanoir continued, leading up to an expansion of his definition, but there could well be treason without murder, 'for it is treason to assault someone or to cause grievous injury during a truce or in violation of a safe-conduct or by ambush; or to bear false witness in order to cause someone's death or disinheritance or banishment, or in order to cause his lord to hate him; or for many other similar causes'.[1] Treason, then, as Beaumanoir defined it, was an unexceptional if still malicious crime that he naturally enough classed with the other felonies.[2] It was for him what we should call 'petty treason'. Nowhere, unfortunately, does he broach the topic of treason against the king or the kingdom, doubtless because his primary concern was to explain the customs of the Beauvaisis.

One will find that Beaumanoir differed little from the discussions on treason in such other contemporary works of customary law as

[1] Philippe de Beaumanoir, *Coutumes de Beauvaisis*, ed. A. Salmon (2 vols., Paris, 1899 and 1900), I. 430. For the date of composition see A. Esmein, *Cours élémentaire d'histoire du droit français* (14th edn, Paris, 1921), p. 695.

[2] *Coutumes de Beauvaisis*, I. 104, 429.

the *Etablissements de Saint Louis*, the *Usage d'Orlenois*, or the *Livres de jostice et de plet*. The first two of these, however, had gone further than Beaumanoir in asserting unequivocally that 'treason is not by words', and in the implicit definition of certain treasons as violations of an inferior–superior relationship.[3]

To the customary law notion of treason was added the more formal feudal law concept of treason as 'infidelity' – a breach of faith, a violation of a sworn oath to one's lord.[4] The crime in feudal law known as 'felony' was also precisely this breach of adjured fidelity.[5] Equivalent in meaning to 'infidelity' and 'felony' was 'perjury'. This did not signify, as it does today, the wilful giving of false evidence while under oath, but rather the violation of an oath of fealty already made.[6]

Insofar as royal authority was concerned, there was an inherent weakness in a doctrine of treason based wholly on the breach of a sworn oath of fidelity, for 'infidelity' was strictly speaking only an *unwarranted* breach of faith. Loyalty (*fides*, *foi*), it should be stressed, was not absolute and unconditional, but had become the expression of a voluntary, bilateral contract of vassalage cemented by a personal bond. Should a vassal feel grieved, he could seek justice through rebellion by offering formal defiance (*diffidatio*, *défi*), which meant literally a withdrawal of loyalty. Thus the vassal who resorted to war in defence of what he perceived as his rights could not be guilty of treason.[7]

Clearly a conception of suzerainty that legitimized rebellion in such a way could not augur well for the future of royal authority. According to the theocratic view of kingship, however, he who has a sovereign must obey the sovereign's law as a command; he is a

[3] *Etablissements de Saint Louis*, ed. P. Viollet (S.H.F.) (4 vols., Paris, 1881–6), II. 47, 49, 357–8, 454–6; *Usage d'Orlenois* (published in the *Etablissements*, I. 495–520), pp. 499, 517; *Li livres de jostice et de plet*, ed. Rapetti (C.D.I.) (Paris, 1850), pp. 83, 104, 109, 287–90.

[4] E.g., *L'ancienne coutume de Normandie*, ed. W. L. de Gruchy (Jersey, 1881), p. 42; *Summa de Legibus Normannie*, ed. E.-J. Tardif (Soc. de l'hist. de Normandie) (Rouen and Paris, 1896), pp. 38–9.

[5] E.g., B.N., ms. fr. 5040, fol. 172r–v.

[6] Joannes Andreas, *In Sex Decretalium Libros Novella Commentaria* (3 vols., Venice, 1581), Lib. III, Tit. *De Feudis*, cap. 1: 'vassalus dicitur perfidus, id est proditor, et periurus, quia fidelitatem expressam et iuratam violat'.

[7] W. Ullmann, *The Individual and Society in the Middle Ages* (London, 1967), pp. 27–8, 64–5; W. Ullmann, *Principles of Government and Politics in the Middle Ages* (4th edn, London, 1978), p. 152; F. L. Ganshof, *Feudalism*, trans. P. Grierson (New York, 1964), pp. 69–101.

subject (*subditus*) and can commit treason by his disobedience.[8] Somehow the vassal had to be turned into a subject. For if the king were to have extensive legal powers to crush opposition by declaring it treasonable, with all the severe penalties that this would entail, restive barons might then have second thoughts about disregarding royal authority. The key to solving this problem of obedience was found in the Roman doctrine of treason. If one is to understand fully how the jurists, the lawyers, the treatise-writers, the royal officials, indeed the kings themselves comprehended the nature of treason, one must turn, albeit briefly, to the Roman concepts that helped inform their notions and justify their actions.

'Those whom we call "enemies" ', wrote the jurist Gaius, 'the ancients used to call "perduelles", indicating by that word those with whom there could be a relationship of war.' Eventually the external enemy was called *hostis*, while *perduellis* designated the internal one – the traitor. In Roman political thought, *perduellio* was the earliest term for crimes against the state, and, as treason, was essentially military in nature.[9] *Crimen maiestatis*, which came into existence after *perduellio* as a term for treason, proved to be the more comprehensive of the two, however. *Maiestas*, derived from *maior*, represented the sovereignty and *superioritas* of its bearer, which was the *populus Romanus* in republican Rome and the *princeps* in imperial Rome. More than this, it was a confirmation that its bearer was the elect of the gods.[10] Generally speaking, the *crimen maiestatis* was an act or plot the goal of which was to diminish the greatness or security of the sovereign power; and the crime was tinged with sacrilege.[11] Although the *crimen maiestatis* absorbed and superseded *perduellio*, jurists and scholars ever since Ulpian in the third century have argued

[8] G. de Lagarde, *La naissance de l'esprit laïque au déclin du moyen âge* (new edn, 5 vols., Louvain, 1956–70), I. 143; Ullmann, *Principles*, pp. 131–2.

[9] Gaius was quoted in Latin in P. M. Schisas, *Offences against the State in Roman Law* (London, 1926), p. 5 n. 3; see also *ibid.*, pp. 5–7; C. L. von Bar *et al.*, *A History of Continental Criminal Law*, trans. T. S. Bell *et al.* (London, 1916), p. 16; F. S. Lear, *Treason in Roman and Germanic Law* (Austin, Texas, 1965), pp. 10–11; T. Mommsen, *Le droit pénal romain*, trans. J. Duquesne (3 vols., Paris, 1907), II. 244–51.

[10] J. Hellegouarc'h, *Le vocabulaire latin des relations et des partis politiques sous la république* (Paris, 1963), pp. 317–18; R. Bauman, *The Crimen Maiestatis in the Roman Republic and Augustan Principate* (Johannesburg, 1970), pp. 6–8; J. Gaudemet, 'Maiestas Populi Romani', *Synteleia Vincenzo Arangio-Ruiz* (2 vols., Naples, 1964), II. 699–709.

[11] *Digesta Justiniani Augusti*, ed. T. Mommsen (2 vols., Berlin, 1870), 48, 4, 1: 'Proximum sacrilegio crimen est, quod maiestatis dicitur. Maiestatis autem crimen illud est, quod adversus populum Romanum vel adversus securitatem eius committitur.'

that the latter remained a distinct, if not the most important, component of the former.[12] One does come across the term *perduellio* in the later middle ages, but such instances are admittedly rare.[13]

Of all the Roman legislation on treason, that attributed to Julius Caesar[14] was of cardinal importance for the later medieval French law of treason. Although unfortunately there is no extant version of it, the extracts from the commentaries *ad legem Juliam maiestatis* in Book 48 of the *Digest* do make possible a reconstruction of the law. The following crimes are described therein as treason: bearing arms against the state; sedition, armed or otherwise; communicating with the enemy to the detriment of the state; giving material or financial aid to the enemy; desertion or defection; refusing to fight in war; surrendering fortified places; leading an army into an enemy ambush; raising troops or waging war without the authority of the prince; usurping magisterial authority; refusing to leave a province or hand over an army on the appointment of a successor; alienating friendly nations; obstructing the submission of an enemy or a foreign king; killing a magistrate or other person holding *imperium*; executing hostages without the authority of the prince; helping a convicted criminal to escape from prison; and defacing the consecrated statues of the prince.[15]

There was another Roman law, the *lex Quisquis*, from which the later medieval French law of treason drew much of its content. Originally promulgated by the emperors Arcadius and Honorius in 397, it appeared in the *Codex Theodosianus* and was incorporated without abridgement in the *Codex Justinianus*. It stressed that the assassination of the emperors' councillors was treason, 'for they are a part of our body' (*nam et ipsi pars corporis nostri sunt*). It is best known, however, for its provisions on punishment. The traitor was to be executed and his property confiscated to the imperial fisc. Although

[12] *Digest*, 48, 4, 11; Jacobus Gothofredus [Jacques Godefroy], *Discursus Historicus ad Legem Quisquis Cod. ad l. Iuliam Maiestatis* (Geneva, 1654), p. 44; Mommsen, *Le droit romain*, II. 235–6; Lear, *Treason in Roman and Germanic Law*, p. 26.

[13] I have found only five examples: L. Ménard, *Histoire civile, ecclésiastique et littéraire de la ville de Nismes* (7 vols., Paris, 1750–68), II. 23 n. xii; S. Luce, *Jeanne d'Arc à Domremy* (Paris, 1886), *preuve* xx, p. 65; A.N., x2a 8, fol. 321v; B.N., ms. fr. 5040, fol. 172r; n.a. fr. 1001, fol. 76v.

[14] J. E. Allison and J. D. Cloud, 'The lex Julia Maiestatis', *Latomus*, XXI (1962), 711–31; J. D. Cloud, 'The Text of Digest XLVIII, 4 Ad Legem Iuliam Maiestatis', *Zeitschrift der Savigny-Stiftung für Rechtsgeschichte, romanistische Abteilung*, LXXX (1963), 206–32.

[15] *Digest*, 48, 4, 1–6.

the sons, too, ought to be executed because of the corruption of blood now known to exist, their lives were to be spared, but otherwise attainder was to be enforced. Incapable of succession to any property whatsoever, 'they shall forever be needy and poor, the paternal infamy shall accompany them always, they shall never attain any honours', and their existence would be such that 'death shall be a solace and life a death-sentence'. Wives, however, were to recover their dowries, and all the daughters together were to receive a fourth of their mother's property according to the *lex Falcidia*. The females were to be treated with relative leniency on the grounds that punishment 'ought to be softer against those who we trust will dare less because of the infirmity of their sex'.[16]

Except for one example,[17] and even in its weakest form as a synonym for *infidelitas*, the Roman concept of treason had negligible influence in France from the sixth to the eleventh centuries;[18] and it seems to have disappeared altogether after that until the reign of Louis IX. By approximately 1250, however, the notion of lese-majesty had again become familiar in France due to the zeal for learning in Europe that made the study of Roman law not only attractive but relevant as well. English jurists also were not unaffected by Roman notions of treason. For the author known as Glanville, treason was the crime 'quod in legibus dicitur lese maiestatis'. Bracton, too, the most influential of the medieval English jurists, followed Glanville in calling high treason *laesa maiestas*. In England practice was to differ from theory, for the Roman law doctrine of lese-majesty never exerted any real influence.[19] In France, by contrast, though both the intellectually inferior feudal notion of infidelity and that quality of treachery evinced by Beaumanoir, the

[16] *Codex Theodosianus*, ed. G. Haenel (2 vols., Bonn, 1840–2), 9, 14, 3; *Codex Justinianus*, ed. P. Krueger (Berlin, 1877), 9, 8, 5; *Imperatoris Justiniani Institutionum Libri Quattuor*, ed. J. B. Moyle (Oxford, 1903), 2, 22 for the *lex Falcidia*.

[17] J.-F. Lemarignier, 'A propos de deux textes sur l'histoire du droit romain au moyen âge', *B.E.C.*, CI (1940), 157–8.

[18] M. Lemosse, 'La lèse-majesté dans la monarchie franque', *Rev. du moyen âge latin*, II (1946), 5–24; for examples see Gregory of Tours, *Histoire ecclésiastique des Francs*, ed. and trans. J. Guadet and N. Taranne (S.H.F.) (4 vols., Paris, 1836–8), II. 274, 486; III. 282; IV. 88–98; *Capitularia Regum Francorum*, ed. A. Boretius and V. Krause (Monumenta Germaniae Historica) (2 vols., Hanover, 1883–97), I. 205; *Recueil des historiens des Gaules et de la France*, ed. M. Bouquet *et al.* (24 vols., Paris, 1738–1904), III. 323; VI. 179; Richer, *Histoire*, ed. and trans. J. Guadet (S.H.F.) (2 vols., Paris, 1845), II. 223–45; B.N., ms. fr. 7593, fols. 1r–8v; ms. fr. 18425, fols. 11r–15r.

[19] Bellamy, *The Law of Treason*, pp. 4–8, 11, 14.

Etablissements de Saint Louis and the *Usage d'Orlenois*, for example, remained important, it was the Roman notion of lese-majesty that from the second half of the thirteenth century began to play a truly central rôle not only in French thinking on treason but also in political life. For, as we shall now see, 'lese-majesty' had become bound up with the interrelated notions of sovereignty, obedience and war that, having evolved from the vigorous study and exegesis of the texts of Roman law, were the underpinnings of the later medieval French law of treason.

II

In France, as elsewhere on the continent, claims for independence were argued with reference to that most serviceable of maxims, *rex in regno suo princeps est*. This apophthegm, which first appeared in the second half of the twelfth century,[20] rested on two conceptual pillars: *plenitudo potestatis* and *superiorem non recognoscens*. As early as the first years of the thirteenth century an official fillip to French sovereignty was given by Innocent III: in the decretal *Per Venerabilem*, published in 1202, the pope stated, perhaps none too happily, that 'the king certainly does not recognize a superior in temporal matters'.[21] By the late thirteenth century, furthermore, there existed the word *souveraineté*, in which were combined conceptually the two notions of supreme authority and refusal to recognize a superior.[22] Logically the conclusion to the claim that the king of France was independent of all external powers was that he should enjoy all the

[20] G. Post, *Studies in Medieval Legal Thought* (Princeton, 1964), p. 469; M. David. *La souveraineté et les limites juridiques du pouvoir monarchique du IXe au XVe siècle* (Paris, 1954), pp. 57–8. For the debate on the origin of the maxim see F. Ercole, 'L'origine francese di una nota formola bartoliana', *Archivio storico italiano*, LXXIII (1915), 241–94; F. Ercole, 'Sulla origine francese e le vicende in Italia della formola "rex superiorem non recognoscens est princeps in regno suo" ', *Arch. stor. it.*, LXXXIX (1931), 197–238; F. Calasso, 'Origini italiane della formola "rex in regno suo est imperator" ', *Rivista di storia del diritto italiano*, III (1930), 213–59; F. Calasso, *I glossatori e la teoria della sovranità* (3rd edn, Milan, 1957); E. M. Meijers, *Etudes d'histoire du droit*, ed. R. Feenstra (4 vols., Leyden, 1956–73), IV. 191ff, 202ff. See also generally W. Ullmann, 'This Realm of England is an Empire', *Journ. Ecc. Hist.*, XXX (1979), 175–8; W. Ullmann, 'Arthur's Homage to King John', *E.H.R.*, XCIV (1979), 356–64; H. Quaritsch, *Staat und Souveränitat*, vol. I (Frankfurt, 1970), pp. 79–82.

[21] Calasso, *I glossatori*, pp. 44, 123.

[22] David, *La souveraineté*, p. 67. see also J. R. Strayer, 'The Laicization of French and English Society in the Thirteenth Century', *Speculum*, XV (1940), 76–86. For the notion of sovereignty in its European context, see W. Ullmann, 'The Development of the Medieval Idea of Sovereignty', *E.H.R.*, LXIV (1949), 1–33.

prerogatives of the emperor. Because such ideas were engendered by the study of Roman law, it was surely the Roman emperor of late antiquity, the absolute *princeps* of the *Corpus Juris Civilis*, rather than the 'medieval chimera of the Western emperor' that one had in mind. This seems to be the best interpretation of *princeps* in the maxim.[23] If the king of France was indeed the juridical equal of a *princeps*, then one clear sign of his independent status and plenitude of power would be that the *crimen laesae maiestatis* could be committed against him. As early as 1199 that opinion was implicitly if rather casually proffered, and again it was Innocent III who was the source.[24]

The first French jurist to take up the interrelated notions of obedience, sovereignty and war was Jean de Blanot, who was almost certainly at one time a *magister* in the legal *studium* at Bologna.[25] He began by asserting without cavil in his *Commentaria super Titulum de Actionibus*, written *c.* 1256, that the king of France had absolute jurisdiction over all the inhabitants of the realm. Then he posed an hypothetical problem: a baron rebels against the king, enjoining his vassals to come to his aid by virtue of their oath of fidelity to him. Are they obliged to obey him? At first Blanot suggested that it would seem so because, as he argued, it would indeed be a serious offence to break one's oath, especially one that had not excluded the king. But Blanot was only playing the devil's advocate here. A baron who rebelled against the king, he stated, would be guilty of treason under the *lex Julia maiestatis* 'because he is deemed to have plotted the death of a magistrate of the Roman people, or more correctly, because he is deemed to have acted directly against the *princeps*, for the king of France is a *princeps* in his own kingdom, since he does not recognize a superior in temporal matters'. Clearly, as far as Jean de Blanot was concerned the king of France was wholly independent *de iure* as well as *de facto*; and, as the equal of a *princeps*, he ruled not as *primus inter pares* but as a sovereign over subjects. With this status of sovereign came the attributes of the Roman emperor, among which was *maiestas*. Since the hypothetical baron

[23] Ullmann, *Principles*, p. 206.

[24] *Innocentii III Romani Pontificis Opera Omnia*, ed. J.-P. Migne (Patrologia Latina) (4 vols., Paris, 1855), I. cols. 809–10.

[25] Calasso, *I glossatori*, p. 114. For a biographical sketch of Blanot see R. Caillemer, 'Jean de Blanot', *Mélanges Ch. Appleton* (Lyon and Paris, 1903), pp. 51–101.

had no right to levy war, his action would be lese-majesty, and his vassals would naturally in this casc be absolved from their oaths of allegiance.[26]

This passage from the *Commentaria* is in stark contrast to the discussion of the same problem in the *Etablissements de Saint Louis.* There it was stated that the baron's liege men must first seek an audience with the king in order to find out whether or not there had been a *déni de justice.* If there had been, they could then join their lord; but if not, they must abstain from all hostile activity.[27] The *ius resistendi*, hinging on a denial of justice, was thus clearly allowed in the *Etablissements de Saint Louis.* Jean de Blanot, however, would brook no exception: war, any war, against the king by a subject of the realm was treason, for in essence it compassed the death of the king. This treason, moreover, was not primarily infidelity but lese-majesty.

The opinions of Jacques de Révigny, who taught at the University of Orléans *c.* 1270–90,[28] differed markedly from those of Blanot, though Révigny did acknowledge that the ideas which he opposed were rather widely held. Addressing himself to the problem posed by Blanot, he faithfully reproduced the former's conclusion. But although Révigny would not accept Blanot's asseveration, he did allow that lese-majesty would nonetheless have been committed, 'not because the king is a *princeps*, as they [Blanot *et al.*] argue, but because the crime is committed against a magistrate of the *princeps*, for France and Spain have once been and therefore shall always be under the empire'.[29] He admitted elsewhere that *de facto* the king of France did not recognize a superior, but about all this he said, perhaps in exasperation, 'I could not care less'. Although Révigny emphatically

[26] Joannes de Blanosco, *Commentaria super Titulum de Actionibus in Institutis* (Mayence, 1539), fols. 44v–45r; cf. Blanot's *Tractatus de Homagiis*, published in J. Acher, 'Notes sur le droit savant au moyen âge', *Nouv. rev. hist. de droit fr. et ét.*, XXX (1906), 160–1. See also R. Feenstra, 'Jean de Blanot et la formule "Rex Franciae in regno suo princeps est" ', *Etudes d'histoire du droit canonique dédiées à Gabriel Le Bras* (2 vols., Paris, 1965), II. 885; M. Boulet-Sautel, 'Jean de Blanot et la conception du pouvoir royal au temps de Louis IX', *Septième centenaire de la mort de Saint Louis: actes des colloques de Royaumont et de Paris*, ed. L. Carolus-Barré (Paris, 1976), pp. 62–3.

[27] *Etablissements*, II. 75–7.

[28] M. Fournier, *Histoire de la science du droit en France* (Paris, 1892), p. 120. For a biographical sketch of Révigny see Meijers, *Etudes*, III. 59–80; and P. Tourtoulon, *Les oeuvres de Jacques de Révigny (Jacobus de Ravanis) d'après deux mss. de la B.N.* (Paris, 1899), pp. 1ff.

[29] B.N., ms. lat. 4427, fol. 73r, ed. by R. Feenstra as 'Quaestiones de materia feudorum de Jacques de Revigny', *Studi Senesi*, LXXXIV (1972), 394.

denied that France was *de iure* independent of the empire,[30] he could still conceive of treason against the king of France in terms not of infidelity but of lese-majesty.

Apart from Jean de Blanot, another jurist with whom Jacques de Révigny disagreed was no doubt Guillaume Durand, bishop of Mende, whose *Speculum Juris* first appeared *c.* 1271.[31] That Durand was very much influenced by Jean de Blanot is unquestionable. Like Blanot he asserted that the king of France had absolute jurisdiction in his realm.[32] He, too, used the concept of the *princeps*, and there are indications that his *princeps*, like Blanot's, was synonymous with sovereign, for it is the *princeps* who is said to possess the *merum imperium, suprema et generalis iurisdictio, imperium generalis iurisdictionis*, and *auctoritas suprema*.[33] Under the rubric *De Appellationibus*, moreover, and using as his authority the decretal *Per Venerabilem*, Durand expressly stated that the king of France was independent of the emperor. Blanot's influence is most evident in Durand's handling of the problem of the rebellious baron, for the relevant passage in the *Speculum Juris* is almost word for word the same as that in Blanot's *Commentaria*. There was this one difference, however: Durand did not mention at all that aspect of the *crimen laesae maiestatis* that included attacks on the magistrates of the *princeps*. Levying war against the king was treason against the sovereign plain and simple, 'for the king of France is *princeps* in his kingdom, since he does not recognize a superior'.[34]

Of course not every jurist accepted that the Roman law of treason could apply to the king of France. Pierre Jame, a lawyer of the next generation, expressed in his turn a view that was different from those of Blanot, Durand or Révigny. In his opinion the Roman crime of lese-majesty was valid only for the Roman emperor and his

[30] M. Boulet-Sautel, 'Le concept de souveraineté chez Jacques de Révigny', *Actes du congrès sur l'ancienne Université d'Orléans* (Orléans, 1962), pp. 25–6; cf. Post, *Studies in Medieval Legal Thought*, pp. 474, 481.

[31] For a biographical note on Durand see (Dom.) J. Vaissete and (Dom.) C. Devic, *Histoire générale de Languedoc*, ed. and annotated by A. Molinier *et al.* (16 vols., Toulouse, 1872–1905), x. 45–9.

[32] Gulielmus Durandus, *Speculum Juris* (Frankfurt, 1592), Lib. IV, Pars III, *De Feudis*, no. 28 (p. 309).

[33] M. Boulet-Sautel, 'Le *Princeps* de Guillaume Durand', *Etudes dédiées à Gabriel Le Bras*, II. 805–6.

[34] Durandus, *Speculum Juris*, Lib. II, Pars III, *De Appellationibus*, p. 480; Lib. IV, Pars III, *De Feudis*, no. 29 (p. 310); see also Boulet-Sautel, 'Le *Princeps* de Guillaume Durand', pp. 811–12.

magistrates in the strictest sense. By no construction of the law would Jame accept that it could be committed against the king of France. Although the king might be a sovereign, he was not an emperor, even if he wanted to be one; and since, according to Jame, France had never been subject either *de facto* or *de iure* to the Roman people or the emperor,[35] the king was not a *magistratus* either. Yet Jame had clearly not rejected sovereignty for the king of France, having affirmed in several places that the king did not consider the Holy Roman Emperor as his superior.[36] Jame might therefore have attributed to the king the prerogatives of a *princeps*; Jean de Blanot and Guillaume Durand, after all, had done just that. But for Jame it was out of the question. In his rather narrow and fundamentalist interpretation of the law, he proved to be slightly more rigid than Jacques de Révigny. Unfortunately the terms in which he did think of treason against the king are not known, but his brief comments on sovereignty and lese-majesty bear witness to the vigour of the debate that had been begun by Blanot, Durand and Révigny.

Speculation on sovereignty and lese-majesty was not of course confined to France. Italian jurists were influenced by and in their turn influenced the legal and political thinking in France. One might assert, as did the Italian scholar Calasso, for example, that the Sicilian, Marinus de Caramanico, was the first jurist to develop fully the concept *rex in regno suo princeps est* as a general principle. Writing *c.* 1280, Marinus made his contributions to prevailing notions in his *Proemium in Constitutiones Regni Siciliae.* He arrived at the same conclusions in arguing for the independence of the king of Sicily as did his French colleagues for the king of France: the monarch was *princeps* in his own kingdom, and consequently the crime of lese-majesty could be committed against him.[37] More to the point, the Neapolitan jurist Andreas de Isernia upheld the view that the king of France was a sovereign and enjoyed the prerogatives of a Roman emperor. 'There are those nowadays', he wrote,

[35] E. Perrot, *Les cas royaux* (Paris, 1910), p. 29 and n.1; E. Chénon, 'Le droit romain à la *curia regis* de Philippe-Auguste à Philippe le Bel', *Mélanges Fitting* (2 vols., Montpellier, 1907 and 1908), I. 211 and n.4; Post, *Studies in Medieval Legal Thought*, p. 477.

[36] Petrus Jacobi, *Aurea Practica Libellorum* (Cologne, 1575), pp. 163, 165–6, 285.

[37] Calasso, 'Origini italiane', pp. 218–29; Calasso, *I glossatori*, pp. 28, 127–64; Marinus de Caramanico, *Proemium in Constitutiones Regni Siciliae*, in *Utriusque Siciliae Constitutiones* (Venice, 1590), unpaginated.

who declare that the law with regard to *lèse-majesté* applies only to the king of the Romans, that is the Emperor, because all the laws which speak of royal majesty are speaking of the Emperor; but this position is not tenable in law, for the king's law is mightier in his kingdom than the Emperor's in the empire, and kings in practice distrain traitors by their persons and their goods.

Baldus, too, asserted that the king of France was an emperor in his own kingdom, by reason of which all the texts of Roman law could indeed apply to him. And of major importance was Bartolus's treatise on treason, his *Qui Sint Rebelles*;[38] Jean de Terre-Vermeille, whom we shall discuss later in this chapter, drew heavily from this work when he composed his own tractate, *Contra Rebelles Suorum Regum*, in the early fifteenth century.

The maxim *rex in regno suo princeps est* was to have a long history in France. Originally formulated for use in upholding the king's independence *vis-à-vis* the empire and the papacy, it was also used quite naturally in theory and in practice for internal purposes. Sovereignty, for the lawyers, was nothing less than the *imperium* in the Roman sense, the *plenitudo potestatis* that, it should be stressed, bound to the king all the inhabitants of the kingdom, without exception, in the status of subject.[39] It was imprescriptible, inalienable, absolute, *sui generis* and, for Guillaume Durand as for others, not to be placed within the conceptual confines of a feudal hierarchy.[40] As we have seen, the attribution of *maiestas* to the king followed naturally from the maxim. This would enable him to proscribe previously legitimate political activity, such as the right of a baron to wage war in defence of his prerogatives, because such activity would be *laesa maiestas*, and *laesa maiestas* was treason. Although there was undoubtedly a good deal of wishful thinking about the real powers of the monarchy, the very use of this concept of *maiestas* was indicative, it can be argued, of changing political

38 M. H. Keen, *The Laws of War in the Late Middle Ages* (London and Toronto, 1965), p. 76 (Isernia); Chénon, 'Le droit romain', p. 211 and n.5 (Baldus); Bartolus of Sassoferrato, *Qui Sint Rebelles*, in *Glosa in Extravagantes* (Venice, 1489).

39 A. Bossuat, 'La formule "Le roi est empereur en son royaume". Son emploi au XVe siècle devant le Parlement de Paris', *R.H.D.F.E.*, 4th series, XXXIX (1961), 371–81; B.-A. Pocquet du Haut-Jussé, 'Une idée politique de Louis XI: la sujétion éclipse la vassalité', *R.H.*, CCXXVI (1961), 383–98.

40 Boulet-Sautel, 'Le *Princeps* de Guillaume Durand', p. 806; P. Chaplais, 'La souveraineté du roi de France et le pouvoir législatif en Guyenne au début du XIVe siècle', *M.A.*, LXIX (1963), 451; P. Riesenberg, *Inalienability of Sovereignty in Medieval Political Thought* (New York, 1956).

attitudes[41] at least on the part of those who favoured a more powerful monarchy. Treason – lese-majesty – not only pointed to the gulf that separated the king from his subjects but also was increasingly perceived as an impersonal crime. More than mere flesh and blood, the king was a symbol of authority and continuity as well.[42] The prosecution of treason could therefore be construed not as personal vengeance but as a necessary measure to maintain public order.

III

The later medieval French law of treason, nourished by the authority of Roman law, was thus very much the child of royal claims to sovereign rights. From the *Corpus Juris Civilis* the legists, exemplified by Blanot, Durand and to a lesser extent by Révigny, fastened on the notion of a puissant monarchy that might trample some ancient liberties underfoot but that by the same token could also banish violence and disorder. In the process of constructing this new public law to the detriment of feudal principles the legists did not only invoke Roman law; they appealed as well to a higher principle, that of the public good.

Blanot, Durand and Révigny all referred to the *utilitas publica* when they considered the problematic question of divided allegiance. The king of France, it was posed, is at war with the king of the Romans; while a magnate of France is at war with an enemy of his. Both the king of France and the magnate request of the men in the latter's jurisdiction – who are obliged simultaneously to both of them – that they provide service in arms. Who is to be obeyed? Both Blanot and Durand, each using much the same words, argued ultimately that the king ought to be obeyed 'because the king, to whom belongs the administration of the kingdom, summons them for the common good, indeed for the defence of the common country [*patria*] and of the crown'. Durand, carrying his argument even further, asserted that 'for the defence of the *patria* it is permissible to kill one's father'.[43]

41 See Ullmann, *Individual and Society*, p. 27, and *Law and Politics in the Middle Ages* (London, 1975), pp. 102–3.

42 E. Kantorowicz, *The King's Two Bodies: A Study in Medieval Political Theology* (Princeton, 1957).

43 Durandus, *Speculum Juris*, Lib. IV, Pars III, *De Feudis*, no. 30 (p. 310); Blanot, *Tractatus de*

In contrast Jacques de Révigny approached the issue differently, for he did not see it as simply as they did. Apparently the king was to be obeyed, because 'public utility is to be preferred to private utility, and for the defence of the realm one must leave father and mother and children'. But, Révigny then added, what if the Mongols, for example, invaded Burgundy? To whom should one proffer one's assistance then, 'since public utility is in question in both cases'? Although neither Blanot nor Durand posed this question, one might hazard a guess that they would still have given preference to the king. Révigny, however, while not denying to France the quality of common country (*communis patria*), argued that in this case the clear duty of the vassal was to defend his own *patria* first.[44]

Révigny was clearly not as disposed to support a monarchical position as were Blanot and Durand, but he as well as they gave credence to the notion of the public good, which was to have a definite bearing on the law of treason. Throughout the fourteenth and fifteenth centuries, official documents such as indictments, *arrêts*, pardons, or letters of donation regularly contained the charge *inter alia* that the alleged or proven treason had been committed against the public welfare.[45]

Another conceptual element that appeared in the writings of the jurists and in charges of treason in the later middle ages is that of the 'crown' (*corona*). Jean de Blanot referred to it, as did Guillaume Durand; and Jacques de Révigny spoke of the 'corona regis' as the 'communis patria'.[46] What exactly was the crown? Metaphysical, symbolic, even mystical, the crown represented the spiritual union of the king with the community of the realm. Neither wholly

Homagiis, in Acher, 'Notes', pp. 161–2. See also F. H. Russell, *The Just War in the Middle Ages* (Cambridge, 1975), p. 50; and G. Dupont-Ferrier, 'Le sens des mots "patria" et "patrie" en France au moyen âge et jusqu'au début du XVIIe siècle', *R.H.*, CLXXXVIII (1940), 89–104.

[44] Feenstra, 'Quaestiones de materia feudorum', pp. 395–6; see also Boulet-Sautel, 'Le concept de souveraineté chez Révigny', p. 23; and Tourtoulon, *Les oeuvres de Révigny*, pp. 49–50.

[45] E.g., *Thesaurus Novus Anecdotorum*, ed. E. Martène and U. Durand (5 vols., Paris, 1717), I. cols. 1334–6; 'Choix de pièces inédites', ed. H. Duplès-Agier *et al.*, *B.E.C.*, 4th series, III (1857), 271; *Documents inédits pour servir à l'histoire du Maine au XIVe siècle*, ed. A. Bertrand de Broussillon, *Arch. hist. du Maine*, V (1905), pp. 152–4; A.N., JJ 162, no. 362; JJ 170, no. 178; B.N., ms. fr. 10238, fol. 1r.

[46] Blanot, *Tractatus de Homagiis*, in Acher, 'Notes', p. 162; Durandus, *Speculum Juris*, Lib. IV, Pars III, *De Feudis*, no. 30 (p. 310); Révigny, in Feenstra, 'Quaestiones de materia feudorum', p. 395.

separated from nor exactly identical with *rex* or *regnum*, it was common to both. Yet because it was eternal, the crown was therefore distinct from and superior to the physical king and the geographical kingdom.[47] The concept of the crown was thus one more element that served to depersonalize the crime of treason. For the traitor was injuring not only the mortal king but also the immortal and sacred union of king and kingdom.

Admittedly there was some time-lag between theory and application, as the evidence pertaining to treason indicates that the notion of the crown did not appear with any regularity until the 1340s and early 1350s.[48] Thenceforth, however, and particularly during the regency and reign of Charles V, the concept was much used. Pierre Puisieux, for example, advocate in the Parlement of Paris and an adherent of Etienne Marcel, was executed in August 1358 because he was 'false and a traitor to our said lord [Jean II], to us and to the crown of France'. In 1359 Pierre de la Chapelle, mayor of Hesdin, was accused of having plotted 'treasons and alliances against the crown of France in favour of [Charles the Bad,] king of Navarre'.[49] Numerous other documents of the period attest to the importance attached to the notion.[50] In the next century the mystical, religious content in the concept of the crown was made explicit in a letter of Louis XI. Writing to the Parlement on 11 June 1479 the king referred to the late duke of Nemours, who had wanted 'to have me killed and to destroy the holy crown of France'.[51] The king, endowed with a sacred aura, was God's anointed, a theocratic ruler whose duty was to preserve the divinely ordained hierarchy of existence.[52] The implication of all this was clear: treason against the king and the crown was coloured with the hue of sacrilege.

47 Kantorowicz, *The King's Two Bodies*, p. 341; Ullmann, *Principles*, p. 179; Bellamy, *The Law of Treason*, index *sub* 'crown'.

48 For examples see e.g., A.N., X1a 8, fol. 272r–v; X1a 12, fols. 343v–345r; X2a 4, fols. 113v and 220r: JJ 82, no. 601; JJ 87, no. 92; *Actes du Parlement de Paris (1328–1350)*, 2nd series, ed. H. Forgeot (2 vols., Paris, 1920 and 1960), II. no. 4671.

49 A.N., JJ 90, no. 210 (Puisieux); no. 328 (la Chapelle; this document is partially published in *Recueil de pièces servant de preuves aux mémoires sur les troubles excités en France par Charles II, dit le Mauvais, roi de Navarre et comte d'Evreux*, ed. Secousse (Paris, 1755), pp. 158–9).

50 E.g., A.N., JJ 86, nos. 151, 179; JJ 87, nos. 81–2, 106. For some examples from the later fourteenth and fifteenth centuries see JJ 100, no. 27; JJ 111, no. 325; JJ 179, no. 377; JJ 180, nos. 1, 61.

51 *Lettres de Louis XI*, ed. E. Charavay, J. Vaesen and B. de Mandrot (Société de l'histoire de France) (11 vols., Paris, 1883–1909), VIII. 25–6.

52 A. Luchaire, *Histoire des institutions monarchiques de la France sous les premiers capétiens* (2

By divine right the *defensio regni* belonged to the king, and his prerogatives thereto enabled monarchical authority to increase; *defensio regni*, it has been argued, was the thirteenth-century prodrome of the sixteenth-century *raison d'état*.[53] Connected to *defensio regni*, the redoubtable theory of the *cas royaux* was elaborated in the thirteenth and fourteenth centuries in order to extend the jurisdiction of royal courts, particularly the Parlement of Paris.[54] Treason was obviously the most important of the *cas royaux*. Apart from high treason against the king, which by the second half of the fourteenth century could be called lese-majesty in the first degree,[55] there were such other royally defined treasons as insults to or rebellions against royal officers; the counterfeiting of the king's seal and coin; the violation of safe-conducts and safeguards; private war; and crimes committed on public highways. Some examples will be given in the following chapter, but one should note here that the crimes listed above were not always considered treasonable.

Notwithstanding the categories mentioned above, the *cas royaux* were never clearly defined or enumerated, for they were meant to encompass the total dignity and function of the king as public majesty and authority. The vagueness in this matter was no doubt deliberate. That it was vexatious to the feudality was apparent from the first years of the fourteenth century. On the death of Philippe IV the nobles revolted, venting the resentment that they had accumulated over the last thirty years at having had their power, authority and traditional rights reduced. But the charter given by Louis X to the Champenois, for example, in May 1315, and which was meant to assuage them, still reserved to royal justice all those cases that 'touch our royal majesty'.[56] Couched in such general language this provision did not satisfy the numerous nobles who were already apprehensive of the encroachment of royal justice. Attempting to clarify this point and set the jurisdictional lines for cases concerning the monarchy,

vols., Paris, 1891), I. 41–6; A. J. and R. W. Carlyle, *A History of Medieval Political Theory in the West* (6 vols., London, 1903–36), III. 182; M. Bloch, *Les rois thaumaturges* (Paris, 1924).

53 J. R. Strayer, 'Defense of the Realm and Royal Power in France', *Studi in onore di Gino Luzzatto* (4 vols., Milan, 1949–50), I. 289–96.

54 Perrot, *Les cas royaux*.

55 *Le grand coutumier de France*, ed. E. Laboulaye and R. Dareste (Paris, 1868), p. 92; *Ordonnances*, V. 479.

56 C. Dufayard, 'La réaction féodale sous les fils de Philippe le Bel', *R.H.*, LIV (1894), 241–72; LV (1895), 241–90; A. Artonne, *Le mouvement de 1314 et les chartes provinciales de 1315* (Paris, 1912), p. 77.

Louis X declared in September 1315 that 'royal majesty is under stood in those cases that by law or ancient custom may and must belong to a sovereign prince and to no other.'[57] This was no less vague, but Louis was obviously not going to be any more specific.

Naturally enough the feudality could not have been expected to swallow whole these new developments without distaste. Rebellion against the king, because undertaken normally only by the most powerful of magnates, would continue notwithstanding the perilous consequences of defeat. But the lawyers and other writers like Christine de Pisan and Honoré Bovet in the late fourteenth century continued to hammer home the argument that any war other than one levied on the authority of the sovereign was not a true, just war, a *bellum hostile*.[58] This was the principle implied but unexpressed by Jean de Blanot, Guillaume Durand and Jacques de Révigny; and Pierre Jame quite probably shared this opinion. Only the king, as sovereign, could declare public war, because only the king represented public authority. Vanquished rebels, it was clear, could be treated not simply as defeated enemies but rather as traitors.

Just as the sovereignty of the king meant that only he could declare public war, it meant too that only he was ultimately responsible for preserving the *tranquillitas regni*. Indeed, ever since the early middle ages the *raison d'être* of monarchical authority had been the king's functions as preserver of the peace and dispenser of justice.[59] Any infraction of the peace such as private war was therefore an injury to the king, albeit an indirect one, and could be assimilated to treason.[60]

[57] *Ordonnances des roys de France de la troisième race* (21 vols., Paris, 1723–1849), I. 606.

[58] N. A. R. Wright, 'The *Tree of Battles* of Honoré Bouvet and the Laws of War', *War, Literature and Politics in the Late Middle Ages: Essays in Honour of G. W. Coopland*, ed. C. T. Allmand (Liverpool, 1976), p. 22; Keen, *Laws of War*, pp. 68–9, 72, 77; P. Contamine, *Guerre, état et société à la fin du moyen âge* (Paris and The Hague, 1972), p. 203; P. Contamine, 'L'idée de guerre à la fin du moyen âge: aspects juridiques et éthiques', *Comptes rendus de l'Académie des Inscriptions* (1979), 70–86.

[59] See e.g. C. Pfister, *Etudes sur le règne de Robert le Pieux 996–1031* (Paris, 1885), pp. 155–61.

[60] E.g., *Ordonnances*, I. 57. But private war was not easy to extirpate; see *ibid.*, I. 56–8, 328, 390, 492–3, 538, 655–6; II. 61–3. See also Contamine, *Guerre, état et société*, p. 318; R. Cazelles, 'La saisie de la Bourgogne en 1334', *Ann. de Bourgogne*, XXXII (1960), 169–82; R. Cazelles, 'La réglementation royale de la guerre privée de St-Louis à Charles V et la précarité des ordonnances', *R.H.D.F.E.*, 4th series, XXXVIII (1960), 530–48.

IV

In the fourteenth and fifteenth centuries the *coutumiers* and the legists' lucubrations exemplified yet more lucid thinking on the subject of treason. In his *Stilus Curie Parlamenti*, written *c.* 1330, Guillaume du Breuil in effect gave a broad definition when he wrote about the crime of fraud that it 'was not a crime of lese-majesty because it was not intended against the *princeps* or his agent or the public weal'. Clearly he had the *lex Julia maiestatis* in mind here. In a passage from a *coutume* of Anjou and Maine, redacted *c.* 1390, there were definite echoes of the *lex Quisquis*, too. 'A case of majesty', it was asserted,

> is when one plots, conspires or actually effects the death of one's prince or of the men of the prince's council or household or of those who are close to him, because they are called the limbs of the prince; or when one commits any treason against the prince or the aforesaid persons, or to the prejudice of the prince.[61]

Though strictly speaking not a juridical work, the polemical *Songe du verger*, written in the later fourteenth century, is of some interest for its brief comments on treason because the anonymous author synthesized the Roman concept of treason with the feudal notion of infidelity, placing all the while considerable emphasis on the sovereignty of the king of France.[62] The king of England, it was asserted, was guilty of lese-majesty for having falsely claimed sovereignty and jurisdiction without appeal in Guyenne, for having broken his oath 'to keep and affirm the treaty of Calais', and for having supported troops engaging in warlike activities inside France. The retention of lands taken from the English was therefore justified, because 'the crime of lese-majesty is one of the greatest crimes that can be in this century, as it is written *codice ad legem iuliam maiestatis, lege, Quisquis*'. Furthermore, all the subjects of Guyenne, obliged to recognize the sovereignty of the king of France, were thus required to hand over cities, towns and castles to him, for otherwise the king could repute them as 'traitors and rebels'.

[61] Guillaume du Breuil, *Stilus Curie Parlamenti*, ed. F. Aubert (Paris, 1909), p. 122; *Coutumes et institutions de l'Anjou et du Maine antérieures au XVIe siècle*, ed. C.-J. Beautemps-Beaupré (4 vols. in 8, Paris, 1877–97), I (1), 214.

[62] For what follows see *Songe du verger*, in *Traitez des droits et libertez de l'église gallicane*, ed. P. Dupuy (edn of J.-L. Brunet, 4 vols., Paris, 1731–51), II. 162–3, 170, 173; see also J. Quillet, *La philosophie politique du Songe du Vergier (1378)* (Paris, 1977), pp. 21–3.

Jean de Montfort, duke of Brittany, was also castigated in the *Songe du verger* and described as a 'rebel and traitor to the crown of France... who gave counsel, comfort and aid to Edward of England'. Not only had he maintained Edward's men in his towns and fortresses, thereby violating the law and his oath of fidelity to the king of France, who was his sovereign lord, but he also formally defied the king and made war on him in the company of the king's enemies. These, incidentally, as we shall see in chapter 4, were the actual charges to be laid against Montfort at his trial in December 1378. For the author of the *Songe du verger*, then, one committed treason by rejecting the sovereignty of the king of France, and by infidelity; that is, by giving aid and comfort to the king's enemies, and by levying war against him in his realm.

The first comprehensive treatment in the later middle ages of the crime of treason, and one that clearly shows the influence of Roman law, is that to be found in Jean Boutillier's *Somme rural*, written *c.* 1390.[63] Although Boutillier preserved a distinction between *trahison* and *lèse-majesté*, the former had a very limited meaning for him: it was premeditated murder or attempted murder of one's lord, or of anyone else for that matter. When *trahison* was committed against the king it then became *lèse-majesté*, which, apart from that most heinous crime of premeditated regicide, was for Boutillier 'to plot, scheme or conspire in any way soever against the noble majesty of the king our lord'. Additionally, Boutillier's discussion of sedition and conspiracy left no doubt that as in the *lex Julia maiestatis* they were to be included as crimes of lese-majesty when they injured the king or his interests. It is clear, too, that for Boutillier sacrilege was akin to lese-majesty.

So strongly was the crime of treason to be condemned, in Boutillier's opinion, that accomplices of the traitor, or those who consented to the crime, or those who merely had knowledge of the treason but failed to denounce it, should also suffer the capital punishment of the traitor. Even 'if someone so much as thought of committing treason', he, too, should be punished capitally. Punishment as envisaged by Boutillier was gruesome indeed, for he meant it to be so severe and shameful that no one would ever contemplate

[63] For what follows see Jean Boutillier, *Somme rural*, ed. L. Charondas Le Caron (Paris, 1603), I. 28 (pp. 170–5); I. 39 (pp. 279–80).

committing treason. Convicted traitors would be flayed alive, then quartered or burned, and their property would be confiscated to the king. Furthermore, a traitor's children, particularly the males, would suffer a *mort convenable*, 'and the reason is that so horrible and detestable is the crime of the traitor that by its very nature it infects the seed; and therefore the root, stock and seed must be destroyed'. Boutillier did allow, however, that the king by his generosity could spare the lives of the traitor's children, although the king did not thereby have to leave them with their estates intact. Provision would be made only for the daughters, who were to have just one-quarter of their mother's property. Boutillier took most of this straight from the *lex Quisquis*, repeating from that law the argument concerning the weakness of feminine nature; but he added to it by suggesting that females who were guilty of treason should be punished even more severely than men 'because for a woman to think of such wickedness is a thing too inhuman'.

Immediately upon the assassination of Louis, duke of Orléans, on 23 November 1407, and at the behest of John the Fearless, duke of Burgundy, Jean Petit composed his notorious *Justification*.[64] The thrust of Petit's thesis was that the duke of Orléans had been guilty of lese-majesty and therefore deserved death at anyone's hands. Yet apart from the sophistry in the *Justification*, Jean Petit's general remarks on treason are worthy of note because they illustrate concisely some main currents of thought on the subject.

Lese-majesty, he first asserted, echoing the *Songe du verger* and Boutillier's *Somme rural*, was one of the worst of all possible crimes 'because royal majesty is the most noble and dignified thing that can be, and one can commit no greater sin, no greater crime than to injure royal majesty'. The crime, moreover, he divided into degrees: the first degree was direct injury against the king; the second, direct injury or insult to the queen; and the third, treasonable activities against *la chose publique*.[65] Specifically, Petit attainted as traitors those

[64] The *Justification* was published in Enguerran de Monstrelet, *Chronique*, ed. L. Douët-d'Arcq (S.H.F.) (6 vols., Paris, 1857–62), I. 178–242. See A. Coville, *Jean Petit: la question du tyrannicide au commencement du XVe siècle* (Paris, 1932); A. Coville, 'Le véritable texte de la Justification du duc de Bourgogne par Jean Petit (8 mars 1408)', *B.E.C.*, LXXII (1911), 57–91.

[65] Monstrelet, *Chronique*, I. 187–8. There could be differences about the three degrees of lese-majesty. The anonymous author of a *mémoire* prepared for the case of Jean Balue in 1469 argued that the second degree was against 'la chose publique universelle', which 'at present resides in the sovereign prince, since the people have granted him their *ius* and *imperium* and

who made attempts on the life of the king, those who openly maintained alliances with the king's enemies or who obstructed military operations against them, and those who secretly gave aid and comfort to the enemy. Retaining *gens d'armes* that pillaged, murdered and raped; raising taxes only to embezzle them from the royal treasury; and helping convicted traitors to escape from prison were also treasonable in his opinion.[66] In much of this Petit strayed little from the texts of Roman law or the other later medieval writers. But he was innovative in one respect. Although magical practices were included as crimes of *laesa maiestas* in imperial law,[67] and although, as we shall see in the next chapter, they were in fact condemned as such in France from at least the mid-fourteenth century, Jean Petit was the first French writer specifically to describe sorcery and witchcraft as treason when their object was the king. Because, in his opinion, this particular treason was also sacrilege, the death penalty should be a double one: physical death and eternal damnation.[68]

For Petit, one could not punish traitors too severely, though unlike Boutillier he did not have a standard punishment in mind. He argued that the closer one was to the king by blood or office, the greater was one's obligation to him; and therefore the punishment for treason ought to be commensurate with the nature of that relationship. Furthermore, he added, the machinations of those who were close to the king, and who consequently had great power and authority, were much more perilous than the scheming of insignificant men, 'and because more perilous, should entail greater punishment'. Although Petit was obviously thinking here of Louis d'Orléans, his observations were nevertheless natural ones that could be accepted as general principles.

Jean Petit's *Justification* is not the only polemical treatise from which one can glean contemporary attitudes on treason; the *Contra Rebelles Suorum Regum* of Jean de Terre-Vermeille is equally instructive. The author, who had obtained his licentiate in law from

potestas', and that the third degree included crimes against the collaterals of the king; against royal officers; against 'la chose publique particuliere'; and 'in many other ways' described in the civil law (B.N., n.a. fr. 1001, fol. 76r–v; see also H. Forgeot, *Jean Balue, cardinal d'Angers (1421?–1491)* (Bibl. de l'Ec. des Hautes Et: 106) (Paris, 1895), p. 90).

66 Monstrelet, *Chronique*, I. 218–19, 222.

67 C. E. Smith, *Tiberius and the Roman Empire* (London, 1972), p. 179.

68 Monstrelet, *Chronique*, I. 203, 217; for what follows see I. 204–5.

the University of Montpellier in 1395,[69] was inspired to write his treatise by the civil war between the Burgundians and the Armagnacs. Replete with references to the major texts of Roman law and such influential post-glossators as Bartolus, the tractate, though an invective against the Burgundians, illustrates better than any other French source the fusion of the Roman and feudal notions of treason in the later medieval French conception of that crime. With regularity 'crimen laesae maiestatis' and 'infidelitas', or 'proditio' and 'infidelitas' appeared, if not in juxtaposition, at least in proximity the one to the other. Jean de Terre-Vermeille also added a certain theological flavour to his treatise. Again with regularity he referred to the *corpus mysticum* of the kingdom and to the king as the *caput mysticum*.[70] The use of these theological notions in a political context was not new with Terre-Vermeille, for it dated at least from Vincent de Beauvais. It was a perfectly natural conjunct to the mysticism that enshrouded the French monarchy and that was unmistakably evident during and after the reign of Charles V. By illuminating the sacramental functions of French kingship, the theological notions reinforced a widely held attitude that treason was sacrilege. Jean de Terre-Vermeille and Jean Petit certainly thought so, as did Jean Gerson in 1405 and the Parlement of Paris in 1490.[71]

Considering Terre-Vermeille's conception of the divine monarchy, one will not be surprised at his strong opinions on treason. For him, 'omnis infidelitas, proditio, inobedientia aut rebellio commissa per subditum contra principen suum et dominum caput regni Francie . . . aut regni mystici honorem, statum, regimen, potestatem prosperitatemve causat crimen lese maiestatis'.[72] Towns as well as individuals could commit treason, not only by conspiring against the king but also by usurping royal prerogatives. But what specifically constituted treason for Jean de Terre-Vermeille? In his vilification of John the Fearless and the Burgundians he followed

[69] A. Gouron, 'Les juristes de l'école de Montpellier', *Ius Romanum Medii Aevi*, part IV, fasciculum IIIa (Milan, 1970), p. 27.

[70] Joannes de Terra-Rubea, *Contra Rebelles Suorum Regum*, ed. J. Bonaud (Lyon, 1526), fols. 36v, 65v, 68v, 70r, 74v, 77r, 92v, 93v.

[71] Kantorowicz, *The King's Two Bodies*, pp. 208–18; P. S. Lewis, *Later Medieval France* (London, 1968), p. 87; P. S. Lewis, 'Jean Juvenal des Ursins and the Common Literary Attitude towards Tyranny in Fifteenth-Century France', *Medium Aevum*, XXXIV (1965), 105.

[72] Terra-Rubea, *Contra Rebelles*, fol. 74v; for what follows see fols. 36v–37r, 57v, 68v, 70r–72r, 74v, 82r.

closely the categories set out in the *lex Julia maiestatis* and the *lex Quisquis*. Helping by word or deed to introduce armed men into Paris was treason, as were the occupation without warrant of fortified places; incitement to sedition; raising troops or waging war without royal authorization; and the usurpation of public authority in general. If illicitly occupying fortified places was treason, so too and *a fortiori* was delivering the same to the enemy, or refusing to hand them over to the king even after a legitimate occupation. Openly adhering to the king's enemies was patently a treason, and desertion from the field of battle, for Terre-Vermeille as for others, was a most serious treason, particularly when it resulted in the loss of a strategic place. All forms of providing aid and comfort to the enemy, such as sending money or munitions, transmitting state secrets, or preventing the king from properly resisting the enemy, were also treasonable. Obviously bearing in mind the passage in the *lex Quisquis* that began 'de nece etiam virorum illustrium', he included as treason the murder of royal officers; and on this point he was most surely thinking of the assassinations in 1407 and 1418 of Louis d'Orléans and Bernard d'Armagnac, constable of France. Terre-Vermeille also asserted that any opposition whatsoever to royal authority was treason. Here, though, he added a new twist by arguing that treason could be committed as much by omission as by commission; and he would even go so far as to label as traitors those who would not orally and publicly defend the king.

The political and legal writers who followed Jean de Terre-Vermeille added little of significance to the previous notions of treason. Jean Juvenal des Ursins, for example, openly expressed what many perhaps thought, that revolts like the War of the Public Weal were treasonable. It was treason, too, he suggested, to assemble the Estates without permission, because this would be an arrogation of authority that belonged to the king alone. Jean Masuer, a jurist who became chancellor of the duke of Auvergne, spoke of lese-majesty in the first and second degrees against the king and the kingdom respectively, but he did not elaborate on this. Gui Pape, the notable Dauphinois jurist of the mid-century, wondered, in spite of what was by then a commonly held opinion, whether the *lex Julia maiestatis* applied to others than the emperor. It did, he concluded, to those who in fact or law recognized no superior. Since the dauphin as heir to the throne of France had a quasi-sovereign status in his appanage of Dauphiné, it therefore followed that the attempted murder of members of the Parlement of Grenoble, which was a sovereign court, was lese-majesty 'tanquam delinquentes in magistratum [principis]'. Helping a convict escape from prison was also lese-majesty in his opinion, as was the *porte d'armes notable*.[73] But in none of what Pape, Juvenal des Ursins or Masuer wrote were there any significant departures from previous thinking.

From Jean de Blanot to Jean Boutillier to Gui Pape the concept of treason in the juristic thought of later medieval France was, with few exceptions, that derived from Roman law. Essentially it was the king, as the embodiment of public authority, against whom lese-majesty could be committed, but the treatise-writers and legists would include in that crime injuries to the king's family, to his officers, to the kingdom, and to the crown – that legal fiction representing the eternal, spiritual union of the king and the realm.

Yet though the concept of lese-majesty lay at the centre of the later medieval French law of treason, one should remember that the aspects of treachery and infidelity were notionally still very prominent. On 8 September 1369, for example, the royal chancery explained to the *bailli* of Saint-Pierre-le-Moûtier and Bourges that the knight Renier de Saint-Julien had forfeited his property because 'in going against his faith and loyalty, [he] adheres to the party of our enemies . . . of England . . . thus committing the crime of lese-majesty'. The same close association of concepts is evident in a letter written by Charles VII on 28 September 1457 to Pierre de Brézé, *grand sénéchal* of Normandy. Several inhabitants of Caen, he recounted, had been passing sensitive information to the English, and they had done so, 'in going against their oath and loyalty, committing the crime of lese-majesty'. Twenty years later, on 24 June 1477, Antoine Dupont, a proctor and secretary of the town of Lyon, described for the councillors of his city the execution in effigy at Paris of Jean de Chalon, prince of Orange. Beneath the burning effigy, he related, was the published sentence that declared the prince

[73] Lewis, 'Jean Juvenal', pp. 113, 117; see now generally Jean Juvenal des Ursins, *Ecrits politiques*, ed. P. S. Lewis (S.H.F.), (1 vol. published, Paris, 1978). For Masuer see Jean Masuer, *Practica Forensis* (Lyon, 1577), p. 345; there is a brief biographical note on him in A. Bardoux, *Les légistes: leur influence sur la société française* (Paris, 1877), p. 40; Gui Pape, *Decisiones* (Lyon, 1613), pp. 319–20, 404, 525.

guilty of the 'crime of public treason, perjury, felony, infidelity and lese-majesty'.[74]

Thus far we have examined the theoretical framework of the law of treason in later medieval France. Let us now consider evidence from the historical record in order to establish precisely what the range of treasonable offences was.

[74] A.N., JJ 100, no. 106 (Saint-Julien); B.N., ms. fr. 22469, no. 60 (Caen; I owe this reference to Dr C. T. Allmand); Arch. Municipales de Lyon, AA 98, no. 18 (Orange).

Chapter 2

THE CRIMES OF TREASON

I

The English Statute of Treasons, promulgated in 1352,[1] did not have a counterpart in France. This is not to say, however, that there was no French legislation at all: from time to time, as we shall see, the kings of France did indeed publish various kinds of documents, having the force of law, that clarified contentious issues or created precedents. But for the most part, in the absence of a fundamental piece of legislation comparable to the English Statute of Treasons, French royal officials used the adopted Roman laws – the *lex Julia maiestatis* and the *lex Quisquis* – and made their own constructions upon them.

Regicide was obviously the gravest of all treasons. Although all the French kings of the later middle ages died in their sick-beds, in one instance, the death of Philippe IV, charges of criminal responsibility were brought against two of the late king's principal officers: Pierre de Latilly, bishop of Châlons and chancellor of France; and Raoul de Presles, advocate-general. Unfortunately, little is known about this affair. It is clear enough, though, that the accusation was groundless and had proceeded from the enmity of their political opponents, chief of whom was Charles de Valois. De Presles was released in September 1315 for lack of evidence; and the bishop, after a long and desultory trial conducted by ecclesiastical justice that had not finished in 1318, was also released, returning to his see by 1320.[2]

Real or alleged assassination attempts occurred often enough in the fourteenth and fifteenth centuries. Some of these, to be discussed more fully in later chapters, can be briefly mentioned here for the sake of illustration. In late 1355, for example, there was a plan by

[1] Bellamy, *The Law of Treason*, pp. 59–101.

[2] *Registres du Trésor des Chartes*, ed. R. Fawtier *et al.* (3 vols., Paris, 1958–78), II. nos. 299 and 328; F. J. Pegues, *The Lawyers of the Last Capetians* (Princeton, 1962), pp. 67–83.

Charles the Bad, king of Navarre, and several others including possibly the dauphin Charles, to seize Jean II, imprison him in a tower 'and there take away his life'.[3] The king pardoned the conspirators; but at Rouen on 5 April 1356 he arrested Navarre and had four of Navarre's Norman intimates beheaded on suspicion of a similar treason.[4] Poison was a favoured means in attempted assassination, as in 1385 when Charles the Bad plotted to have Charles VI, the royal dukes and other princes murdered with arsenic.[5] In late 1473 the Burgundian agent Jean Hardi tried to have Louis XI poisoned, but like Navarre's agent he too was discovered and paid with his life for his treason.[6] Several years later Louis XI was not able to capture and punish Jean de Chalon, prince of Orange, but he proceeded against him *in absentia*. 'The Prince of Thirty Pennies wanted to poison us', he wrote to the Parlement on 6 June 1478, 'as you shall see from [the transcript of] the investigation that we are sending you so that you can have it read in open court . . . so that everyone can know of [his] great treason.'[7]

To compass the destruction of the dauphin, too, was treason. In late August 1358, soon after the future Charles V regained control of Paris, he wrote to his brother-in-law Amadeus VI, count of Savoy, vehemently denouncing the 'wicked and false treasons' committed by the Parisian rebels at the instigation of Charles the Bad. Foremost were the charges that they had contrived not only 'to have [Jean II, who was then captive in England] die in prison over there', but also 'to . . . murder us and take away our heritage'.[8] In 1476 Jean Bon, the would-be assassin of the dauphin Charles, was fortunate not to be punished capitally, though he did have his eyes gouged out. Injuries to other royal relatives were assimilable to treason. In 1308 one of the charges against Guichard, bishop of Troyes, was that he had poisoned Queen Jeanne of France, who had died in 1305. Mere scandalous behaviour involving members of the royal family could also be construed as treason. Thus in 1314 Philippe and Gauthier Aulnay, minor nobles of Philippe IV's household, were executed as

3 B.N., ms. fr. 7598, fol. 137r.
4 R. Delachenal, *Histoire de Charles V* (5 vols., Paris, 1909–31), I. 150–5.
5 *Recueil*, ed. Secousse, pp. 493–503.
6 Jean de Roye, *Journal, dit Chronique scandaleuse*, ed. B. de Mandrot (S.H.F.) (2 vols., Paris, 1894 and 1896), I. 303–9; A.N., z1h 16, fols. 128r, 141r, 143r.
7 *Lettres de Louis XI*, VII. 90–1.
8 Published in Delachenal, *Hist. de Charles V*, II. 424–32.

'the worst kind of traitors' for their adulterous relationships with the king's daughters-in-law.[9]

Hardly less serious than attempted assassination of the king was conspiracy to seize his person, depose him, or replace him at the helm of government. The persistent machinations of Charles the Bad; the treason of Louis d'Amboise in 1429; the Praguerie; the War of the Public Weal; and the conspiracy of 1474–5, for example, will be discussed in later chapters. Here, however, we can cite the one plot that was not spawned by domestic political intrigue. During the siege of Caen in 1450 Edmund Beaufort, duke of Somerset, promised 4000 *écus* and £50 to Robin Campbell and four other Scots archers of Charles VII's bodyguard if they would help to capture the king and several others in his retinue. Although the plan failed, the treason of the Scots was not discovered until late 1454 at the earliest. After being tried in the Parlement, Robin and John Campbell were condemned on 8 August 1455 to be drawn, beheaded and quartered.[10] Their execution precipitated a minor diplomatic crisis between France and Scotland just as Charles VII and James II were trying to co-ordinate their policies to take advantage of the disturbed situation in England. James II informed Charles VII that the execution of the Campbells and the continuing detention of the others had caused a few people in Scotland to talk 'most evilly' about fomenting a rift between France and Scotland. James therefore made two suggestions: that the transcript of the trial be given to his ambassadors, who would then bring it to Scotland for disclosure in order better to explain Charles VII's actions; and that those still in prison be released. Although Charles VII assented to the first proposal, he was reluctant to be clement with the prisoners. The matter was a most serious one, a royal *communiqué* elucidated, for it touched 'the person of the king . . . and the perdition of the whole army, and from [it] irreparable harm could have happened to the public welfare of his kingdom'.[11] What the *communiqué* did not express, indeed need hardly have expressed, was the fact that the treason was all the more serious for

[9] Roye, *Chron. scan.*, II. 30–1 (Bon); A. Rigault, *Le procès de Guichard, évêque de Troyes (1308–1313)* (Paris, 1896); Guillaume de Nangis, *Chronique de Guillaume de Nangis et de ses continuateurs*, ed. H. Géraud (S.H.F.) (2 vols., Paris, 1843), I. 404–5 (Aulnays).

[10] B.N., ms. fr. 3876, fols. 199r–v; M. G. A. Vale, *Charles VII* (London, 1974), p. 138.

[11] *Letters and Papers Illustrative of the Wars of the English in France*, ed. J. Stevenson (Rolls Series) (2 vols. in 3, London, 1861–4), I. 319–51; see also Vale, *Charles VII*, p. 138.

having been plotted by those who were responsible for the king's safety.

It happened that conspiracies such as the Praguerie or the War of the Public Weal led to armed insurrection. But conspiracy or no, the levying of war against the king was treason for three reasons. In the first place it compassed at least implicitly the destruction of the king or the kingdom. Secondly, it was a violation of the allegiance that a subject owed to his king. And thirdly, it was an arrogation of sovereignty, for the display of banners, the firing of cannon at a siege, the taking of spoil, the holding of prisoners to ransom, the wasting of land, were all part of public war. Since no French subject had the right to resist the king in arms, any acts of public war committed by the former clearly identified as treason his opposition to the crown.[12]

The levying of war does not seem to have been a treason during the reign of Philippe III, nor during the first twenty years of Philippe IV's rule; not even Gui de Dampierre, count of Flanders, was treated as a traitor.[13] The turning point came in the second decade of the fourteenth century, at the time of renewed conflict between the kings of France and Robert de Béthune, count of Flanders since his father's death in 1305. On 11 August 1314, for example, a royal proclamation made it quite clear that the fractious count and his allies, who 'have gone into rebellion against us and are waging war', were committing treason. Once in person, in 1312, and once *in absentia*, in 1315, Robert de Béthune was tried for treason.[14]

Nor did *diffidatio* any longer afford legal protection. Philippe de Navarre, count of Longueville, and other Norman adherents of Charles the Bad learned this after May 1356, and so did Jean de Montfort, duke of Brittany, in the late 1370s.[15] In the fifteenth century Louis XI twice imputed to Charles the Bold, duke of Burgundy, the treasonous levying of war. On the second occasion Louis XI, in his instructions to the Parlement to begin posthumous

12 Keen, *Laws of War*, p. 92; 'Treason Trials under the Law of Arms', *T.R.H.S.*, 5th series, XII (1962), 94–7; C. A. J. Armstrong, 'La Toison d'Or et la loi des armes', *Publication du centre européen des études burgundo-médianes*, V (1963), 77.

13 C.-V. Langlois, *Le règne de Philippe III le Hardi* (Paris, 1887); E. Boutaric, *La France sous Philippe le Bel* (Paris, 1861); F. Funck-Brentano, *Les origines de la guerre de Cent ans: Philippe le Bel en Flandre* (Paris, 1896), pp. 181ff.

14 A.N., JJ 50, no. 62: 'et ont encouru le crime de nostre roial majeste blecie'; *infra*, pp. 95–6.

15 A. N., JJ 84, nos. 606, 640; M. Jones, *Ducal Brittany 1364–1399* (Oxford, 1970), pp. 79–85.

proceedings against the duke, explained *inter alia* that in 1465 Charles, then count of Charolais, 'came in arms against us, took by force ... several places, towns and castles ... laid siege against us before our good town of Paris, and committed publicly ... all exploits of hostility and war'.[16] Warfare against the king, warfare against the kingdom, both were equally treasonable. One can mention as a final example the Breton war of the late 1480s. On 3 June 1487, when the Parlement issued a summons to the prince of Orange, it stated in unequivocal terms that he and the other magnates who were 'in open rebellion of war and have taken up arms against the king' were 'committing by these things the crime of lese-majesty, sedition, treason, rebellion and disobedience'.[17] Nothing could be more clear than this on the treasonous nature of armed insurrection. All the above treasons – attempted assassination of king or dauphin, scandalous liaisons with members of the royal family, levying war against the king, attempts to seize the king or traitorously destroy his army – were also treasons in England.[18]

Unlike open warfare against the king, private war was an indirect affront to him, for his authority could be undermined by unchecked disruptions of public order. Yet although private war was formally proscribed as treasonable, particularly during time of general war,[19] it could in fact be tolerated provided that three conditions were met: the dispute had to be lawful; there had to have been a *déni de justice*; and the conflict had to be limited to physical combat between the parties in conflict. If, however, either of the disputants was known to have committed acts of public war, he would be guilty of treason for the third reason mentioned above, that is, for arrogating sovereignty to himself.[20] A number of cases that came before the Parlement illustrate this point. In Thomas Pineau *v.* Gauthier Carnot in 1362, the king's proctor, also joining issue with the latter, argued that Carnot was guilty of conspiracy, treason and lese-majesty because he had taken spoil and prisoners. In another case the Parlement confirmed in December 1367 that the count of Forez's men had committed treason by having attacked the town of Pouilley-les-Vignes

[16] *Ordonnances*, XVIII. 397 (11 May 1478); for the other instance see *ibid.*, XVII. 353.
[17] A.N., X2a 51, unpaginated.
[18] Bellamy, *The Law of Treason*, pp. 23–58, 87.
[19] A.N., X2a 7, fol. 64r; X2a 13, fol. 171v; Keen, *Laws of War*, pp. 73–4, 92.
[20] Keen, *Laws of War*, p. 109.

'cum armis et vexillis patentibus ad modum guerre'. The law could obtain for magnates as well as for the minor nobility. Archambaud V, count of Périgord, in 1397 and his son Archambaud VI in 1399; Charles, duke of Lorraine, in 1412; and Jean IV, count of Armagnac, in 1441 were all convicted of treason for their private wars against the towns of Périgueux, Neufchâtel and Millau respectively.[21] Although obviously the law by no means deterred all private wars, it was not entirely without effect, for the crown could confiscate the property of those who persisted in flouting its authority. In England private war does not seem to have fallen within the scope of the law of treason. Nor for that matter did free-booting;[22] this is in contrast with the situation in France.

Here, there was a thin line that separated private war at its worst from free-bootery, and a thinner line yet separating free-bootery from outright brigandry. What made the free-booting soldiers' offences treasonable was not the individual felonies but the cumulation of crimes *ad modum hostilitatis.* Thus a pardon granted to the *routier* Guillaume de Cheverouche in December 1371 cited his 'pillaging, robberies, larceny, murders, rapes, spoliations of churches . . . ransoming of people, arson and . . . all other kinds of crimes . . . against us . . . our subjects . . . and our kingdom, committing the crime of lese-majesty'. Lyon Duval's pardon in August 1359 was even more explicit. He and his companions had

> seized and occupied, burned, pillaged and wasted, by treason and otherwise, castles, towns and fortresses, houses and places . . . [they] assaulted, beat, mutilated and murdered several persons . . . secular, religious and clergymen as [much as] others; [they] raped virgins, maidens, nuns, widows and married women; [they] took and imprisoned people, tortured them and took large ransoms from them; [they] broke into prisons and led away the prisoners . . . and committed . . . other serious crimes . . . in doing which . . . they have been guilty several times over . . . of the crime of lese-majesty.[23]

It is worthwhile to mention here the case of the notorious *routier* Mérigot Marchès, for it illustrates some points already discussed in this chapter, and others – the violation of truces and the problem of

[21] A.N., x2a 7, fols. 63v–66v (Pineau *v.* Carnot); x2a 8, fols. 23r–24v (Pouilley-les-Vignes *v.* Forez); L. Dessalles, *Périgueux et les deux derniers comtes de Périgord* (Paris, 1847), *preuves*, pp. 8–30, 77–93; Luce, *Jeanne d'Arc, preuve* xx, pp. 30–72 (Lorraine); J. Artières, *Récits, documents et études sur l'histoire de la ville de Millau. Ière partie: Annales de Millau depuis les origines jusqu'à nos jours* (Millau, 1894–9), pp. 95–9.

[22] Bellamy, *The Law of Treason*, pp. 90–1.

[23] A.N., JJ 103, no. 7 (Cheverouche); JJ 90, no. 240 (Duval).

allegiance – to be considered presently. After a truce organized by Jean de Blaisy in south-central France in 1390, Mérigot not only took possession of the fort of La Roche Vendeux but also waged open war in the vicinity. Eventually taken into custody, he was sent to Paris for trial. At the Châtelet in July 1391 his judges rejected his claim of English allegiance, having established that he had been born in France. Moreover, since he was a Frenchman 'who is not the head of a war, the king can have no formal war and has no defiance from him. Rather has he (the prisoner) by way of treason taken, raised and levied *appatiz* and ransoms in the king's realm, and has done so since the truces were cried.' Mérigot was therefore sentenced to death and was executed as 'a great traitor to the king and his realm, and a great robber, murderer and incendiary'.[24] The trials of Mérigot Marchès and a few others notwithstanding,[25] the prosecution of *routiers* was desultory and ineffectual until the 1440s, and pardons were easily obtained. For until Charles VII set about to create a disciplined standing army and to suppress the *routier* bands, the crown needed to employ many for whom free-booting was a way of life.

Illicit public and private war and the activities of the free-booters were encompassed by the laws of war. In this domain of military law there were a number of other crimes, more strictly military in nature, that could also be punished as treason. Not only those who claimed the right to wage war against the king but also their adherents were guilty of treason, and for the same reason: a breach of allegiance if not the implicit imagining of the king's death.[26] To bear arms against the king himself was patent treason. It was on this account that some twenty-five defenders of the castle of Saint-Maixent were executed in April 1440 after it fell to the royal forces that were led by Charles VII in person. Bearing arms in other circumstances was construed as treason for compassing the destruction of both the kingdom and the king. In March 1373, for example, Charles V granted to Arnaud-Amanieu, lord of Albret, all the property in Gascony of the lord of Puyanne, 'our enemy and rebel', who had been captured at La Rochelle 'making war against us and

[24] Keen, *Laws of War*, pp. 97–9; the translations are Dr Keen's.

[25] E.g., *Confessions et jugements de criminels au Parlement de Paris (1319–1350)*, ed. M. Langlois and Y. Lanhers (Paris, 1971), p. 172; *Registre criminel du Châtelet de Paris*, ed. H. Duplès-Agier (2 vols., Paris, 1861 and 1864), I. 14–35; II. 92–100.

[26] Keen, *Laws of War*, p. 92.

our kingdom with our enemy of England . . . committing the crime of lese-majesty'.[27] It should be noted here that consorting in arms with the enemy was an accusation often made by plaintiffs to afforce charges of treason in cases of private war that came before the Parlement of Paris.[28]

As in England, desertion, particularly during the heat of battle, was most treasonable,[29] and if captured, deserters could hope for little mercy. When the dauphin Louis took Dieppe in 1443 he had eight French men-at-arms, four archers and two cannoneers executed for having fought with the English. In 1477 Denis Lepage, executioner at Mâcon, received four pairs of gloves for having executed some soldiers who had deserted to the prince of Orange and to Maximilian, archduke of Austria;[30] presumably the gloves were to protect his hands in the course of all the judicial killing that he was doing. Encouraging desertion or even thinking about it was treasonable;[31] and an ordinance of Charles V from the mid 1360s declared that so, too, was going absent without leave.[32] During time of war, furthermore, it was forbidden for anyone to travel outside the kingdom 'for a feat of arms or for a long voyage' 'on penalty of forfeiting [one's] property and being reputed [a] traitor'. The same punishment would be meted out to all holders of royal fiefs and subfiefs who did not respond to the *ban* and *arrière-ban*.[33]

The capture of strategic places by the enemy was most serious if brought about by treason. For having enabled Jean V d'Armagnac to take Lectoure in October 1472 Charles d'Albret, lord of Sainte-Bazeille, was executed as a traitor in April 1473.[34] It was also treason for a captain to surrender his place without undergoing siege.[35] In one of the first cases of lese-majesty in the later middle ages, Alain de

27 Mathieu d'Escouchy, *Chronique*, ed. G. du Fresne de Beaucourt (S.H.F.) (3 vols., Paris, 1863–4), III. 13 (Saint-Maixent); A.N., JJ 104, no. 103 (Puyanne).

28 E.g., A.N., X2a 8, fols. 24v, 110r; Dessalles, *Périgueux, preuves*, p. 78; Keen, *Laws of War*, p. 109, n. 1.

29 B.N., ms. fr. 2913, fol. 86r; H. Sée, *Louis XI et les villes* (Paris, 1891), p. 88 n. 4. For the case of Nicholas de Segrave in England see Bellamy, *The Law of Treason*, p. 55.

30 M. Thibault, *La jeunesse de Louis XI* (Paris, 1907), p. 311; C. Rossignol, *Histoire de la Bourgogne pendant la période monarchique (1476–1483)* (Dijon, 1853), p. 156.

31 Roye, *Chron. scan.*, II. 83–4; Contamine, *Guerre, état et société*, p. 216.

32 A.N., JJ 99, no. 337; see also Contamine, *Guerre, état et société*, pp. 61–2; *Lettres de Louis XI*, VI. 203–4.

33 Contamine, *Guerre, état et société*, pp. 4, 372; B.N., ms. fr. 26095, no. 1340.

34 Roye, *Chron. scan.*, I. 294–5.

35 Keen, *Laws of War*, p. 124; Bellamy, *The Law of Treason*, pp. 109–11.

Roucy in 1259 was adjudged guilty 'according to the written law' because he had surrendered the castle of Montréal in Albigeois to the heretics. 'At that time', it was stated, 'there was a large garrison and sufficient provisions in the castle . . . and it could have been defended.'[36] But neither honour nor the law required a garrison to fight to the last man: once an honourable defence had been made, both the besieged and the attackers could enter into a binding legal agreement for the surrender of the place on an appointed day if a relieving force did not come to give battle before then.[37] Jean de Belon, captain of La Roche-sur-Yon in Poitou, had made and fulfilled just such an agreement with the English in late 1369, yet he was executed for treason in January 1370. Wherein lay his crime? Froissart informs us that it was for having received 6000 francs for the provisions. It was treason for Belon to have accepted money in any circumstances, and all the more treason to have surrendered after only one month of siege: the provisions, Froissart pointed out, could have lasted for a full year.[38]

Unsuccessful attempts to deliver strategic places were no less treasonable for their failure. One of the reasons why Charles de Melun was beheaded in 1468 was for allegedly having left open the Saint-Antoine gate during the siege of Paris in 1465 so that the enemy could gain entry. One also committed treason by seizing or remaining in possession of a place against the king's will. In 1442 Charles VII had Maurice de Ploesquellec arrested because of his illicit occupation of Taillebourg; unlike Jean de Bonneil, however, who was executed in 1363 for having unlawfully held the fortress of Vallières, Maurice suffered only imprisonment and forfeiture of his property.[39] To refuse entry to royal troops, as at Le Mans in 1368, Brive in 1373, and Laon in 1380, was another treason.[40]

36 *Les Olim*, ed. le comte Beugnot (C.D.I.) (3 vols. in 4, Paris, 1839–48), I. 461.

37 Keen, *Laws of War*, pp. 125, 128–9.

38 Jean Froissart, *Chroniques*, ed. S. Luce *et al.* (Société de l'histoire de France) (15 vols., published, Paris, 1869–1975), VII. pp. lxxiii–lxxiv, 160–2; A.N., JJ 102, no. 4; *Recueil des documents concernant le Poitou contenus dans les registres de la chancellerie de France*, ed. P. Guérin (vols., XI, XIII, XVII, XIX, XXI, XXIV, XXVI, XXIX, XXXII, XXXVIII, XLI, XLIV, L, LVI of *Archives historiques du Poitou*), XVII. 387–9.

39 B.N., ms. fr. 2921, fol. 21r (Melun); A.N., JJ 96, no. 185 (Bonneil); X2a 24, fols. 73r–74v; P 2298, fols. 1213–23 (Ploesquellec).

40 *Documents pour servir à l'hist. du Maine*, ed. Broussillon, pp. 152–4 (Le Mans); J.-F. Perol, 'Six siècles avant nous: la tragédie briviste de 1374', *Lemouzi*, 5th series, LIII (1975), 52–9; A.N., JJ 123, no. 85 (Laon).

The violation of a truce could also be treasonable because it was a blatant affront to the king's majesty and honour. One will remember that this was one of the charges against Mérigot Marchès, and it was a telling one. A case at the turn of the fifteenth century involving Jean de Beaufort, lord of Limeuil, is also worth mentioning in this regard. In the late 1390s, in violation of a truce between the English and the French, Beaufort had given his castles of Campagne and Alleyrat to two captains of English allegiance. Because he had taken prisoner two other English captains, the first two carried out a series of reprisal raids, using Beaufort's castles as a base. Renaud de Pons, *vicomte* of Turenne and conservator of the truces in Périgord, Saintonge and Angoumois, held Beaufort responsible for this turn of events and brought suit against him. At the Parlement of Paris the king's proctor as well joined issue with Beaufort, castigating his actions as 'perjury and the crime of lese-majesty'. On 3 December 1412 the court convicted Beaufort as charged, levying a fine of 18,000 *l.t.*, banishing him and confiscating his property.[41]

II

Most treasons involved a breach of loyalty. One will recall that Mérigot Marchès had tried to use in his defence the argument that he was of English allegiance and was therefore to be treated not as a traitor but as an enemy. On the face of it this particular argument seems reasonable enough, since the region from which he came – the Limousin – was disputed territory. But it was precisely because the kings of France had never renounced their sovereignty over the Limousin and other contested areas, never accepted the English claim that Guyenne, for example, was an allodium,[42] that they could consider as traitors the inhabitants of these lands who adhered to the English, especially in time of war. Not only in regions like Guyenne but also in the territories adjacent to the disputed areas, indeed even in the regions unquestionably in French control, the English had their partisans. Nor were they the only adversaries adherence to whom constituted treason. In Normandy, Brittany and Burgundy the followers of Charles the Bad, Jean de Montfort and Charles the Bold

[41] A.N., x2a 16, fols. 221v–23v.

[42] M. G. A. Vale, *English Gascony 1399–1453* (Oxford, 1970), pp. 2–3.

respectively also could find themselves reputed traitors. It is not surprising, then, that the treason which one encounters most frequently in the later middle ages was that of adhering to the enemy. As can be expected, this was also a most common treason in England.[43]

One could adhere to the enemy in more ways than by taking up arms. In the trial of Jacques Coeur one of the charges against him was that he had sold to the Turks military equipment with which they had won a battle against the Christians. Other examples indicate that there was little distinction between supplying arms and engaging in commercial transactions with the enemy. In 1344, for instance, Jean Maillet was accused of treason for having sent 'wheat, apples, wine, onions . . . and other things' to the English and to the Flemings. In the late 1350s Raoul de Rully, an apothecary from Senlis, was similarly charged for having provisioned the English garrisons of Creil and Pont-Saint-Maxence.[44] Acquiescence in such activity could be as treasonable as the act itself.[45]

Espionage was certainly treasonable. Although Cibeuf de Chaponnères in October 1356 was fortunate enough to obtain a pardon, the crown normally punished this crime severely. Hennequin du Bos, for example, who had been recruited to spy for the English when he was in Scotland with Jean de Vienne in 1385, was drawn and beheaded on 18 August 1390 after being tried in the Châtelet.[46] Even when given under compulsion, active assistance to the enemy was treason. The pardon given to Jean Aimery in March 1374 left no doubt that by serving the English in arms for two years in order to acquit himself of his ransom he had committed 'treason against us and our royal majesty'.[47] Apparently what won him his pardon was his plea that he had served the English out of fear of being killed. But when Jean le Restis was being prosecuted at the Châtelet in 1389 he made no such defence, pleading only that he had spied for the English

[43] Bellamy, *The Law of Treason*, index *sub* 'adhering to the king's enemies'.

[44] P. Clément, *Jacques Coeur et Charles VII* (2 vols., Paris, 1853), II. *p.j.* xii. 296; A.N., X2A 4, fol. 119v (Maillet); JJ 91, no. 19 (Rully).

[45] E.g., A.N., JJ 72, no. 318.

[46] A.N., JJ 84, no. 627 (Chaponnères); *Reg. crim. du Châtelet*, I. 379–93 (du Bos). For some other examples see Roye, *Chron. scan.*, I. 206; B.N., ms. fr. 25997, no. 303/3; ms. fr. 26091, no. 699; *Preuves pour servir à l'histoire de la maison de Chabannes*, ed. H. de Chabannes (4 vols., Dijon, 1892–7), II. 432–3.

[47] A.N., JJ 105, no. 192. For some other examples see JJ 82, no. 372; JJ 91, no. 480; JJ 95, no. 39.

because he could not pay his ransom. He was consequently executed 'as a traitor'. For those same prosecutors in the Châtelet the behaviour of Guillaume de Bruc was even more treasonous: not only had he served the king's enemy Geoffroy Tête-Noir, captain of Ventadour, in order to discharge himself of his ransom; but also he had remained with the enemy in spite of having had several opportunities to escape. Since his personal honour should have ceded to his duty to remain loyal, he was executed on 6 October 1389 'as a traitor of the king our lord and of his kingdom'.[48]

When no specific acts of treason could be ascertained the crown simply declared people guilty for having given 'counsel, comfort and aid', or for notoriously adhering to the enemy.[49] One example indicates to what extent the crown might go in this regard. In early 1340 Tomasso Barri and Angelo Soderini, and Niccolo Francesco and Filippo Pucci, factors of the Peruzzi and Bardi firms respectively, were imprisoned in the Châtelet because their firms had lent money to the English and to the Flemings, and had thereby given 'aid and comfort to [the enemy] during the war'. But no doubt because he realized the folly of biting the hand that fed him, Philippe VI pardoned the Italians and had them released in July.[50]

Even without giving active assistance to the enemy, persons could be reputed traitors if they had property in land of French obedience but nevertheless chose to live in enemy territory. This was true whether or not they had made oaths of allegiance to their new masters. Thus in the late 1350s Pierre Beauché and his wife forfeited their property 'because they went to live in the Cotentin in the land occupied by the king of Navarre'. In July 1366, even before the war with the English broke out anew in 1369, Guillaume Varenne and his sister Agnès forfeited all their property because 'of their own free will . . . [they] lived with the English'. After 1369, of course, many people in Poitou and elsewhere had their property confiscated for living voluntarily in English-controlled territory. Guillaume Quatre-Sous, for example, forfeited a house and six acres of land in the *vicomté* of Caen because he had gone to live in England.[51] At

[48] *Reg. crim. du Châtelet*, I. 14–35 (du Bruc); I. 119–25 (le Restis); Keen, *Laws of War*, p. 162.

[49] E.g., A.N., JJ 90, no. 401; JJ 104, no. 188; JJ 179, no. 377; K 70, no. 56.

[50] A.N., JJ 71, no. 352.

[51] A.N., JJ 87, no. 98 (Beauché); JJ 100, no. 101 (Quatre-Sous); Guérin, *Arch. hist. Poitou*, XVII. 351–4 (Varenne).

least in the fourteenth century the law was rigorously applied in this respect.[52]

There was one group of people – Englishmen who held lands in France – whose status appears to be dubious. Were they, too, considered traitors? The answer to this seems to be that with regard to their persons they were not: if captured they were treated as enemies and were allowed the right to ransom themselves. With regard to their lands, however, they were indeed considered traitors, and their property could be confiscated for that reason.[53] The crown also appears to have treated with strictness the French wives of Englishmen or English adherents. In July 1372, for example, the property of a certain Périnelle and that of her son Mathieu from her first marriage was confiscated for treason after she had gone to live in England with her second husband, the English knight Hugh Scot. The attitude of the crown is typified by a case from the 1430s. Just before Paris fell to the French in 1436 a young Parisienne married an Italian merchant who was closely connected with the English. When the newly-wed couple went with them to Rouen their property in Paris was confiscated. The young woman's mother contested the forfeiture in the Parlement of Paris, arguing that by cleaving to her husband her daughter was only following the dictates of divine law. But the king's proctor replied that nothing superseded the public interest, and that therefore the young woman was guilty of lese-majesty. The Parlement agreed.[54]

III

The problem of allegiance and treason in Lancastrian France is perhaps best treated within the context of English history. Since, however, the kings of England claimed to be 'roys de France' and therefore ruled in their French territories according to French law, it is of some interest to this study to examine, albeit briefly, how the Lancastrian administration applied the law of treason.

While considerable efforts were made to conciliate the Normans after 1417, Henry V and his successors were just as determined to punish the recalcitrant. The heart of the matter, of course, lay in the

[52] For some other examples see A.N., JJ 76, no. 57; JJ 100, no. 111; JJ 103, no. 38; JJ 122, no. 338; JJ 124, no. 26.

[53] Keen, *Laws of War*, pp. 91–2.

[54] A.N., JJ 103, no. 178; J. H. Shennan, *The Parlement of Paris* (London, 1968), pp. 158–9.

problem of allegiance, and English policy was a clear one: all Frenchmen in lands of English obedience were obliged to take an oath of fealty, records of which were kept; those who did not swear allegiance either because they had become rebels or because they had taken up residence in lands of French obedience were liable to have their properties confiscated.[55]

The extent of such forfeitures will be discussed more fully in chapter 5, but some examples can be given here. In February 1418 Richard Drayton, esquire, obtained the fortress and lordship of Coulombiers that had been confiscated from the knight Olivier de Coulombiers, 'qui adhuc contra nos rebellem se tenet'. On 28 March 1419 Richard Fitz-James was given the property, worth some 1200 *écus*, confiscated from the knight Guillaume Montauban, 'adhuc rebellis'. On 6 November 1420 the manor of Tournebu in the *bailliage* of Gisors was confiscated from Louis d'Harcourt, archbishop of Rouen, 'huc usque inobediens', and granted to the esquire Brian Cornwall. Charles de Saint-Clair and his mother, 'huc usque absentes', forfeited their property in the *bailliage* of Gisors in 1419, as did Marie de la Ferrière in the *bailliage* of Alençon, Lancelot de Harenvilliers in the *bailliage* of Evreux, and Richard de Buret in the *bailliage* of Caen. In 1424 one Colin du Bosc obtained that part of his paternal inheritance that should have gone to his brother Jean but which was forfeited by the latter because he lived with the French enemy.[56] The policy of Henry V could be rather severe on the question of residence: on 8 December 1421 he directed the *baillis* of Normandy to expel from the duchy all women whose husbands lived in enemy territory.[57]

[55] R. Jouet, *La résistance à l'occupation anglaise en Basse-Normandie (1418–1450)* (Cahiers des Annales de Normandie: 5) (Caen, 1969); E. Burney, 'The English Rule in Normandy 1435–1450' (unpublished Oxford. B.Litt. thesis, 1958); R. Newhall, 'Henry V's Policy of Conciliation in Normandy 1417–1422', *Anniversary Essays in Medieval History by Students of Charles Homer Haskins*, ed. C. H. Taylor and J. L. LaMonte (Boston and New York, 1929), pp. 205–29; F. de Fontaine de Resbecq, 'Les rapports du gouvernement anglais et de la noblesse normande dans la vicomté de Valognes pendant l'occupation 1418–1450', *Mém. soc. archéol., artist. litt. et sc. de l'arrondissement de Valognes*, IX (1907–12), 17–42; H. de Frondeville, 'La vicomté d'Orbec pendant l'occupation anglaise (1417–1449)', *Etudes lexoviennes*, IV (1936), 1–115.

[56] *Rotuli Normanniae*, ed. T. D. Hardy (London, 1835), p. 247 (Coulombiers); 'Rôles normands et français et autres pièces tirées des archives de Londres par Bréquigny', *Mém. soc. des antiquaires de Normandie*, XXIII (1858), nos. 341 (Montauban), 887 (Harcourt), 382 (Saint-Clair), 384 (Ferrière), 387 (Harenvilliers), 392 (Buret); A.N., Coll. Lenoir 26, fol. 155r (du Bosc).

[57] Newhall, 'Henry V's Policy', pp. 227–8.

The oath of allegiance could be an important matter, for, as in France generally, a distinction could be drawn between a person and his property. Those who had taken the oath and later rebelled were traitors pure and simple. By contrast those who had not taken the oath could be considered as enemies insofar as their persons were concerned, and thus could be put to ransom if captured; but they were traitors insofar as their lands were concerned, and these could be confiscated.[58]

As in both France and England, notoriety was enough to convict a person of treason. In March 1418, for example, the property of the knight Richard Sully, 'rebellis ut dicitur', was confiscated and granted to William Ayleston, esquire. Also in that month Guillaume d'Assy, esquire, 'qui erga nos de presenti se tenet rebellem ut dicitur', forfeited his property, which was granted to the esquire William Porter. Many other such examples can be cited.[59]

Brigandage was a major problem that plagued the Lancastrian government throughout the years of occupation. Of course not all those designated as brigands were French partisans,[60] for one must remember that for years prior to the English invasion brigands had been causing disorder in Normandy.[61] Yet the brigands were not all mere criminals either. Effectively there are three ways in which one can distinguish the common brigands from those who were also traitors in the eyes of the English. The first way is that when the former were meant the documents spoke only of 'brigands', or 'brigands and thieves', or 'brigands and highway-robbers';[62] whereas the latter were described more fully as 'traitors and brigands', 'traitors, thieves and brigands', 'traitors, brigands, enemies and adversaries', or 'traitors, thieves, brigands, highway-robbers, enemies and adversaries of the king'.[63] The second way of differentiating

[58] *Ibid.*, pp. 210–16.

[59] *Rot. Norm.*, p. 265 (Sully); 'Rôles normands', no. 74 (d'Assy). For other examples see *Rot. Norm.*, pp. 258–9, 261–2, 264–5, 271–2, 277–81; 'Rôles normands', nos. 122, 129, 130, 139, 172, 178, 180.

[60] See G. Lefèvre-Pontalis, 'La guerre des partisans dans la Haute-Normandie (1424–1429)', *B.E.C.*, LIV (1893), 475–521; LV (1894), 239–305; LVI (1895), 433–508; LVII (1896), 5–54; XCVII (1936), 102–30.

[61] Newhall, 'Henry V's Policy', p. 211.

[62] B.N., ms. fr. 7645, nos. 20, 22, 31, 32.

[63] A.N., Coll. Lenoir 29, fols. 19–20; Frondeville, 'Orbec', appendix II, pp. 70–9; Jouet, *La résistance*, pp. 23–4; *Chronique du Mont-Saint-Michel (1343–1468)*, ed. S. Luce (2 vols., Paris, 1879–83), II. 25–6.

between the traitors and the common criminals is, arguably, by the manner of their execution. The latter were usually hanged, the former decapitated and sometimes drawn as well; as we shall see in chapter 5, this latter form of execution was characteristic for crimes of treason. Thus at Orbec in 1431 'two traitors, brigands, enemies and adversaries of the king' were 'decapitated as traitors, and, since they were thieves, their bodies were hanged on the gibbet'. At Caen in 1436 Jean du Bois and Jean Radigues, thieves and highway-robbers, were only hanged, while Guillaume le Maître was drawn, beheaded and hanged as a 'traitor, thief, murderer, enemy and adversary'.[64] The third way of distinguishing is that a traitor's property would be confiscated to the crown, whereas that of a common criminal went to his immediate lord.[65]

One can object at this point in the argument that in view of the profits to be gained by the crown, royal officers would incline to condemn all brigands as traitors. No doubt there was some cynical afforcing of charges in order to obtain convictions for treason, but on the whole it seems that there was a clear enough distinction between traitors and criminals, or traitors and partisans, and English policy seems to have been consistent, if not fair.[66]

English policy was also firm with regard to treasonous conspiracies in the towns. In 1418–19 traitors at Louviers, Rouen and Dieppe were executed for plotting to deliver those towns to the French. There were subsequent similar conspiracies, followed by executions of the guilty, at Rouen in 1422, 1427 and 1432,[67] Paris in May or June 1422, Le Mans in 1428, Lisieux in 1431,[68] Paris again in 1430 and 1433, Pont-de-l'Arche in 1439, and Vernon in 1443.[69] The

64 Jouet, *La résistance*, p. 25 (Orbec); Stevenson, *Letters and Papers*, II (1), LXII (Caen).

65 Jouet, *La résistance*, pp. 23–4.

66 B. J. Rowe, 'John, duke of Bedford, and the Norman "Brigands"', *E.H.R.*, XLVII (1932), 583–99; see also *Actes de la chancellerie d'Henri VI concernant la Normandie sous la domination anglaise (1422–1435). Extraits des registres du Trésor des Chartes aux Archives Nationales*, ed. P. Le Cacheux (Soc. de l'hist. de Normandie) (2 vols., Rouen, 1907 and 1908), I. nos. 4, 12, 28, 39, 73, 96, 122, 153; II. nos. 201, 244.

67 Newhall, 'Henry V's Policy', p. 217; L. Puiseux, *L'émigration normande et la colonisation anglaise au XVe siècle* (Caen, 1866), pp. 56–8; *Les cronicques de Normandie (1223–1453)*, ed. A. Hellot (Rouen, 1881), pp. 79–80, 242–3 n. 238.

68 Jean Le Fèvre, *Chronique*, ed. F. Morand (S.H.F.) (2 vols., Paris, 1876 and 1881), II. 58 (Paris); *Journal d'un bourgeois de Paris (1405–1449)*, ed. A. Tuetey (Paris, 1881), p. 226 (Le Mans); Frondeville, 'Orbec', appendix II, p. 71 (Lisieux).

69 *Paris pendant la domination anglaise (1420–1436)*, ed. A. Longnon (Paris, 1878), nos. 145–6, 173–5; *Journ. d'un bourgeois*, pp. 251–2 (Paris); A.N., Coll. Lenoir 16, fol. 377r (Pont-de-l'Arche); *ibid.*, 74, fol. 223 (Vernon).

non-revelation of traitorous plots could as well expose a person to charges of treason.[70]

Serving the French, even involuntarily, was certainly treasonable. On 1 April 1433, for example, one Henri Dacinet was executed at Lisieux as a traitor for having acted as a guide for the French. In the 1420s the cleric Robert le Changeur was imprisoned for treason because, having been taken prisoner by the French, and being incapable of paying a ransom, he had served them for one year. Numerous other persons, however, received pardons for similar offences.[71] It seems that slanderous speech, too, could be construed as treason. In 1426 one Jean Desmarest was beheaded at Paris 'because he had said that the people can make a king, but a king cannot make a people'.[72] Such treason by words could also be committed in France, as we shall see presently. Generally speaking, then, in its application of the law of treason the Lancastrian administration stayed well within the boundaries established by French practice.

IV

There were a number of crimes in France that, constituting usurpation or disregard of the king's sovereignty, could thus be treasonable. The illicit convocation of assemblies was one such. In the late 1350s it was argued that Robert Le Coq, bishop of Laon, committed lese-majesty in the first degree by having been the prime mover of the Estates-general. In the period of tension after the assassination of Louis d'Orléans in 1407, Charles VI emphasized that even the dauphin would be guilty of treason if he convoked an assembly without royal approval.[73] It was also treasonous to negotiate agreements independently with the enemy, or even to be in secret communication with him. One of the treasonable acts of Jean IV d'Armagnac in the 1440s was his negotiation of a truce with the English; and both he and Jean, duke of Alençon, secretly tried to

[70] *Actes d'Henri VI*, II. nos. 206, 214; Seine-Maritime, *Inventaire sommaire*, ed. Ch. de Robillard de Beaurepaire, vol. II (Paris, 1874), 142.

[71] Frondeville, 'Orbec', appendix II, p. 73 (Dacinet); Seine-Maritime, *Inventaire sommaire*, II. 141–2 (le Changeur); for other examples see *Actes d'Henri VI*, II. nos. 277, 293, 294; *Paris pendant la domination anglaise*, no. 111.

[72] Seine-Maritime, *Inventaire sommaire*, II. 141.

[73] L. Douët-d'Arcq, 'Acte d'accusation contre Robert Le Coq', *B.E.C.*, II (1840), 374–6; *Ordonnances*, XII. 224–5.

arrange marriage alliances with the English.[74] In the late 1350s the abbess of Saint-Nicolas in Bar-sur-Aube, though both a woman and a cleric, was not immune from prosecution for having been in traitorous communication with the king's enemies.[75] At least in the early fourteenth century the extreme royal position was that the kings of England, because they were dukes of Guyenne, could be considered traitors for making alliances to the prejudice of France.[76]

In the fifteenth century, French magnates who in general acted as sovereign lords were liable to find themselves prosecuted as traitors. Jean IV d'Armagnac's other usurpations of sovereignty – his use of the title 'count by the grace of God'; his granting of letters of pardon, ennoblement and legitimation; his coining of money; his refusal to allow his subjects to contribute to *aides* for the war; his private wars – all finally led to his arrest in 1444. In the 1450s his son Jean V renewed the exercise of these regalian rights, and he too was tried for treason. Yet another Armagnac, Charles, *vicomte* of Fezansaguet, was prosecuted on these same grounds in the 1470s.[77] If it is not stretching the point too far one might argue that, at least for Louis XI, usurpation alone was sacrilege. As the king declared in May 1478, the late Charles, duke of Burgundy, had been 'following the example of Lucifer' in trying 'to usurp and arrogate to himself the right of sovereignty that belongs to us in the lands that he holds . . . from us and the crown'.[78] But the kings of France had to tread warily against living dukes of Burgundy or Brittany.

From as early as 1309 the violation of the king's safeguard was considered treasonable because, like the breach of a truce, it was an affront to the king's honour and majesty.[79] The obstruction of legal appeals to the king or his courts was another treason of this type. There are several examples from Guyenne in the fourteenth century; the Black Prince's interference with the appeals of the Gascon lords

74 Escouchy, *Chronique*, III. 130, 142 (Armagnac); *Recueil général des anciennes lois françaises*, ed. Isambert, Jourdain and Decrusy (29 vols., Paris, 1822–33), IX. 345ff (Alençon).

75 A.N., JJ 90, no. 197.

76 P. Chaplais, 'Règlement des conflits internationaux franco-anglais au XIVe siècle (1297–1327)', *M.A.*, LVII (1951), 293 n. 3.

77 Escouchy, *Chronique*, I. 61–5; II. 290–6; C. Samaran, *La maison d'Armagnac au XVe siècle et les dernières luttes de la féodalité dans le Midi de la France* (Paris, 1908), pp. 90–8, 114–30, 210ff.

78 *Ordonnances*, XVIII. 399.

79 E.g., A.N., X2a 2, fols. 11v–12r; X2a 3, fols. 87r–v, 159v–160r; X2a 6, fols. 144r–v, 167v–169r; X2a 7, fols. 133r–134r; X2a 9, fols. 216v–219r.

in the 1360s is the best known one.[80] Such treason was clearly more reprehensible when the offender was himself a royal officer. In March 1454 Louis de Courcelles, lord of Breuil and *bailli* of the mountains of Auvergne, was convicted of lese-majesty, treason and rebellion for having hanged Pons Mercier sometime in the 1430s in disregard of Mercier's appeal to the Parlement of Poitiers.[81] In February 1418 the Parlement of Paris declared that to appeal to the Roman Curia could also be treasonous.[82]

V

According to the *lex Quisquis* it was treason to assault a royal councillor ('nam et ipsi pars corporis nostri sunt'). Jean Le Coq confirmed that, on the basis of this law, Jean Louvart, in 1393, was executed as a traitor for his attempted assassination of Robert d'Acquigny, a councillor in the Parlement, 'quia domini Parlamenti, maxime exercendo suum officium, sunt pars corporis regis'. A better-known example is Pierre de Craon's attempted assassination of the constable Olivier IV de Clisson in June 1392. Craon was convicted of treason *in absentia* on 26 August on the grounds that Clisson, 'a person so privileged because of his office of constable . . . [was] in the singular protection and safeguard of the king, [whose] person he represents as his lieutenant'. This principle of immunity, derived from the *lex Quisquis*, had been extended ever since the early fourteenth century to minor royal officials. It seems that in 1323 what finally impelled the crown to bring the Gascon rebel Jourdain de l'Isle-Jourdain to justice for treason was his murder of a royal sergeant who was bearing a mace decorated with the *fleur de lis*.[83]

The case in 1406 of Jean, lord of Fontaines, confirms the fact that

[80] Anselme de Sainte-Marie (le Père), *Histoire généalogique et chronologique de la maison royale de France*, continued by M. du Fourny (9 vols., Paris, 1726–33), II. 586–8. For other examples see *Reg. du Trésor*, I. nos. 2011, 2027–8, 2030.

[81] A.N., X2a 26, fols. 343r–345v. For a brief note on Courcelles see G. Dupont-Ferrier, *Gallia regia, ou état des officiers royaux des bailliages et des sénéchaussées de 1328 à 1515* (7 vols., Paris, 1942–65), I. 184.

[82] Clément de Fauquembergue, *Journal*, ed. A. Tuetey and H. Lacaille (S.H.F.) (3 vols., Paris, 1903–15), I. 58–60.

[83] *Questiones Johannis Galli*, ed. M. Boulet [-Sautel] (Paris, 1944), pp. 363–4 (Louvart); A.N., K 54, no. 20 (Craon); *Les grandes chroniques de France*, ed. J. Viard (S.H.F.) (10 vols., Paris, 1920–53), IX. 16–17 (Jourdain de l'Isle-Jourdain). For other examples see *Registres du Trésor*, I. nos. 2005, 2026.

the display of royal insignia was very important in determining whether treason had been committed. Pierre de Picquigny, lieutenant of the *bailli* of Amiens, suspected that Fontaines, a former *bailli* of Mâcon and *sénéchal* of Lyon, was harbouring a felon named Pierre Fenin. When Picquigny and several royal sergeants went to Fontaines's *hôtel* to arrest Fenin, a skirmish took place, during the course of which Picquigny and the sergeants were disarmed and beaten. Legal proceedings were then initiated against Fontaines. On 23 March 1406 the king's proctor in the Parlement of Paris asserted in his presentation for the crown that Picquigny had disclosed the nature of his orders to Fontaines, and moreover that the sergeants' staves had been clearly visible. Fontaines was thus guilty of treason, the proctor argued, because 'whoever obstructs justice and harms the public good, especially when it is ascertained that [the royal officer had] the king's mandate or that of his sovereign court, commits the crime of lese-majesty in the first degree'.[84]

One could symbolically resist the king's authority by desecrating royal insignia. One proof of the duke of Lorraine's treason in his private war against the town of Neufchâtel in the early 1400s was the fact that his men had seized the royal pennants that were a sign of the king's safeguard and had then trampled them in the mud. A similar charge was laid against Jean IV d'Armagnac in the 1440s. In the mid 1350s, during Etienne Marcel's rule at Paris, Laurent de Veullettes took an escutcheon that was emblazoned with the *fleur de lis*, 'spat on it and pierced it with a dagger and an arrow from a crossbow, in contempt of . . . [Jean II, the dauphin Charles] and the whole royal line'.[85] The traitorous symbolism of his actions was all too clear.

Laurent de Veullettes's treason was in fact a double one, for he had also uttered 'ugly, villainous and injurious words too dishonourable to record'. As in England,[86] scandalous speech by itself was indeed treasonable and need not have been accompanied by overt acts, since it could be construed as compassing the death or disinheritance of the

84 A.N., x2a 14, fols. 308v–309v.

85 Luce, *Jeanne d'Arc, preuve* xx, p. 48 (Lorraine); Escouchy, *Chronique*, III. 129–30 (Armagnac); A.N., JJ 86, no. 233 (Veullettes).

86 Bellamy, *The Law of Treason*, pp. 116–20; D. Thornley, 'Treason by Words in the Fifteenth Century', *E.H.R.*, XXXII (1917), 556–61; S. Rezneck, 'Constructive Treason by Words in the Fifteenth Century', *American Hist. Rev.*, XXXIII (1928), 544–52.

king, or the destruction of the kingdom. Thus in July 1346 Simon Pouillet, a rich burgess of Compiègne then living in Paris, was brutally executed for having said that 'the right to the kingdom belonged more to Edward, king of England, than to Philippe de Valois'.[87] In 1358 Pierre le Prêtre, a royal *sergent à verge* in the Châtelet, was also prosecuted but was ultimately pardoned for having uttered 'most horrible and villainous words that . . . cannot even be set down'. One case from the reign of Charles VII indicates how sensitive that king could be, at least in the last years of his life, about his image. In 1459 members of the *grand conseil*, acting as a royal commission, conducted an investigation of Yves Philippe, *chirurgien* of the king, because he had said that Charles VII was stricken with leprosy and would have died had he, Philippe, not treated him. When Philippe fled the kingdom, his case was sent to the Parlement, which condemned him *in absentia* of treason on 14 August 1460.[88]

The general royal position on treason by words was summed up in 1432 by Jean Barbin, king's proctor in the Parlement of Poitiers, in the prosecution of the Fleming Hennequin Bize. 'By word and by deed', he began, 'one commits the crime of lese-majesty: by deed when one makes an attempt on the person of the *princeps*; and by word when one speaks sinisterly of him or his acts.' Barbin asserted furthermore that it was worse 'to disparage by word than to injure by deed', but he neglected to explain why. Turning to the specifics of the case, Barbin alleged that what Hennequin had said – that 'the duke of Burgundy was good and loyal and . . . had not done anything that a good knight ought not to do, since the king had traitorously had his father murdered' – made Hennequin guilty twice over of lese-majesty in the first degree: firstly for having spoken maliciously against the person of the king; and secondly for having favoured by his words the king's enemies.[89]

In certain circumstances there was clearly no difference between treason by words and inciting to sedition. In December 1346 Jean,

[87] *Grandes chron.*, IX. 269–70; *infra*, p. 117.

[88] A.N., JJ 86, no. 431 (Prêtre); X2a 29, fols. 127r–128v (Philippe).

[89] A.N., X2a 18, fol. 308r. For some other cases of treason by words see A.N., JJ 84, no. 245; JJ 90, no. 206; JJ 109, no. 28; X2a 6, fol. 265v; X2a 11, fols. 34r–v; 39 r–v; X2a 12, fol. 387v; X1a 9317, no. 111; R. Fédou, 'Fidélité lyonnaise et propagande bourguignonne au temps de Louis XI', *Mélanges Fugier* (Lyon, 1968), pp. 71–80.

duke of Normandy, affirmed that Guillaume de Varonne, who had tried 'to have the inhabitants of . . . Saint-Clément become rebels and disobedient' at the time of Edward III's invasion of Normandy, and who had been executed for that reason by the townspeople, was indeed an 'enemy and traitor to our most dear lord and father'. After the tax revolt at Laon in the early 1380s Oudart Trousset was one of those prosecuted for treason for having incited to riot. Seditious written words, too, could precipitate charges of treason against their author. In 1378 Charles V declared that Robert Porte, bishop of Avranches and a partisan of the king of Navarre, was a traitor because *inter alia* he procured sedition of the people as much by letters and messages as by publicly spoken words and other means. The Parlement of Paris in July 1417 stopped short of calling the duke of Burgundy himself a traitor, but it did assert that the manifesto which he had recently circulated to the towns was 'seditious, scandalous and offensive to the royal majesty'.[90]

If it was treasonable to sow discord between the king and his subjects, and his army in particular,[91] it was certainly treasonable to cause dissension between the king and the dauphin. This was one of the principal *gravamina* against Robert Le Coq, bishop of Laon, in the late 1350s.[92] And therein, one might argue, lay in part the treason of the magnates in the Praguerie. Louis XI added a new, vindictive twist: no sooner was he enthroned than he began to purge as traitors some of the men who, remaining loyal to Charles VII, had opposed his bids for power when he was dauphin. Antoine de Chabannes, whose case will be discussed in chapter 10, was the most notable victim. A number of Louis's former subjects in the Dauphiné also suffered. The lord of Le Bouchage, arrested immediately in September or October 1461 for having refused to support Louis's rebellion in 1456, died a prisoner in December 1461. His confiscated lordship of Le Bouchage was later granted to the *courtier* Ymbert de Batarnay. At about that time Louis XI appointed a commission to try the eminent jurists Gui Pape and Jean Bâle, presidents in the Parlement of Grenoble, and René Thomassin, another member of that court.

90 A.N., JJ 81, no. 109 (Varonne); X2a 11, fols. 53v–54r, 240r–v; X2a 12, fols. 54r–57v (Trousset); *Thesaurus Novus Anecdotorum*, I. cols. 1529–31 (Porte); Fauquembergue, *Journal*, I. 30–4 (Burgundy).

91 Roye, *Chron. scan.*, I. 78.

92 Douët-d'Arcq, 'Acte d'accusation', p. 368.

Convicted of felony and lese-majesty on 2 June 1462, they were removed from their offices and were ordered to pay back all the wages they had received since Louis's flight to Flanders in 1456; furthermore, all their property was confiscated, and they were banished from the Dauphiné.[93]

VI

Popular disturbances could be considered treasonable. There are indications that the Jacquerie was viewed in this light; so too, at least in popular opinion, was the revolt of the Tuchins in the 1380s. 'It means as much to say "Tuchin" as "rebel" or "traitor" ', explained a man who had murdered another for having called him just that.[94] But it was more especially urban revolts that brought charges of treason down upon the heads of the civic rebels. After the battle of Cassel in 1328, for example, Philippe VI was clearly intent on confiscating the property of all who had fought there against him. The Flemish rebels of the 1380s seem to have been treated just as severely.[95] At Rouen around 1350 twenty-three burgesses were executed as traitors for having instigated a riot against the tax-collectors.[96] In 1378–9 there were a series of tax revolts at Nîmes, Montpellier and several other places in the south of France that were also punished under the law of treason. The same was true of the revolts that broke out in Normandy, the Ile-de-France and the north-east in 1382,[97] and at Bourges in 1474.[98] These urban revolts were all perceived as

[93] B. de Mandrot, *Ymbert de Batarnay, seigneur du Bouchage* (Paris, 1886), pp. 7–11; B.N., ms. fr. 16536, fol. 165r–v (Pape *et al.*).

[94] A.N., JJ 86, nos. 152–3 (Jacquerie); C. Portal, 'Les insurrections de Tuchins dans les pays de langue d'oc, vers 1382–1384', *Ann. du Midi*, IV (1892), 467–8; see also M. Boudet, *La Jacquerie des Tuchins 1363–1384* (Riom, 1895).

[95] *Le soulèvement de la Flandre maritime de 1323–8* (documents inédits), ed. H. Pirenne (Brussels, 1900); A.N., JJ 121, no. 285 *bis*: *infra*, pp. 122–3.

[96] A.N., JJ 81, nos. 309, 517; JJ 87, no. 92; Pierre Cochon, *Chronique normande*, ed. Ch. de Robillard de Beaurepaire (Soc. de l'hist. de Normandie) (Rouen, 1870), pp. 75–6; N. Valois, *Le conseil du roi aux XIVe, XVe et XVIe siècles* (Paris, 1888), pp. 6–7.

[97] L. Mirot, *Les insurrections urbaines au début du règne de Charles VI (1380–1383)* (Paris, 1905); Delachenal, *Hist. de Charles V*, v. 294ff.

[98] The full references for this revolt are B.N., ms. fr. 2896, fol. 85r: ms. fr. 2897, fol. 9r; ms. fr. 2907, fol. 6r; ms. fr. 2912, fols. 1r–31v; ms. fr. 2914, fol. 1r; *Lettres de Louis XI*, v. 265–8, 273–4; A. Leguai, 'Emeutes et troubles d'origine fiscale pendant le règne de Louis XI', *M.A.*, LXXIII (1967), 461–9; L. Raynal, *Histoire du Berry* (4 vols., Bourges, 1844–7), III. 109–24; H. Sée, *Louis XI et les villes* (Paris, 1891), pp. 179–81; Mandrot, *Ymbert de Batarnay*, pp. 50–3.

tending to the destruction of the kingdom and the crown as well as of the king. Furthermore, particularly at Bourges in 1474 and at Rouen in 1382, it was not only the rioters themselves and those who gave them aid who were considered traitors, but also those who by remaining passive were deemed to have favoured the rioters.[99] In each case the insurrections provided the king with the pretext to restructure the municipal organization in the crown's favour. Especially after the riots of the 1380s the huge fines levied on the towns filled the royal coffers.

One further point can be made on urban revolts: the towns corporately, not only their individual inhabitants, could be held guilty of treason. This was all the more true if a town had adhered to the enemy. Pardons for such treason were given to Port-Sainte-Marie, for example, in December 1354, Saint-Antonin in March 1354, Lisieux in December 1465 and Montdidier in January 1477.[100] As we shall see in chapter 9, the towns of Normandy after 1449–50 and of Guyenne after 1451 and again after 1453 also had to supplicate for pardons.

Some towns did not stop with merely receiving the enemy within their gates, but actively took part in hostilities. For such treasonable alliance with the English, Saint-Jean-d'Angély was pardoned in August 1351. The inhabitants of Capdenac, who in the early 1440s had supported Jean IV d'Armagnac against the dauphin 'and engaged in all kinds of hostility and war', were pardoned their treason in April 1446. The list of crimes imputed to the inhabitants of Saint-Macaire after Talbot's descent in 1452 is telling. The pardon to that town, addressed to the 'gens deglise, nobles, bourgois, manans et habitans' in April 1454, described how

> during that time they waged war with our enemies against us and our loyal subjects, took our subjects prisoner and put them to ransom ... they beat, mutilated and killed some of them, and seized from them all kinds of cattle, food and other things ... [they] supported, counselled, aided and favoured our said enemies, and committed every other misdeed and malfeasance, committing the crime of lese-majesty, rebellion and disobedience.[101]

99 B.N., ms. fr. 2912, fol. 5r (Bourges); P. Chéruel, *Histoire de Rouen pendant l'époque communale 1150–1382* (2 vols., Rouen, 1843–4), II. 452.

100 A.N., JJ 84, no. 23 (Porte-Sainte-Marie); B.N., Coll. Doat 2, fol. 102 (Saint-Antonin); H. Stein, *Charles de France, frère de Louis XI* (Paris, 1921), *p.j.* xxii, pp. 562–3 (Lisieux); V. de Beauvillé, *Histoire de la ville de Montdidier* (3 vols., Paris, 1875), I. 544–5.

101 A.N., JJ 82, no. 233 (Saint-Jean-d'Angély); JJ 177, no. 236 (Capdenac); JJ 191, no. 17 (Saint-Macaire).

In addition to what has been discussed so far in this chapter, there were a number of miscellaneous crimes that could amount to treason. In 1336, for example, Hugues de Crusy, first president in the Parlement of Paris, was executed for lese-majesty on charges of having accepted bribes.[102] Peculation, too, was treasonable. In this category one can mention the cases of Arnaud Serène, *clavaire royal* of Montréal in Albigeois, in 1343; Jean Barillet, lord of Saincoins, *receveur-général* of Charles VII, in 1450–1; and of course Jacques Coeur in 1451–3.[103] Like Glanville, Bracton, *Fleta* and *Britton*, Jean Boutillier thought that counterfeiting coin was treason; and so did the judges in the Châtelet at the end of the fourteenth century.[104] In the *chambre des monnaies* in 1443 the king's advocate, Jean Dauvet, opposed the registration of a pardon given to the 'maistre particulier de nostre monnoie', Millet Blondelet, because in making coin of weak alloy Blondelet had committed 'crimes of lese-majesty against the king's welfare and in prejudice of the entire public weal'. Jeanne, countess of Boulogne, was convicted of lese-majesty in 1422 for having counterfeited coin as well as for having tried to make an alliance with the king of Portugal.[105] But however much the crown lawyers in the Parlement of Paris castigated false-coining as treason, it was not until the sixteenth century that the court definitively declared it as such.[106] Although there is little evidence on the counterfeiting of the royal seal, it seems that this crime, too, could be considered treasonable. In England the situation was much clearer: counterfeiting coin or the king's seal was always treasonable.[107]

At least since the affair of the lepers in 1321 the poisoning of wells was a treasonous offence. That plot, Philippe V thought, was lese-majesty 'contra rem publicam' and 'in mortem nostram'; this attitude of the king is most interesting, for by 'in mortem nostram' he

[102] *Actes du Parlement*, 2nd series, II. no. 5613; *Documents parisiens du règne de Philippe VI de Valois (1328–1350)*, ed. J. Viard (2 vols., Paris, 1899 and 1900), I. 264–5; *Chron. de Guill. de Nangis*, II. 153.

[103] *Actes du Parlement*, 2nd series, II. 5160 (Serène); *infra*, pp. 206–9 for Saincoins and Coeur.

[104] Bellamy, *The Law of Treason*, pp. 5, 15; Boutillier, *Somme rural*, I. 39 (p. 280); *Reg. crim. du Châtelet*, I. 480–94.

[105] A.N., Z1b 60, fols. 49v–50r; *Lettres de Louis XI*, I. 14–15 (Blondelet); Valois, *Le conseil du roi*, pp. 307–8 (Boulogne).

[106] A.N., X2a 22, fol. 51v; Perrot, *Les cas royaux*, pp. 238–40; P.-C. Timbal, 'La confiscation dans le droit français des XIIIe et XIVe siècles', *R.H.D.F.E.*, 4th series, XXII (1944), 42.

[107] A.N., X2a 2, fol. 26v; Escouchy, *Chronique*, I. 137–8; III. 265–341; Perrot, *Les cas royaux*, pp. 238–40; Bellamy, *The Law of Treason*, p. 85.

could only have meant his public, political body. In the 1350s the affair of the lepers was the one crime of lese-majesty that Jean Bergonho, a notary of Rodez, could remember.[108] For having poisoned the wells in the region around Chartres in the 1390s, a number of persons were tried at the Châtelet and executed as traitors.[109]

As in England, one could commit treason by necromancy when the object of such magical practices was the king or the royal line. In 1340 a Master Robert Langlois and two Cistercian monks from Germany 'plotted the death of the king and queen, and the perdition of the whole kingdom by wicked art and invocation of the devil'; and one of the fourteen treasons imputed to Jean de Chalon, prince of Orange, in 1478 was his use of 'diabolical arts'. Langlois, the monks and Orange escaped punishment, but Master Jean Cimar, a converted Aragonese Jew living in Paris, was executed as a traitor in 1399 'because he was a sorcerer, idolator, necromancer, invoker of enemies and defamatory words against the honour of those closest to the blood royal'.[110]

From the second half of the thirteenth century until the mid fourteenth century and probably beyond, crimes committed on public roads were treasonable.[111] It was treason, too, according to Gui Pape and Jean Petit, to help a convicted traitor escape from prison, and it was as traitors that those who had helped Antoine du Lau escape in 1468 were executed.[112] The latter offence but generally not the former was also treasonable in England.[113] Persons making false accusations of treason were themselves liable to be punished as traitors.[114]

For all crimes of treason, but particularly for the serious ones, those persons who, though uninvolved themselves, failed to reveal their knowledge could be charged with complicity. Thus in 1340

108 'Choix de pièces inédites', ed. Duplès-Agier, p. 271; B.N., Coll. Doat 8, fol. 118r; A. Bristow, 'Fourteenth-Century Rodez', (unpublished Oxford D.Phil. thesis, 1976), p. 211.

109 *Chron. de Saint-Denys*, I. 682ff; *Reg. crim. du Châtelet*, I. 419–80; II. 1–6.

110 *Confessions et jugements*, pp. 145–7 (Langlois); Arch. Mun. de Lyon, AA 98, no. 18 (Orange's other treasons are not described); H. Sauval, *Histoire et recherches des antiquités de la ville de Paris* (3 vols., Paris, 1724), III. *preuves*, 258 (Cimar); Bellamy, *The Law of Treason*, p. 126.

111 E.g., *Actes du Parlement de Paris (1254–1328)*, 1st series, ed. E. Boutaric (2 vols., Paris, 1863 and 1867), I. no. 615; 2nd series, I. no. 4496; A.N., X2a 3, fols. 40v–41v.

112 *Infra*, p. 216 and n. 20.

113 Bellamy, *The Law of Treason*, pp. 14, 91, 131, 208.

114 B.N., n.a. fr. 3360, fol. 13r; Roye, *Chron. scan.*, I. 173–4.

Hennequin Lallemand was put in the pillory for his knowledge of Robert Langlois's treasonous necromancy, and in 1314 there were many executions of those who had known of the Aulnay brothers' scandalous liaison with the daughters-in-law of Philippe IV. In the 1470s the extent of the treasonous conspiracies so disturbed Louis XI that on 22 December 1477 he finally codified in law the principle that knowledge alone of treason was no less treason. In England it was not before the fifteenth century that the concealment of treason was assimilated to the crime itself.[115]

The scope of treasonous offences in France as in England was thus a wide one: any action that injured the king, the royal line, or the kingdom, or that otherwise diminished the authority of the crown – or was intended to do so – was treason. Most certainly this interpretation of treason was a wide one by design. First of all the kings could thus invoke the law of treason more readily to punish, if not to deter, political opposition and disloyalty at all levels of society. Deterrence and punishment were also central to a second motive: by extending the severe penalties for treason to a broad range of crimes, the kings could hope better to maintain public order and, perhaps as importantly, to be known to be doing so. As we shall see in the following chapter, the wide scope of treasonous offences also enabled the crown to contest the jurisdictional claims of municipal, seigneurial and ecclesiastical justice. The better the kings could protect themselves and their prerogatives, the greater would be their power and the authority of the crown. To these essentially political considerations can be added a material one: the confiscation of property to the crown was always a part of the punishment for treason. From all points of view the broadest interpretation of treason was in the best interests of the kings personally and of the crown.

[115] *Confessions et jugements*, p. 145 (Lallemand); *Chron. de Guill. de Nangis*, I. 404–5 (Aulnays); *Ordonnances*, XVIII. 315–17; Bellamy, *The Law of Treason*, p. 222.

Chapter 3

JURISDICTION

I

The authority of the French crown in the later middle ages can in part be measured by the extent to which the crown could successfully claim for itself jurisdiction in the prosecution of crime. Since treason was the public crime *par excellence*, only the king – as the embodiment of public authority – or his delegated officers and institutions could have competence to try it. Such at least was the opinion of most legal theorists and *coutumiers*.[1] In practice, however, although a multiplicity of royal jurisdictions did indeed take cognizance in most cases of treason, the crown on occasion still had to assert its rights against the pretensions of municipal, seigneurial and above all ecclesiastical courts. But before we examine these conflicts of jurisdiction, let us first consider the variety of royal jurisdictions.

The kings of France by themselves and without any further legal restraint could exercise their authority to pass sentence on accused traitors. The execution of Olivier III de Clisson in August 1343 'by judgement of the king' is a case in point. Not many months later Philippe VI instructed the *prévôt* of Paris to execute twelve recently arrested supporters of Jean de Montfort 'because we condemn them as traitors'.[2] During the first years of Jean II's reign there were more summary executions by royal order. On 18 November 1350, within months of ascending the throne, the new king had the constable, Raoul de Brienne, count of Eu, beheaded for treason.[3] Perhaps the best-known incident of royal judgement without judicial process was the decapitation at Rouen of Jean V, count of Harcourt, Jean Malet, lord of Graville, and two others on 5 April 1356. By these executions and the arrest of Charles the Bad, Jean II provoked open

[1] E.g., *Le grand coutumier*, p. 100; Boutillier, *Somme rural*, I. 28 (p. 170); *Coutumes de l'Anjou et du Maine*, I(1), 205; see also Perrot, *Les cas royaux*, p. 232n.

[2] Froissart, *Chroniques*, III. pp. ix–x nn.

[3] Gilles Le Muisit, *Chronique et annales*, ed. H. Lemaître (S.H.F.) (Paris, 1905), p. 281.

rebellion in Normandy and drove Navarre's Norman adherents into the eager arms of the English.[4] A valuable lesson, however, was learned from these disastrous results of Jean II's ill-considered actions: from that time onward the kings of France did not avenge themselves on their principal political enemies in such an arbitrary and personal manner, but tried rather to represent the repression of treason as the impartial, legal prosecution of public crime.

This is not to say that summary executions by royal command no longer occurred, for indeed they did; but they were for violations of the laws of war, and did not involve the greater magnates. After the capture of Soissons in May 1414, for example, Charles VI had Enguerran de Bournonville, the Burgundian captain of that town, beheaded for having appeared in arms against him.[5] But this and other examples[6] notwithstanding, conviction by the king's record did give way to more formal procedures when accused traitors were to be punished capitally. It should be noted, though, that the same was not true with regard to forfeitures. Throughout the fourteenth and fifteenth centuries, whenever a traitor escaped the reach of the law his property could be confiscated on the king's word alone. This will be discussed further in chapters 4 and 5.

More common than the summary justice of the king acting alone was the judicial process before the king and council. One finds here the feudal procedure *par excellence*. Bernard Saisset, bishop of Pamiers, was so tried in 1301,[7] as were Enguerran de Marigny in 1315;[8] Béraud de Mercoeur in 1319;[9] the Normans Richard de Percy, Guillaume Bacon and Jean de la Roche-Tesson in 1344;[10] Martin Pisdoe in 1359;[11] Waleran de Luxembourg, count of Saint-Pol, in 1380;[12] Nicolas d'Orgemont, Robert de Belloy and Renaud Maillot in 1416;[13] and Jean IV d'Armagnac in 1445,[14] to name the most important cases. Some persons, like Raoul de Presles in 1315–17[15] and Jacques Coeur in 1451–3[16] were prosecuted by a royal

[4] Delachenal, *Hist. de Charles V*, I. 151ff.

[5] *Chron. de Saint-Denys*, V. 328.

[6] E.g., *supra*, p. 34; *infra*, p. 197.

[7] *Infra*, pp. 73–5.

[8] J. Favier, *Un conseiller de Philippe le Bel: Enguerran de Marigny* (Paris, 1963), pp. 208–17.

[9] *Reg. du Trésor*, II. no. 1487.

[10] L. Delisle, *Histoire du château et des sires de Saint-Sauveur-le-Vicomte* (Valognes, 1867), *p.j.* lxxii.

[11] A.N., JJ 90, no. 369; Delachenal, *Hist. de Charles V*, II. 173–5.

[12] *Chron. de Saint-Denys*, I. 36.

[13] *Infra*, pp. 72–3.

[14] Escouchy, *Chronique*, I. 61–5.

[15] *Reg. du Trésor*, II. no. 299.

[16] R. Guillot, *Le procès de Jacques Coeur* (Paris, 1975).

commission before finally being judged by the king and council. The prosecution of treason before the king's council in France was considerably different from that in England. There the king's council acted more as a 'clearing house': since it could not decree a capital sentence it would direct cases of treason to any of the proper judicial organs; its rôle was essentially to elicit information.[17]

Most of the trials before king and council occurred in the fourteenth century; and there is a probable explanation for this: because of the burdens of other affairs, because of the increasing sophistication of the legal process, and because of an obvious desire publicly to dress prosecution in the cloth of legality, the kings of France later looked increasingly to other royal jurisdictions. Foremost among these was the Parlement of Paris, which, as the judicial outgrowth of the feudal *curia regis*,[18] was naturally competent to try cases in the first instance as well as on appeal. Until the third quarter of the fourteenth century few significant cases came before the Parlement. One can mention only those of Jourdain de l'Isle-Jourdain in 1323;[19] Godefroy d'Harcourt twice, in 1344 and 1356;[20] Jean de Marconnay, bishop of Maillezais, in 1349;[21] and Guillaume de Poitiers, bishop of Langres, in 1354.[22] But beginning with the trial of Jacques de Rue and Pierre du Tertre in 1378,[23] most of the major treason trials and many minor cases were prosecuted before the Parlement, or at least were judged by it.[24] Although no persons, not even clerics, were exempt from its jurisdiction, only the peers had the right to be tried exclusively in the Parlement, with the court 'suffisament garnie de pairs'.[25]

The general judicial burdens on the Parlement in its turn led to the

[17] Bellamy, *The Law of Treason*, pp. 151–4.

[18] See G. Ducoudray, *Les origines du Parlement de Paris et la justice au XIIIe et XIVe siècles* (Paris, 1902). On the Parlement in general see F. Aubert, *Histoire du Parlement de Paris de l'origine à François I* (2 vols., Paris, 1894); F. Aubert, *Le Parlement de Paris de Philippe-le-Bel à Charles VII (1314–1422): sa compétence, ses attributions* (Paris, 1890); F. Aubert, *Le Parlement de Paris de Philippe-le-Bel à Charles VII (1314–1422): son organisation* (Paris, 1887); E. Maugis, *Histoire du Parlement de Paris de l'avènement des rois Valois à la mort d'Henri IV* (3 vols., Paris, 1913–16).

[19] *Grandes chron.*, IX. 16–18.

[20] Delisle, *Hist. de Saint-Sauveur-le-Vicomte*, *p.j.* lxxvi, lxxxix.

[21] *Actes du Parlement*, 2nd series, II. no. 8975.

[22] A.N., JJ 82, no. 216; B.N., Coll. Dupuy 339, fols. 29r–32r.

[23] Delachenal, *Hist. de Charles V*, V. 207ff.

[24] These cases are too numerous to cite. They are referred to throughout this study.

[25] The trial of peers will be discussed in detail in chapter 4.

creation of Grands Jours and provincial Parlements,[26] sovereign courts that were also competent to try treason. In 1456, for example, the case of Pierre Rebouil, a Gascon who was accused of having been an adherent of the English, came before the Grands Jours of Bordeaux.[27] Among the provincial Parlements, that at Toulouse was most active. During the 1420s, just after the future Charles VII had established it, this court had as one of its main tasks the prosecution in the south of France of men like one Pierre de Gibbert who were staunch partisans of the Burgundian faction. After 1444, the court turned its attention to Guyenne and to the people accused of collaborating with the English. But except perhaps for Pons de Castillon, lord of Bruch, all those against whom charges were brought were minor figures.[28] The only important case tried by the Parlement of Toulouse came at the turn of the sixteenth century, against Pierre de Rohan, lord of Gié and marshal of France.[29] By no means were the other Parlements inactive. During the English occupation of Paris the royal Parlement of Poitiers naturally tried cases of treason.[30] And the Parlement of Grenoble, particularly after the death of Charles the Bold, was empowered to bring to justice such traitors as Jean de Chalon, prince of Orange.[31]

At the local level the tribunals of the *baillis*, *sénéchaux* and *prévôts*, which were most often presided over by their lieutenants, had the competence to try crimes of treason, but these cases seem to have been rather minor ones. Prosecution could be undertaken on the initiative of the *bailli* himself;[32] or at the request of the king,[33] the

[26] *Actes du Parlement*, 1st series, I. pp. cxciv–cci; Aubert, *Hist. du Parlement à François I*, I. 268; *Histoire des institutions françaises au moyen âge*, vol. II (*Institutions royales*), ed. F. Lot and R. Fawtier, (Paris, 1958), 470.

[27] M. G. A. Vale, 'A Fifteenth-Century Interrogation of a Political Prisoner', *B.I.H.R.*, XLIII (1970), 80.

[28] A. Viala, *Le Parlement de Toulouse et l'administration royale laïque 1420–1525 environ* (2 vols., Albi, 1953), II. 147–8.

[29] *Procédures politiques du règne de Louis XII*, ed. R. de Maulde La Clavière (C.D.I.) (Paris, 1885), pp. v, xc–cxxvii, 3–565.

[30] E.g., A.N., x2a 18, fols. 179r–184r, 274r; x2a 21, fols. 113v, 122v (King's Proctor *v.* Pierre Caillerot; 1429–31); x2a 18, fols. 308r–309r; x2a 20, fols. 46v–47r; x2a 21, fols. 171r, 179r (King's Proctor *v.* Hennequin Bize; 1431–2); Y. Lanhers, 'Deux affaires de trahison défendues par Jean Jouvenel des Ursins (1423–1427)', *Mélanges Pierre Tisset* (Montpellier, 1970), pp. 317–18. On the Parlement of Poitiers in general see D. Neuville, 'Le Parlement royal à Poitiers 1418–1436', *R.H.*, VI (1878), 1–28, 272–314.

[31] *Lettres de Louis XI*, VI. 154–5.

[32] What applies for the *baillis* also applies for the *sénéchaux* and *prévôts* and their lieutenants: *Actes du Parlement*, 2nd series, II. no. 5160; *Archives anciennes de la ville de Saint-Quentin*, ed.

Parlement,[34] or the king's proctor in the *bailliage*.[35] At least one case indicates that the *bailli* did not always have a free hand. In 1346 or 1347 Guillaume Richier, *bailli* of Gisors, imprisoned Jean de Lyons for having said that Edward III should be king of France 'because he cured scrofula'. Lyons's wife quickly obtained royal letters for his release and presented them at the balival assizes of November 1347. Although Richier was prepared to set Lyons free, he would only do so 'with reservation for the rights of the king's proctor'. The latter, however, stating that 'he was not advised on this matter', asked to examine 'the plea of the said Jean, the investigations and the entire *procès* . . . in order to . . . obtain the advice of the king's council'. A full six years went by before the proctor reported at the assizes of 2 December 1353 that he had shown the *procès* to the king's council and that he had thereupon been instructed not to pursue the case. Only then did the *bailli* release Lyons.[36]

The one royal officer whose power to prosecute traitors became extensive indeed was the *prévôt* of Paris. Since he was the principal officer of the Châtelet – jurisdiction of which originally covered only the *prévôté* of Paris, but which effectively became a sovereign court for the whole kingdom – he was far more powerful than any *bailli* or *sénéchal*.[37] Yet although the Châtelet, like the Conciergerie, was used from the early fourteenth century as a prison for accused traitors who were awaiting trial,[38] it was not until the summer of 1359 that the *prévôt* was vested with competence to prosecute for treason. Of this date one can be reasonably sure. At that time Jeanne Ploybaude, an inhabitant of Amiens held in the Châtelet on charges of treason, sent a complaint to the Parlement, protesting her innocence and objecting strenuously to her imprisonment. The *prévôt*, it was clear, had been refusing to judge her on the grounds that since she was accused of treason, her case did not come within his general jurisdiction. The Parlement acknowledged her letter and wrote to the *prévôt* on 19 July. Brushing aside his objections, the Parlement concurred with Ploybaude that her continuing detention was 'a

E. Lemaire (2 vols., Saint-Quentin, 1888–1910), II. 201; A.N., JJ 71, no. 382; JJ 75, no. 45: JJ 90, no. 351; X2a 11, fols. 275v–277v.

33 A.N., JJ 79A, no. 29.

34 A.N., X2a 2, fols. 26v, 39r.

35 A.N., JJ 77, no. 145.

36 A.N., JJ 82, no. 25.

37 L. Batiffol, 'Le Châtelet de Paris vers 1400', *R.H.*, LXII (1896), 227–32; P. Viollet, *Histoire des institutions politiques et administratives de la France* (3 vols., Paris, 1890–1903), III. 280.

38 A.N., X2a 3, fols. 40v–41r, 149r–v, 196v–197r; X2a 6, fol. 265r.

delay of justice, and great prejudice to [her]'. It therefore instructed the *prévôt* to proceed with 'punishment, conditional release or absolution' because more pressing matters that could not be put aside were occupying the regent and the *grand conseil*, who might otherwise have considered the matter.[39] This grant of authority, made rather casually, it seems, for a specific case, was added to several weeks later: when the regent Charles bestowed privileges on the *arbalétriers*, exempting them from the jurisdiction of the *prévôt* of Paris, he made an exception for the crime of treason.[40] The precedents had now been set.

It is a pity that most of the evidence pertaining to the Châtelet no longer exists. But from what little there is one might assume that at least in the later fourteenth century the *prévôt* of Paris presided over a fair number of cases like those of the spy Hennequin du Bos and the *routier* Mérigot Marchès.[41] By the early fifteenth century the *prévôt*'s responsibility for prosecuting treason was greater still. In 1409 Pierre des Essarts tried no less a figure than Jean de Montagu, *grand maître de l'hôtel*.[42] On 14 October 1411, during the war between the Armagnacs and the Burgundians, Charles VI empowered this same *prévôt* to punish the Armagnac princes and their adherents, who 'have committed the crime of lese-majesty against us and our lordship and crown'.[43] The powers of the *prévôt* reached their peak towards the middle of the fifteenth century. By virtue of royal letters patent published on 5 April 1438 he acquired 'full power, authority and special mandate' to seek out traitors and other criminals anywhere in the kingdom, to have them brought to the Châtelet and to punish them accordingly.[44]

Since the *prévôt* of Paris could preside at the Châtelet over cases of treason from anywhere in the kingdom, one is reasonably led to ask what decided whether a trial would take place in the Châtelet or in the Parlement. There are three parts to the answer. In the first place, except for the trial of Jean de Montagu, which took place at a time of civil war and was conducted by the Burgundian sympathizer Pierre des Essarts, none of the political treason trials were prosecuted in the Châtelet. Secondly, while many of the cases that were taken

[39] A.N., x2a 6, fol. 406v.

[40] *Ordonnances*, III. 361.

[41] *Reg. crim. du Châtelet*, I. 379–93; II. 177–213.

[42] A.N., J 369, no. 5.

[43] *Ordonnances*, IX. 640–2.

[44] *Recueil général des anciennes lois*, VIII. 861–2.

before the Parlement could be prosecuted *ad finem civilem*,[45] this was not true of the cases in the Châtelet. And thirdly, several of the trials in the Châtelet that ultimately ended in convictions for treason had in fact been initiated on other charges such as theft; the treasons were only discovered accidentally during the course of interrogations under torture.[46] Again, one cannot say this of the Parlement.

As in England,[47] in the military sphere numerous officers could take cognizance. If treason was within the jurisdiction of captains in the field,[48] it was *a fortiori* within the competence of the royal lieutenants and captains-general,[49] the constable,[50] the marshal,[51] the provost-marshal,[52] the *maître des arbalétriers*,[53] and their lieutenants.[54] The military officers of the realm zealously prosecuted treason. Indeed, at least in the mid fourteenth century they were too zealous; for as a result of the confused situation that marked the late 1350s and early 1360s, they were encroaching on civil jurisdictions in cases that were not strictly military. For example, in a suit arising from the Jacquerie, the knight Geoffroy de Saint-Gaubert had some subjects of the duke of Orléans taken before the marshal's court in spite of the fact that they were exempt from that tribunal's jurisdiction. When the case went on appeal to the Parlement of Paris the marshals' proctor argued that the marshals 'have been accustomed to take cognizance in [the king's] name of each and every case, and its dependencies, that arise from wars and rebellions among [his] subjects'.

[45] These are cases of private war or breach of safeguard in which plaintiffs claim damages, and in which the king's proctor also joins issue with the defendants. See e.g., A.N., x2a 6, fols. 449v–452v; x2a 7, fols. 344v–346r; x2a 9, fols. 216v–219r; x2a 16, fols. 221v–223v.

[46] E.g., *Reg. crim. du Châtelet*, I. 14–35, 52–73, 119–25; II. 92–100.

[47] Keen, 'Treason Trials'.

[48] *Recueil*, ed. Secousse, pp. 149–50.

[49] E.g., A.N., JJ 73, no. 57; JJ 80, no. 686; JJ 105, no. 73; B.N., ms. fr. 26018, no. 246; *Preuves de la maison de Chabannes*, II. 176–80.

[50] *Chronographia Regum Francorum*, ed. H. Moranvillé (S.H.F.) (3 vols., Paris, 1891–7), II. 43–4; A.N., JJ 84, no. 67; JJ 113, no. 242. On the constable's jurisdiction in general see J. H. Mitchell, *The Court of the Connétable* (New Haven, Connecticut, 1947), pp. 12–13; Contamine, *Guerre, état et société*, p. 519; G. Le Barrois d'Orgeval, *La justice militaire sous l'Ancien Régime. Le tribunal de la connétablie de France du XIVe siècle à 1790* (Paris, 1918).

[51] A.N., JJ 81, no. 194; JJ 82, no. 519; A. Chérest, *L'archiprêtre: épisodes de la guerre de Cent ans au quatorzième siècle* (Paris, 1879), pp. 16–19 and *p.j.* iii. For the jurisdiction of the marshal in general, see Contamine, *Guerre, état et société*, p. 519.

[52] Roye, *Chron. scan.*, I. 78; A.N., J 950, nos. 8–10, 20.

[53] A.N., JJ 80, no. 412.

[54] B.N., ms. fr. 26091, nos. 669–70; Bibliothèque Sainte-Geneviève, ms. 2000, fols. 76r–85v. Although I have not come across any evidence of cases tried by the admiral or the lieutenants of the constable and the marshal, it is likely that they too had competence.

This was a far-reaching claim indeed, and the court appropriately rejected it.[55] On the other hand, even cases to which a military tribunal had jurisdictional entitlement could be tried in civil courts. It should be noted, though, that in such instances the allegation of treason was not the principal cause of prosecution but rather a line of attack followed by one of two parties to prove that the other was an enemy of the king and thus fell under the laws of war with regard to ransom.[56]

In prosecuting treason the king could delegate authority to royal officers and non-royal jurisdictions not normally competent in this matter. During the reign of Louis XI the *prévôt de l'hôtel du roi* was more than once given the authority to prosecute traitors.[57] And on at least one occasion – the trial of Jean Hardi in 1474 – the king empowered the *prévot des marchands* and the *échevins* of Paris to conduct the prosecution.[58] But such instances are admittedly rare. With regard to cognizance being granted to non-royal jurisdictions, the affair of the lepers in 1321 can serve as an example, although here Philippe V was in fact ratifying a situation that already existed. The barons in Languedoc, faced with the immediate need to repress the lepers, who were accused of a gigantic conspiracy with the Jews to poison the wells, had ignored royal jurisdiction in bringing many of these poor wretches to justice. When officers of the crown complained to the king about this he levied a fine against the barons for their judicial usurpation 'because it was understood in our council that the jurisdiction and punishment of all the lepers in our kingdom belong to us as for the crime of lese-majesty'. But later, since certain people were unsure if the crimes were in fact lese-majesty, and, more importantly, because 'the seriousness of the crime . . . requires swift punishment', Philippe V on 18 August 1321 granted to the barons the right to prosecute all who were accused even of crimes of lese-majesty.[59]

In England, among the extraordinary jurisdictions with competence to prosecute treason, there were commissions of oyer and

[55] Le Barrois d'Orgeval, *La justice militaire*, *p.j.* iv; see also Keen, *Laws of War*, pp. 63–4.

[56] E.g., A.N., x2a 22, fols. 12r–13v; x2a 23, fols. 2v–3r, 376r–v; x2a 26, fols. 56r–v, 177r, 184r–v, 219v–220r, 332v, 367r–371r; Lanhers, 'Deux affaires de trahison'.

[57] Roye, *Chron. scan.*, II. 30–1; *Lettres de Louis XI*, VI. 203–4.

[58] A.N., z1h 16, fols. 128r, 141r, 143v; B.N., ms. fr. 5908, fol. 143r; Roye, *Chron. scan.*, I. 303–9.

[59] *Ordonnances*, XI. 481–2; B.N., Coll. Doat 8, fols. 118r–120r.

terminer, which did operate under the common law, and special commissions, which need not. In France the kings were similarly not limited to the permanent jurisdictions; they too had unrestrained authority to appoint special commissions.[60] The functions and composition of these commissions were not all uniform. The commissioners could have investigative rôles alone;[61] they might be empowered to act in concert with certain royal officers,[62] members of the Parlement or the king's council;[63] or they could have full authority from beginning to end in the prosecution of accused traitors;[64] but unlike in England, they all followed the inquisitorial procedure. Whatever the case, the value of commissions, particularly to Charles VII and Louis XI, was in the swiftness of their procedure and the control that the kings could exercise over them.

Although it was not unusual for commissions to be empowered to deal with urban or local rebellions – as at Rouen *c.* 1350, Paris in 1358, Normandy and the north-east in the early 1380s, and Bourges in 1474[65] – most of the commissions were appointed to try individuals. These could be barons and great lords like Louis d'Amboise in 1431, Charles de Melun in 1468, Charles d'Albret in 1473, Louis de Luxembourg in 1475, Jacques d'Armagnac in 1476–7, or René d'Alençon in 1481–3;[66] civil servants like Jean de Saincoins in 1450, Jacques Coeur in 1451–3, or Jacques de Canlers, *contrôleur* of the *argenterie*, in 1465;[67] a jurist like Gui Pape in 1462;[68] or a royal physician like Yves Philippe in 1459.[69] Some rather insignificant

[60] For commissions in England see Bellamy, *The Law of Treason*, pp. 147–51. On commissions in general in France see G. Dupont-Ferrier, 'Le rôle des commissaires royaux dans le gouvernement de la France spécialement du XIVe au XVIe siècle', *Mélanges Paul Fournier* (Paris, 1929), pp. 171–84.

[61] A.N., x1a 12, fols. 413v–414r; *Actes du Parlement*, 2nd series, I. no. 9049; A.N., x2a 23, fol. 65r–v.

[62] E.g., with a *bailli* (A.N., JJ 79A, no. 29); the *grand sénéchal* of Normandy (B.N., ms. fr. 22469, no. 60); with the provost-marshal (B.N., ms. fr. 2921, fols. 29r *et seq.*).

[63] B.N., ms. fr. 16541, fols. 313ff (Jacques Coeur); ms. fr. 3869, fols. 1r–3r (Louis de Luxembourg).

[64] Jean Chartier, *Chronique de Charles VII*, ed. A. Vallet de Viriville (3 vols., Paris, 1858), III. 49–50.

[65] A. N., JJ 81, no. 309 (Rouen); *Recueil*, ed. Secousse, pp. 80–1 (Paris); A.N., JJ 123, no. 85; JJ 124, no. 70; Mirot, *Les insurrections urbaines*, pp. 198–9 (Normandy and the north-east); B.N., ms. fr. 2912, fol. 5r (Bourges).

[66] *Infra*, pp. 106–12 (Nemours and Alençon); 195–6 (Amboise); 217–18 (Melun), 221–2 (Albret); 224–7 (Luxembourg).

[67] *Infra*, pp. 206–9 (Saincoins and Coeur); 215–16 (Canlers).

[68] B.N., ms. fr. 16536, fol. 165r–v.

[69] A.N., x2a 29, fol. 127v.

people, too, like the papal sergeant-at-arms Pierre Vital in 1344, the 'simple man' Jean le Meunier in 1358, and Laurent de Mory in 1465 could also be tried by commissioners.[70]

In the most important political cases the king or the Parlement would pronounce sentence in order to lend greater authority to the decision. Amboise and Coeur, for example, were judged by the king, while Louis de Luxembourg was condemned by the Parlement. Jacques d'Armagnac and René d'Alençon, both of whom had claims to the peerage, were also sentenced in the end by the Parlement of Paris, but in both cases the king was represented by his chosen lieutenant.

Although a commission could be composed of as little as one person,[71] or as many as seventeen,[72] the norm was about six to eight. The members were usually drawn from the royal household, the Parlement, the king's council, the Châtelet, the higher military officers, and occasionally the local officers. Thus when the regent Charles appointed a commission in August 1358 to prosecute the traitors in Paris, he chose a president of the Parlement, three *maîtres des requêtes de l'hôtel*, three councillors in the Parlement, the *bailli* of Troyes and Meaux, and the *prévôt* of Paris.[73] In 1469 the commissioners chosen for the prosecution of Jean Balue, cardinal of Angers, reflected the gravity of the case. They were the chancellor Guillaume Juvenal des Ursins; the *grand maître des arbalétriers* Jean d'Estouteville; Guillaume Cousinot, lord of Montreuil; Jean de la Driesche, president of the *chambre des comptes*; Jean Le Boulanger, president in the Parlement of Paris; the future chancellor Pierre d'Oriole, then *général des finances*; the provost-marshal Tristan l'Hermite; and Guillaume Allegrin, a councillor in the Parlement.[74] In general there was one defect in trials by commission: some commissioners, like Antoine de Chabannes in the prosecution of Jacques Coeur, and Ymbert de Batarnay in that of Jacques d'Armagnac,[75] knew that they would profit materially from the condemnation of the accused.

[70] A.N., JJ 75, no. 52 (Vital); JJ 90, no. 206 (Meunier); Roye, *Chron. scan.*, I. 69 (Mory).
[71] A.N., JJ 81, no. 309.
[72] Bibl. Ste-Geneviève, ms. 2000, fols. 105r–117r (trial of Nemours, 1477).
[73] *Recueil*, ed. Secousse, pp. 80–1.
[74] Forgeot, *Jean Balue*, *p.j.* v.
[75] A.N., X2a 32, fol. 102r; Clément, *Jacques Coeur*, II. 189–90; Mandrot, *Ymbert de Batarnay*, pp. 70–1.

II

At the beginning of this chapter it was said that the crown had to be ever on the alert to assert its authority against the encroachments of municipal, seigneurial and ecclesiastical justice. Let us now consider these in order. In March 1346, for example, the consuls and inhabitants of Montauban were constrained to supplicate for a pardon because they had usurped royal jurisdiction by having executed the traitor Jacques Carbonnel.[76] A few years later there was a similar episode at Mirebeau in Poitou. Two men sent from Lusignan to spy on the town for the English were decapitated as traitors by order of Aimery Chauverel, *garde de la justice*, who was subsequently imprisoned for having usurped royal jurisdiction.[77] Another example from the fourteenth century illustrates how the crown actually contended with a town for its rights. Peyre Robi and Ramon Enargau, sergeants of the Bourg of Rodez, having charged each other with treason, were summoned in early 1350 to a judicial duel by the officers of that town's common court. In May, when this encroachment on royal jurisdiction came to the attention of Philippe VI, he instructed the *juge-mage* of Marvéjols to make an investigation. The latter then summoned the *sénéchal* of Rouergue for the king, and the proctor of the common court for the town of Rodez. To the *sénéchal*'s contention that 'from ancient times' the king had jurisdiction in cases of treason, the proctor Gaffinel replied that 'in the present town of Rodez my lords have high, low and every other kind of jurisdiction, indeed jurisdiction in the first instance in the most important cases'. Since no solution to these conflicting arguments could be found, a commission of inquiry was sent to Rodez in 1352. But the case had become moot before the commissioners arrived, since the two sergeants had proceeded to fight their duel. Bitter feelings, however, remained between the municipal and royal officers.[78]

Although it is not evident from the above examples, there was in

[76] A.N., JJ 76, no. 264, published in M. Bertrandy, *Etude sur les chroniques de Froissart* (Bordeaux, 1870), pp. 227–8.

[77] A.N., JJ 82, no. 33; Chauverel was pardoned in December 1353.

[78] Bristow, 'Fourteenth-Century Rodez', pp. 206–7. Philippe VI and not Jean II was king in May 1350 (*Chroniques des règnes de Jean II et de Charles V*, ed. R. Delachenal (S.H.F.) (4 vols., Paris, 1910–20), I. 25 n. 2).

fact one way in which the crown did justify its rights in a town, and that was by specifically excluding jurisdiction for treason from the privileges granted in a town's municipal charter. Thus in 1261 the Parlement of Paris informed the *échevins* of Roye that they could not judge a burgess of their town who was accused of having attacked a cleric on a public road: this was a crime of treason, it was argued, and according to the town's charter the cognizance of it thus belonged to the king. In 1370, in the charter granted to Saint-Antonin, Charles V stipulated that only the crown could punish treason. Even in the late fifteenth century Louis XI had to remind a town like Chartres that treason was definitely not in its jurisdiction.[79]

But because towns were jealous of their privileges, royal officers, when they successfully asserted their rights to jurisdiction, had to take this into account. In November 1346, for example, when the *prévôt* of Saint-Quentin was about to execute a traitor named Morel de Fonsomes, he assured the mayor and *jurés* that this would not be to their prejudice.[80] In spite of its sometimes graceful insistence on its exclusive jurisdiction, the crown could also on occasion authorize a town to take cognizance, as on 14 October 1411, when Charles VI instructed the *capitouls* of Toulouse to punish as traitors the adherents of the Armagnacs in that town.[81]

III

The crown could specifically reserve to itself jurisdiction in cases of treason when making grants of land to both magnates and minor nobility.[82] But conflicts did occur whether or not such reservations had been made. For the most part the disputes were resolved in the Parlement of Paris, and not surprisingly in the crown's favour. In the 1330s, for example, the *dame* of Cassel unsuccessfully claimed competence in the case of Guillaume Dupont, who, normally subject to her jurisdiction, had been imprisoned by the *bailli* of Montreuil on charges of treason for having instigated the murder of the castellan

79 *Actes du Parlement*, 1st series, I. no. 615 (Roye); *Ordonnances*, VI. 502 (Saint-Antonin); *ibid.* XVIII. 656 (Chartres).

80 *Archives anciennes de Saint-Quentin*, II. 201.

81 Ville de Toulouse, *Inventaire des archives communales antérieures à 1790*, vol. I, ed. E. Roschach (Toulouse, 1891), 485.

82 *Ordonnances*, V. 429, 479; *Reg. du Trésor*, I. no. 1508.

of Franleu.[83] Another case, with the rôles reversed, came before the Parlement after the outbreak of hostilities between the English and the French in the late 1360s. Berengar d'Arpajon, who had imprisoned Auger de Caumont for having tried to deliver the place of Caumont to the English, was ordered by the Parlement on 23 July 1370 to hand him over to royal justice. Arpajon refused, whereupon the court instructed the *sénéchal* of Rouergue on 16 November to obtain Caumont's release so that he could be brought to Paris for trial. Since, the court declared, this was a case of treason, 'the cognizance of which belongs to [the crown]', Arpajon was expressly prohibited from proceeding further in this matter. But still he continued to claim jurisdiction. On 13 September 1371 the court again ordered that Caumont be transferred to the *sénéchal*'s prisons.[84] One can assume that this was finally done, since nothing more is heard of the case.

There was a similar, though slightly more complicated, episode in the later 1350s. Shortly after the murder of Etienne Marcel on 31 July 1358 Guy de Châtillon, count of Saint-Pol and royal lieutenant in Picardy, the Beauvaisis, 'and generally in the area around the river Oise', arrested Pierre de la Chapelle, mayor of Hesdin, on charges of adhering to the king of Navarre. On the basis of Saint-Pol's report, the council of the regent Charles on 8 February 1359 commissioned Fauvel de Badencourt, a royal councillor and *maître des requêtes*, to conclude the prosecution of la Chapelle. At about that time Saint-Pol was replaced as royal lieutenant by the constable Robert de Fiennes, who asked him to deliver the prisoner into his custody. In spite of Saint-Pol's assent to do so he kept putting off the constable, trying at the same time to win the support of the regent. Although Charles had to back Fiennes, since Saint-Pol was now only a private person, Saint-Pol still refused to give up jurisdiction in the case. Not long afterwards, the *bailli* of Amiens was sent with royal letters for the release of the prisoner to the constable, but to no avail, since la Chapelle had escaped from prison. Eventually, however, he did appear before the constable and was pardoned.[85] In the fifteenth century, too, at least in the south of France, the nobility of middle

[83] A.N., X1a 6, fol. 358r; *Actes du Parlement*, 2nd series, I. no. 825.

[84] A.N., X2a 8, fol. 238r–v.

[85] A.N., JJ 90, no. 46; X2a 6, fol. 401r–v; *Recueil*, ed. *Secousse*, pp. 158–9.

rank – lords like Jean, count of Astarac – had to be reminded by the Parlement of Toulouse that they could not claim competence in cases of lese-majesty.[86]

The greatest lords also sought to have jurisdiction over crimes of treason. Charles the Bad had such pretensions in the town and barony of Montpellier;[87] but in this as in other matters the crown had to be most watchful of the dukes of Burgundy. On 17 May 1390, for example, the king's proctor in the Parlement of Paris expressly declared that when 'there is a crime of lese-majesty . . . my lord of Burgundy cannot have cognizance'. And in 1463 a *mémoire* presented by the royal *bailli* of Sens reiterated that 'to the king our lord and to his *baillis*, *prévôts* and officers belong the cognizance, punishment and correction of all cases and crimes of lese-majesty'.[88] Another problem, though a minor one, was the pretensions of certain lords to have injuries against themselves treated as crimes of lese-majesty. The crown could perhaps argue successfully against a count of Candale or a cardinal of Montserrat,[89] but there was little that it could do about a duke of Brittany or Burgundy.[90]

IV

The most intense conflict was not with the towns nor with the nobility but with the church, which claimed to be competent not only for all treasons committed by clerics but also for treasons committed within its general jurisdiction. With regard to the second of these two claims the crown needed only to invoke the principle, as expressed by Guillaume du Breuil, that 'temporal jurisdiction cannot be impeded by spiritual jurisdiction'.[91] But treason by clerics was a more complex issue on which the legists and *coutumiers* were not of one mind. Both the anonymous author of the *Livre des droiz et des commandemens d'office de justice* and a *coutume* of Anjou and Maine

[86] Viala, *Le Parlement de Toulouse*, II. 40. [87] *Le grand coutumier*, p. 100.

[88] Quoted in J. Faussemagne, *L'apanage ducal de Bourgogne dans ses rapports avec la monarchie française (1363–1477)* (Lyon, 1937), pp. 195, 197.

[89] Viala, *Le Parlement de Toulouse*, II. 14.

[90] B.N., ms. fr. 4773, fols. 33r–40v; Fr. baron de Reiffenberg, *Histoire de l'Ordre de la Toison d'Or* (Brussels, 1830), pp. 45–6.

[91] Breuil, *Stilus Curie Parlamenti*, p. 210; see also P. Fournier, 'Les conflits de juridiction entre l'église et le pouvoir séculier de 1080 à 1328', *Rev. des quest. hist.*, XXVII (1880), 432–64. For an example see A.N., X2a 12, fols. 14v, 108v; *Reg. crim. du Châtelet*, I. 381–2.

made the absolute assertion that clerical privilege did not obtain.[92] Jacques d'Ableiges, author of the *Grand coutumier de France*, made some concession to the church, arguing that a cleric should be handed over to the official of his diocese, but he added significantly that 'the latter shall be prohibited from examining the former without calling in the king's men'.[93] Jean de Terre-Vermeille, on the other hand, asserted that only the pope could sit in judgement.[94] How indeed did the crown deal with treason by clerics?

At the end of the thirteenth century royal justice allowed ecclesiastical courts to have exclusive cognizance of treason committed by clerics. In 1297, for example, at the request of Philippe IV the pope instructed the archbishop of Rouen, the bishop of Auxerre and the abbot of Saint-Denis to punish several accused clerics.[95] In the fourteenth and fifteenth centuries there was only one case to my knowledge – and this a minor one – in which an ecclesiastical tribunal proceeded without the prior knowledge or interference of royal officials. In the early 1350s the official of Angers prosecuted Benoît le Galois, who had been accused of having given valuable aid and information to Walter Bentley, Edward III's lieutenant in Brittany. Yet although this ecclesiastical officer acquitted le Galois, he did not have the full authority to pardon crimes of treason; le Galois's absolution had to be confirmed by the king.[96]

The crown generally acceded to ecclesiastical claims of jurisdiction, but rarely did it do so unreservedly or without prior legal action. After the death of Philippe IV, Pierre de Latilly, bishop of Châlons, was tried in the court of his superior the archbishop of Reims, then by the bishops of Cambrai, Amiens, Mende and Arras, and finally by the pope, but there was constant interference by royal officers, and even by Louis X himself.[97] In 1344 one of Philippe VI's *maîtres des requêtes*, Henri de Malestroit, who had defected to the Montfortists and was later captured at Quimper, was first interrogated and

[92] *Le livre des droiz et des commandemens d'office de justice*, ed. C.-J. Beautemps-Beaupré (2 vols., Paris, 1865), II. 282; *Coutumes de l'Anjou et du Maine*, I(I), 435.

[93] *Le grand coutumier*, p. 102; L. Delisle, 'L'auteur du Grand coutumier de France', *Mém. soc. hist. de Paris et de l'Ile de France*, VIII (1881), 140–60.

[94] Terra-Rubea, *Contra Rebelles*, fol. 66r.

[95] R. Genestal, *Le Privilegium Fori en France du Décret de Gratien à la fin du XIVe siècle* (2 vols., Paris, 1921 and 1924), II. 162. On conflict of jurisdiction generally see R. Genestal, *Les origines de l'appel comme d'abus* (Paris, 1951).

[96] S. Luce, *Histoire de Bertrand du Guesclin et de son époque* (Paris, 1876), *p.j.* iii.

[97] Pegues, *The Lawyers of the Last Capetians*, pp. 67–73.

detained for some time in royal prisons before being turned over to the bishop of Paris.[98] In January 1439 the English captured the castle of Saint-Germain-en-Laye. It was royal officers who later arrested Carbonnet, prior of Nanterre, who had treasonably helped the English, but it was an ecclesiastical court that sentenced him to prison on bread and water.[99] All these episodes occurred in or near Paris and the central organs of government. A case from the reign of Louis XI illustrates the hesitations of local royal officers faced with the demands of ecclesiastical officers. During the War of the Public Weal the *bailli* of Tournai arrested Ostelet Brumin, a labourer from Waterloo who had boasted that he was going to join the count of Charolais's army and would bring back Louis XI's head. The officials of the ecclesiastical court of Tournai claimed him as a cleric, but the *bailli*, unwilling to act without the consent of the king, wrote to Louis XI on 4 August 1465 and requested instructions. At the same time, he sent Brumin's confession to the chancellor. Nor was this the first time that the *bailli* had so acted: a month earlier he had made a similar request for guidance concerning David Jacques, a religious of Saint-Quentin charged with fomenting sedition in that town.[100] Unfortunately nothing more is known of these two episodes.

Most often the crown reserved for itself a rôle, greater or lesser depending on the exigencies of the case, in the prosecution of clerics accused of treason. In 1371, or thereabouts, royal officers arrested Robert de la Bourse on charges of consorting with the English at Calais, inciting to riot and revealing state secrets, and imprisoned him in the Châtelet. Although the crown eventually allowed the official of Paris to take custody of la Bourse, the king's proctor and advocate were delegated to participate in the ecclesiastical prosecution.[101] Another trial from that period exemplifies how a compromise between crown and church could be reached. Bastin de Brabant, a cleric and royal officer, was being held in the prisons of the bishop of Paris on charges of peculation, clipping coins and counterfeiting the royal seal. At the same time as the bishop brought suit in the Parlement of Paris for release to himself of Bastin's property, which was

[98] *Grandes chron.*, IX. 249–51; *Chron. Reg. Franc.*, II. 208; *Confessions et jugements*, p. 156.
[99] *Journal d'un bourgeois*, pp. 343–4.
[100] A.N., J 1021, nos. 4, 28.
[101] A.N., JJ 103, no. 191; at the request of the count of Flanders, the king voided the prosecution and pardoned him in August 1372.

being distrained by the *prévôt* of Paris, he had to defend his claims to jurisdiction in the case. The thrust of his argument was that the crimes fell within the civil law, and that Bastin should in this case enjoy benefit of clergy. Arguing in rebuttal for the *prévôt* of Paris, the king's proctor asserted that even if the case were civil – which he strenuously denied – the crown would have cognizance, since Bastin was a royal officer. But not only was the case criminal, it was also one of treason 'because of the horses and weapons that [Bastin] has recently sold to the enemies of the king'. Although the Parlement decided in favour of the bishop on both issues it did stipulate that councillors from the court would be present throughout the course of Bastin's trial.[102]

The more serious the treason, the greater the rôle of the crown. Bernard Délicieux, a Franciscan monk who had been arrested and tried for treason in 1305 on charges of fomenting sedition in Carcassonne and elsewhere in the south, was arrested again in 1318 on a similar charge, and was also accused of heresy, necromancy and poisoning Benedict XI. The commission instituted to try him included the archbishop of Toulouse; the bishops of Pamiers, Saint-Papoul and Laon; Jean, count of Forez; the *sénéchals* of Toulouse and Carcassonne; and several other ecclesiastics and secular lords. On 8 December 1319, having been convicted of all but the last charge, he was degraded and imprisoned for the rest of his life. He died in March 1320.[103]

Better examples of this type are the trials of Jean Fusoris and Nicolas d'Orgemont in 1415–16, for they illustrate well the manner by which the crown could manage the prosecution of accused clerics while yet appearing to accede to ecclesiastical claims of jurisdiction. Jean Fusoris, canon of Notre-Dame of Paris, Master of Arts, Medicine and Theology, was arrested on 6 September 1415 by order of the *grand conseil* on suspicion of having had traitorous relations with the English since their invasion that summer. Commissioners from the Parlement and the *prévôté* of Paris were appointed to conduct the prosecution, and for the moment ecclesiastical justice was completely brushed aside. On 15 September the dean of Notre-Dame went to

[102] A.N., X1a 1469, fols. 489v–490r.

[103] J. B. Hauréau, *Bernard Délicieux et l'inquisition albigeoise* (Paris, 1877), pp. 97–101, 105–30, 156–65; Vaissete, *Hist. de Languedoc*, IX. 391–3; P. Lehugeur, *Histoire de Philippe le Long, roi de France (1316–1322)* (2 vols., Paris, 1897 and 1931), I. 440–5.

the Châtelet, where Fusoris was being detained, to remonstrate with the commissioners. Robert de Maugis, first president in the Parlement and one of the commissioners, responded that he did not have the authority to deliver Fusoris to the church, since it was the *grand conseil* that had ordered his arrest. But after repeated protestations by the dean, the chancellor Henri de Marle decided on 22 January 1416 to hand Fusoris over to the chapter.[104] One can only speculate why he chose to deliver Fusoris at that particular time. The most probable explanation is that Marle realized that there was not enough hard evidence to convict Fusoris: by seeming to yield to the chapter of Notre-Dame he was thus exerting subtle pressure on it to punish Fusoris in some way. To ensure that the ecclesiastical prosecution would indeed be rigorous the chancellor stipulated that four or five councillors from the Parlement would be deputed not merely to observe but to take part in the ecclesiastical procedure.[105]

On 27 January 1416 the chapter of Notre-Dame appointed its prosecutors, who for the next several months gathered witnesses' depositions. But the accusation against Fusoris could not be proved because of discrepancies in the statements. Finally on 24 June the chapter assembled in order to conclude the trial. The dean declared that while on the one hand there was not enough evidence for conviction, on the other hand a full acquittal was impossible. Fusoris was therefore constrained to reside at Mézières-sur-Meuse or within a five-mile radius of it; and, on penalty of being convicted of the crimes with which he was charged, he was not to leave there unless the chapter decided otherwise.[106]

In the case of Nicolas d'Orgemont, another canon of Notre-Dame, we have the example of a cleric first being condemned and punished civilly before being handed over to ecclesiastical justice for canonical punishment; but even then royal interference did not cease. During the spring of 1416 Orgemont became involved in a Burgundian plot to deliver Paris to John the Fearless, and he was arrested along with many others on 21 April. On the following day his chapter claimed jurisdiction. Orgemont had confessed fully, however,

[104] L. Mirot, 'Le procès de Maître Jean Fusoris', *Mém. soc. hist. de Paris et de l'Ile de France*, XXVII (1900), 161–6; Mirot published the transcript of the trial (A.N., LL 85, fols. 1r–59v) at pp. 173–279.

[105] *Choix de pièces inédites relatives au règne de Charles VI*, ed. L. Douët-d'Arcq (S.H.F.) (2 vols., Paris, 1863 and 1864), I. 377.

[106] Mirot, 'Le procès de Jean Fusoris', pp. 166–9.

and the king acted swiftly. In a session of his council on 23 April Charles VI declared Orgemont guilty of lese-majesty, 'a crime which is privileged' – that is, one for which there was no clerical immunity – 'and the cognizance of which belongs to the king'. By virtue of the royal judgement Orgemont was stripped of all his public offices and was fined 80,000 *écus*. Furthermore, the sentence required that he witness the executions of two of his co-conspirators, Robert de Belloy and Renaud Maillot. Like Orgemont the latter was also a cleric, but one of considerably lesser status. After this, Orgemont's condemnation would be read out in public. Then and only then could the chapter take cognizance.[107] The sentence was carried out on 24 April, but in spite of the theoretical transfer of jurisdiction the king did not allow the chapter to take physical custody of Orgemont, who he insisted must stay in the Bastille. Since it was most difficult in such circumstances for the whole chapter to conduct a trial, it therefore appointed five commissioners, but even then their freedom of action was curtailed by the five royal officers who joined them at the insistence of the king. The ensuing process was brief: on 30 April the full chapter deprived Orgemont of his ecclesiastical offices and sentenced him to life imprisonment on bread and water. Completely broken, Orgemont died in November of that year.[108]

Royal officers, if not the king himself, played a yet more active rôle in the prosecution of prelates. The first such case, and perhaps the most important one, was that of Bernard Saisset, bishop of Pamiers, in 1301. Since much has been written about this affair and the church–state dispute that it provoked,[109] only the essential and neglected details that are germane to this study and to this chapter in particular need be mentioned.

Not only was Saisset's the first important treason trial of a cleric in later medieval France, it was also the first 'state trial' of any person, cleric or lay, in the period. Saisset's alleged conspiracy with the count

[107] Mirot, 'Le procès du Boiteux d'Orgemont', 4th part, *M.A.*, xxv (1912), 363–75; B.N., Coll. Dupuy 480, fol. 23r.

[108] Mirot, 'Le procès d'Orgemont', pp. 375–81; Nicholas de Baye, *Journal*, ed. A. Tuetey (S.H.F.) (2 vols., Paris, 1885 and 1888), II. 248–9; *Journal d'un bourgeois*, pp. 70–1; Genestal, *Privilegium Fori*, II. 180–92.

[109] E.g., P. Dupuy, *Histoire du differend d'entre le pape Boniface VIII et Philippes le Bel roy de France* (Paris, 1655); G. Digard, *Philippe le Bel et le Saint-Siège de 1285 à 1304* (2 vols., Paris, 1936), *passim*; J. Rivière, *Le problème de l'église et de l'état au temps de Philippe le Bel* (Louvain and Paris, 1926), *passim*; J.-M. Vidal, *Bernard Saisset (1232–1311)* (Paris and Toulouse, 1926).

of Foix was perhaps the most important charge against him, but much emphasis was given as well to his slanderous remarks about Philippe IV: the king would lose his kingdom; 'he was worth nothing'; he was 'neither man nor beast, but a phantom'; he was descended from bastards and therefore had no right to the throne.[110] Here we have the first case of constructive treason by words in the later middle ages. The actual language of the accusation is also worthy of note, for here we find the fusion of the Roman and feudal concepts of treason. Saisset's crime, described as 'laesa maiestas', 'proditio', and 'conspiracio', was conceived 'contra fidelitatem ad quam domino Regi tenetur'. The bishop, moreover, was 'proditor' not only 'patriae suae', but also 'domini Regis et regni Franciae'.[111]

Having learned of Saisset's treasonous behaviour, both by means of a secret investigation and from witnesses personally interrogated by himself, Philippe IV convoked his council. On the advice of the prelates and the magnates he summoned Saisset to appear at Senlis on 6 October 1301 in order to justify himself. On 24 October, before an assembly of ecclesiastical and secular magnates, knights and clerics, Pierre Flote read out the indictment in the presence of Saisset. Although Philippe IV then expressed his desire that Gilles Aicelin, archbishop of Narbonne, take custody of Saisset, at the same time he made it clear that he wanted secular as well as ecclesiastical judges to prosecute the bishop. In the face of the king's threat to act unilaterally if he refused, the archbishop reluctantly agreed.[112]

Philippe IV then sent an embassy to the pope to justify his actions and to request papal co-operation. The king, it was declared, had the authority to punish 'talem proditorem suum', since 'tantus reatus omne privilegium, omnem dignitatem excludat'. Philippe IV would for the moment defer to the pontiff, but the king's ambassadors conveyed his expectation that the pope would degrade Saisset so that the king 'de illo proditore Dei et hominum . . . possit Deo facere per viam justiciae sacrificium optimum'.[113] This was hardly a request

110 *Gallia Christiana*, ed. D. Sammarthan *et al.* (16 vols., Paris, 1715–1865), XIII. instr. xvi, cols. 116–18; instr. xviii, cols. 120–31.

111 A.N., J 336, no. 9, published in Dupuy, *Hist. du differend*, p. 627; *Gallia Christ.*, XIII. instr. xvi, col. 118.

112 Vidal, *Bernard Saisset*, pp. 78–87; Dupuy, *Hist. du differend*, pp. 628–30, 633–51, 656; *Gallia Christ.*, XIII. instr. xvi, col. 118; instr. xvii, cols. 118–20.

113 Dupuy, *Hist. du differend*, p. 630; see also Genestal, *Privilegium Fori*, II. 163–7.

calculated to mollify the already incensed pope, who in his turn demanded on 6 December 1301 from an equally intransigent Philippe IV that Saisset be tried in Rome. In the event, the fate of the bishop was reduced to an issue of minor importance as the king and the pope confronted each other over weightier matters. By the summer of 1302 Saisset was out of France and at the papal curia, where he remained until his death in 1311.[114] But Philippe IV had made his point that even prelates were not exempt from secular prosecution.

When Guichard, bishop of Troyes, was arrested in 1308 for allegedly having poisoned Queen Blanche of Navarre in 1302 and Queen Jeanne of France in 1305, there were parallel proceedings by secular and ecclesiastical tribunals. The royal officers, however, were clearly the most zealous in examining witnesses and drawing up the indictment. Indeed, the ecclesiastical prosecution was initiated only because Philippe IV again let the pope know that justice would be done in any case. All the while that Guichard's trial was in progress he remained in royal custody at the Louvre. As in the case of Saisset, no judgement was reached, the affair having become moot when the pope translated Guichard to the see of Diakovar in Bosnia in 1314.[115]

In the fifteenth century the cases of Jean Balue, cardinal of Angers; Guillaume de Haraucourt, bishop of Verdun; and Jean d'Armagnac, bishop of Castres, exemplify further the crown's *de facto* exercise of jurisdiction, and its efforts at the same time to have the papacy formally condemn the accused. Balue and Haraucourt were arrested in April 1469 when it was learned that they were involved in a conspiracy to form a new league against Louis XI. On 8 May the king appointed an eight-man commission 'to arrive at the truth . . . and to mete out punishment'. He preferred, however, to have the pope condemn them, and so to this end he immediately sent Pierre Gruel, president in the Parlement of Grenoble, to inform the pope of the details of the arrest. In November Gruel was joined in Italy by one of the commissioners – Guillaume Cousinot, lord of Montreuil – and by Guillaume Lefranc, doctor of laws.[116]

The pope received them for the first time on 1 December 1469,

114 Dupuy, *Hist. du differend*, pp. 661–2; Vidal, *Bernard Saisset*, pp. 94–7, 119.

115 Rigault, *Le procès de Guichard, évêque de Troyes.*

116 Forgeot, *Jean Balue*, pp. 70–86; *p.j.* v.

but the crucial part of their embassy came around 15 December in an audience with the cardinals. The king and his officers, Cousinot asserted, have always arrested traitors whatever their status. It was therefore by royal grace that papal commissioners would be allowed to conduct a prosecution for the church, though this would still have to be done in the presence of royal officers. Once the papal commissioners pronounced their sentence, the king's officers would then complete the royal prosecution and decree punishment; 'and the two jurisdictions by this means would remain in accord'. Cousinot furthermore suggested that Balue and Haraucourt be degraded, asserting that such an action would not be contrary to custom.

In their turn the cardinals stressed that the jurisdiction of the church was inviolable: even if the accused confessed to their treason 'it was not before competent judges'. To this Cousinot reiterated that the king could not only arrest clerics of even the highest status but could also punish them corporally. To soften the severe directness of this statement Cousinot tried to make it clear that the cardinal and the bishop were for the moment merely being detained until the pope could act to avoid a scandal to the kingdom, the church and the papacy.[117]

An undated and anonymous *mémoire*, which was surely prepared for Cousinot's embassy, presented the arguments both for and against the accused prelates. On their behalf it was at first posited that they had not committed treason 'because they did not conspire to kill the king, to [seize] him, to take away his crown, to make war against him, to have his enemies invade France, to seize his places or his sovereignty'. Nor did they do anything against his public person, the universal or particular good, his collaterals, or in any way as described in the third degree of lese-majesty. On the other hand, however, the anonymous author of the *mémoire* drew on the texts of *Digest* 48, 4 and Bartolus to assert that the prelates were indeed guilty of treason in all three degrees. Again on behalf of the prelates it might be argued that they could not be guilty of lese-majesty against the king because their only sovereign was the pope: it was against him alone that they could commit treason; royal justice could have jurisdiction only after their degradation. But the anonymous author argued that this was not so, because 'every man is by natural law a

[117] B.N., ms. fr. 10971, fols. 295, 315–45.

liege subject of his king . . . as soon as he is born . . . and this natural law is immutable'.[118]

The cardinals eventually conceded that Louis XI had proceeded properly against the prelates. In January 1470 Paul II appointed commissioners to investigate the charges against Balue and Haraucourt, but as soon as the papal *commissarii* arrived in France there were disputes between them and the royal officers. Rebuked by the *grand conseil*, the *commissarii* returned to Rome. Louis XI went through the motions of requesting new envoys, but as far as is known nothing ever came of this second, half-hearted *démarche*, nor of a third that he made to Sixtus IV in 1471. No judgements were ever pronounced in the case,[119] and the two prelates remained in prison for over a decade. Balue was released at last in 1480, and Haraucourt gained his liberty two years later.[120]

Jean d'Armagnac, bishop of Castres, brother of Jacques d'Armagnac, duke of Nemours, was implicated in the duke's treason in 1474–5. As far as Louis XI was concerned the bishop was a 'traitor who had been party two or three times to attempts to capture me and make me a prisoner'. The bishop prudently fled to Rome, but the king did not let the matter rest there. In 1478 Armagnac was cited before the Parlement of Paris; and in 1480 Louis XI tried to have the pope prosecute the bishop or at least transfer him to another see. Louis XI persisted at the papal curia in 1481 through the protonotary Jean Cabourdelli, and in 1483 through a Master Albertin. As in so many other prosecutions for treason, the end of the affair is unclear, though it does appear that the bishop was in fact tried *in absentia* by the Parlement.[121]

In the prosecution of Geoffroi de Pompadour, bishop of Périgueux, and Georges d'Amboise, bishop of Montauban, in 1487, the crown tolerated papal participation without having sought it. The bishops had been arrested in January on charges of being in treasonous

118 B.N., n.a. fr. 1001, fols. 76r–82r; cf. Coll. Dupuy 762, fol. 287r; see also Forgeot, *Jean Balue*, pp. 90–3.

119 Forgeot, *Jean Balue*, pp. 93–5; J. Combet, *Louis XI et le Saint-Siège 1461–1483* (Paris, 1903), pp. 87–8.

120 *Lettres de Louis XI*, VIII. 335–6 (Balue); Thomas Basin, *Histoire de Louis XI*, ed. and trans. C. Samaran and M.-C. Garand (Classiques de l'hist. de France au moyen âge) (3 vols., Paris, 1963–72), III. 297 n. 5.

121 P. Ourliac, 'The Concordat of 1472: an Essay on the Relations between Louis XI and Sixtus IV', *The Recovery of France in the Fifteenth Century*, ed. P. S. Lewis (London, 1971), pp. 164–5.

communication with the rebellious Louis, duke of Orléans. They were interrogated first by the officers of the archbishop of Tours[122] and then by several members of the Parlement. Commissioners from that court were then instructed to examine all witnesses and to collect evidence. At about that time the pope sent several nuncios to Charles VIII. Although the king refused them their request – that the bishops be tried in Avignon by the nuncios alone or in conjunction with the archbishop of Bourges – he did allow them a rôle in the royal prosecution. But friction between them and the royal commissioners militated against progress being made in the case.[123] The bishops remained thereafter in royal custody, in legal limbo as in the prosecution of Balue and Haraucourt. By February 1489, seven months after the battle of Saint-Aubin-le-Cormier and the disintegration of the Orléanist opposition to the crown, they were released, but not acquitted.[124]

Volens-nolens the crown thus allowed the church some degree of involvement in the prosecution of clerics accused of treason. But because the more serious treasons merited penalties greater than those envisaged by canon law, the church could defer to royal justice in the matter of punishment. Thus after Etienne de Beaurepaire was convicted of treason in 1464 by the bishop of Paris, who had incidentally been 'assisted' by councillors from the Parlement, his case came back to that court for sentencing: he was banished, with confiscation of his property.[125] When clerics were to be punished corporally, they first had to be degraded.[126] There is however only one known example of this for the crime of treason. In 1398 two Augustinian canons with reputations as physicians almost killed Charles VI by performing some kind of trepanning operation on him. When a combined secular and ecclesiastical commission established that they were idolators as well as charlatans and self-proclaimed sorcerers, they were handed over to the bishop of Paris

[122] Guillaume de Jaligny, *Histoire de Charles VIII*, in *Histoire de Charles VIII*, ed. D. Godefroy (Paris, 1684), pp. 14–15.

[123] B.N., n.a. fr. 2398, fols. 23v–24r; Coll. Baluze 272, fol. 3r; R. de Maulde La Clavière, *Histoire de Louis XII* (6 vols., Paris, 1889–93), II. 206.

[124] Jaligny, *Hist. de Charles VIII*, p. 69; B.N., n.a. fr. 2398, fol. 24v.

[125] B.N., ms. fr. 5908, fol. 117v.

[126] E. Daniel, *Le procès de Jacques Coeur. Du crime de lèse-majesté et des juridictions séculière et ecclésiastique au XVe siècle* (Bourges, 1889), p. 47. Genestal, *Privilegium Fori*, II. pp. iii–iv, 124, 136ff.

for degradation, and then to the *prévôt* of Paris to be decapitated and quartered.[127] This was clearly not a common occurrence, for according to Juvenal des Ursins, 'many were surprised that they were degraded and handed over to secular justice'. However, 'it was said by notable clerics that, in view of what they had done against the person of the king, it was justice'.[128]

Thus far we have been considering the cases of clerics in which the church participated to a greater or lesser degree. In fact the crown could conduct prosecutions without any reference to ecclesiastical justice, since in theory a cleric accused of treason forfeited his privilege of clergy *ipso facto*.[129] When a cleric was not brought to trial but had his property confiscated on being reputed a traitor by the king,[130] there was clearly nothing that the church could do. Furthermore, royal courts, officers or special commissions might take cognizance without any apparent interference by the church. In the second half of 1358, for example, a royal commission prosecuted Raoul d'Ailly, royal councillor and *maître* in the *chambre des comptes*, for complicity in Robert Le Coq's efforts to hold Laon for the king of Navarre.[131] Nor did prelates escape the exclusive jurisdiction of the crown. Jean de Marconnay, bishop of Maillezais, in 1349;[132] Guillaume de Poitiers, bishop of Langres, in 1354;[133] Robert Porte, bishop of Avranches, in 1378; and Charles de Martigny, bishop of Elne, in 1481[134] were all tried in the Parlement, for example. Even a cleric in the physical custody of the church could be pursued by royal justice. Although the abbess of Saint-Nicolas at Bar-sur-Aube was held in the prisons of the bishop of Langres in the late 1350s, she was nevertheless prosecuted by Jean de Chalon, royal lieutenant in the *bailliage* of Sens, Troyes, and Chaumont.[135] There is also evidence that some clerics accused of treason were executed

[127] *Chron. de Saint-Denys*, II. 542ff, 662ff. Sauval (*Hist. de Paris*, III. *preuve* 258) identifies the canons as Pierre Tasan and Lancelot Martin.

[128] Jean Juvenal des Ursins, *Histoire de Charles VI*, ed. D. Godefroy (Paris, 1653), p. 136.

[129] Genestal, *Privilegium Fori*, II. 202.

[130] E.g., A.N., JJ 74, no. 54; JJ 98, no. 141; JJ 170, no. 150; Guérin, *Arch. hist. Poitou*, XIII. 339–42; *Recueil*, ed. Secousse, pp. 85–6.

[131] *Recueil*, ed. Secousse, pp. 119–20; he was pardoned in December, 1358.

[132] A.N., X1a 12, fols. 343v–345r.

[133] A.N., JJ 82, no. 216; B.N., Coll. Dupuy 339, fols. 29r–32r; *Gallia Christ.*, IV. col. 623; see also JJ 82, nos. 102, 346, 565; JJ 110, no. 269.

[134] *Infra*, pp. 177–8, 232.

[135] A.N., JJ 90, no. 197; she was pardoned in June 1359.

without first being degraded. In the late 1340s the sub-deacon Raymond-Bernard de Pestillac, 'who had been captured fully armed', was executed 'by way of justice . . . as a traitor to [Philippe VI], the crown of France and the public weal'. It is certain that Guillaume Mauvinet, a tonsured cleric involved in the conspiracy at Laon in 1358, was not degraded before being executed,[136] and it is likely that the other clerics who were also executed were not degraded either.[137]

Claims of clerical privilege could readily be rejected. In the late 1350s Raoul de Rully, an apothecary from Senlis, was accused of having provisioned the English at Creil and Pont-Saint-Maxence in defiance of a royal warning that anyone caught taking supplies out of Senlis would be considered a traitor. Hauled before a judicial commission sitting at Paris, he feebly protested his innocence and argued that as a tonsured cleric who wore clerical garb he should be judged by the official of Senlis. He quickly paid a fine of 200 francs, however, when the king's proctor made it clear that his claim of privilege would not be respected.[138] Similarly in the 1440s Jean le Sellier did not benefit from his clerical status. Canon and treasurer of the church of Laon, he was arrested for having spoken against the king, '[his] most dear and beloved companion the queen, and against [his] majesty and royal authority'. In spite of his appeal to his chapter, le Sellier remained in the royal prison at Laon until Charles VII pardoned him in April 1451.[139] In some cases the church added threats to its claim of jurisdiction, but these might only serve to stiffen the resolve of royal officers. When the priest Robert Godet was being held at Les Andelys in 1451 on unspecified charges of treason, the archbishop's court at Rouen issued a 'warning and citation' to Jean de Hely, lieutenant of the *bailli* of Gisors, threatening him with excommunication if he did not release Godet. Hely then consulted with other royal officials in Rouen, and together they decided not only not to hand over Godet to ecclesiastical justice but also to take measures to have the warning lifted.[140]

[136] A.N., JJ 81, no. 309 (Pestillac); JJ 90, no. 212 (Mauvinet).

[137] Froissart, *Chroniques*, v. p. xl n. 4.

[138] A.N., JJ 91, no. 19.

[139] A.N., JJ 185, no. 70. But on 13 April 1451 the king's proctor in the Parlement of Paris requested that the court quash his pardon and have him banished from the kingdom (B.N., ms. fr. 5908, fol. 64v).

[140] B.N., ms. fr. 26080, no. 6341; ms. fr. 26081, no. 6498; cf. B.N., ms. fr. 25998, no. 515, and *Gallia Christ.*, XIII. 313.

Although clerical privilege did not obviate criminal prosecution by the crown, it is clear that with few exceptions it provided some safeguard. The degradation and execution of the Augustinians in 1398 is the only known case of its kind; and there were not many executions without degradation. Canonical penalties were of course much less severe than those meted out by the crown. To be tried in an ecclesiastical court, even one to which royal officers would be seconded, was often the last hope of desperate men faced with aggressive royal prosecution. But if the crown was most reluctant to admit claims of clerical privilege in the cases of men who were undisputed clerics, it was hardly likely to be more amenable in the cases of men whose claims were weak at best and risible at worst.

Although the *routier* Maurice de Ploesquellec, for example, asserted in 1445 that he was a cleric, the king's proctor on 23 December peremptorily rejected the bishop of Paris's motion to be given jurisdiction in the case. 'The function of a cleric and the privilege [thereof]', the proctor said, 'is given for the duty that Maurice does not at all undertake but [does] the contrary. Moreover, the bishop cannot have cognizance of the crimes with which Maurice is charged.'[141] Jacques Coeur also asserted, with stronger reason, that he had been tonsured and should thus be subject to ecclesiastical jurisdiction. But his motion was quashed even though letters of tonsure were produced on his behalf.[142] Although during the first years of Louis XI's reign a group of jurists agreed that the case against Jacques Coeur could with justice be re-opened, significantly they did not think that there had been any irregularity in denying him clerical privilege, 'because he did not comport himself like a cleric'.[143]

Proof of clericature was thus clearly not enough. The king's advocate Jean Simon made this point forcefully in 1459 in the prosecution of Jean V d'Armagnac, who, having had his claim for the privilege of peerage rejected on 14 December 1458,[144] made the surprising assertion in February 1459 that he was a cleric and should be tried in an ecclesiastical court.[145] Even if Armagnac could produce

141 A.N., x2a 24, fol. 101r.

142 A.N., x2a 32, fols. 83v–84r.

143 B.N., ms. fr. 16541, fol. 652r.

144 A.N., x2a 29, fol. 35r–v.

145 A.N., x2a 28, fol. 233v. It is not clear exactly when the claim was made; Simon merely revealed on 27 February that Armagnac 'se dit clerc'.

proof of tonsure, argued Simon, he would not enjoy clerical privileges 'because of the [incestuous] relationship between him and his sister. Moreover, he has always worn lay habit, abjuring clerical habit, and he is a knight, the which status is contrary to that of a cleric'.[146] As a final example there is the claim to clerical privilege of Jacques d'Armagnac, duke of Nemours, in mid-February 1477. Obliged to take action, the Parlement on 22 February deputed Etienne Dubois, a councillor of the court, to investigate the matter. Presented on 19 April,[147] his report confirmed that Nemours had indeed been tonsured by the bishop of Castres some twenty years earlier. The court was thrown into a quandary: since the proofs of Nemours's clericature were valid, should the case be transferred to an ecclesiastical court? At least one clerical member of the Parlement thought so. 'Even though [Nemours] had appeared in arms against the king', he argued, 'nevertheless he ought not to lose his clericature.' Another went so far as to insist that 'if my lord of Nemours is a cleric he cannot have committed the crime of lese-majesty'.[148] The Parlement deliberated inconclusively on 21 April, but on 7 May it pronounced that Nemours would not enjoy privilege of clergy and that the court would proceed with his trial.[149] Extra-legal pressure from Louis XI must surely have influenced that decision, but the court nevertheless had valid legal precedents in the cases of Maurice de Ploesquellec, Jacques Coeur and Jean d'Armagnac: in order to enjoy the privilege of clergy one must live like a cleric.

In England it is clear that though petty treason was clergyable until 1497, the privilege of clergy was not admitted in cases of treason against king, crown or kingdom. Sir John Gerberge in 1347, Anketil de Hoby in 1352, and Thomas Merks, bishop of Carlisle, in 1401 were all unsuccessful in pleading their clergy.[150] In Lancastrian

146 A.N., x2a 28, fol. 233v. In a reference that I could not find in the registers of the Parlement, Bernard de Mandrot ('Jacques d'Armagnac, duc de Nemours', *R.H.*, XLIV (1890), 296 n. 1) quotes Simon as having argued that anyone who had 'grands cheveux et grande barbe et un chaperon à gros borrels et une jacquette sans collet et qui est marié ne doit pas jouir du privilège de clerc, *car clericus neque comam neque barbam mutare debet*'.

147 Dubois received 80 *livres* 4*s* 2*d* for his expenses (C. Samaran, 'Les frais du procès et de l'exécution de Jacques d'Armagnac, duc de Nemours', *Mém. soc. hist. de Paris et de l'Ile de France*, XLIX (1927), 151).

148 B.N., Coll. Duchesne 108, fol. 63r–v.

149 Mandrot, 'Jacques d'Armagnac', *R.H.*, XLIV (1890), 295–8; Bibl. Ste-Geneviève, ms. 2000, fols. 439r–469r.

150 Bellamy, *The Law of Treason*, pp. viii–ix n. 6, 61–3, 92; see also pp. 72, 138, 153.

Normandy the jurisdictional conflicts and their resolution followed the French rather than the English pattern, for the church seems to have had some success in asserting its claims. Royal proctors would of course claim ultimate jurisdiction for the crown, and royal officers would act accordingly, imprisoning clerics accused of treason, even going so far, in the case of the abbess of Saint-Antoine in 1432, as to seize her from ecclesiastical sanctuary.[151] Nor were benefices immune from confiscation.[152] But perhaps because one English policy goal in Normandy was to win and keep the support of the clergy, concessions were made to ecclesiastical claims of privilege.

Let us take the case of Jean de Saint-Avit, for example, who was arrested in May 1431 on suspicion of being an accomplice to a plan to deliver Rouen to the French. After the archbishop of Rouen, Hugues d'Orges, claimed him in vain, *démarches* were made at the Parlement and the University of Paris, with the bishops of Normandy and the chancellor Louis de Luxembourg, even at the council of Basle. Ultimately the English government yielded. On 26 March 1433 a royal order instructed the *bailli* of Rouen to deliver Saint-Avit to the archbishop for trial. There was one condition, however: that two members of the king's council, to be appointed by Bedford, participate in the interrogation.[153]

That the *échiquier* of Normandy played a not insignificant rôle as a court of appeal in cases of conflict between royal and ecclesiastical justice can be illustrated by the following example. Sometime in the mid-1420s Pierre Poulin, lieutenant-general of the *bailli* of Rouen, had two clerics, Richard Cheloe and Jean de la Mare, executed for treason in spite of the protestations of the archbishop of Rouen, 'saying that the punishment and execution belonged to the king'. Yet although it was too late for the clerics, the royal council on 6 August 1426 sent the matter, which had now become one of principle, to the *échiquier*. In such cases the crown had the difficult

[151] C. T. Allmand, 'The Relations between the English Government, the Higher Clergy and the Papacy in Normandy 1417–1450' (unpublished Oxford D.Phil. thesis, 1962), pp. 90–3; Seine-Maritime, *Inventaire sommaire*, II. 142; *Chron. du Mont-Saint-Michel*, II. 128–9; Fauquembergue, *Journal*, III. 65.

[152] Allmand, 'English Government and Higher Clergy in Normandy', pp. 1–15. For an example see *Paris pendant la domination anglaise*, no. 47.

[153] *Rouen au temps de Jeanne d'Arc et pendant l'occupation anglaise (1419–1449)*, ed. P. Le Cacheux (Soc. de l'hist. de Normandie) (Rouen and Paris, 1931), pp. cxi–cxii. Saint-Avit was ultimately declared innocent and released.

task of asserting its judicial rights at the same time as it tried to pose as the defender of ecclesiastical privilege.[154]

In France as a whole, jurisdiction in cases of treason thus had its administrative and its political aspects. Administratively, the prosecution of treason was not and could not be channelled into one or two or even three principal jurisdictions. Because treason was a crime that took so many forms and – as will become even more clear in the following chapters – was so widespread, virtually all the judicial resources of the crown were necessary to cope with it. In this respect France compares favourably with England. The king – alone or with his council – the Parlements and Grands Jours, the Châtelet, the *baillis*, *sénéchaux* and *prévôts*, and the military officers of the crown all regularly prosecuted treason in the first instance. For local rebellions or for treasons in which the kings took a special interest, royal commissions would be established. On occasion, too, the kings might look to jurisdictions not normally competent to try treason. Specific cases might thus be assigned to particular jurisdictions; or, as with treasons committed under the law of arms, they might come naturally within the competence of certain tribunals. But apart from these instances, it appears that the cognizance of a case would belong to whichever royal jurisdiction first instituted proceedings in it.

Conflicts among royal jurisdictions would have been an administrative problem. But between the crown and the municipal, seigneurial and ecclesiastical jurisdictions that opposed it, the conflicts were political in nature, for the administration of justice was – as it still is – a manifestation of power and authority. Whereas the crown had a large measure of success in deflating the pretensions of the towns and lay lords, it had to be considerably more circumspect in dealing with the church. Although at times the crown could act aggressively on its claims of exclusive jurisdiction in cases of treason committed by clerics, on most occasions it allowed the church to participate in or, less frequently, independently to conduct the prosecution. But whether the crown did so as a result of pressure or from a desire to have the church itself pronounce sentence, it conceded nothing in principle.

154 *Ibid.*, no. XLVI; Allmand, 'English Government and Higher Clergy in Normandy', p. 104.

Chapter 4

PROCEDURE AND THE TRIAL OF PEERS

I

There was no single procedure in the prosecution of treason in later medieval France that was followed to the exclusion of all others. Generally speaking, one can discern seven basic types of legal procedure: summary judgement; trial by battle; *procédure ordinaire; procédure extraordinaire*; trial before the king and council; state trials; and the trial of peers. Any combination of several factors could determine the manner of proceeding: the tribunal before which a case was tried; the status of the accused; the nature of the treason; the evidence; or the political *desiderata* of the crown.

'By denunciation, present misdeed, accusation by formal party, and public notoriety':[1] the prosecution of treason, like that of other felonies, could be initiated for any one of these reasons. The most simple and sure way of proceeding was of course summarily. As we learned in the last chapter, the kings of France could have capital sentences adjudged on their own record, but after the mid fourteenth century they exercised this prerogative in military rather than in political cases.

Apart from the kings it was characteristically the military officers of the crown and their subordinates who meted out summary punishment. The treasons for which they had jurisdiction were mostly those committed under the law of arms,[2] though of course there were exceptions. On 14 April 1477, for example, seventeen burgesses of Arras who had tried to meet secretly with Mary of Burgundy were executed by order of the provost-marshal Tristan l'Hermite.[3] Non-military commissioners, particularly those with

[1] Boutillier, *Somme rural*, I. 34 (pp. 221–3).

[2] E.g., *Chronique normande du XIVe siècle*, ed. A. and E. Molinier (S.H.F.) (Paris, 1882), p. 57; A.N., JJ 74, no. 53; JJ 90, no. 231; B.N., ms. fr. 26018, no. 246; ms. fr. 26091, no. 669.

[3] A.N., J 950, no. 20; on this see also Jean Molinet, *Chroniques*, ed. G. Doutrepont and O. Jodogne (3 vols., Brussels, 1935–7), I. 187–8. For another example see *Preuves de la maison de Chabannes*, II. 176–80.

power to prosecute urban revolts, could also be mandated to proceed summarily to judgement.[4] In the late 1340s and early 1350s Simon de Bucy so abused his authority in this regard that he had to seek a pardon in March 1352 in order to forestall prosecution against himself for murder.[5]

Although clearly not all accused traitors could be taken into custody, the king could still execute summary justice against those at large simply by recording their guilt, for his word was incontrovertible. Such judgement by decree was a neat legal device that could be used to confiscate the property of traitors. Let us take the example of Jean de Galard, lord of Limeuil. After defecting to the English in the last years of Philippe VI's reign, Galard was pardoned in June 1350; but within six months he had again gone over to the English. In December 1351, when Jean II granted his lordships of Limeuil, Clarens and Miremont to Roger Bernard, count of Périgord, he merely declared that Galard's treason was so notorious 'that there is no doubt that he has committed the crime of lese-majesty and that all his property is confiscated to us'.[6] Evidence of cases like Jean de Galard's is rare before the outbreak of the Hundred Years War,[7] but once hostilities began, and thereafter throughout the later middle ages, royal judgement by notoriety was an integral part of the law of treason. One can count the examples in the hundreds.[8]

In some cases, as in Jean de Galard's, the relevant document contained a phrase that pointed to the notoriety of the treason. Thus in July 1376, when Charles V granted to the esquire Jean Coutier a rent of 100 *s.t.* that normally accrued to Jean de Sainquennaux of Bergerac, the justification was that the latter was 'our rebel . . . and adheres notoriously and publicly to . . . our enemies of England'. Similarly Marie Thorelle of Libourne forfeited her property in the 1380s because she was 'notoriously our traitor and rebel'. In 1465, after Louis XI had confiscated the property of Pierre d'Amboise, lord of Chaumont, he declared that Amboise had 'taken up arms and rose against us and participated in several machinations . . . in order

[4] E.g., A.N., JJ 86, no. 431; JJ 125, no. 244; B.N., ms. fr. 2912, fol. 5r.
[5] A.N., JJ 81, no. 309.
[6] *Documents historiques sur la maison de Galard*, ed. J. Noulens (5 vols. in 4, Paris, 1871–6), I. 501–9. For further details on Galard see *ibid.*, I. 510–15, 522; A.N., JJ 89, nos. 305, 308.
[7] A.N., X2a 3, fol. 3v (Ramfred de Durfort) is the only example that I have discovered.
[8] See especially A.N., JJ 86–90, 100–4, *passim*.

to injure us and our loyal subjects . . . the which deeds are extremely notorious'.[9] But it was not necessary in all cases that a traitor's crimes be notorious: it was enough that the king simply have knowledge of a treason in order to pass judgement on his own record. Evidence for examples of this type might contain a phrase such as 'si comme len dit', 'si comme nous entendons', or 'ut dicitur'.[10]

Often, of course, the denouncer of a traitor profited from the ensuing forfeiture,[11] but the eagerness, if not the cupidity, of such informers, and the king's or regent's too willing acceptance of unsubstantiated accusations, could cause innocent people to suffer. Thus on 14 April 1359 the future marshal Mouton de Blainville and several other royal officers wrote to the regent Charles on hearing that Raoul d'Esneval had been accused of treason and that his property of Alainville had been given to Jeanne de Vendôme, *dame* of Béthencourt. 'We are indeed amazed that you have been told such a thing', they protested diplomatically, 'because we certify that the said lord Raoul is true and loyal to you.' As a result of this testimonial Charles restored Alainville to Esneval on 10 May; and in doing so he admitted that he had made the grant to Béthencourt 'because, as she said and maintained, the said lord Raoul had become a traitor, rebel and enemy of my lord [Jean II], us and the crown of France'.[12] Esneval was fortunate; but there must have been more than a few falsely accused persons who had nobody of influence to vouch for their loyalty.

When a formal accusation of treason could not be proven by witnesses or by evidence, the appellant could request a trial by battle to settle the issue. The first known instance of such a procedure in the later middle ages occurred in the spring of 1293, when Roger Bernard III, count of Foix, was appealed by Bernard VI, count of Armagnac. The substance of the charges, however, is not known. The battle took place at Gisors in the presence of Philippe IV and the barons, but it was stopped by the king before the two could fight to a decision, and the affair seems to have ended there.[13]

[9] A.N., JJ 109, no. 105 (Sainquennaux); JJ 128, no. 126 (Thorelle); K 70, no. 36 (Amboise).

[10] E.g., A.N., JJ 86, no. 565; JJ 87, no. 119; JJ 96, nos. 67, 129, 355; Luce, *Bertrand du Guesclin*, *p.j.* xix.

[11] E.g., A.N., JJ 90, no. 175; JJ 187, no. 340.

[12] A.N., JJ 90, no. 548 (partially published in *Recueil*, ed. Secousse, p. 40).

[13] *Chron. de Guill. de Nangis*, I. 282–3.

Although in 1307 Philippe IV ordered the Parlement to take cognizance of cases that would previously have been resolved through trial by battle, he did not absolutely forbid such judicial resort to arms.[14] Indeed, for the years 1317–22, an anonymous chronicler recorded several duels for treason. Ferri de Picquigny was involved in one in 1317, and Jourdain de l'Isle-Jourdain was involved in another in 1320, but neither of these was fought to a conclusion. The only battle that did end decisively resulted in the defeated traitor, an esquire named Guillaume Mauferas, being hauled off to prison in the Châtelet by order of the king. His fate after that is not known.[15]

From the accused traitor's point of view – and from the crown's, too – trial by battle was a procedure whereby he could vindicate his honour: if he was not vanquished in battle he would not be subject to further legal proceedings. This is made clear by a case in 1331. Bernard Ferrand of the *sénéchaussée* of Toulouse, having appealed Pierre-Bertrand Jourdain of notorious treason as well as of the murder of Thomas d'Hermenonville, was granted his request for a trial by battle. But he did not appear on the appointed day, whereas Jourdain did and so was given unconditional leave to depart.[16] This case was quite probably the last one in which treason was prosecuted by this procedure. However much trial by battle might have been used to settle other issues,[17] there is no evidence that it was used beyond the mid fourteenth century in cases of treason. This is in contrast to practice in England, where trials by battle in cases of treason not only were more common generally, particularly during the reign of Richard II, but also continued at least through the mid fifteenth century.[18]

At the Parlement of Paris and the courts of the *baillis* and *sénéchaux*, treason was prosecuted by either the *procédure ordinaire* or the *procédure extraordinaire*. With few exceptions – for example the trials of Jean Maillet in 1344–50, Jean de Fontaines in 1406,[19] and several that were prosecuted in the absence of the defendants[20] – all the cases

[14] Boutaric, *La France sous Philippe le Bel*, p. 55.

[15] *Chronique parisienne anonyme de 1316–1339*, ed. A. Hellot (*Mém. soc. hist. de Paris et de l'Ile de France*, XI (1885), pp. 31–2, 39, 54–5, 60, 70.

[16] A.N., X2a 3, fol. 149v.

[17] See Keen, *Laws of War*, pp. 41–2.

[18] Bellamy, *The Law of Treason*, pp. 143–7.

[19] *Confessions et jugements*, p. 25 n. 1 (Maillet); A.N., X2a 14, fols. 308v–309v (Fontaines).

[20] E.g., A.N., X2a 5, fol. 113r; X2a 26, fols. 343r–345r; JJ 147, no. 113.

that were tried by the *procédure ordinaire* were initiated on accusation by formal party, that is to say by persons acting privately.[21] The treason alleged by the plaintiff was for him not the primary issue but rather, as mentioned in the previous chapter, a peg on which to hang his claim either to a ransom or to punitive damages for a breach of safeguard, a violation of a truce, or his losses in a private war. For the king's proctor, on the other hand, the treasonous nature of the alleged crime was indeed the primary matter, and he would therefore also join issue with the defendant.

Briefly, in the *procédure ordinaire*[22] the witnesses would have their depositions taken down in writing by the *examinateurs*, and the results of the inquest would be communicated to the accused. The prosecution and the defence would then argue in open court, but whereas the plaintiff's case would most likely be presented *ad finem civilem*, the king's proctor would seek to have stiff criminal penalties adjudged, at least in the more serious cases. Thus in the dispute between Guillaume de Cardaillac and the Murat brothers in the late 1360s over the succession to the *vicomté* of Murat, the king's proctor accused Cardaillac of treason because of his depredations against the Murats, and also for having adhered to the English. He demanded that Cardaillac pay a fine of 100,000 francs to the Murats, that he be executed or banished if he could not be captured, and that his property be confiscated.[23]

One should note that treason trials under the *procédure ordinaire* could differ from trials for other felonies under the same procedure in one important respect: the number of defaults allowed before conviction for contumacy was awarded. For crimes other than treason a defendant was normally permitted four defaults; but as the king's proctor asserted in the case of Charles, duke of Lorraine, in the early 1400s, 'where there is a notorious case of treason . . . there is need of only one default to obtain an *arrêt*'. Lorraine was in fact condemned after four defaults, as were many others, but Jean de Montfort was judged guilty in December 1378 after only one

[21] E.g., A.N., x2a 6, fols. 144r–v, 167r–169v; x2a 7, fols. 63v–66v; x2a 9, fol. 39r–v; x2a 22, fol. 12r–v; x2a 26, fols. 367r–371r.

[22] For this in detail see A. Esmein, *A History of Continental Criminal Procedure*, trans. J. Simpson (London, 1914), p. 126; Aubert, *Hist. du Parlement à François I*, I. 28–39, 211–19; A. Tardif, *La procédure civile et criminelle aux XIIIe et XIVe siècles* (Paris, 1885), pp. 141–3.

[23] A.N., x2a 8, fols. 24v–26r.

default.[24] The most defaults prior to conviction were the nine decreed in the case of Jacques de Pons in the 1440s.[25]

The *procédure extraordinaire* could be followed only when the accused was in custody.[26] Herein lies the reason why, as long as the accused could not be apprehended, his case would be prosecuted by the *procédure ordinaire*. The *procédure extraordinaire* was used at the Châtelet,[27] by royal commissions,[28] by military tribunals,[29] at the courts of the *baillis* and *sénéchaux*,[30] and at the Parlement of Paris as well.[31] For some particularly important cases that were tried by the Parlement or by royal commissions, the chancellor would head the prosecution and usually be assisted by the king's most trusted officers and *courtiers*.[32] The rôle of the chancellor was a key one in such cases, for he was the principal legal officer of the crown as well as its chief political officer.

The *procédure extraordinaire* differed from the *procédure ordinaire* in two fundamental ways. In the first place the proceedings were conducted in a secret inquisitorial manner. The accused would be interrogated without being apprised of the specific charges against him, although from either his own guilt or the questioning he would have a rather good idea of what they were. He would of course attempt to exculpate himself during his interrogation, but he was not allowed to produce witnesses on his own behalf. Although he

[24] Luce, *Jeanne d'Arc, p.j.* XX. pp. 30–72 (Lorraine); A.N., X1a 1471, fols. 134v–136v, printed as Appendix XXIX in *Chron. de Jean II et Charles V*, III. 213–19 (Montfort). For others convicted after four defaults see A.N., X2a 7, fols. 344v–346r (Pierre d'Oradour; 1367); X2a 8, fols. 110r–114r (Jean de Lessarges *et al.*; 1370); X2a 26, fols. 343r–345r (Louis de Courcelles; 1454).

[25] A.N., X2a 26, fols. 41v–43v. A. Robinet de Manteville was convicted in 1357 after two defaults (JJ 87, no. 333); Jean V d'Armagnac in 1460 after three defaults (X2a 29, fols. 107r–118v, printed in A. Lancelot, *Mémoires concernant les pairs de France* (2 vols. in 1, Paris, 1720), *preuves*, pp. 780–805); Yves Philippe in 1460 after five defaults (X2a 29, fols. 127r–128v); Armagnac again in 1470 after seven defaults (X2a 36, fols. 308v–309v, printed in Philippe de Commynes, *Mémoires*, ed. Lenglet-Dufresnoy (4 vols., Paris, 1747), III. 141–5).

[26] For the *procédure extraordinaire* see Tardif, *La procédure*, pp. 144–9; Aubert, *Hist. du Parlement à François I*, II. 218; Esmein, *Hist. of Continental Crim. Procedure*, p. 128; G. Dupont-Ferrier, *Les officiers royaux des bailliages et sénéchaussées et les institutions monarchiques locales en France à la fin du moyen âge* (Bibl. de l'Ec. des Hautes Etudes: 145) (Paris, 1902), pp. 393–400.

[27] *Reg. crim. du Châtelet, passim.*

[28] E.g., Guillot, *Jacques Coeur*; B.N., ms. fr. 2921 (Melun; 1468); A.N., J 949, no. 6 (René d'Alençon; 1481–3).

[29] Bibl. Ste-Geneviève, ms. 2000, fols. 75r–86r.

[30] A.N., JJ 79A, no. 29; X2a 11, fols. 53v–54r.

[31] A.N., X2a 6, fol. 265v; X2a 11, fol. 34r–v; P. Guérin, 'Pierre d'Urfé, grand écuyer de France, et Jean de Jaucourt', *Le cabinet historique*, XXVI (1) (1880), pp. 115–17.

[32] B.N., ms. fr. 3869 (Saint-Pol; 1475); ms. fr. 18442, fols. 3r *et seq.* (Ch. d'Albret; 1473).

might be allowed to submit written evidence, this was not common.[33] There was no constraint on him to confront the crown's witnesses, but he could do so if he wished; whatever the case he could not obtain communication of their testimony. In none of the trials was the defendant permitted to be assisted by counsel; and there were of course no pleadings in open court.

The second distinguishing feature of the *procédure extraordinaire* was the use of torture to extract a confession. The standard method seems to have been some combination of the rack and the pouring of water down the throat of the accused, though there was always room for innovation: Miquelot Fauvel, the messenger of Saint-Pol and Nemours in the 1470s, was tortured by tongs – presumably red-hot ones – applied to his heels.[34]

At various stages in the *procédure extraordinaire* the transcript of the interrogation would be read back to the accused so that he could retract from or add to his statements.[35] In the major political trials during the reign of Louis XI the commissioners would seek guidance from the king. Indeed, in the trial of Charles de Melun in 1468 Louis XI actually testified as a witness.[36] Once all the evidence in a trial was gathered the *greffier criminel* or the *rapporteur* would prepare a report for the commissioners, who, if they themselves did not render judgement, passed it on to the Parlement, the Châtelet, or the court of the *bailli* or *sénéchal*.[37] A provisional sentence would then be handed down. In the Parlement it was known as the *dictum*, was written in French and was subject to revision by the king.[38] It became definitive only when it was published by a president of the Grand' Chambre; this, the *arrêt*, was written in Latin.[39] Thus the *dictum* against Louis de Luxembourg, count of Saint-Pol, was pronounced on 16 December 1475, and the *arrêt* was published on the 19th. Similarly the *dictum* against Jacques d'Armagnac, duke of Nemours,

[33] E.g., Guillot, *Jacques Coeur*, p. 28; ms. fr. 2921, fol. 112r (Melun; 1468).

[34] E.g., *Reg. crim. du Châtelet*, I. 487; B.N., ms. fr. 2921, fol. 117r. For Fauvel see Bibl. Ste-Geneviève, ms. 2000, fol. 84r.

[35] In the trial of René d'Alençon in 1481 this was done every day that he was interrogated (A.N., J 949, no. 6, fol. 16r).

[36] *Lettres de Louis XI*, VI. 88–91; B.N., ms. fr. 2895, fol. 9r–v; Bibl. Ste-Geneviève, ms. 2000, fols. 232r–v, 481v–482r (Nemours); A.N., J 949, no. 6, fol. 142v (René d'Alençon); B.N., ms. fr. 2921, fol. 114r–v (Melun).

[37] B.N., ms. fr. 3869, fol. 34r–v (Saint-Pol); *Reg. crim. du Châtelet, passim*; Dupont-Ferrier, *Les officiers royaux*, p. 400.

[38] E.g., B.N., ms. fr. 5908, fol. 131v.

[39] Aubert, *Hist. du Parlement à François I*, II. 134.

was pronounced on 10 July 1477, and the *arrêt* was published on 4 August.[40] In the Châtelet and in the courts of the *baillis* and *sénéchaux* the presiding officer would review the evidence, take counsel from the crown lawyers and others, and then pass sentence.[41]

The prosecution in 1378 of Charles the Bad's agents Jacques de Rue and Pierre du Tertre does not quite fit any pattern discussed thus far. Having been tried by a royal commission, and having confessed to their treason, they could have been sentenced and executed forthwith. But for political, propagandist reasons Charles V decided to have them judged in the Parlement in what can only be described as a state trial. It was in fact the first such proceeding for treason since the trial in 1315 of Robert de Béthune, count of Flanders, and the only one that did not involve a peer of France.

On 16 June the Parlement assembled, having put aside all other business that day. Charles V himself did not attend, but those present were the chancellor Pierre d'Orgemont; the presidents of the Parlement; the archbishops of Sens and Rouen; the bishops of Beauvais, Condon, Bayeux, Thérouanne and Evreux; the count of Harcourt; the *vicomte* of Thouars; several other knights and ecclesiastics; the *prévôt* of Paris; magistrates of the Châtelet and all the other members of the Parlement; masters of the *chambre des comptes* and the *requêtes de l'hôtel*; the *prévôt des marchands*; the *échevins* of Paris and other civic officials; and two papal envoys. The transcripts of the traitors' interrogations and confessions were read out by prior order of the king and his council, after which both Jacques de Rue and Pierre du Tertre confirmed the veracity of their statements and swore that their confessions had been given without constraint. When Charles V was informed of this he instructed the Parlement to condemn them to death and to have the sentence executed that day.[42] How this process differed from the other state trials will be seen when in section II of this chapter we discuss the trial of peers.

Trials before the king and council were not all conducted alike. Formal indictments were read out against Bernard Saisset, bishop of

[40] B.N., ms. fr. 3869, fol. 37v; G. Périnelle, 'Un texte officiel sur l'exécution du connétable de Saint-Pol', *Mélanges d'archéol. et d'hist. de l'Ecole française de Rome*, XXIII (1903), 430; Mandrot, 'Jacques d'Armagnac', *R.H.*, XLIV (1890), 302–4.

[41] *Reg. crim. du Châtelet, passim*; Dupont-Ferrier, *Les officiers royaux*, p. 400.

[42] A.N., X1a, 1471, fol. 54; *Recueil*, ed. Secousse, pp. 373–437; Delachenal, *Hist. de Charles V*, V. 187–218.

Pamiers, and against Enguerran de Marigny; as far as one can tell, none was issued in any of the other trials, though in the proceedings against Jean IV d'Armagnac in 1445 the king's proctor did present the case for the crown.[43] Béraud de Mercoeur in 1319, Alexandre de Bassac in 1357, and Waleran de Luxembourg in 1380 were allowed to defend themselves personally, and Jean IV d'Armagnac was allowed to do so by proxy.[44] But Saisset; Marigny; the Normans Jean de la Roche-Tesson, Guillaume Bacon and Richard de Percy in 1344; Martin Pisdoe in 1359; and Nicolas d'Orgemont, Robert de Belloy and Robin Maillot in 1416 were all denied the right to defend themselves. The Normans and Orgemont and his co-defendants, though in custody, were not even present at their trials; nor did Jacques Coeur make any appearances when Charles VII and his council took over the prosecution of the case.[45] Both Marigny and Pisdoe were executed, but the former, unlike Pisdoe, had not made a confession, which was normally necessary for capital punishment to be adjudged. Although the Norman barons were also condemned to death, their treason was so manifest – they had been captured in arms while defending Quimper in Brittany for Jean de Montfort – that no further proof was needed.

A principle of Roman law that was accepted by the jurists[46] and carried out in practice was that the crown could pursue an accused traitor at law after his death. Such posthumous prosecution thus enabled the crown to confiscate the property that a traitor would inevitably have forfeited but for his demise. The procedure involved was usually a simple matter of reputing the deceased person a traitor,[47] but more formal proceedings could be instituted. In September 1476, for example, shortly after Jean de Luxembourg, count of Marle, was killed in the Burgundian disaster at Murten, the Parlement of Paris received royal letters patent 'by which the king our lord instructs

[43] Dupuy, *Hist. du differend*, pp. 653–6; Favier, *Marigny*, pp. 210–11; Escouchy, *Chronique*, I. 61–5 (Armagnac).

[44] R. Cazelles, *La société politique et la crise de la royauté sous Philippe de Valois* (Paris, 1958), pp. 41–2 (Mercoeur); A.N., x2a 6, fols. 278v–279r (Bassac); *Chron. de Saint-Denys*, I. 36. (Luxembourg); Escouchy, *Chronique*, I. 61–3 (Armagnac).

[45] Dupuy, *Hist. du differend*, pp. 621–31 (Saisset); Favier, *Marigny*, p. 212; Delisle, *Hist. de Saint-Sauveur-le-Vicomte*, *p.j.* lxxii (the Normans); Delachenal, *Hist. de Charles V*, II. 173–5 (Pisdoe); B.N., Coll. Dupuy 480, fol. 23 (Orgemont *et al.*); Guillot, *Jacques Coeur*, p. 54.

[46] *Digest*, 48, 4, 11; Masuer, *Practica Forensis*, p. 345.

[47] E.g., A.N., JJ 118, no. 239.

that an investigation be made concerning the crimes of treason and others . . . perpetrated by the late count of Marle against the said lord, his crown, and the public weal of his kingdom'.[48] There is no further evidence of the Parlement's actions in this case, but in the first months of 1477 Louis XI granted Luxembourg's county of Marle and other properties to the marshal Pierre de Rohan, lord of Gié.[49] More elaborate proceedings were followed in the cases, which we shall discuss presently, of the peers Charles the Bad and Charles the Bold in 1387 and 1478 respectively.

II

Feudal custom provided that a peer could be tried in the *curia regis* by the other peers when his life or his fief were in question. Strictly speaking, as we shall see, this was a privilege and not a right, for the king could confiscate the lands of a peer without convoking the other peers. And again strictly speaking, there never existed a *cour des pairs* separate from the *cour du roi*, for apart from the peers there had always been others who participated in the judgements.[50] Indeed the custom by which the peers themselves pronounced sentence fell into desuetude during the fourteenth century. On the whole, however, perhaps because in the political mythology of France the peers had a distinct and exalted position, the trials of such persons were to be momentous, ceremonial occasions. In England, in contrast, although some peers, like the Despensers in 1321 and Suffolk in 1450, could be tried in Parliament with all the formalities, others, like the earl of Oxford in 1462, could be tried by the constable in the court of chivalry; and still others, like the earl of Lancaster in 1322 and the duke of Clarence in 1478, could be condemned more or less summarily.[51]

48 A.N., X1a 1487, fol. 118v.

49 A.N., X1a 8607, fols. 53v–54r, 58v–59v, 60v–62r. H. Stein wrongly identified the deceased Luxembourg as Louis, Jean's father (*Inventaire analytique des ordonnances enregistrées au Parlement de Paris jusqu'à la mort de Louis XII* (Paris, 1908), nos. 1028, 1033).

50 M. Boulet-Sautel, 'Le rôle juridictionnel de la cour des pairs aux XIIIe et XIVe siècles', *Recueil de travaux offert à M. Clovis Brunel* (2 vols., Paris, 1955), II. 508–14; Funck-Brentano, 'Les pairs de France à la fin du XIIIe siècle'; F. Funck-Brentano, *Etudes d'histoire du moyen âge dédiées à Gabriel Monod* (Paris, 1896), pp. 352–3.

51 Bellamy, *The Law of Treason*, index *sub* Despenser, Suffolk, Oxford, Clarence, peers; L. W. Vernon Harcourt, *His Grace the Steward and the Trial of Peers* (London, 1907), caps. 9–12; Keen, 'Treason Trials'.

The conflict between the kings of France and the counts of Flanders provides us with the earliest evidence on the prosecution of a peer for the crime of treason. In May 1300, when Count Gui de Dampierre and his son Robert de Béthune put themselves on the mercy of Philippe IV after having rebelled and allied with the English, no formal proceedings were instituted against them. Treated as vanquished enemies rather than as traitors, they were only confined to prison; and their captivity was a rather luxurious one at that.[52] The groundwork for a change in royal policy towards rebellion was prepared in 1305, when, upon the death of Gui de Dampierre, Philippe released Robert de Béthune from prison and on 23 June concluded with him the treaty of Athies. The one important clause for our purposes was the one which provided for a trial if Robert were to break the treaty; the matter, it was agreed, would be judged not by the Parlement but by the peers. The very fact that this had to be specified is an indication of just how much the king had been using the Parlement to supplant the *juridiction pariale.* Significantly, too, there was included the provision that the king could appoint twelve men from his council to equal the number of peers.[53] This clause meant that in fact the *gens du roi* would outnumber the peers, because only eleven of the latter would be acting as judges.

In January 1312, after the renewal of hostilities in 1310–11, Robert de Béthune was summoned to justify himself before the court of peers. He appeared in Paris and though he defended himself ably, he was still fined 60,000 *livres*; this penalty was rescinded, however, when he signed the treaty of Pontoise on 11 July 1312. He went into rebellion once more in July 1314 and yet again after the accord signed at Marquette on 3 September 1314.[54] This time Louis X, having succeeded Philippe IV in November 1314, decided to proceed at law against the count. On 15 February 1315 he summoned Robert to appear on 20 May before 'nostre cour garnie de nos pers et autres bonnes gens et grands de nostre conseil'. A long preamble specified the count's treasons: he had repeatedly broken his oath to keep the peace; he had allied with the enemies of the king, had given them aid and comfort, and had waged open war against the king; and he

[52] Funck-Brentano, *Les origines de la guerre de Cent ans*, pp. 181–347.
[53] *Ibid.*, pp. 499–501. [54] *Ibid.*, pp. 573–670.

had given refuge to his son Louis de Nevers, himself a convicted traitor banished from the kingdom. 'Whether or not he comes before us', Louis X added, 'we shall go forward in this matter.'[55]

The king and the peers – with the exception of Edward II, the bishop of Noyon and the bishop of Châlons[56] – assembled with the twelve chosen prelates and barons on the day assigned. The abbot of Selebècque, acting as proctor for the absent count, made his excuses for him. Although the king's proctor then requested immediate judgement, the *cour garnie* deferred decision until 25 May. On that day the king followed custom and instructed that judgement be rendered by the peers and in their name. This was most significant, for Louis X was explicitly stating that he was not present as a judge. The sentencing was postponed several more times until 30 June, when at last Robert de Béthune was declared guilty as charged; a punishment only of forfeiture, however, was decreed.[57]

Several points are to be noted in this case. Firstly, the repetition of the phrase 'nous pers de France, la cour garnie, selon la forme de ladite paix' stressed the legality of what was patently a relatively new procedure. And as we shall see, it was but a small step from trial in the *cour garnie* to trial in the Parlement *garnie*, for the Parlement was the judicial offspring of the *curia regis*. Secondly, the sentence was pronounced by the *cour garnie* at the behest of the king, and apparently without his participation. We shall see, too, how important this particular issue was to be at the trials of Jean de Montfort in 1378 and Charles the Bad in 1387. Lastly, the penalty was only one of forfeiture, and even that could not be implemented; at least as far as the peers were concerned, there was as yet no question of corporal punishment.

The criminal trial of Robert d'Artois in 1331–2, though not for treason, was nevertheless of great importance as a legal precedent for future treason trials of peers. Different in form from that of the prosecution of Robert, count of Flanders, it was judged in the Parlement by the king and the peers, this time with the king pronouncing sentence. Artois was in fact later condemned for treason, in March 1337, for having allied with Edward III, but at that time

[55] Anselme, *Hist. généalogique*, II. 812–15.

[56] The bishop of Châlons was himself being prosecuted for treason; *supra*, pp. 28, 69.

[57] Anselme, *Hist. généalogique*, II. 815–17.

he had long been deprived of his peerage, and the judgement against him took the form of a royal decree.[58]

In May 1337, when Philippe VI ordered that the duchy of Guyenne be sequestrated because of the treason of Edward III, who was a peer of France as duke of Guyenne, he came to his decision 'per maturam deliberationem magni consilii nostri'. In 1369 and again in 1370 Charles V's decrees of confiscation of the duchy were issued in the same way: 'cum nostro consilio ac pluribus peritissimis ac magnis scientibus viris, deliberatione super hoc praehabita diligenti'.[59] In neither case was there formal process at law by the king and the peers. In 1356, when Charles the Bad, a peer of France as count of Evreux, was clapped into prison, no legal action against him was undertaken or even envisaged. But with the prosecution of Jean de Montfort in 1378 there was a return to the formal procedure established at the trial of Robert d'Artois. Even so the king's proctor still asserted that no formal proceedings at all need have been instituted.

The studied neutrality that Montfort had maintained at the outbreak of the war in 1369 gave way to a secret alliance with the English, and finally to open collusion with them. He was incapable, however, of resisting the French offensive launched against him in 1372. By April 1373 the royal army had occupied most of his duchy, and he fled to England. In spite of the successful campaign, Charles V took no decisive action at that time, partly in order to leave open the door to reconciliation, and partly because he preferred to have the duchy administered by Anjou, du Guesclin, Clisson, and other Breton barons than to pronounce in favour of a Penthièvre successor. By the summer of 1378, however, buoyed by his successful campaign in Normandy against the Navarrese, Charles V was ready to institute legal proceedings against Montfort, who in the winter of that year had taken part in Buckingham's expedition.[60]

Although the trial was to have begun on 4 December, the opening session was postponed for a few days because of inadequate

[58] Kervyn de Lettenhove, 'Procès de Robert d'Artois', *Bull. de l'acad. roy. de Belgique*, 2nd series, x (1860), 641–69; xi (1861), 107–25; G. Callies, 'Le procès civil et criminel de Robert III d'Artois', *Position des thèses soutenues à l'Ecole Nationale des Chartes* (1932), pp. 35–41; Lancelot, *Mémoires concernant les pairs, preuves*, pp. 472–4.

[59] Anselme, *Hist. généalogique*, II. 583–4; *Ordonnances*, VI. 508–10.

[60] Jones, *Ducal Brittany*, pp. 68–84.

attendance.[61] On 9 December 1378 Charles V held his *lit de justice* in the Parlement. Seated 'in his royal majesty in the accustomed manner when he sits in justice', he was flanked on his right by the dauphin and three lay peers – the dukes of Burgundy and Bourbon and the count of Etampes – and on his right by the six ecclesiastical peers – the archbishop of Reims, and the bishops of Beauvais, Châlons, Laon, Langres and Noyon. A further seventeen prelates and barons were also present. No mention was made of other participants but it is certain that members of the Parlement were there.[62] Although Montfort was clearly not going to appear, he was nevertheless summoned, after which the king's proctor Guillaume de Saint-Germain presented the case for the crown 'en elisant conclusions civiles'. The principal charge was of course Montfort's treasonable alliance with the English and his participation in Lancaster's *chevauchée* of 1373 'with banners unfurled, from Calais to Bordeaux, not war in fact but depredation'. Because of the notoriety of the facts, Saint-Germain continued, the king could have proceeded summarily, but wishing to act scrupulously, Charles V had decided to summon Montfort 'to his noble court of Parlement before himself and the peers'. In conclusion Saint-Germain demanded that Montfort forfeit his peerage and his duchy for his notorious crimes of lese-majesty, felony and perjury.

During the next several days the proctor for Jeanne de Penthièvre contended that since Montfort had no right to the duchy, he could not in fact forfeit it. At some point in the proceedings – it is not clear when – the peers 'maintained before the king that the decision, determination and judgement of the case belonged to them'. They requested that it be so declared or that they be given a letter to the effect that 'if the king determined the case and gave the judgement and the *arrêt*', this would not derogate from their privileges nor bestow a new right on the king. Charles V agreed to this request, but although the letter apparently was drawn up, it was never delivered.[63] In the end it was the king alone who passed judgement, declaring confiscation of the duchy on 18 December.[64]

[61] For this paragraph and the first sentence of the following one see A.N., X1a 1471, fols. 134v–136v, published as Appendix XXIX in *Chron. de Jean II et Charles V*, III. 213–19. Delachenal gives a clear summary of the trial (*Hist. de Charles V*, v. 241–51); see also Jones, *Ducal Brittany*, p. 85.

[62] Anselme, *Hist. généalogique*, III. 258–9.

[63] A.N., X1a 1473, fol. 294r. Delachenal was not aware of this entry.

[64] Delachenal, *Hist. de Charles V*, v. 251.

The trial of Charles the Bad in the first days of March 1387 was similar in form and procedure to the trial of Jean de Montfort. It is of additional interest not only because it was posthumous – Navarre had died on 1 January – but also, and more significantly, because of the renewed conflict between the king and the peers over the right to judge.[65] For two weeks before the trial began, Philippe, duke of Burgundy, representing the other peers in his capacity as doyen, remonstrated with the king about the letter that had been promised to the peers at the trial of Montfort but that had never been produced. The chancellor Pierre de Giac then convoked the *grand conseil* on two occasions – once in his *hôtel* and once in the Parlement – in order to deliberate on the matter. Finally it was decided that the letter of non-prejudice would be produced on the opening day of the trial, and that it would mention the precedent set by the Montfort trial.

Charles VI held his *lit de justice* on 2 March, but before the proceedings could begin the duke of Burgundy brought up the issue of the letter of non-prejudice: if it were not delivered now, he threatened, he and the other peers would depart immediately. In view of the decision already taken by the *grand conseil* the king instructed that the letter be produced for the peers and for the king's proctor as well. This done, and the obligatory summons having been made, Oudart de Moulins, king's advocate, presented the case against Navarre.

From natural law he argued that those who commit the crime of felony forfeit their fiefs 'because the vassal renders himself unnatural in going against his lord, especially when [his lord] is the king, who is the head of the public weal'. From Roman law he explained that lese-majesty was so detestable that it could even be prosecuted posthumously. Treason was sacrilege, he implied, because 'the king is sacred and anointed'. Furthermore, the facts of Navarre's treason – his whole political life – were so notorious that no further prosecution

[65] Froissart, *Chroniques*, XIV. 187–8 gives a vivid description of his death. The legal proceedings against Navarre had in fact begun before his death; the first summons had been issued on 7 August 1386 (A.N., Coll. Lenoir 8, fol. 297r; *ibid.* 20, fols. 41–2). There are two sources for Navarre's trial, the one an extract from A.N., X1a 1473, fols. 294r–295r, published with some errors in D. and T. Godefroy, *Le ceremonial françois* (2 vols., Paris, 1649), II. 435–7; and the other an extract from a criminal register of the Parlement. This register no longer exists, but the extract fortunately was published by the Godefroys (*Ceremonial françois*, II. 437–40). What follows is a collation of the two texts.

was necessary. In the same way that Guillaume de Saint-Germain argued at the trial of Montfort, so did Oudart de Moulins assert that although forfeiture could therefore now be declared, the king preferred to proceed formally. Unfortunately, there is no trace of further legal action in this case, but it is probable that an *arrêt* of confiscation was published, for otherwise one can think of no other reason for the trial.

From the first days after the arrest of Jean II, duke of Alençon, on 27 May 1456[66] until the royal commissioners completed their interrogations of various witnesses and of Alençon's agents in December 1456,[67] Charles VII was not sure how to proceed against the duke. All he knew, as he wrote in a letter of 2 June 1456 to Pierre I, duke of Brittany, was that he would proceed 'par bon conseil et advis ainsi quil appartiendra par raison'.[68] When the full extent of Alençon's treason was appreciated, Charles VII decided to institute a full-scale trial of the duke. It had been almost seventy years, however, since the last trial of a peer – that of Navarre – and the formalities had been forgotten.[69] On 24 December 1456, therefore, the *grand conseil* sent to the king's proctor, Jean Dauvet, and to the king's advocate, Jean Simon, a letter 'along with a *mémoire* of the doubts and difficulties that have been brought up concerning the case . . . of Alençon'. A similar letter was sent to the presidents of the Parlement. Specifically, Jean Tudert, a royal councillor and *maître des requêtes de l'hôtel*, posed six questions concerning Alençon: does he hold his duchy in peerage, and if so, does he have the same prerogatives as the twelve ancient peers? Before what judges ought the peers of France to be tried? Do the other peers have to be summoned to the trial? If so, do they have to attend in person, or can they send representatives? Was the presence of the king a necessity? And if there was a crisis affecting the public weal, could the king then delegate a lieutenant to preside over the trial?

Together with Dauvet, Simon and several notables, the presidents discussed the problems at length. On 28 December Dauvet and

66 Escouchy, *Chronique*, II. 320–1; not 31 May.

67 B.N., ms. fr. 18441, fols. 1r–125v.

68 B.N., n.a. fr. 6525, no. 4.

69 For the rest of this paragraph and for the following three see B.N., ms. fr. 2811, fol. 35r; and A.N., X1a 1484, fol. 1v, now badly damaged, but fortunately published in Anselme, *Hist. généalogique*, III. 258–9.

Simon wrote back to the *grand conseil*, explaining that 'because it is a question of great import and consequence, it has seemed expedient to us to search in the registers of the Parlement, in the *trésor des chartes*, in the *chambre des comptes* and wherever else one is likely to find . . . a solution to the said questions and difficulties'. Their opinions and advice, and those of the presidents, would then be sent in writing to the *grand conseil*.

It took over a year for the Parlement to make its report, which was presented on 20 April 1458 and which on most points referred to the precedents set by the trials of Artois, Montfort and Navarre. Alençon was indeed a peer, it declared, and there should be no distinction made between him and the ancient twelve peers of France. When a peer was a defendant in a case that concerned his life or his dignity as a peer, the trial should be conducted in the Parlement by the king and the peers, with the participation of other notables, prelates and members of the royal council. All the peers should be summoned to the trial; if they did not respond to the summons, however, the king was not obliged to delay the proceedings. The peers could not appear by proxy, for they were summoned by virtue of the 'authority, dignity and prerogative of their persons and lordships, [and they] cannot and should not subrogate others in their place'. Although there was no constraint on the king to preside in person, nevertheless the peers and the others had never proceeded without him. And although there were precedents for the commission of notable men to conduct the preliminaries of the trial, 'such as to make investigation, interrogate accomplices [and so on] . . . with regard to the . . . interlocutory or definitive judgements, it is found that the kings have always been present'. It was thus 'most expedient, appropriate and reasonable' that it be so in this trial of Alençon. In the event that the king might want to delegate a lieutenant because of some crisis, the court thought it preferable that the trial be prorogued.

There was a seventh question in Tudert's *mémoire*: should the cases of the princes of the blood be treated in the same way as those of the peers? Although Tudert had not specifically named Jean V d'Armagnac, he had clearly asked this question with Armagnac in mind, for the count had only recently been summoned to appear in the Parlement to answer for his rebellion and treasonous usurpation of royal authority.[70] When the Parlement replied to the other questions on 20 April 1458 it avoided this particular problem 'because there is a trial in progress . . . over just such an issue, and the deliberation of this article would in effect decide the case'. Before continuing with the trial of Alençon let us pause here to consider briefly those aspects of Armagnac's case that bear on the trial of peers.

After defaulting on two summonses Armagnac gave himself up in Paris on 8 December 1457.[71] From the start, however, he denied that the Parlement alone could have competence in his case. Through his proctor, Pierre Poignant, he demanded that he be judged by the king, or by the king and the peers, or by the king and the peers in the Parlement. In mid-March 1458 Poignant argued in the Parlement on the count's behalf, informing the court that on his mother's side Jean V was the great-great-grandson of Jean le Bon: those who descended in the female line, he asserted, were every bit as close to the king as those in the male line. Indeed, he argued, custom and usage have set the precedents for trial by peers: 'if such great solemnity was maintained for a simple crime of fraud', he contended, referring to the trial of Robert d'Artois in 1331–2, 'it seems that in the present case it ought to be maintained even more'.[72]

In reply the king's advocate Jean Simon declared that since the Parlement was a sovereign court and represented the king, no one could decline its jurisdiction. As for the argument that the king must personally take cognizance of cases concerning the princes of the blood, 'this is not so [because] there is no privilege or ordinance in any court register or in the *trésor des chartes* or in the *chambre des comptes*' to support this. Nor could Poignant argue so from custom and usage: Armagnac could not use the case of Artois as a precedent, Simon declared, because 'it was the good will and pleasure of the king' to convoke the peers; he was certainly not bound to do so. In any case, Simon added, Artois was a peer and descended in direct male line from Louis IX: if the peers had been summoned to sit in judgement it was precisely because of these two reasons. The privileges accruing to the direct descendants in the male line 'cannot

[70] A.N., x2a 29, fol. 116r. R. Jackson ('Peers of France and Princes of the Blood', *French Historical Studies*, VII (1971), 34 and n. 14) knew of Tudert's *mémoire* and the answers by the Parlement but he was not aware of the prosecution of Armagnac.

[71] A.N., x2a 29, fols. 107v–108r.

[72] A.N., x2a 28, fols. 202r–205r for this and the following paragraph.

be extended to those descended from daughters'. The one point especially worthy of note in Simon's argument was that just one month before the Parlement gave its replies to Tudert's questions – replies that Simon himself helped to formulate – he could argue that for the trial of one peer the king was not obliged to summon the others.

While the Parlement continued its prosecution of Armagnac, the venue for the trial of Alençon was changed, first to Montargis, then to Vendôme, where on 21 August 1458 Charles VII made his entrance.[73] On 26 August, in a chamber the walls, floor and benches of which were covered with blue cloth decorated with golden *fleur de lis*, Charles VII opened the proceedings in a *lit de justice*.[74] Notwithstanding the answer given in April concerning the participation of the peers, the king allowed the Burgundian delegation of Jean de Croy, lord of Chimay, Simon de Lalaing, Jean l'Orfèvre, proctor of Burgundy, and Toison d'Or to take up seats in the chamber; it is unlikely, however, that they were permitted to participate in the judgement. Alençon was then brought into the chamber, and the trial proper began. After swearing an oath, the duke was interrogated in open court, and he confessed to the main points of his intrigue to have the English invade Normandy.[75] Because of some obfuscation on his part, however, he was confronted with at least one witness. He was allowed the unusual privilege of calling witnesses to testify on his behalf.[76]

On 14 September Jean l'Orfèvre delivered the Burgundian plea for clemency. In a learned discourse replete with references to the

[73] Anselme, *Hist. généalogique*, III. 261–2; Beaucourt, *Hist. de Charles VII*, VI. 187. The entry is described in detail in Jacques Duclercq, *Mémoires*, ed. Fr. Baron de Reiffenberg (4 vols., Paris, 1826–7), II, 260–2.

[74] For a concise iconographical analysis of the *lit de justice* see Vale, *Charles VII*, pp. 204–7. The seating plans described by G. du Fresne de Beaucourt (*Histoire de Charles VII* (6 vols., Paris, 1881–91), VI. 187–9) and by Vale (*Charles VII*, pp. 207–8) are taken from contemporary but truncated descriptions (B.N., ms. fr. 5738, fols. 17r–19r; ms. fr. 5943, fols. 33v–34r; ms. fr. 6750, fol. 5r). The only complete seating plan is preserved in the College of Arms, MS Arundel 48, fols. 222r–224v as an addendum to the 'Fastolf Relation' (see C. A. J. Armstrong, 'Politics and the Battle of Saint-Albans', *B.I.H.R.*, XXXIII (1960), 3–4). I owe this reference to Mr Armstrong, and I should like to thank Mr J. P. Brooke-Little, Richmond Herald, for allowing me to consult the MS.

[75] Beaucourt, *Hist. de Charles VII*, VI. 41–59 summarized from B.N., ms. fr. 18441, fols. 1r–125v the details of the duke's treason. See also *idem*, 'La conspiration du duc d'Alençon (1455–1456)', *Rev. des quest. hist.*, XLIX (1891), 410–33.

[76] *Recueil général des anciennes lois*, IX. 344–5, 351–2.

Bible, the Decretals, John of Salisbury's *Policraticus*, Virgil, Cato and Seneca, he put forward four reasons why the king should be inclined to mercy: the sublimity of the king's majesty; the kinship between the king and Alençon; the services to the crown by Alençon and his ancestors; and the lack of true malice on the duke's part. The king's response, spoken for him by the bishop of Coutances, did not augur well for Alençon. It was precisely because of the king's majesty, the bishop began, that Charles VII was bound to do justice, 'for kings reign through justice'. As for the bonds of parentage put forward by Orfèvre, Alençon was 'all the more bound to the good of [the king] and his kingdom, and his offence is therefore all the greater'. This general argument, one will remember, was made by Jean Petit in his *Justification*. In addition, the duke had not followed the example of his ancestors, 'and just as the children should not suffer for the crimes of their father . . . they should not therefore profit from his fame and merit'. Finally, it was not at all true that Alençon had acted with no evil intent. On the contrary he had persevered in his treason 'by great malice and his too great subtlety'.[77]

Another plea for mercy was made by the poet-prince Charles, duke of Orléans.[78] His self-effacing, erudite, impassioned and sensitive speech concluded with the wistful suggestion that if the king were to convict Alençon, he would do better to have him executed than to have him imprisoned. 'Death', the duke of Orléans explained, 'would deliver him from the pain and sorrow of this world, for I myself know from my imprisonment in England . . . that to escape the affliction in which I found myself, I often wished that I had died at the battle [of Agincourt] where I was taken.'[79] A third plea came from Artur de Richemont, duke of Brittany and constable of France. At first Richemont had refused to attend the trial, arguing that he was not a peer and was not obliged to participate; but succumbing to the entreaties of the duchess of Alençon, he did eventually go to Vendôme after the trial had begun.[80]

[77] G. Chastellain, *Oeuvres*, ed. Kervyn de Lettenhove (8 vols., Brussels, 1863–6), III. 468–76; see also Beaucourt, *Hist. de Charles VII*, VI. 190–1.

[78] The full text of this speech is in B.N., ms. fr. 5738, fols. 23r–34r. There is a brief summary of it in Beaucourt, *Hist. de Charles VII*, VI. 192–3; see also Vale, *Charles VII*, pp. 208–9.

[79] B.N., ms. fr. 5738, fol. 32v.

[80] (Dom.) P.-H. Morice, *Histoire ecclésiastique et civile de Bretagne* (2 vols., Paris, 1750 and 1756), II. 65; E. Cosneau, *Le connétable de Richemont (Artur de Bretagne) (1393–1458)* (Paris, 1886), pp. 448–9.

By the time that Jean Juvenal des Ursins, archbishop of Reims, made his speech on behalf of Alençon on 8 October, 'several notable persons . . . from [the] court of Parlement and [the] council, and others' had argued strongly for application of the penalties for treason: execution and forfeiture. Because of the clerical prohibition against shedding blood, some, but not all, of the prelates, clerical *maîtres des requêtes* and clerical councillors of the Parlement absented themselves from the trial. This probably occurred at the conclusion of the prosecution and at the beginning of the deliberation on Alençon's fate. Like Jean Juvenal des Ursins, however, some ecclesiastics did remain; but although they might have pleaded for clemency, they would not take part in the formal judgement. Probably at this point in the proceedings, the duchess of Alençon presented written petitions to the king, who had them read out in court. And the duke himself got down on his knees to beg for mercy.[81]

On 10 October the chancellor Guillaume Jouvenel des Ursins, 'rising to his feet and turning to face the king, whom he reverenced in genuflection, and then turning to face the assembly, began to read the sentence',[82] which the king had arrived at 'à tresgrande et meure délibéracion de nostredicte court, garnie comme dessus'. Although the sentence was one of death and forfeiture, the king was content to defer the capital punishment 'jusques à nostre bon plaisir'. The extent of forfeiture was also modified. The *vicomtés* of Domfront and Verneuil were incorporated into the royal domain; retained by the king, though not incorporated like the two *vicomtés*, were all the other lands and appurtenances of the duchy of Alençon, the land of Semblançay in Touraine and the duke's rights in Tours. But Charles VII left to René d'Alençon the county of Le Perche in tail male, though without privilege of peerage; and to Alençon's other children, who were to be royal wards until they reached the age of majority, the king left the duke's remaining properties. His moveables were to be enjoyed by the duchess as well as by the children.[83] Alençon himself was not present at the reading of the *arrêt*. Precise

81 For this paragraph see Anselme, *Hist. généalogique*, III. 264–8. Juvenal des Ursins's speech is summarized in Beaucourt, *Hist. de Charles VII*, VI. 193–5.

82 Chastellain, *Oeuvres*, III. 478.

83 The *arrêt* is published in *Recueil général des anciennes lois*, IX. 341–54. In July 1460 Alençon's daughter ceded to the king the rights to her portion in return for a one-time payment of 8000 *l.t.*, a life-rent of 500 *l.t.*, and a grant of some lands in Normandy for her lifetime only (A.N., J 779, no. 5).

instructions were later given to Guillaume de Ricarville, captain of the castle of Loches, on the terms of the duke's imprisonment.[84]

Pardons that Alençon received from Louis XI in October 1461 and again in December 1467–January 1468 stipulated that he would forfeit all privilege of peerage for any future treason.[85] Thus when he was arrested in February 1473 for again having conspired with the English, he was at first prosecuted by a royal commission and then, from January 1474, by the Parlement. This time there was no question of a trial in the *cour garnie de pairs*. The *procédure extraordinaire*, albeit without torture, was followed.[86]

The prosecutions of Jacques d'Armagnac, duke of Nemours, in 1476–7, and of René d'Alençon in 1481–3 were based on the precedent set by the second trial of Jean d'Alençon: that a peer could forfeit his legal privileges by committing treason in violation of a written pledge. Unlike the second trial of Alençon, however, the proceedings against Nemours and René d'Alençon were a new form of state trial. Let us consider them in turn.

At Saint-Flour on 17 January 1470 the duke of Nemours had made his submission to the king's lieutenant, Antoine de Chabannes, count of Dammartin, after having been in rebellion with the count of Armagnac. One important clause of the peace agreement stipulated that for any future treason not only would Nemours forfeit his pardon, but the king could then proceed against him 'as [against] a purely private person having no privileges, prerogatives or dignities, and [he could] punish Nemours corporally . . . without it being necessary for [him] to have the Parlement *garnie de pairs* assembled, nor to observe any other solemnities'.[87]

Nemours had been a principal in the conspiracy of 1474–5, and after the execution of Saint-Pol in December 1475 Louis XI turned his attention towards the duke. Besieged in his castle of Carlat since February 1476, Nemours surrendered to Pierre de Beaujeu in March. On 22 September Louis XI appointed the chancellor Pierre d'Oriole and seventeen others to prosecute Nemours.[88] Their commission

[84] B.N., ms. fr. 23838, fols. 318r–320r; see also P. Odolant-Desnos, *Mémoires historiques sur la ville d'Alençon et sur ses seigneurs* (2 vols., Alençon 1787), II. 122–3.

[85] A.N., JJ 198, no. 36; J 776, nos. 13–15; J 779, nos. 6–7; Commynes, *Mémoires*, ed. Lenglet-Dufresnoy, II. 347–52; *Ordonnances*, XVII. 53–4, 58–66.

[86] Anselme, *Hist. généalogique*, III. 274–9.

[87] *Ibid.*, III. 402.

[88] Mandrot, 'Jacques d'Armagnac', *R.H.*, XLIV (1890), 274–7, 280–1.

was not one simply to conduct preliminary investigations, but was indeed one with full authority to prosecute and sentence Nemours as if the king himself were there.[89] One cannot say that the presence of a president and several councillors from the Parlement gave the process the status of a trial in that court: at this stage the prosecution was nothing more nor less than trial by commissioners. In fact the chancellor d'Oriole opposed this procedure and wanted the case to be tried in the Parlement, but for the moment Louis XI firmly opposed this suggestion.[90]

On 7 November the commissioners, having first interrogated other witnesses, decided to begin the questioning of Nemours. The duke demurred about taking the oath, however, when he realized that they were going to proceed against him 'par forme de proces'. He reminded them that he was a peer and that should they persist he would appeal to the king to protect his privileges. He also asked for the assistance of counsel because 'he was not terribly wise, for if he had been wise he would not be there'. D'Oriole denied him this request; but when he assured Nemours that the taking of the oath would not prejudice his rights, the duke finally agreed to co-operate. Nevertheless, throughout the first part of the trial, which lasted from November to January 1477, Nemours adhered to his protest and to his appeal to the king.[91]

In mid-December the commissioners as a group, not just d'Oriole, advised Louis XI that the case should be sent to the Parlement.[92] On 24 January 1477 the king's proctor-general Michel de Pons presented to the commissioners a letter that Louis XI had written on 7 January after deliberation of his council. Determinedly the king rejected the claims of Armagnac – Louis XI no longer called him the duke of Nemours – to the privileges of peerage. The commissioners, he added, were to proceed against Armagnac on the basis of the Saint-Flour agreement, 'by ordinary or extraordinary procedure, as against any private person, until final sentence'. Although this was clearly a mandate to put Nemours to torture, there is no evidence that it was actually done.

89 Bibl. Ste-Geneviève, ms. 2000, fols. 105r–107r.
90 *Lettres de Louis XI*, VI. 88–91.
91 Bibl. Ste-Geneviève, ms. 2000, fols. 266r–270r, 283r–382r; Mandrot, 'Jacques d'Armagnac', *R.H.*, XLIV (1890), 285.
92 Bibl. Ste-Geneviève, ms. 2000, fol. 232r–v.

Even before Louis XI had written that letter of 7 January, Nemours, no doubt broken by the harsh conditions of his prolonged imprisonment and by the merciless resolve of the king, began to confess in detail to his treason. On 27 January, with the sure knowledge that Nemours's confessions would guarantee conviction in any court of law, Louis XI issued letters patent by which he allowed the Parlement to judge the case.[93] It was clear, however, that the Parlement would not be *garnie de pairs*; nor was there any hint of a departure from the normal practice of the Parlement in the *procédure extraordinaire*. And though the Parlement was given the right to judge Nemours, the king's commissioners were still to conduct the prosecution.

A document that one can date at about March–April 1477 indicates that some members of the Parlement thought that Louis XI's concessions to due process at law were inadequate. One councillor argued that 'the king ought to have Nemours judged as a peer of France'. Another spoke 'more dishonourably, saying that a member of the Parlement should never give an opinion if the king was not present in the Parlement accompanied by the twelve peers, and that he should pardon Nemours, considering that he has shown contrition'. The king should seek no further vengeance, it was added, because that is what the people of the kingdom were asking, 'and the Parlement should please the people'.[94]

In a further concession to the members of the Parlement and others who were agitating for a more solemn procedure, Louis XI declared on 20 May that he was going to have the case brought before himself or his lieutenant, in the Parlement, and that members of his council would also take part. In so doing, the king explained, he was following the example of his father Charles VII in the trial of Jean, duke of Alençon.[95] This was a brazen misrepresentation, however, for Louis XI knew full well not only that Charles VII had presided in person, but also that the peers of France had been in attendance. No mention of the peers was made here.

On 20 June Boffile de Juge, viceroy of Roussillon, and Guillaume de Cerisay, *greffier civil* in the Parlement, appeared in Noyon, where

[93] *Ibid.*, fols. 249v–254v; Mandrot, 'Jacques d'Armagnac', *R.H.*, XLIV (1890), 291–5.
[94] B.N., Coll. Duchesne 108, fol. 63r–v.
[95] Bibl. Ste-Geneviève, ms. 2000, fols. 470v–472r; Mandrot, 'Jacques d'Armagnac', *R.H.*, XLIV (1890), 298–9.

the trial of Nemours was to take place. They informed the court that because the king was occupied in Hainault and Artois, he had delegated his son-in-law Pierre de Beaujeu to preside as his lieutenant in the case. On 26 June Beaujeu presented the powers given to himself and to sixteen royal officers by letters patent dated 4 and 22 June: as far as Louis XI was concerned Nemours was guilty, and there remained nothing but to pronounce the sentence.[96] From 27 June to 8 July the evidence was read out in court. During the deliberations on 8 and 9 July the clerical members of the court absented themselves because of the possible death penalty. Nemours was convicted on 9 July and the *dictum* was pronounced on the 10th. On 22 July, after rejecting a plea by Nemours for clemency, Louis XI ordered Beaujeu, d'Oriole and the court to return to Paris to carry out the sentence. The *arrêt* was published in the Parlement on 4 August and Nemours was beheaded that day.[97]

Even before Jean d'Alençon died in 1476 Louis XI had restored to René d'Alençon all the lands that his father had forfeited in 1474, with the exception of Pouancé, Domfront and Sainte-Suzanne; René, furthermore, was recognized as a peer in spite of the proctor-general's contention that Jean II's recidivism had disqualified his heirs from succeeding to his privileges.[98] But in spite of René's ostensible status, when Louis XI had him arrested in August 1481 on charges of treason, he did not intend to have Alençon tried in the Parlement *garnie de pairs*. Instead he appointed a commission headed by the chancellor, reserving final judgement for himself; in a letter to d'Oriole on 29 August the king advised him not to write back until the prosecution was completed.[99]

For his part Alençon insisted adamantly on 4 September that 'for nothing in the world would he depart from [his privileges]'. What his father had done 'could not be to his prejudice, and therefore he is not obliged to reply before any judge whatsoever except the king and the peers of France and the court of Parlement'. The commissioners would not be put off, however, emphasizing that they had a proper commission from the king, and asserting that since

[96] Bibl. Ste-Geneviève, ms. 2000, fols. 473v–478v; *Lettres de Louis XI*, VI. 187–9.
[97] Mandrot, 'Jacques d'Armagnac', *R.H.*, XLIV (1890), 301–5.
[98] A.N., KK 893, fol. 42; *Additions aux recherches d'Alençon et du Perche*, ed. G. Bry de la Clergerie (Paris, 1621), p. 23.
[99] Commynes, *Mémoires*, ed. Lenglet-Dufresnoy, IV. 76; *Lettres de Louis XI*, IX. 69–70.

Jean II had forfeited his peerage, René could hardly inherit it; furthermore they insinuated cunningly that should he refuse to co-operate, he would be giving 'evident presumption of wanting to hide the truth'. After some further arguing Alençon relented and answered several questions on peripheral matters. The next day he promised that if he were guilty of treason he would renounce his privileges as a peer, but he would do so only after being taken to the king.[100]

By 20 October 1481, when it seemed to Alençon that the commissioners were not merely gathering evidence prior to a trial elsewhere or to the granting of a pardon, but were proceeding against him 'par forme de proces', he again claimed his privileges as a peer. Rejecting the competence of the commissioners, he demanded a trial by the king, the peers and the Parlement. To assuage him the commissioners insisted that they were not there to judge him but to take down his statements in writing to be forwarded to the king. Again told that his obduracy made a bad impression, Alençon agreed to answer their questions fully but without prejudice to his privileges.[101]

On 13 March 1482 Louis XI instructed the chancellor to send him the *procès* of Alençon. By 19 March, at the latest, the king had made up his mind to allow the Parlement to judge the case, for on that date he advised the court that he was deputing Beaujeu to take part in the trial, and that they should proceed together with him.[102] Although it was not said explicitly, it was clear that Beaujeu was to act as the king's lieutenant as he had done in the trial of Nemours. Again, as in the case of Nemours, there was to be no participation by the peers, and the king's commissioners were not to take second place to the Parlement in the prosecution. Beaujeu appeared in the Parlement on 26 March to communicate the king's will, but since the court wished for more formal authorization, it decided on 1 April to obtain letters patent from Louis XI empowering it to judge the case. In addition it sought the letters patent that Alençon claimed had been given to his father and by which Jean II's privileges as a peer had allegedly been restored.[103]

[100] A.N., J 949, no. 6, fols. 12v–15r, 18v–21r; these and other key extracts from the trial are published in *Additions aux recherches d'Alençon*, pp. 27–56.

[101] A.N., J 949, no. 6, fols. 39v–42r.

[102] *Lettres de Louis XI*, IX. 189–90, 192–3.

[103] A.N., J 949, no. 6, fol. 142v.

On 9 July 1482 Boffile de Juge, now count of Castres, replaced Beaujeu.[104] From 10 to 16 July the *procès* was read in the Grand' Chambre of the Parlement. When this was done the court decided to remove to the castle of Vincennes, where Alençon was being held, in order to read the *procès* to him. Brought to a room above the dungeon on 18 July, Alençon stood by his claim of peerage and rejected the competence of the court. At this point the presidents and councillors thought it best to read to Alençon the pardon given to Jean II on 11 October 1461; the amplification of December 1462; and the letters of 31 December 1467, 20 and 27 January 1468 that *in toto* pardoned him for his treasonous alliance with François II, duke of Brittany. Since in all but the pardon of 1461 there was in fact no specific mention of the peerage, the court took these omissions in the later pardons to mean that the king had definitely not restored the peerage to Jean II. But René d'Alençon insisted that there were indeed documents by which the king had granted to him, René, the privileges of peerage. One of these letters, he asserted, had been given to him at the Estates-general of Tours in 1468, though he did not have it published at the time or later for fear of causing shame to his father. The Parlement, however, refused to accept his argument; referring to the renunciation clause in the pardon of October 1461 to Jean II, they voided René's claim to peerage.[105]

Because Louis XI meanwhile was becoming impatient with the pace of the proceedings, the court on 12 August 1482 sent Boffile de Juge to inform him that it was indeed working diligently to conclude the trial. On 29 September Louis XI formally rejected Alençon's claim to peerage. For the moment Alençon was not informed of this, and the Parlement and the commissioners continued their interrogation of him and of other witnesses. On 20 November, Gaillardet de Montaulin, *écuier de l'écurie*, presented to the court royal letters patent, dated 14 October, by which he was delegated to replace Boffile de Juge; the court, furthermore, was to keep Louis XI advised of its proceedings.[106]

Having recited the indictment and the evidence for the proctor-

[104] For the rôle of Boffile de Juge in the trial of René d'Alençon see P.-M. Perret, 'Boffile de Juge, comte de Castres, et la république de Venise', *Ann. du Midi*, III (1891), 204–9.

[105] A.N., J 949, no. 6, fols. 143r–172v.

[106] *Ibid.*, fols. 178r–181r. The letter of 14 October is published in *Lettres de Louis XI*, IX. 82–3 from B.N., Coll. Dupuy 38, fol. 126v, but is wrongly dated 14 October 1481.

general on 13 December 1482, the king's advocates informed the Parlement that the case was ready to be judged. The court, however, continued to drag its heels. On 13 February, Boffile de Juge returned to the court with instructions from the king to expedite the case. Four days later a delegation from the Parlement went to Vincennes to tell Alençon that the king had rejected his claim of peerage and that the court was to proceed against him as against any private person.[107] The *arrêt*, pronounced on 22 March 1483, reflected the court's inclination to be lenient with Alençon: he was 'condemned' to beg pardon from Louis XI, to swear loyalty to him until death, and to remain in prison until all this was done.[108] Whether or not he carried out the terms of his sentence, he was still in prison when Louis XI died on 30 August 1483. One of Charles VIII's first acts was to have him released.[109]

After Charles the Bold died on the battlefield at Nancy on 5 January 1477, Louis XI tried to incorporate his appanage into the royal domain by invoking the principle of reversion in default of a male heir.[110] At the same time, and in order to provide himself with a firm legal foundation in his attempt to confiscate the whole French heritage of Charles's daughter Mary, Louis XI instituted formal proceedings against the late duke. In a letter written to the Parlement on 11 May 1478 the king set forth his *gravamina* under the guise of repeating remonstrations made to him by the proctor-general. Ever since the War of the Public Weal, the king began, Charles had gone 'directly against all divine, natural and human laws, his faith and his honour . . . and incited to sedition several princes, lords and others . . . against us and the public weal of our kingdom'. After the death of his father Philippe, duke of Burgundy, he renewed his 'damnable and, to speak more properly, more diabolical than human intentions'. He invaded Normandy and waged open war, and at Péronne in 1468 'he demonstrated clearly that there was no treason nor disloyalty too great, no crime too high, too enormous nor too detestable that he would not . . . commit'. Again in 1472 he waged open

[107] A.N., J 949, no. 6, fols. 179r–183v. [108] A.N., J 860, no. 8.

[109] A.N., J 777, no. 14. This pardon of 26 September 1483 did not specify restitution of Alençon's property; he had to make a further supplication and received his lands back on 15 October (B.N., ms. fr. 2832, fols. 109r–111r).

[110] P. Saenger, 'Burgundy and the Inalienability of Appanages in the Reign of Louis XI', *French Historical Studies*, x (1977), 1–26.

war and committed all sorts of atrocities, showing that his behaviour was not that of a 'Catholic and Christian prince, but of a most execrable, inhuman and cruel tyrant'. Moreover, he had allied with the English, accepting the Order of the Garter, and had feloniously tried to usurp sovereignty in his French lands. Most treasonably he had conspired with the English, with the constable Louis de Luxembourg and with others 'to destroy . . . us and our posterity, and to subvert the whole state and tranquillity of the public weal'. In all this Charles had committed 'the greatest, most enormous crime of lese-majesty humanly possible', and by law his lands were forfeit to the crown. Because of the notoriety of the treason, the king added, there was no need to proceed beyond this present declaration. Although Louis XI did not say so, he had very good precedents in the cases of Jean de Montfort and Charles the Bad, in particular. Yet 'so that all should better know our right, the great reasons and the justice that we wish to preserve in this matter', Louis XI would have the case taken up in the Parlement, 'which is the sovereign court of justice in our kingdom where . . . the matters concerning the peers should be judged'.

That same day, 11 May, Louis XI instructed the presidents of the Parlement to inform themselves of Burgundy's treason. If necessary the king's proctor would provide them with details in writing. Furthermore, they were to hear the witnesses whom the proctor-general would produce, and they were to communicate the results of these investigations and interrogations to the *gens du Parlement*.[111] In another letter of 11 May the king instructed his advocates and the proctor-general to inform the chancellor if they thought that anything needed to be added to, removed from, or changed in his letter to the Parlement.[112] At the request of the proctor-general, Louis XI commissioned the royal advocates and the proctor-general on the one hand, and the Parlement as a whole on the other hand, to examine witnesses. In addition, the king felt that the Parlement ought to create its own commission for this same purpose 'because that which will be done by the authority of the court will be more certain'.[113]

On 28 May Simon Davy and Guillaume Dauvet, royal councillors

[111] *Ordonnances*, XVIII. 396–402. [112] *Lettres de Louis XI*, VII. 53–4.

[113] U. Plancher, *Histoire générale et particulière de Bourgogne* (4 vols., Dijon, 1739–81), IV. *preuve* cclxxx.

and *maîtres des requêtes de l'hôtel*, and Jean le Beauvoisin, a councillor in the Parlement and president of the *chambre des enquêtes*, were commissioned to examine witnesses concerning the interview of Péronne. They began their task immediately, questioning over the next few days Antoine de Crèvecoeur; Philippe de Crèvecoeur, lord of Esquerdes; Baudouin, bastard of Burgundy; and Antoine, grand bastard of Burgundy, among others.[114] Unfortunately this is the last that is known of the posthumous prosecution of Charles the Bold. Clearly, though, the proceedings were initiated as a means of bringing pressure to bear on Mary of Burgundy. From the legal point of view the significant aspect of the prosecution was that no special form was envisaged for, no rôle given to, nor even contemplated for, the peers. For all intents and purposes the process was to be one of *procédure ordinaire*.

The hallowed process of trial by peers thus never really existed in a pure form in later medieval France. Although the peers did render judgement at the trial of Robert de Béthune, count of Flanders, in 1315, and had been enjoined to do so by the king, the fact remains that twelve prelates and barons who were appointed by the king also took part in the trial by virtue of the treaty of Athies. The precedent was a most important one. Two further changes are noticeable at the trials of Jean de Montfort, Charles the Bad and Jean d'Alençon. Firstly, it was the king who pronounced judgement: the peers had only an advisory, if not simply a decorative, rôle. For all that the peers objected to this development at the trials of Montfort and Navarre, they seem meekly to have accepted the situation at the trial of Alençon: in all but form they had abandoned their right to render judgement. The second point is that trial by peers had become transformed into a trial not merely by the king and the peers accessorily, but by the king and the peers in the Parlement, with the attendance of other prelates, barons and royal councillors selected by the king. This was the form that future treason trials of peers were to take: those of Brittany and Orléans in 1488, and Bourbon in the 1520s, for example.[115]

It is most evident that the prosecution of peers took place in the Parlement because such trials thereby received the greatest sanction

114 B.N., ms. fr. 5042, fols. 4r–9r.

115 Godefroy, *Le ceremonial françois*, II. 450–1 (Brittany and Orléans); II. 455–7, 474–8; A.N., J 954 (Bourbon).

of the law, for the Parlement was the highest court in the kingdom. In the cases of Jean d'Alençon in 1474, Jacques d'Armagnac and René d'Alençon, the Parlement, though not *garnie de pairs*, was nevertheless empowered to conduct the final stages of the prosecution for that same reason. There may have been much mutual enmity between Louis XI and the Parlement, but he was not unaware of the authority with which that court was endowed, and he could use it masterfully for his own purposes.

Chapter 5

PUNISHMENT, FORFEITURE AND PARDON

I

In 1610, for having assassinated Henri IV, François Ravaillac was condemned by the Parlement of Paris to a most horrible death.

> His breasts, arms [and] thighs... were plucked by red-hot pincers, his right hand that held the knife [was] burned by sulphur-fire, and on the places where he [was] plucked by the pincers, molten lead, boiling oil, burning pitch, and molten wax and sulphur were poured. This done, his body was dismembered by four horses, [and] his limbs and corpse [were then] consumed by fire, reduced to ashes [and] thrown to the wind.[1]

In later medieval France there was no punishment for treason that matched this in cruelty, but the penalties inflicted on traitors were often not much less severe.

Decapitation and/or hanging were not uncommon,[2] but as in England[3] a traitor's death could be clearly distinguished from that of other felons by the additional penalties of drawing and/or quartering. The execution in 1323 of Jourdain de l'Isle-Jourdain, lord of Casaubon, who was stripped naked, drawn on a hurdle from the Châtelet to the gibbet, and hanged there, left a vivid impression on a contemporary chronicler. 'One cannot remember nor can one find it written in the *gestes* of France,' he remarked, 'that a man as high-born as my lord Jourdain has ever suffered such a death since the time of Ganelon.' Another example confirms that drawing was a hallmark of the punishment for treason. In April 1328 Pierre Remi, chief treasurer of the late Charles IV, was sentenced to be hanged for maladministration. Just as he was about to be executed he admitted 'that he had committed treason against the king and the kingdom in

[1] *Arrest de la cour de Parlement contre le tres-meschant parricide François Ravaillac* (Paris, 1610), p. 4.

[2] E.g., Favier, *Marigny*, pp. 216–17 (hanging); J. Andrieu, *Histoire de l'Agenais* (2 vols., Agen, 1893), I. 225 (decapitation); *Chron. normande*, p. 75 (decapitation); Roye, *Chron. scan.*, I. 295 (decapitation); I. 360 (decapitation); A.N., x2a 56, fol. 87r (hanging); *Reg. crim. du Châtelet*, I. 469, 474–5; II. 6 (decapitation and hanging); B.N., ms. fr. 26091, no. 670 (decapitation and hanging).

[3] Bellamy, *The Law of Treason*, pp. 18, 23, 26, 39, 47, 116–17, 152.

Gascony'. Because of his confession he was immediately taken down from the gibbet, 'tied to the tail of the four-horse chariot that had transported him [there], drawn from [that gibbet] to the new [one], which he himself had caused to be built, and was the first one to be hanged there'.[4] Unlike Jourdain de l'Isle-Jourdain he was not drawn on a hurdle, for this, as one learns from the execution of Mérigot Marchès in 1391, was done only in the case of a 'gentilhomme'.[5]

It is clear that quartering was another characteristic penalty in the punishment of treason. In prosecuting Louis de Courcelles in the early 1450s the king's proctor demanded that he be drawn, decapitated, quartered 'as is customary' and hanged. At the trial of Jean d'Alençon in 1458 Jean Juvenal des Ursins remarked that 'according to the usage observed in the kingdom' traitors could be punished by beheading and quartering. And although the Parlement of Paris in December 1475 condemned Louis de Luxembourg only to be decapitated, it had declared that 'given the enormity of these great and execrable crimes of lese-majesty ... he should be quartered'.[6]

One of the first known examples of quartering in France dates from 1346, when Simon Pouillet was executed for having indiscreetly said in public that Edward III rather than Philippe de Valois should be king of France. 'Like a side of meat in a butcher shop,' he was 'stretched and bound on a slab of wood ... and was there beheaded and dismembered, first his arms, then his legs, and then his head; and finally [his corpse] was hanged on the gibbet.' This execution, it was noted in the *Grandes chroniques*, was 'such as had never before been done in the kingdom of France'.[7] Mérigot Marchès in 1391 and the Scots archer Robin Campbell in 1455, having first been drawn and beheaded, were also quartered, after which their corpses were hanged. The would-be poisoner Jean Hardi suffered perhaps the most severe punishment in the reign of Louis XI. On 31 March 1474 he was 'drawn on a hurdle from [the Conciergerie] to the gate of [the Louvre], and from there taken in a tumbrel to the Place de Grève', where he was 'decapitated [and] quartered. His head [was then impaled] on the end of a lance, and each of his four limbs

[4] *Chron. parisienne anon.*, p. 88 (Jourdain); *Chron. de Guill. de Nangis*, II. 85 (Remi).
[5] *Reg. crim. du Châtelet*, II. 208.
[6] A.N., X2a 26, fol. 344r (Courcelles); Anselme, *Hist. généalogique*, III. 264 (Alençon); B.N., ms. fr. 3869, fol. 37v (Saint-Pol).
[7] *Grandes chron.*, IX. 269.

was taken to the four towns closest to the extremities of the kingdom.' His dismembered corpse was then burned, reduced to ashes and scattered to the wind.[8]

There were of course other corporal punishments. Women were burned at the stake,[9] and clerics especially were drowned;[10] but there does not seem to have been any disembowelling and burning of entrails as in England.[11] Not all the penalties were capital: one could be put in the pillory[12] or on the wheel,[13] or have one's eyes gouged out.[14] Because treason could take many forms, the punishment could be made to fit the crime. For their adulterous liaison with the daughters-in-law of Philippe IV, the Aulnay brothers were 'vivi excoriati, eisque virilibus una cum genitalibus amputatis, caesisque capitibus ad commune patibulum tracti, cunctisque omnino corio denudatis, per spatulas et brachiorum compagines suspenduntur'. And in 1390 the counterfeiter Jean Jouye was boiled alive, presumably because his crime involved the melting down of coin.[15]

Imprisonment, rarely a punishment in the first instance,[16] was usually the result of a commuted death sentence, as in the cases of Louis d'Amboise in 1431, Jacques Coeur in 1453, and Jean, duke of Alençon, in 1458 and again in 1474.[17] When an accused traitor could not be apprehended, a sentence of banishment would be pronounced.[18] In only one instance was there execution in effigy. On 24 June 1477 a proctor and secretary of the town of Lyon described how at Paris he had seen 'the portraiture of my lord the prince of Orange, who, fully armed, was hanged on a gibbet by his left foot. His bowels [were] protruding from his stomach, his head [was]

[8] *Reg. crim. du Châtelet*, II. 208 (Marchès); B.N., ms. fr. 3876, fol. 199r–v (Campbell); ms. fr. 5908, fol. 143r (Hardi; see also Roye, *Chron. scan.*, I. 308–9).

[9] *Reg. crim. du Châtelet*, I. 479–80.

[10] Beaucourt, *Hist. de Charles VII*, III. 170; Roye, *Chron. scan.*, I. 73–5; A.N., Coll. Lenoir 29, fol. 111.

[11] Bellamy, *The Law of Treason*, index *sub* 'punishment'.

[12] *Confessions et jugements*, p. 145.

[13] *Chron. de Guill. de Nangis*, II. 103–4.

[14] Roye, *Chron. scan.*, II. 30–1.

[15] *Chron. de Guill. de Nangis*, I. 404–5 (Aulnays); *Reg. crim. du Châtelet*, I. 493–4 (Jouye).

[16] Philippe de Commynes, *Mémoires*, ed. Mlle Dupont (S.H.F.) (3 vols., Paris, 1840–7), III. *preuves*, 146–8 (Commynes in 1489 is one of the few cases).

[17] A.N., J 366, no. 1 (Amboise); Clément, *Jacques Coeur*, II. *p.j.* xii. pp. 307–8; *Recueil général des anciennes lois*, IX. 352 (Alençon, 1458); Anselme, *Hist. généalogique*, III. 279 (Alençon, 1474).

[18] E.g., A.N., X2a 4, fol. 221r; X2a 29, fol. 128r–v; Lancelot, *Mémoires concernant les pairs, preuves*, pp. 804–5; Commynes, *Mémoires*, ed. Lenglet-Dufresnoy, III. 141–5.

enveloped in flames, and a devil, using an iron tong, was holding the said prince by the tongue, which was pulled from his throat.' At Dijon, Thibaut le Lièvre, a painter and stained-glass artist, was paid 40 *s.t.* for having produced four similar paintings.[19] At Caen the artists Jean de Haguais and Jean Picard received 50 *s.* for an effigy of the prince; and for 35 *s.* Jean Paumier provided 'two ells of cloth for a fitted and damasked robe' to clothe this effigy, which, after being paraded around the streets of Caen, was hanged by its feet on a mock gibbet that had cost 10 *s.* to erect.[20]

Fines in the range of 500–18,000 *l.t.* could be levied for minor treasons such as breach of safeguard, private war or violation of a truce, though most of the money would go to the plaintiffs rather than to the crown.[21] Larger fines were assessed for peculation, and these of course were payable to the crown. Jean de Saincoins in 1450, for example, was condemned to pay 60,000 *écus*; the marshal Joachim Rouault, who in 1476 was prosecuted for 'other great crimes . . . against the king, the crown, the kingdom and the whole public welfare' as well as for peculation, was fined 20,000 *l.t.*; and Jacques Coeur was fined the enormous sum of 400,000 *écus*, which of course he could not pay.[22]

Beginning with Carcassonne in 1305[23] towns corporately might have to pay financially for the treason of their inhabitants; but except for the early 1380s, when the royal uncles exacted about a million francs from the towns that had rebelled against the new taxes,[24] the crown does not seem to have enriched itself in this manner on a regular basis.

[19] Arch. Mun. de Lyon, AA 98, no. 18; 'Exécution en effigie de Jean de Chalons, prince d'Orange', *Le cabinet historique*, IX (1) (1863), 47. A Jean François made similar pictures at Mâcon; see Rossignol, *Hist. de la Bourgogne*, p. 82.

[20] P. Carel, *Histoire de la ville de Caen depuis Philippe-Auguste jusqu'à Charles IX* (Paris, 1886), p. 181.

[21] E.g., A.N., X2a 7, fol. 346r; X2a 8, fol. 193v; X2a 16, fol. 223v; *Actes du Parlement*, 2nd series, I. no. 4496.

[22] Chartier, *Chronique*, II. 245 (Saincoins); B.N., Coll. Dupuy 751, fols. 66r–67v (Rouault); Clément, *Jacques Coeur*, II. *p.j.* xii. pp. 307–8.

[23] A.N., J 335, no. 4 (Carcassonne was fined 60,000 *livres*); see also Vaissete, *Hist. de Languedoc*, IX. 279.

[24] A.N., JJ 123, no. 85; JJ 125, no. 244; *Chron. de Jean II et Charles V*, III. 31–2; Chéruel, *Hist. de Rouen*, II. 445; E. Perroy, *The Hundred Years War*, trans. W. B. Wells (London, 1965), p. 190.

II

Whatever the punishment for treason, confiscation of all moveable and immoveable property to the benefit of the crown was an integral part of it.[25] Such complete confiscation in France contrasts with the practice in England, where distinctions could be made between entailed estates and lands held in fee simple, dowers, uses, jointures and a wife's inheritance.[26] The evidence on forfeiture in France is far from complete, however, and is one-sided: there is much information about grants of confiscated lands,[27] considerably less about restitutions, and hardly any concerning forfeited property that remained in the royal domain. Because of the eighteenth-century fire in the *chambre des comptes* there no longer exist the thirty-two volumes, for example, in which were recorded the value of property that had been confiscated during the reigns of Charles VI and Charles VII; all that remains is a useless index.[28] Those volumes were only the most notable loss; much else was destroyed during the French Revolution. Yet although no meaningful calculation of royal revenue from forfeitures can be attempted, and although little other statistical analysis can be done, one can still discuss some of the main features and facts of confiscation in later medieval France.

In spite of the *lex Quisquis*, which, as we have seen, was a principal source for the later medieval French law of treason, it seems that the crown confiscated the property of wives as well as that of the traitors themselves. This was most certainly so with regard to the widow of Jean de la Roche-Tesson. Shortly after he was executed in April 1344 she petitioned the king, arguing that 'according to written law a married woman ought not to lose her dowry because of the crime of her husband, be it for treason or otherwise'. Her only income for herself and her two small children, she added, was the rent of 200 *l.t.* that she was allowed to receive from the forfeited property. On 8 January 1345, after consultation with the Parlement, Philippe VI annulled all grants of land made on her dowry, and instructed the

[25] Generally see Timbal, 'La confiscation'.

[26] Bellamy, *The Law of Treason*, pp. 191–5; Lander, 'Attainder and Forfeiture'; C. D. Ross, 'Forfeiture for Treason in the Reign of Richard II', *E.H.R.*, LXXI (1956), 560–75.

[27] Mostly in the JJ series of the A.N.

[28] A. Bossuat, 'Le rétablissement de la paix sociale sous le règne de Charles VII', *M.A.*, LX (1954), 141; for the index see A.N., P 943.

bailli of the Cotentin to seise her of the property that was hers.[29]

Philippe VI's decision in that case did not permanently change royal policy, however, for other evidence from the fourteenth and fifteenth centuries indicates that forfeiture continued to be enforced against the wives of traitors.[30] The examples of Jacques Coeur, Jean d'Alençon, and Antoine de Chabannes, count of Dammartin, will illustrate this. Although the *arrêt* against Jacques Coeur declared that only his property was to be confiscated, we find his sons almost immediately afterwards supplicating for the return of their mother's property. When Alençon was arrested in 1456 Charles VII instructed Louis d'Harcourt, archbishop of Narbonne, and Jean Le Boursier, *général des finances*, who had been commissioned to administer the duke's lands, to provide for the duchess and her children from the revenues; this would hardly have been necessary if her property was to remain untouched. Similarly in 1461, when Louis XI began the prosecution of Antoine de Chabannes, he gave instructions for the maintenance of the count's wife and children. Indeed, if a contemporary source is to be believed, after Chabannes was convicted in 1463 his wife was left so destitute that 'if it had not been for a common labourer . . . who helped her nourish [her two-year-old son Jean], she would have suffered a great deal'.[31]

There are indications that royal policy with regard to the property of a traitor's wife was being reversed in the last years of Louis XI's reign. After the death of Charles the Bold in 1477 disputes had arisen over the forfeited property of the late duke's adherents. On 8 February 1478 the chancellor and members of the *grand conseil* wrote to the *chambre des comptes* for clarification of royal policy. In its turn the *chambre des comptes* deferred to the king, who on 14 March declared that while the wives of traitors could not gain possession of any properties forfeited by their husbands, they could recover their dowries.[32]

Although lands held by a traitor in lieu of a debt did not in fact belong to him and therefore could not be included in the forfeiture,

[29] B.N., ms. fr. 25698, no. 130.

[30] E.g., A.N., JJ 86, no. 228, JJ 90, no. 88; JJ 96, no. 67; JJ 100, no. 605; JJ 157, no. 18; JJ 122, no. 142; JJ 168, no. 101; JJ 171, no. 93.

[31] *Les affaires de Jacques Coeur. Journal du procureur Dauvet*, ed. M. Mollat (2 vols. in 1, Paris, 1952–3), I. 30–1; B.N., ms. fr. 20371, fol. 82r (Alençon); *Preuves de la maison de Chabannes*, II. 93–4; Roye, *Chron. scan.*, II. 162–3 (Chabannes).

[32] *Ordonnances*, XVIII. 366–8.

the king would replace the traitor as the creditor.[33] All other debts owed to a traitor would, of course, also be transferred to the king. One has only to read through the journal of Jean Dauvet to see how thorough royal officers could be in enforcing the king's rights.[34] As for debts encumbering a traitor's property, there was no policy as late as 1343,[35] but by 1380 it could be stated in the chancery that the king was certainly not obliged to acquit such debts; this position was supported by contemporary jurists.[36] In the last years of Louis XI's reign it became possible for creditors to collect the debts that a traitor had incurred before committing his crime,[37] but by the sixteenth century, if not sooner, there was a return to the royal policy whereby all debts whatsoever were cancelled upon forfeiture.[38]

When forfeitures were declared against groups of people it was usual for a royal commission to be established. Immediately after the battle of Cassel in July 1328, for example, Philippe VI empowered three royal officers to make an inventory of the property of all those who had fought there. But since the application of forfeitures to the crown rather than to the immediate lord was an unaccustomed practice in Flanders, and since Philippe VI did not want to alienate the count of Flanders, who was his ally, he consented to share the confiscations with him. From September 1328 the count received a third of the forfeitures. His son Robert de Cassel also profited from the forfeitures: from 20 December he obtained a third of the confiscations in his own appanage.

On 14 October 1328 the Lombard, Vane Guy, whose function was to receive the monies due to the crown from the forfeited properties, sent 3400 *l.* 12 *s.p.* to the *chambre des comptes* in Paris; and in February 1331 he delivered the complete inventory of the property of the approximately 3200 men who had been killed at the battle. Most of the properties were quite small, being roughly two hectares on average. By 1336 the commissioners were still trying to track down some forfeited property in the castellanies of Bourbourg, Furnes, Bergues, Dunkirk and Cassel. They never did finish their task, however, for in the next year Philippe VI renounced what was

33 A.N., JJ 100, no. 125; see also *Ordonnances*, XVIII. 366–8.
34 *Les affaires de Jacques Coeur*. 35 A.N., JJ 74, no. 489.
36 A.N., JJ 116, no. 111; Timbal, 'La confiscation', XXII (1944), 57.
37 *Ordonnances*, XVIII. 366–8.
38 B.N., ms. fr. 11221, fols. 2r–3v.

still owing to him, hoping thereby to keep the Flemings from allying with the English.[39]

Within days of recovering Paris on 2 August 1358 the regent Charles confiscated the property of Etienne Marcel and his principal adherents. On 4 November, having already made a number of donations from these forfeitures, he commissioned Jean Mouche, a royal clerk and secretary, and Michel le Ferron, *receveur* for Paris, to seek out and sell all the property of Marcel's other accomplices.[40] Similarly after the recovery of Paris in 1436, Charles VII appointed Arnaud de Marle and Regnier de Bouligny as commissioners for confiscated property.[41] Through 1438 there were some 125 forfeitures.[42]

One can follow more closely the work of the royal officers whom Charles V appointed after the executions in June 1378 of Navarre's agents Jacques de Rue and Pierre du Tertre. On 7 July the king commissioned Robert Assire, *maître des eaux et forêts* in Normandy, to seize the property in that duchy of those two traitors, together with 'all the other lands of all the other allies of our said enemy [Charles the Bad] in Normandy [and in every] other part of our kingdom'. Assire was furthermore instructed to make an inventory of the properties, to detail their worth in land and rents, and to send this to the king or the *gens des comptes* at Paris. In an amplification, Charles V stated that forfeiture was to be applied to the properties of all those who since the battle of Cocherel in 1364 had remained in, gone into or died in rebellion.[43]

Assire began his task immediately. In August he was in Illeville-sur-Montfort to confiscate the property of one Geoffroy Corbin.[44] Nothing else, however, is known about this first part of his commission, which lasted until late 1379 or early 1380. Charles V meanwhile was making donations from the forfeited properties of the better-known adherents of Navarre. On 22 July 1378 he granted to Louis, duke of Bourbon, the castellany of Millac in Clermont that had been confiscated from Robert de Picquigny and that was worth 800 *l.t.* annually. From the property of Pierre de Sacquenville's

[39] *Le soulèvement de la Flandre*, ed. Pirenne, pp. xxiv–lxv, 1–162, 195–206.
[40] A.N., JJ 90, no. 101; *infra*, p. 165 for the donations.
[41] Bossuat, 'Le rétablissement de la paix', p. 155. [42] A.N., PP 118, fols. 1–16.
[43] A.N., J 1050, no. 16; *Chron. de Jean II et Charles V*, III. Appendix XXXII, pp. 226–8.
[44] B.N., ms. fr. 26015, no. 2412.

son-in-law Jean Tesson the king made equal grants of 500 *francs d'or* and life-rents of 200 *l.t.* to both Jean d'Estouteville the younger, royal *valet tranchant*, and to Renaud d'Angennes, first *valet tranchant* of the dauphin. Two further grants from Tesson's property were made to the esquires Le Galois de Givry and Jean de Brovillart, each of whom received lands worth 50 *livres* annually.[45]

Although the records of Assire's initial efforts have not been preserved, he clearly achieved little, for the king was dissatisfied when Assire presented his report. The properties described therein, Charles V complained, 'do not amount to much'. Certain that there were other, more rich lands in Normandy and elsewhere, he wanted a fuller investigation to be made. Therefore on 19 February 1380 he issued a new commission, this time to Assire and to Nicolas de Plancy, a royal notary and *clerc des comptes*. They were to seize all lands of Charles the Bad's partisans, sell them to the king's profit, send the contracts of sale to the *chambre des comptes* for approval, and collect all debts owing to the traitors.[46]

Again the surviving records of the *chambre des comptes* tell us nothing about this second commission, but there is some scattered evidence on it in the chancery registers. On 8 March 1380 the two commissioners were in Evreux, whence they issued orders to all royal officers concerned with confiscations to implement the king's orders.[47] From 15 May until at least 23 May Assire and Plancy were in Bernay, where they made three known sales totalling 2120 *francs d'or*.[48] At Bernay, again, on 16 June the commissioners sold to Yon, lord of Garencières, for 800 *francs d'or*, the land of Branville and other properties in the *bailliage* of Evreux that had been confiscated from Jean Tesson and his wife Isabelle de Sacquenville. Three days later, Garencières paid 220 *francs d'or* for the land of Le Pin in the *vicomté* of Orbec which Jean de Fourneaux had forfeited, and 200 *francs d'or* for Pierre du Tertre's land of Le Moulin-Geoffroy.[49]

More sales were made in July and August.[50] By September 1380 Assire and Plancy were back in Evreux. Gui de Barreux, lord of Tillières, bought Pierre du Tertre's fief of Garnaville in the castellany

[45] A.N., JJ 113, no. 28 (Bourbon); no. 72 (Estouteville); JJ 145, no. 447 (Angennes); JJ 113, no. 178 (Givry and Brovillart).

[46] *Chron. de Jean II et Charles V*, Appendix XXXII.

[47] A.N., JJ 118, no. 353.

[48] A.N., JJ 118, nos. 112, 239; JJ 119, no. 280.

[49] A.N., JJ 157, no. 18.

[50] A.N., JJ 124, no. 18; JJ 146, no. 364.

of Breteuil for 400 *francs d'or*. In January 1381 the prior of Sainte-Catherine de Paris paid 800 *francs d'or* for his land of Cathelon.[51] We lose trace of the commissioners after February 1381,[52] but it is not unlikely that by then they had done all that they could do.

The kings of France made good use of confiscations to supplement the incomes of their closest relatives. Louis X, for example, granted much of Enguerran de Marigny's property to his uncle Charles de Valois; to his brother Charles de La Marche; to his cousin Philippe de Valois; to his wife Clémence of Hungary; to his cousin Louis de Clermont; and to another uncle, Louis d'Evreux.[53] From the property of Pierre Remi, Philippe VI gave 8600 *l.p.* to Charles d'Alençon; 1600 *livres* to the duke of Bourbon; and three properties to Charles d'Evreux, count of Etampes.[54] In 1344 Louis de Poitiers, count of Valentinois and Diois, received 3600 *l.t.* annually in lands and rents from the confiscated property of Olivier III de Clisson and Jeanne de Belleville.[55] The land of Belleville alone, situated in north-west Poitou, and which was given by Philippe VI to Jean, duke of Normandy, was valued at 20,000 *l.t.* annually. In the 1350s Jean II bestowed this land on his son Jean, the future duke of Berri,[56] who in the 1370s also received the castles of Gençay and Mortemer in Poitou; in 1391 he acquired the property of the *routier* Mérigot Marchès as well.[57] Not surprisingly, the grasping Louis, duke of Orléans, seems to have profited from forfeitures more than any other prince in the later middle ages. From 1392 and presumably until his death in 1407 he received 4000 *livres* annually from confiscations. In that first year lands worth 1500 *l.t.* came to him from the property of Pierre de Craon alone; and at the turn of the century Charles VI granted to him the county of Périgord that had been confiscated in

51 A.N., JJ 119, no. 265 (Barreux); JJ 118, no. 353 (prior of Sainte-Catherine).

52 There had been another commission, in the *bailliage* of Amiens. The *receveur*, Pierre le Serre, owed approximately 1700 *l.p.* for the period ending 26 August 1381. Since he had not turned this sum over to the treasury, his lands were seized and sold (A.N., JJ 120, no. 172).

53 J. Petit, *Charles de Valois (1270–1325)* (Paris, 1900), p. 153; Artonne, *Le mouvement de 1314*, p. 37 n. 3; Favier, *Marigny*, pp. 219–20.

54 A.N., KK 2, fols. 78v, 149v; J. Viard, 'Les domaines de Vaux de Pierre de Remi', *Annuaire Bulletin de la soc. de l'hist. de France* (1921), pp. 145–9; Cazelles, *La société politique*, p. 284.

55 A.N., JJ 75, no. 20; 'Rapports à Philippe VI sur l'état de ses finances', ed. H. Moranvillé, *B.E.C.*, XLVIII (1887), 389.

56 A. Lefranc, *Olivier de Clisson, connétable de France* (Paris, 1898), p. 30; Delachenal, *Hist. de Charles V*, IV. 34.

57 A.N., JJ 109, no. 10; J 187A, no. 8; J 187B, no. 45.

1399 from Archambaud VI.[58] In 1460 and again in 1470 Jean, duke of Bourbon, acquired Jean V d'Armagnac's county of Isle-Jourdain.[59] In 1465 Louis XI granted to the duchess of Orléans the lordships of Chaumont and two others, all in the county of Blois, that had been confiscated from Pierre d'Amboise.[60] Donations could be used as bribes, not only as rewards. In 1469 and 1470 Louis XI was transparently trying to buy off his troublesome brother Charles by giving him 9000 *livres* from the property of Jean Balue, cardinal of Angers, and all the lands of the count of Armagnac 'deça la riviere de Garonne'.[61]

The principal crown officers and the kings' favourites and political supporters, as well as royal relatives, quite often received considerable grants of confiscated property. In 1344 Robert de Dreux, lord of Beu, *maître d'hôtel*, acquired a rent of 500 *l.t.* from the property of Richard de Percy,[62] one of the Norman barons executed that year. Between 1364 and 1380 Bertrand du Guesclin was rewarded with a number of forfeitures, chief of which was the county of Longueville that had been confiscated from Philippe de Navarre, Charles the Bad's brother.[63] The Norman knight Yon de Garencières, who was so busily buying up forfeited lands in 1380, was a faithful supporter of the crown to whom also several grants were made over an extended period. In July 1356 he received the dowry of Marguerite de Sacquenville, Pierre's daughter, together with some land of hers elsewhere in Normandy valued at 100 *livres* annually. Another 400 *livres* annually from forfeitures in Normandy was given to him as of September 1358. A few months later the dauphin gave him a house in Paris that had belonged to Pierre Puisieux, an advocate in the Parlement of Paris who had recently been executed. On 27 May 1359 Garencières obtained all the property in the castellany of Poissy that had been forfeited by Jean de Vaux, Jean de Bérangeville and the lord of Saint-Leu for having adhered to Charles the Bad. Finally, in April 1378 Charles V gave him a rent of 60 *l.t.* together with a gift of 600 *livres* from the property of Guillaume le Petit,

[58] A.N., QI 1020; J 359, no. 20; Dessalles, *Périgueux, preuves*, pp. 93–6.
[59] *Titres de la maison ducale de Bourbon*, ed. A. Huillard-Bréholles and A. Lecoy de La Marche (2 vols., Paris, 1867–74), II. nos. 6139, 6428.
[60] A.N., K 70, no. 36; P 2299, fols. 557r–558.
[61] Forgeot, *Jean Balue*, *p.j.* xvii, p. 225; B.N., ms. fr. 20430, fol. 45r.
[62] A.N., JJ 68, no. 217.
[63] A.N., JJ 94, no. 51; JJ 98, no. 532; JJ 114, no. 10; Guérin, *Arch. hist. Poitou*, XIX. 388–90.

valet de chambre of the king of Navarre.[64] One could do quite well from other people's misfortune.

For the reign of Charles VI one would expect to find retainers of the royal dukes rewarded by reason of the latter's influence. Thus Gui de La Trémoïlle, chamberlain of the king and the duke of Burgundy, was granted two houses confiscated from Jean des Marès in 1383. In that same year Pierre de Giac, chancellor of Berri, acquired all the property in the Limousin and elsewhere that had belonged to the knight Pierre de Bré. Little is known about forfeitures in the period from 1392 to 1418, at least with regard to grants made to clients of the princes. From 1418, however, as soon as the Burgundians took control of Paris, John the Fearless, acting in the king's name, made numerous donations of former Armagnac property to his own adherents. Charles de Lens, admiral of France, received a number of properties near Paris that were worth *in toto* some 400 *l.t.* David de Brimeu, lord of Humbercourt, *maître d'hôtel* of Burgundy, obtained property valued at 2000 francs. And the duke gave to his own son, the count of Charolais, Bernard d'Armagnac's *hôtel* in Paris.[65]

There is not much information about forfeitures in the first fifteen years or so of Charles VII's reign. From 1436–41 there were some 200 minor confiscations, largely in Paris and in re-conquered parts of Normandy.[66] The first important grant made by this king was that of Taillebourg, confiscated from Maurice de Ploesquellec in 1442 and given to the admiral Prégent de Coëtivy.[67] Pierre de Brézé, the king's favourite, received several forfeitures in the 1440s: as of April 1445 he and Robert de Floquet, *bailli* of Evreux, were together to receive an annual rent of 3000 *l.t.* from the forfeitures in that *bailliage*; and in 1447 and again in 1448, just before his disgrace, he obtained two other forfeitures.[68] The chancellor Guillaume Jouvenel des Ursins obtained a small property in 1466 that had belonged to one Gilles de Gras of Troyes.[69] After Jacques de Pons was

[64] A.N., JJ 84, no. 607 (Sacquenville); JJ 86, no. 351 (Normandy); JJ 90, no. 210 (Puisieux); no. 108 (Vaux *et al.*); JJ 112, no. 193 (le Petit).

[65] Guérin, *Arch. hist. Poitou*, XXI. 213 (La Trémoïlle); A.N., JJ 122, no. 302 (Giac); JJ 171, no. 37 (Lens); JJ 170, no. 190 (Brimeu); no. 160 (Charolais).

[66] A.N., PP 118, fols. 1–26; Coll. Lenoir 25, fol. 77; *ibid.*, 75, fol. 99.

[67] A.N., P 2298, fols. 1213–23.

[68] A.N., Coll. Lenoir 10, fol. 19; A.N., PP 118, fols. 39–40.

[69] A.N., JJ 178, no. 34.

convicted in 1449 the king's *mignon*, André de Villequier, obtained the island-lordship of Oleron and several other of his properties.[70] The progress of the war is reflected in the number of forfeitures during the 1440s and early 1450s: there were as many forfeitures – approximately 140 – in the years 1449–52 as there had been in the years 1441–8.[71] From 1453–61 the number of forfeitures dwindled comparatively to approximately seventy-five.[72] Antoine de Chabannes, count of Dammartin, did quite well for himself in 1453 from the confiscated lands of Jacques Coeur,[73] but Charles VII apparently made few lucrative grants after that. Less than a dozen properties are known to have been distributed in Guyenne after the re-conquest in 1453,[74] and hardly anything was granted away from the forfeitures of Jean d'Alençon and Jean V d'Armagnac.

Louis XI more than any of his predecessors used forfeitures to reward his favourites or to buy the loyalty of others. When Antoine de Chabannes was convicted in 1463 the king gave most of his property to Charles de Melun, *bailli* of Sens, royal lieutenant at Paris and in the Ile-de-France; the rest he granted to Antoine du Lau, *sénéchal* of Beaucaire, Jean de Montespedon, *bailli* of Rouen, and the heirs of Jacques Coeur, from whom their particular allotment had been confiscated in 1453. When Melun in his turn was executed for treason in 1468 Chabannes, now back in favour, obtained, in addition to the restitution of his own properties, all of his dead rival's lands except for one lordship that Louis XI allowed Melun's widow to keep.[75]

In 1469 Charles de France was not the only one to profit from the spoils of Jean Balue's property. Odet d'Aydie, lord of Lescun, whom Louis XI was no doubt trying to wean away from Charles, obtained the munificent sum of 8200 *l.t.* To Tanneguy du Châtel, governor of Roussillon, and to Louis de Crussol, governor of the Dauphiné, the king gave approximately 1100 *livres* worth of tapestries, linen and furs. In addition to a cash grant of 825 *l.* 10 *s.* the future chancellor Pierre d'Oriole also acquired the cardinal's magnificent library

[70] A.N., JJ 185, no. 253; JJ 186, no. 13; B.N., pièces originales 2328, dossier 52504, no. 15.

[71] A.N., PP 118, fols. 26–61.

[72] *Ibid.*, fols. 61–71.

[73] *Preuves de la maison de Chabannes*, II. 103–6.

[74] *Infra*, p. 206.

[75] *Preuves de la maison de Chabannes*, II. 103–11; C. Anchier, 'Charles Ier de Melun, grand maître de France et lieutenant-général du roi Louis XI à Paris et dans l'Ile de France', *M.A.*, V (1892), 83, 110.

of eighty-five volumes. Among the tomes, which bore witness to Balue's erudition, were, apart from the standard works of theology and canon law, three works by Nicolas de Clamanges; the *Defensor Pacis* of Marsiglio of Padua; the *Speculum Historiale* of Vincent de Beauvais; Bartolus's commentaries on the *Digest*; Terence; Suetonius; the tragedies of Seneca; the epistles of Cicero; and the histories of Poggio Bracciolini.[76]

From the major confiscations of the 1470s – those from Jean V d'Armagnac; Louis de Luxembourg, count of Saint-Pol; Jean de Luxembourg, count of Marle; Jacques d'Armagnac, duke of Nemours; Jean de Chalon, prince of Orange – Louis XI made substantial grants to his principal officers and favoured *courtiers*: for example to the marshal Pierre de Rohan, lord of Gié; to Antoine de Chabannes, now *grand-maître*; to Boffile de Juge, viceroy of Roussillon;[77] to Jean Blosset, lord of Saint-Pierre;[78] to Georges de la Trémoïlle, lord of Craon;[79] to Guiot Pot, *bailli* of Vermandois;[80] to Jean Daillon, lord of Le Lude and governor of the Dauphiné; to Gaston de Lyon, *sénéchal* of Lyon; and to Charles d'Amboise, lord of Amboise and governor of Champagne.[81] Grants to Antoine, grand bastard of Burgundy, and to Jacques de Luxembourg, brother of the late constable, were clearly meant as *douceurs*.[82]

Let us consider in detail the lands awarded to Ymbert de Batarnay, to whom Louis XI was particularly generous, and whose principal lordship of Le Bouchage came characteristically from a forfeiture in 1461. From the property of Jean V d'Armagnac he received Salles-Comtaux and Rignac in October 1470; Vicfezansac, Lavardens, Jegun, Lupiac, Castillon, Saint-Paul, Mourède, Lannepax, Roquebrune, Callian, Le Castéra, Valence, Saint-Lary, Cézan and Lalanne

[76] Forgeot, *Jean Balue*, *p.j.* xvii, pp. 222, 225; B.N., ms. fr. 4487, fols. 43v–48v for Balue's library.

[77] A.N., x1a 8607, fols. 53v–54r, 58v–59v, 60v–62r (Rohan); *Preuves de la maison de Chabannes*, II. 241–5 (Chabannes); Mandrot, 'Jacques d'Armagnac', *R.H.*, XLIV (1890), 308 (Juge).

[78] N. Vignier, *Histoire des comtes et ducs de Luxembourg* (Paris, 1619), p. 725; *Titres de Bourbon*, II. no. 6663.

[79] A.N., x1a 8607, fol. 41v; x1a 8608, fols. 4r–5r; *Archives d'un serviteur de Louis XI*, ed. L. de La Trémoïlle (Nantes, 1888), pp. 32–5, 84; Vignier, *Hist. des comtes de Luxembourg*, p. 724.

[80] A.N., x1a 8607, fols. 87v–94r; J 1047, no. 4; JJ 195, nos. 1610–13; Vignier, *Hist. des comtes de Luxembourg*, p. 724.

[81] A.N., x1a 8607, fols. 81r–82v, 133r–134r (Daillon); x1a 8606, fols. 240v–241v (Lyon); JJ 204, no. 155 (Amboise).

[82] A.N., J 794, no. 19; Vignier, *Hist. des comtes de Luxembourg*, p. 725.

in 1472; and Auch, Barran, Aubiet, Saint-Sauvy, Saint-Cricq, Miramont, Saint-Martin-Viague and Saubaignan in 1474. In 1476 and 1477 he obtained the following properties from the forfeiture of the duke of Nemours: Bozouls, Servissac, Fay, Biran, Ordan and Peyrusse-Grande; Châteauneuf, Meslet, Anglards and Turbande in Auvergne; and Clary, Dargies and the forest of Ailly in Picardy. From the property of the prince of Orange he acquired the lordships of Auberive, Falaviers and Anthon. Taken together these lands made Batarnay a wealthy lord practically overnight: the Armagnac properties alone brought in approximately 5000 *livres* annually.[83]

Largesse of this kind on the part of the kings of France was a normal, if irregular, form of political patronage. Of special interest is the extent to which Charles V used forfeitures to reward the lesser nobility who served him in his wars, particularly in Normandy against the Navarrese, and in Poitou and adjacent areas against the English. First as regent and then as king, Charles V is known to have made roughly 300 grants from forfeitures, largely concentrated in the years 1358–60, 1364, 1369–72 and 1378–80.[84] Approximately one hundred of these grants went to esquires, about fifteen of whom were also royal officers or served Jean II or Charles in some capacity; and about ninety-five grants were made to knights, roughly twenty of whom also had official or household positions. The range in value of the donations reflected the status of the recipients: approximately 50–150 *l.t.* annually for the esquires, and 100–150 *l.t.* for the knights.

The rest of the grants made during Charles's regency and reign were distributed not only, as could be expected, among his closest relatives,[85] the greater nobility,[86] and the principal officers of the crown,[87] but also among royal sergeants and clerks,[88] minor household officers and servants,[89] widows of royal adherents,[90] towns,[91] religious and educational institutions,[92] burgesses, and, in keeping with his intellectual interests, manuscript illuminators.[93] Louis XI may well have been more generous to his favourite courtiers, but

83 Mandrot, *Ymbert de Batarnay*, pp. 7–11, 71, 130; Samaran, *La maison d'Armagnac*, p. 224 n. 2.
84 A.N., JJ 86–117, *passim*; *infra*, chapter 7, *passim*.
85 *Supra*, pp. 123, 125. 86 *Infra*, pp. 173, 174, 175. 87 *Supra*, p. 126.
88 E.g., A.N., JJ 86, nos. 86, 347; JJ 87, no. 110; JJ 90, nos. 58, 87, 234.
89 E.g., A.N., JJ 86, no. 328; JJ 87, no. 355; JJ 90, nos. 135, 195.
90 E.g., A.N., JJ 87, no. 343; JJ 96, no. 200; JJ 100, no. 383.
91 E.g., A.N., JJ 88, no. 49 (Amiens, 1360).
92 E.g., A.N., JJ 86, no. 598; JJ 96, no. 165. 93 *Infra*, p. 165.

Charles V more than any other king rewarded and bought support from people at all levels of society. Doing so cost him little, and the return in loyalty and good-will was inestimable. Not by accident was he called the 'well-loved'. The particular importance of forfeitures during the reign of Charles V is a theme to which we shall return in chapter 7.

III

Throughout the period of Lancastrian rule in Normandy numerous grants of confiscated land were made, largely to Englishmen, but also, to a lesser extent, to Normans who remained faithful to the English. As in France such grants served as incentive, payment and reward.[94] By a very rough calculation there were approximately 900 forfeitures for treason in the period 1417–49; over a third of these fell in the first four years.[95] Up to June 1418 there had been roughly ninety forfeitures. From then until early 1419 there were another twenty-eight grants. After the fall of Rouen, however, Henry V applied a much more rigorous policy of confiscation, for it seemed that the English were in Normandy to stay. In the first five months of 1419 Henry V made approximately 200 grants of about 250 fiefs. From June onwards, though the number of forfeitures *per annum* diminished considerably, the crown was ever vigilant. On 6 June 1419, for example, the *baillis* of Normandy were instructed to seize all lands for which royal letters patent had not been granted. On 10 August 1421 instructions were issued to the *vicomtes* of the duchy to proclaim that the property of all rebels would be sold to the king's profit. There was a commission for confiscations at Paris, and at least one, perhaps two, for Normandy generally.[96] By the mid-1440s, however, forfeitures were very few in number, the annual average

[94] C. T. Allmand, 'The Lancastrian Land Settlement in Normandy 1417–50', *Econ. Hist. Rev.*, 2nd series, XXI (1968), 462.

[95] My calculations are based on 'Rôles normands'; *Actes d'Henri VI; Paris pendant la domination anglaise*; and A.N., Coll. Lenoir, vols. 1, 3–5, 13, 14, 21–2, 24–8. On the importance of the Collection Lenoir see C. T. Allmand, 'The Collection of Dom Lenoir and the English Occupation of Normandy in the Fifteenth Century', *Archives*, VI (1964), 202–10; and M. le Pesant, 'Les manuscrits de Dom Lenoir sur l'histoire de Normandie', *Bull. soc. des antiquaires de Normandie*, L (1946–8), 125–51.

[96] Newhall, 'Henry V's Policy', pp. 215, 221, 227; Sauval, *Hist. de Paris*, III. 330; A.N., X1a 4793, fol. 160v; X1a 4794, fol. 47v (I owe these last two references to Mr C. A. J. Armstrong).

being less than ten. In the *vicomté* of Orbec, for example, forfeitures accounted for only 22 *s.* 6 *d.* of the total receipts for Michaelmas 1444.[97]

It was only natural that those of greatest rank or military standing would do handsomely from the conquest. Thus Henry V's brother, the duke of Clarence, obtained the *vicomtés* of Auge, Orbec and Pontaudemer 'avecques toutes les terres des absens d'icelles vicontez'. In July 1418 Thomas Holland, duke of Exeter, was granted the county of Harcourt together with some other properties confiscated from Jean d'Harcourt; and in July 1419 he acquired the lordship of Croisy-sur-Eure that had belonged to Jean de Garencières. John, earl of Huntingdon, in May 1419 acquired all the lands in the Cotentin confiscated from Jean Paynel, to the value of 500 francs; and to these he added the barony of Ivry, confiscated from Artur de Bretagne and given to him in July 1427.[98] Thomas Montague, earl of Salisbury, profited from several forfeitures in addition to the county of Le Perche: in June 1418 he obtained the lordships of Neubourg, Courbon, and la Rivière-de-Thibouville and other properties to the value of 4000 *écus*; in 1423 he was granted the lordship of la Ferté-Fresnel, together with 100 *l.t.* in rent due to Thomas de Carrouges; and he acquired another 100 *livres* in rent in 1425, to which in 1427 were added some properties in Paris of Jean VI de Bretagne and the late Jean Tarenne.[99]

Sir John Fastolf did well for himself, receiving in 1433, for example, a rent of 1560 *saluts d'or* from confiscations. Sir Walter Hungerford did not do too badly either.[100] Such other members of the military élite as Robert Roos, Sir John Popham, Gervaise Clifton, Matthew Gough and William Oldhall also obtained lucrative rewards from forfeitures.[101] Numerous grants were made to lesser figures and to household officers of the magnates. In June 1419 John

[97] 'Compte de Jean Le Muet, vicomte d'Orbec, pour la Saint-Michel 1444', ed. H. de Frondeville, *Etudes lexoviennes*, IV (1936); Burney, 'The English Rule in Normandy', p. 77.

[98] Allmand, 'Land Settlement', p. 463 (Clarence); Allmand, 'Land Settlement', p. 463; 'Rôles normands', no. 621 (Exeter); 'Rôles normands', no. 541; *Actes d'Henri VI*, II. no. 510 (Huntingdon).

[99] Allmand, 'Land Settlement', p. 463; 'Rôles normands', no. 186; *Actes d'Henri VI*, II. nos. 326, 411; *Paris pendant la domination anglaise*, no. 120.

[100] A.N., Coll. Lenoir 26, fol. 219 (Fastolf); Allmand, 'Land Settlement', pp. 463, 465 (Hungerford).

[101] Frondeville, 'Orbec', pp. 83–94 (Roos); 'Rôles normands', no. 132 (Popham); *Actes d'Henri VI*, nos. 613 (Clifton); 616 (Gough); A.N., Coll. Lenoir 4, fol. 215 (Oldhall).

Handford and Clement Overton each received lands to the value of 500 *écus*, while Edmund Norton, John Mortimer, John Skelton and Thomas Burgh were granted lands worth 200 *l.t.*, 400 francs, 600 *écus* and 800 *écus* respectively.[102] William Peck, *clerc de l'épicerie du roi*, in 1432 obtained lands worth 300 *l.p.*, and in 1436 John Russell, a household servant of York, was given lands worth 500 *saluts d'or*.[103] Much smaller grants, particularly in the 1430s and 1440s, could also be made. One William Kilham in 1418 received lands to the value of 80 francs. Property of the same value was granted in 1438 to William Hare, esquire. Smaller yet were the grants, ranging in worth from 15 *l.t.* to 30 *l.t.*, made to the likes of William Wymington, *auditeur des comptes* at Rouen; John Winslow, esquire; William Evington, esquire; and John Hazeldon.[104] Generally speaking, though, the majority of the grants at the lower end of the scale, those, say, worth less than 100 *l.t.*, were made to Frenchmen.[105]

But larger grants, too, could be bestowed on Frenchmen loyal to the Lancastrian régime. In 1419 Jean d'Ouessey, a knight from the county of Mortain, obtained the barony of Orglands, which was worth about 300 *l.t.* Jacques de Montbéron in 1423 received lands worth 600 *l.p.* confiscated from Philippe de Lévis. In 1424 Jean, lord of Saint-Germain-le-Vicomte, was granted lands worth 350 *l.t.* No other grant, however, matched the 4000 *l.t.* in land given in 1430 to Jean de Villiers, lord of l'Isle-Adam.[106] The Lancastrian kings had another way of securing the loyalty, or at least the neutrality, of Norman landholders, and that was to grant to certain members of a family the lands forfeited by their relatives. Thus in 1423 Charles de Jencourt received the lands confiscated in 1422 from his father Pierre, lord of Heubécourt. Jean de Trousseauville in 1427 obtained a rent of 30 *l.t.* confiscated from his late uncle, the knight Olivier du Mesnil. In that same year Jean d'Estouteville and his four brothers

[102] 'Rôles normands', nos. 346 (Skelton); 349 (Burgh); 357 (Handford); 358 (Overton); 374 (Mortimer); 375 (Norton).

[103] *Actes d'Henri VI*, II. no. 624 (Peck); A.N., Coll. Lenoir 5, fol. 71 (Russell).

[104] 'Rôles normands', no. 203 (Kilham); A.N., Coll. Lenoir 4, fol. 345 (Hare); *ibid.* 5, fol. 5 (Wymington); *ibid.* 27, fol. 385 (Winslow); fol. 449 (Evington); *ibid.* 28, fol. 23 (Hazeldon).

[105] E.g., *Actes d'Henri VI*, II. nos. 255, 280, 282, 426, 552; A.N., Coll. Lenoir 4, fols. 193, 195, 227, 335; Allmand, 'Dom Lenoir', 206.

[106] Fontaine, 'Rapports du gouvernement anglais et de la noblesse normande', pp. 34–5 (Ouessey); *Paris pendant la domination anglaise*, no. 50 (Montbéron); no. 149 (Villiers); *Actes d'Henri VI*, II. no. 306 (Saint-Germain).

and sisters gained possession of six fiefs forfeited by their father, Guillaume; this was in addition to the rent of 300 *l.t.*, taken from another property, that had been granted to them in 1422.[107]

The crown did not of course make donations of all the forfeited lands that came into its possession. In November 1431, for example, authorization was given to several members of the royal council to sell lands up to a value of 15,000 *l.t.* for the government.[108] Although clearly the Lancastrians made good use of the property at their disposal, conciliation was still the key-word. Those Normans who wished to make their submission or to return to the duchy could usually expect a pardon and restitution of their property, whether or not they had taken an oath of allegiance. On 26 February 1419, for example, a special proclamation was issued urging all absentee Normans to return to obedience. Another appeal for submission was published at the end of September, and a third was issued by Bedford in 1422. Even until 1427 it was easy for a rebel to obtain a pardon.[109] The evidence for the 1430s and 1440s, however, is rather sparse, though one can assume that by that time the lines had been clearly drawn: by and large those who had opposed the English occupation continued to do so; while those who preferred to live with 'les goddams' had found a way to make their peace.

IV

Although the estates and other properties of some traitors were no doubt incorporated irrevocably into the royal domain or were granted without reversal to third parties, the kings of France did not always enforce the letter of the law, for such a policy would have permanently disinherited a traitor's direct descendants or other kin.[110] Thus even during the lifetime of a traitor some member of his family might receive by royal grace at least a part of his lands. In March 1359, for example, after Jean VI d'Harcourt went into rebellion with the king of Navarre, his brother Louis, *vicomte* of Châtellerault, obtained that portion of the properties in Maine and

[107] *Actes d'Henri VI*, II. no. 283 (Jencourt); no. 514 (Trousseauville); no. 508 (Estouteville).
[108] Allmand, 'Land Settlement', p. 468.
[109] Newhall, 'Henry V's Policy', pp. 220–1, 228; Jouet, *La résistance*, p. 41.
[110] Cf. Lander, 'Attainder and Forfeiture', p. 144.

Touraine which Jean VI had inherited from their mother.[111] In July 1475, while Jean d'Alençon was still in prison, Louis XI restored to his son René all of the duke's confiscated lands except for the lordships of Pouancé, Domfront and Sainte-Suzanne. On 20 April 1479 Louis XI transferred to Jacques, lord of Aubigny, at his request and 'in favour of the house from which he has issued' – Aubigny was a cadet of Bourbon – all the lands of his brother Pierre, lord of Carency, who had been captured at Arras in June 1475 and who had only recently been released from prison.[112] It was not only the great families to whom such politically inspired consideration was shown. In October 1364 Charles V granted to the knight Etienne de Vaux the property near Vernon, worth 50 *l.t.* annually, that had been confiscated from his cousin Jeanne de Perroy, a Navarrese adherent. In December 1369 the esquire Guillaume de Plagny was given the land of Roche-du-Maine in Poitou that had been forfeited by his cousin Baudouin and that was valued at roughly 40 *l.t.*[113]

In the cases of traitors who had been executed or who had died without returning to royal obedience, the kings of France might allow their heirs to recover some, if not all, of their properties. The earliest example of this kind was a royal grace to the children of the traitors who had been executed at Carcassonne in 1305.[114] One can point to a number of other restitutions in full or in part: to Olivier IV de Clisson in the 1360s; in 1377 to Jean le Prestrel, whose father Jacques, treasurer of Navarre, had been executed after the siege of Meulan in 1364; to the widows and children of Pierre des Essarts in 1413 and Robert de Belloy in 1416;[115] to the heirs of Jacques Coeur, Charles de Melun, Jean V d'Armagnac, Louis de Luxembourg, and Jacques d'Armagnac, duke of Nemours, whom we shall discuss at the end of this chapter.

It was certainly possible for convicted traitors themselves, if they were willing to make their peace with the king, to obtain pardons[116]

[111] A.N., JJ 86, nos. 617–19; see also G.-A. de la Roque de la Lontière, *Histoire généalogique de la maison de Harcourt* (4 vols., Paris, 1762), III. 9; *Recueil*, ed. Secousse, pp. 136–7.

[112] A.N., KK 893, fo. 42r (Alençon); K 72, no. 30 (Carency). Both Anselme (*Hist. généalogique*, I. 360) and Dupont (Commynes, *Mémoires*, I. 328) incorrectly dated this act to 1469.

[113] A.N., JJ 96, no. 280 (Vaux); Guérin, *Arch. hist. Poitou*, XIX. 34–6 (Plagny).

[114] A.N., J 335, no. 4.

[115] Lefranc, *Clisson*, pp. 42–5, 63; Delachenal, *Hist. de Charles V*, III. 176 n. 1; A.N., JJ 87, no. 275; JJ 89, no. 698 (Clisson); JJ 110, no. 191 (Prestrel); JJ 167, no. 177 (Essarts); *Choix de pièces*, ed. Douët-d'Arcq, I. 384 (Belloy).

[116] On pardons generally see P. Duparc, *Origines de la grace dans le droit pénal romain et français*

and thereby have their forfeitures reversed. Most pardons were granted to individuals at their own supplication,[117] or at the request of friends or relatives,[118] a patron,[119] or in some cases foreign royalty.[120] The remainder were general pardons to towns[121] and, usually but not always as part of a peace settlement, to the adherents of the king's enemies.[122] The individuals encompassed by a general pardon still had to seek particular pardons for themselves, however, for they were required formally to return to the king's obedience. Through his own efforts, the influence of a patron, or as a result of a general pardon, a convicted or proscribed traitor would normally receive his pardon within a few years of his treason; but some, like a few Gascons who had collaborated with Talbot in 1452–3, might have to wait as long as twenty-five years for their pardons.[123]

Only the king or his lieutenants could grant pardons. But unless a pardon described precisely what the recipient's treason was, its validity could be questioned by the Parlement, the chancery, the *cour des monnaies*, or any other government body where it had to be enregistered to take effect.[124] Even without reference to the specifics of an individual's treason, the Parlement, at least in the fourteenth century, was able successfully to oppose the enregistration of pardons. The best-known example of this is the case of Pierre de Craon in the 1390s.[125]

du Bas-Empire à la Renaissance (Paris, 1942); J. Foviaux, *La rémission des peines et des condamnations* (Paris, 1970). Y.-B. Brissaud's thesis, *Le droit de grace à la fin du moyen âge* (Poitiers, 1971), was not available to me.

117 E.g., A.N., JJ 74, no. 750; JJ 110, no. 120; JJ 204, no. 140.

118 E.g., A.N., JJ 90, no. 401; JJ 163, no. 342.

119 E.g., A.N., JJ 77, no. 129; JJ 82, no. 88; JJ 205, no. 474.

120 E.g., *Reg. du Trésor*, I. nos. 2011, 2016, 2026, 2028, 2030 (at request of Edward II); A.N., JJ 98, no. 267 (at request of the king of Scotland).

121 E.g., A.N., JJ 82, no. 233 (Saint-Jean-d'Angély, 1351); Chéruel, *Hist. de Rouen*, II. 547–9 (1382); A. Germain, *Histoire de la commune de Montpellier* (3 vols., Montpellier, 1851), II. 388–401 (1380); *Ordonnances*, IV. 346–8 (Paris, 1358); *ibid.*, XIV. 270–5 (Bordeaux, 1454).

122 There were at least twenty such general pardons issued between 1337 and 1488; see *infra*, chapters 6–10, *passim*.

123 E.g., A.N., JJ 201, no. 89; X1a 8607, fol. 67r.

124 E.g., A.N., X2a 18, fol. 181v; Z1b 60, fols. 46v–50r; JJ 186, nos. 51, 61.

125 Craon was pardoned on 15 March 1396 (A.N., JJ 149, no. 115), but he failed to have it enregistered in the Parlement (A.N., X2a 12, fols. 298v–300v, 311r–312v, 318r, 320r–325r, 405 *bis* v–406 *bis* r; X2a 13, fols. 278r–284r). He obtained two more pardons in November 1399 and February 1400 (A.N., JJ 154, nos. 604, 686), but he was no more successful with these; see also Bertrand de Broussillon, *La maison de Craon 1050–1480* (2 vols., Paris, 1893), pp. 230–1. For two other cases see *Confessions et jugements*, p. 172; A.N., X2a 8, fols. 24v–29r; JJ 97, no. 192.

Not every pardon provided for restitution in full. Louis XI's pardons to Pierre and Charles d'Amboise in April 1467; to Guillaume de Soupplainville, Odet d'Aydie and other adherents of Charles de France and Jean V d'Armagnac in the 1470s; to Hector de l'Escluse, who had been implicated in the treason of Louis de Luxembourg, all made it clear that they would recover only a portion of their confiscated property.[126] The documents never say more than this, but it is more than likely that Soupplainville and the others were required to surrender some of their lands as the price for recovering the remainder. Furthermore, the fact that certain lands were withheld from a pardoned traitor gave him the incentive to prove his loyalty, for by demonstrated good behaviour he might yet recover the rest of his estates. In England Edward IV in particular followed a similar policy.[127]

The opposition of those to whom confiscated lands had been granted might impede the restitution of property. For example, the forfeitures of Jean V d'Harcourt, Jean Malet, lord of Graville and the others who had been executed at Rouen in April 1356 were to be reversed by virtue of the accord concluded by the dauphin Charles and the king of Navarre on 12 December 1357; although we know from separate acts that this provision was ostensibly carried out, the Graville family did not recover the lordships of Sées and Bernay until after the second condemnation of Jean d'Alençon in 1474.[128] Particularly after the re-conquests of Normandy and Gascony in the mid fifteenth century, restitution could pose quite complex problems.[129]

Let us now look more closely at the cases of Jacques Coeur, Charles de Melun, Louis de Luxembourg, Jean V d'Armagnac and Jacques d'Armagnac, for they illustrate the problems involved in obtaining a reversal. After Coeur's condemnation his three sons and one daughter were relentless in their attempts to have their father's

126 A.N., X1a 8607, fol. 44r–v (Amboise); JJ 197, no. 240 (Soupplainville, 1473); no. 241 (Odet d'Aydie, 1473); no. 379 (Jean de la Molière, 1472); no. 420 (Carbon de Montpezat, 1473); JJ 204, no. 38 (Escluse, 1476).

127 Lander, 'Attainder and Forfeiture', p. 124.

128 *Recueil*, ed. Secousse, pp. 65–8 for the accord; *ibid.*, p. 70; A.N., JJ 89, no. 330; JJ 91, no. 237; *Preuves généalogiques et historiques de la maison de Harcourt*, ed. Dom. P. J.-L. Le Noir and published by the marquis d'Harcourt (Paris, 1907), p. 717 for some restitutions after 1358; A.N., K 71, no. 35; X1a 8607, fols. 1r–2v for the restitutions of Sées and Bernay.

129 Bossuat, 'Le rétablissement de la paix'; C. T. Allmand, 'The Aftermath of War in Fifteenth-Century France; *History*, LXI (1976).

and mother's property returned to them. At last in 1457 they were granted something, but it was only a pittance: four houses in Bourges, a house in Lyon, and the silver and lead mines in the mountain of Pompalieu. They and Guillaume Varie, their father's principal factor, were also allowed to collect the debts that were still owing to Jacques Coeur; but considering the thoroughness of Jean Dauvet in winding up the affairs of the late *argentier*, the sum could not have been much. For so little they had to renounce their claims to the rest of Coeur's property,[130] of which most of the lands had been granted to Antoine de Chabannes.

When Chabannes was disgraced in the beginning of Louis XI's reign Jacques Coeur's sons pressed for a revision of the sentence against their father, as well as for restitution of his property, but they failed to have the judgement reversed.[131] On the condemnation of Chabannes in August 1463, however, Louis XI returned to Geoffroy Coeur the land of Saint-Fargeau and eleven others that constituted the lordship of Puisaye.[132] But when Chabannes escaped from the Bastille in March 1465 he imprisoned Geoffroy Coeur and again, illegally, took possession of the lands. Since Chabannes was soon reconciled to Louis XI, there was little that Geoffroy Coeur could do. After the death of Louis XI Coeur again tried to recover his property by legal action, but he had made no progress by the time that he died in 1488. In the following year, though, his widow and the new count of Dammartin reached an agreement whereby she obtained the lordship of Beaumont-le-Bois and an annual rent of 400 *l.t.*[133]

In 1468 Antoine de Chabannes had also been the principal recipient of Charles de Melun's forfeited property. In the three years that he held the lands he managed to extract 20,000 *écus* from the moveables and 2000 *l.p.* annually in rents. Such rapacity was no doubt common to grantees of confiscated estates: realizing that their tenure was precarious they would try to make it as profitable as possible. But Chabannes did not give up his windfall easily. In spite of the reversal in 1471 he fraudulently kept possession of two lordships, Saint-Marc

[130] *Les affaires de Jacques Coeur*, I. 30–1, 56–7; A.N., JJ 185, no. 335; M. Bonamy, 'Mémoire sur les suites du procès de Jacques Coeur', in Duclercq, *Mémoires*, II. 394–7.

[131] Roye, *Chron. scan.*, II. 157; A.N., X2a 32, fols. 81r–85r, 99v–102v, 132r–v; Beaucourt, *Hist. de Charles VII*, V. 110–11.

[132] *Preuves de la maison de Chabannes*, II. 163–6.

[133] Roye, *Chron. scan.*, I. 40–1; Bonamy, 'Mémoire', pp. 405–6.

and les Fossés. It was not until Charles VIII rehabilitated Melun's memory in 1488, the year that Chabannes died, that those two lands were returned to Melun's heirs.[134]

Although the heirs of Louis de Luxembourg, count of Saint-Pol, were left more or less destitute immediately after his execution in December 1475, they did not remain in that state for long. In August 1477 Mary of Burgundy returned to his children all the lands that had been held by her late father and that were still in her control. Then by the treaty of Arras in December 1482 Louis XI agreed to restore the late constable's French lands.[135] The relevant clause could not be implemented, however, because of the opposition of the grantees; and Louis XI, not wishing to offend these persons, did little to effect the return of the properties. In the year following Charles VIII's accession to the throne the late constable's son Louis petitioned the king for restitution of at least the moveables that had been improperly obtained by certain persons. On 19 August 1484 Jean de Hangest, lord of Genlis, was commissioned to investigate the matter, but it is not known if anything positive resulted from his efforts. A few months later, on 2 October, Jacques de Savoye, count of Romont, pleaded before the king on behalf of his wife, Marie, Saint-Pol's grand-daughter: he requested formally that the counties of Saint-Pol, Ligny and Brienne, and all other properties be restored to her, for since the death of her father Pierre in 1482 she had become the principal heir of the late constable. Guiot Pot, to whom the county of Saint-Pol had been granted, opposed this petition strenuously, and so too, no doubt, did the other grantees. For the moment nothing was done; only in July 1487 did Charles VIII issue letters patent restoring to Marie and to Françoise de Luxembourg, Pierre's other child, all of Saint-Pol's property.[136] Once more there was considerable opposition, but at last on 10 February 1489, after Philip of Austria had interceded on behalf of the sisters, they finally recovered possession of their heritage.[137]

134 B.N., ms. fr. 2921, fols. 5r–12r; Anchier, 'Charles de Melun', p. 110.

135 E. Poncelet, 'L'exécution de Louis de Luxembourg, comte de Saint-Pol, en 1475', *Bull. comm. roy. d'hist.*, XCIX (1927), 183; *Recueil de pièces imprimées sous le règne de Louis XI*, ed. E. Picot and H. Stein (Paris, 1923), facsimiles, p. 212.

136 *Procès-verbaux des séances du conseil de régence du roi Charles VIII*, ed. A. Bernier (C.D.I.) (Paris, 1836), pp. 63, 113, 179–80; *Ordonnances*, XX. 9–14.

137 A.N., X1a 9319, nos. 106, 108; *Lettres reçues et envoyées par le Parlement de Paris (1376–1591)*, ed. S. Clemencet and M. François (Paris, 1961), no. 468; *Recueil général des anciennes lois*, XI. 125.

The fate of Jacques d'Armagnac's property was much the same: Nemours's heirs – his sons Jean and Louis, and his daughters Marguerite, Charlotte and Catherine – had to wait until the advent of Charles VIII to recover their heritage. In Jean Masselin's account of the Estates-general of Tours, their advocate is said to have delivered such an impassioned plea for them on 7 February 1484 that he moved his audience to tears. Four days later, we are told, the eldest of the children, Jean, approached the king and on bended knee presented his petition. Though not made immediately, a decision was not long forthcoming: on 5 March Charles VIII restored to the late duke's heirs the county of Guise and the lordship of Nouvion. Then on 2 August Jean recovered the duchy of Nemours, and the second son Louis became count of Guise. Full restitution of the other properties, except for the county of Castres, which Boffile de Juge managed to keep, was made in July 1491. On the death of Boffile de Juge in 1497 the county of Castres passed to Alain d'Albret, but when he fell out of favour with the crown in the early sixteenth century, the county reverted not to the Armagnacs, who by 1503 had died out in the direct male line, but to the crown.[138]

The final disposition of the Armagnac lands was likewise not settled until the early sixteenth century. Jean V's lands might have devolved on his brother Charles during Louis XI's lifetime, but Charles had been imprisoned for treason in the early 1470s and was not to be released until after Louis XI's death. In 1484, after the Estates-general of Tours, he did recover the Armagnac lands, but when he died in 1497 the direct line of the counts of Armagnac died with him, and the lands were then put under royal administration. A legal contest ensued over the Armagnac succession, with the children of the late Jacques d'Armagnac representing the direct male line, and Charles d'Alençon and Alain d'Albret representing the female line. In 1500 it was declared that the *arrêt* of 1470 against Jean V would stand and that the Armagnac lands were forfeit. The crown did not long keep the lands, however, for by 1515 Charles d'Alençon obtained the whole of the Armagnac patrimony through his wife Marguerite d'Angoulême, sister of François I.[139]

[138] Jean Masselin, *Journal des Etats généraux de France tenus à Tours en 1484*, ed. A. Bernier (C.D.I.) (Paris, 1835), pp. 133–5, 243; Mandrot, 'Jacques d'Armagnac', *R.H.*, XLIV (1890), 311; A. Luchaire, *Alain le grand, sire d'Albret* (Paris, 1877), p. 222.

[139] Samaran, *La maison d'Armagnac*, pp. 242–82, 301–8.

The main features of forfeiture for treason have been presented in this chapter. Although one must bear in mind that the surviving evidence is far from complete, one can still attempt to put forward some tentative conclusions. There were certainly some forfeitures that were never reversed, but it does not seem that the crown made permanent, substantial gains from them. In view of what we know about the likelihood of reversal, income from property that remained 'sous la main du roi' was most assuredly a highly erratic and ephemeral rather than a permanent feature of royal finance. Income from the sales of lands and moveables would exhaust itself with those very sales, though the liquidation of Jacques Coeur's affairs brought in considerable sums. In any case, whether from rents or sales, income from forfeitures could hardly have represented more than a small fraction of the crown's revenues from taxation and other sources.

Forfeitures, then, were used essentially for two political purposes. Firstly the kings of France could distribute confiscated lands to reward those who were steadfastly loyal to the crown, and to win the loyalty of others. In this sense such grants can be said to have alleviated the constant financial pressure exerted on the crown by the exigencies of patronage; but, as Professor Lander has remarked, 'the relief of pressure is . . . a very different thing from the permanent building up of the landed endowment of the monarchy'.[140] Secondly, and more importantly, by decreeing forfeitures and permitting reversals, the kings of France could exercise a measure of political control over the nobility. The one thing more than any other that was likely to render a disaffected person more tractable was the loss of his lands and the prospect of having them restored.

[140] Lander, 'Attainder and Forfeiture', p. 150.

Chapter 6

TREASON AND THE CROWN 1328–1356

I

Thus far we have examined the theoretical framework of the law of treason, the range of crimes encompassed by that law, the administrative and legal aspects of enforcing the law, the legal and political problems raised by the trials of peers and clerics, and the principal features of forfeitures and reversals. In the next five chapters we shall leave the descriptive and analytical paths in order to consider chronologically the prosecution of treason in later medieval France. For the extent and nature of the crown's response to treason can shed some light not only on the political relations generally between crown and nobility, but also perhaps on the characters and policies of individual kings.

The last Capetian kings of France did not on the whole prosecute rebellion and treason with severity. The revolts of the counts of Foix and Armagnac in the early 1270s, and that of the *vicomte* of Narbonne in the early 1280s, for example, were dealt with easily and leniently.[1] It is true that the trials of Bernard Saisset in 1301[2] and the count of Flanders in 1312[3] were indicative of a more aggressive royal policy on treason, particularly in Guyenne;[4] but however important these trials were in their jurisdictional and procedural aspects, and whatever Philippe IV's true intentions were, one cannot say that his treatment of either the bishop or the count was brutal. Indeed, the only known executions for treason during Philippe IV's reign were those in 1305 of the eight consuls and some other inhabitants of Carcassonne, and of about forty people from Limoux, all of whom were implicated in a conspiracy to renounce the sovereignty of France in order to escape the rigours of the Inquisition.[5]

[1] Langlois, *Le règne de Philippe III*, pp. 59–62, 191–5. [2] *Supra*, pp. 73–5. [3] *Supra*, pp. 95–6.
[4] See *Reg. du Trésor*, I. nos. 12, 1059, 2005, 2009, 2011, 2016, 2027–8, 2030.
[5] Vaissete, *Hist. de Languedoc*, IX. 277–9; Hauréau, *Bernard Délicieux*, pp. 97–130.

Louis X and Philippe V were in general able to come to terms with the rebellious nobility of Flanders, Picardy, Artois, Champagne, Normandy and Burgundy by diplomacy and force of arms[6] rather than by formal process at law or arbitrary punishment. The one instance in which recourse to formal proceedings was taken – in 1315 against the count of Flanders[7] – proved to be ineffectual, but Robert de Béthune finally submitted to the crown after a series of military campaigns.[8]

Two examples will illustrate Philippe V's caution in not proceeding with excessive severity against accused traitors, no doubt for fear of provoking yet greater insurrections. In 1317 Ferri de Picquigny, a cadet of a noble Picard family and a supporter of Robert d'Artois, was appealed of treason by his brother-in-law Jean de Varennes 'for [his] alliance with the . . . barons [of Flanders and Artois]'. The two were to have fought in a trial by battle in Paris before the king and the barons, but the contest was called off before any blows could be struck.[9] No further action was taken against Ferri at this time, yet it must surely have been for the same reason that he was arrested in June 1318. He was not put in prison, however, and he soon fled Paris. Captured almost immediately at Montlhéry, he was found to be carrying letters that he himself had written, 'in which [were the king's secrets] and which, if he had not been taken, he intended to send to the Flemings and the barons of Picardy'. Although execution would not have been undue punishment, he was only imprisoned. Again he escaped, this time successfully taking refuge with the count of Flanders.[10]

The second case is that of Béraud de Mercoeur, constable of Champagne. Twice he had revolted against Philippe IV and twice he was only imprisoned until, thanks to the intercession of Charles de Valois, the king pardoned him. On the accession of Louis X he became a member of the king's council, but he soon ran afoul of

[6] Artonne, *Le mouvement de 1314*; Dufayard, 'La réaction féodale'; Lehugeur, *Philippe le Long*, I. 51, 54–8, 96–103, 275.

[7] Anselme, *Hist. généalogique*, II. 812–17.

[8] Lehugeur, I. 54–8; H. Pirenne, *Histoire de Belgique* (5 vols., Brussels, 1972–5), I. 254–63.

[9] *Chron. parisienne anon.*, pp. 31–2.

[10] *Ibid.*, p. 38. Ferri remained in disgrace until Charles IV pardoned him in 1326. Although in 1329 he became governor of Artois under Philippe VI (Cazelles, *La société politique*, pp. 79–80), some of his property remained forfeited at least for another year (A.N., JJ 67, no. 50).

Henri de Sully, *bouteiller* of France and *souverain maître* of the *chambre des comptes*, who in 1318 accused him of conspiring against the king in Burgundy. In November 1318, convinced of the charges, Philippe V empowered the duke of Burgundy to suppress Béraud's rebellion. At the same time, he summoned Béraud to his presence, and he ordered the *baillis* of Auvergne and the mountains of Auvergne to seize Béraud's lands. In a session of the council at Vincennes in June 1319, hot words were exchanged between Béraud and Henri de Sully. Béraud's former patron, Charles de Valois, did not support him this time, and he was forced to make apologies. By order of the king he was then imprisoned in the Châtelet, but that was all. Nor did he remain there for long, since in April 1320 we find him accompanying Philippe de Valois on an expedition to Italy.[11]

The first sign of a change in royal policy towards rebellion came during the reign of Charles IV. Since 1314 the Parlement of Paris and the king's officers in Toulouse, Saintonge and Périgord had been trying to bring an end to the depredations of Jourdain de l'Isle-Jourdain, lord of Casaubon, 'very noble in lineage but ignoble in deed'.[12] In spite of a pardon that he had received at the request of Pope John XXII, whose niece he had married, Jourdain did not desist from his criminal ways, 'that is to say, robberies, homicides, rapes of married women and virgins, being a rebel to the king'. His scorn of royal authority was exemplified by his murder of a royal sergeant, 'who was bearing his mace decorated with the *fleur de lis*, which are the arms of France'.[13] Although the details are probably embellishment, we are told that Jourdain 'avoit bouté la masse . . . parmi le fondement [du sergent], et puis l'eust occis'.

Responding to a summons by the king, Jourdain arrived in Paris in mid-April 1323 'with a great array and with great pride'. The accusations against him were made chiefly by the lord of Albret, the *vicomte* of Lomagne, and the marquis of Ancône, presumably in the king's council. His protestations rejected by the king, Jourdain was imprisoned in the Châtelet. After fifteen days there he was brought before the Parlement, where the king's advocate, Pierre Maucreux,

[11] A.N., JJ 55, no. 31; *Reg. du Trésor*, II. no. 1487; Cazelles, *La société politique*, pp. 41–2.

[12] *Grandes chron.*, IX. 16; *Actes du Parlement*, 1st series, II. nos. 4311, 4771, 5824; A.N., X2a 2, fol. 28r–v.

[13] *Supra*, p. 46; see also *The War of Saint-Sardos*, ed. P. Chaplais *Camden Miscellany*, 3rd series, LXXXVII (1954), *passim* for the wider Anglo-French context of Jourdain's rebellion.

presented the indictment for the crown. Condemned to death, Jourdain was drawn and hanged on 7 May 1323 in the presence of the constable, the marshal, the *prévôt* of Paris and others.[14] This, it should be noted, was the first important treason trial to have taken place in the Parlement. Nor did it go unnoticed that the prosecution and punishment of Jourdain de l'Isle-Jourdain was a marked departure from past practice.[15] The incident was, however, but a solitary one in the reign of Charles IV; apart from several forfeitures,[16] little else has been recorded.

Unlike his predecessors, Philippe VI readily had treason punished, often with the full severity of the law. After the battle of Cassel, for example, there were executions and wholesale confiscations of property, and severe penalties were imposed on the Flemish towns.[17] Most notable was the prosecution of Guillaume de Deken, one of the leaders of the revolt. As burgomaster of Bruges he had been part of the embassies sent to England in 1320, 1324 and 1326 to negotiate an alliance with Edward II. After Cassel he fled to Brabant, seeking help from Duke Jean III, but he was promptly turned over to royal officers. Taken to Paris in December 1328, he was interrogated, probably under torture, and sentenced to a cruel death. After he was placed in the pillory his hands were amputated; he was then tied to a wheel, his severed hands were bound on the rim separately from the rest of his body, and when it seemed that he was about to die from loss of blood, he was taken down, drawn and hanged.[18]

Not surprisingly, the beginning of the Hundred Years War raised the curtain on a drama in which several of the leading actors and many of the minor performers were accused of, if not prosecuted for, treason. In the north-east, Sohier de Courtrai, 'the most courageous knight and the most valiant man in Flanders', was lured to Bruges by Louis de Nevers, count of Flanders, and was arrested there on 6 July 1337 for having tried to persuade the inhabitants of Ghent to ally with the English. When Philippe VI was informed of this sometime later, he sent the constable to Flanders. With Louis de

[14] *Grandes chron.*, IX. 16–18; *Chron. de Guill. de Nangis*, II. 46–7; *Confessions et jugements*, pp. 38–9.

[15] *Chron. parisienne anon.*, p. 88.

[16] E.g., A.N., JJ 65A, nos. 24, 92; JJ 65B, no. 91.

[17] *Le soulèvement de la Flandre*, ed. Pirenne.

[18] *Confessions et jugements*, pp. 43–8; H. Stein, 'Les conséquences de la bataille de Cassel pour la ville de Bruges et la mort de Guillaume de Deken, son ancien bourgmestre (1328)', *Bull. comm. roy. d'hist.*, 5th series, IX (1899), 647–64.

Nevers the constable then went to Rupelmonde, where Sohier was being held, and there on 21 March 1338 they had him beheaded.[19] But if this execution was meant to deter the Flemings from pursuing an English alliance, it was in vain.[20]

In Guyenne, too, treason was being punished from the first months of the war. After the English captured the castle of Parcoul in Saintonge, it became clear that their success had been due to the treason of Arnaud de Marmande, captain of that place. He was subsequently arrested and taken to Paris, where on 8 March 1338 he was beheaded and hanged.[21] Pierre de Belloc was executed for his treason at Le Mas d'Agenais in 1339,[22] and at about that time Guillaume de Cassane, too, paid with his life for having betrayed Lacasson near Agen to the English.[23] At Blaye in 1343 there was a plot to kill the captain and to betray the town to the English, but the conspiracy was discovered and the leader of it, Guillaume Cazans, beheaded.[24] Although Raymond de Pierrelongue and his sons failed to have the town of Montségur delivered to the English, their property was confiscated nonetheless.[25] At least thirty other traitors forfeited their lands in the first years of the war, and already it was clear that those like Renaud de Pons, lord of Ribérac, who remained loyal to the crown would be rewarded from the spoils.[26] Philippe VI did in fact appear willing to pardon repentant traitors like Jean, bastard of Armagnac, Guillaume Raymond, lord of Caumont, and Raymond de Montmirat,[27] but in the first years of the war the repentant were few.

In the north-west in the early 1340s Philippe VI took brutal vengeance on those Norman and Breton lords whom he suspected of favouring the English and who were partisans of Jean de Montfort.

[19] Jean Le Bel, *Chronique*, ed. J. Viard and E. Déprez (S.H.F.) (2 vols., Paris, 1904 and 1905), I. 132–3; *Chron. Reg. Franc.*, II. 42–4; Froissart, *Chroniques*, I. 129–30.

[20] A. Coville, *Les premiers Valois et la guerre de Cent ans (1328–1422)* (vol. IV (1) of *Histoire de France*, ed. E. Lavisse) (Paris, 1911), pp. 44–5.

[21] Richard Lescot, *Chronique*, ed. J. Lemoine (S.H.F.) (Paris, 1896), pp. 44–5; *Grandes chron.*, IX. 160.

[22] A.N., JJ 82, no. 339.

[23] A.N., JJ 71, no. 382.

[24] A.N., JJ 74, no. 53.

[25] A.N., JJ 71, no. 374.

[26] A.N., JJ 74, no. 415. For some other grants see JJ 73, no. 158; JJ 74, no. 634; B.N., ms. fr. 25698, no. 116.

[27] *La Gascogne dans les registres du Trésor des Chartes*, ed. C. Samaran (C.D.I.) (Paris, 1966), no. 595 (Armagnac; December 1339); A.N., JJ 74, no. 756 (Caumont; April 1342); no. 750 (Montmirat; April 1342). For a few other pardons see JJ 71, no. 186; JJ 72, no. 318; JJ 73, no. 57; JJ 74, nos. 256, 384; B.N., ms. fr. 25996, no. 227.

His first victim was Olivier III de Clisson, who, after being captured by the English at Vannes in November 1342, was secretly converted to the Montfortist cause and concluded an alliance with Edward III before the end of that year.[28] According to the *Chronique normande* Philippe VI learned of Clisson's treason from the earl of Salisbury, whose wife, it was alleged, Edward III had recently raped.[29] When the unsuspecting Clisson came to Paris for a joust in the summer of 1343 Philippe VI had him arrested.[30] Confronted with the evidence of his treason, Clisson confessed and was summarily condemned to death by the king. The *procès-verbal* of his execution reads as follows:

> In the year of grace one thousand three hundred and forty-three, on Saturday, the second day of August, Olivier, lord of Clisson, knight, prisoner in the Châtelet of Paris for several treasons and other crimes perpetrated by him against the king and the crown of France, and for alliances that he made with the king of England, enemy of the king and kingdom of France, as the said Olivier . . . has confessed, was by judgement of the king given at Orléans drawn from the Châtelet of Paris to Les Halles . . . and there on a scaffold had his head cut off. And then from there his corpse was drawn to the gibbet of Paris and there hanged on the highest level; and his head was sent to Nantes in Brittany to be put on a lance over the Sauvetout gate [as a sign of his treason].[31]

When Clisson's wife, Jeanne de Belleville, learned of her husband's execution she assembled 400 men-at-arms and massacred the garrison at Brest. Immediately thereafter she took to piracy off the Breton coast.[32] Her actions, though perhaps precipitated by Clisson's death, were only the latest in a series of treasonous offences. As early as March 1343 she and some of her officers and retainers had been summoned to the Parlement to answer for 'rebellions, disobediences . . . and excesses against [the king], the public welfare and [the king's] royal majesty'. After five defaults they were convicted on 1 December 1343 of treason against the king and the crown.[33]

28 *Chron. normande*, p. 58; *Chron. Reg. Franc.* II. 203 n. 1. Clisson's wife Jeanne de Belleville was a personal friend of the countess of Montfort and most likely prepared or at least encouraged his defection (Lefranc, *Clisson*, p. 27).

29 *Chron. normande*, pp. 58–60; see also A. Gransden, 'The Alleged Rape by Edward III of the Countess of Salisbury', *E.H.R.*, LXXXVII (1972), 333–44.

30 *Grandes chron.*, IX. 242.

31 Froissart, *Chroniques*, III. p. ix n. 3.

32 *Chron. normande*, pp. 60–1.

33 A.N., X2a 4, fols. 107v–108r, 113v. For grants on her and Clisson's lands see JJ 75, nos. 20, 135, 141, 338; Lefranc, *Clisson*, p. 29 n. 1; Moranvillé, 'Rapports', p. 389; Morice, *Hist. de Bretagne*, I. 268–9. See Jean Le Bel (*Chronique*, I. 250) for rumours that Philippe VI had Clisson executed in order to seize his lands.

Not long after the execution of Olivier de Clisson a group of Breton nobles attacked Charles de Blois as he was on his way to Paris. Fourteen – among them the two Geoffroys de Malestroit, father and son, Alain de Cadillac, Jean de Montaubon, Fulk de Laval and Henri d'Avaugour – were captured and taken to Paris.[34] Although Philippe VI formally turned the case over to the Parlement, he made sure that the court did as he wished. On 24 November 1343 he advised it that he was sending the *prévôt* of Paris and Jean Richer, *maître des requêtes de l'hôtel*, 'for certain matters regarding the Breton prisoners. We instruct you accordingly,' the king cautioned, 'that you accept what they have to say on our behalf.'

On 29 November the accused appeared in the Parlement, confessed to their treason and were then sent back to the Châtelet without the court having passed sentence. In fact the decision in this case was taken away from the Parlement by the king. On that same day Philippe VI ordered the *prévôt* of Paris to execute the prisoners forthwith, 'because we condemn them as traitors'. Philippe's determination in this matter was patent. In concluding his instructions he wrote: 'take care that there is no slip-up if you do not want to incur our wrath'. Except for Laval and Avaugour, the Bretons were drawn and beheaded that same day; and their corpses were then drawn to the gibbet to be hanged there.[35] These executions had the desired effect on at least some of Montfort's partisans: Jean, eldest son of the count of Vendôme, for example, quickly made his peace with Philippe VI.[36]

Godefroi d'Harcourt, lord of Saint-Sauveur-le-Vicomte, was the most powerful lord in the Cotentin. In the spring of 1343, before the executions of Clisson and the other Bretons, he had incurred royal displeasure because of his private war against the Bertran family. After Harcourt took control of Carentan and Montebourg and put Saint-Sauveur-le-Vicomte in a state of defence, Philippe VI quite possibly began to suspect him of treasonable relations with the English. When royal forces came to suppress his rebellion he fled to his relatives in Brabant,[37] but several of his intimates – Robert de Thibouville, Raoul de Bigars and Guillaume Bacon – were taken

[34] *Grandes chron.*, IX. 246 n. 1; *Chron. Reg. Franc.*, II. 207 n. 1; Morice, *Hist. de Bretagne*, I. 269.
[35] Froissart, *Chroniques*, III. p. x no. 1.
[36] Morice, *Hist. de Bretagne*, I. 269.
[37] Delisle, *Hist. de Saint-Sauveur-le-Vicomte*, pp. 49ff; Cazelles, *La société politique*, pp. 152–3.

into custody.[38] Bacon must have escaped, however, since on 22 April 1343 he was put in default by the Parlement.[39] But he must also have been recaptured (or perhaps he gave himself up), since on 7 May he, Thibouville and Bigars were released from prison.[40] Raoul Patri and Pierre de Préaux, two other intimates of Harcourt who were fugitives from justice, were banished from the kingdom on 2 October.[41]

While the Parlement continued its proceedings against Harcourt, Guillaume Bacon became involved with the Normans Jean de la Roche-Tesson and Richard de Percy. Partisans of Jean de Montfort as well as of Harcourt, the three of them were taken prisoner when Charles de Blois captured Quimper in Brittany in March 1344. Also taken into custody with them was Henri de Malestroit, a *maître des requêtes de l'hôtel.* Malestroit, brother and uncle of the Malestroits executed in November 1343, had defected to Edward III and was thereupon appointed to the captaincy of Vannes.[42] He and the Normans were all imprisoned in the Châtelet, but, unlike the Bretons, they do not seem to have appeared in the Parlement. By judgement of the king and his council, Jean de la Roche-Tesson, Richard de Percy and Guillaume Bacon were drawn, beheaded and hanged on 3 April 1344.[43] Henri de Malestroit, because he was a cleric, was handed over to ecclesiastical justice for trial. On 12 October 1344 the bishop of Paris sentenced him to life imprisonment. Before being incarcerated, however, Malestroit was put on display for the Parisians, who pelted him with stones, ordure 'and other stinking things'. He died from his wounds three days later.[44]

The case of Jean de la Roche-Tesson, Richard de Percy and Guillaume Bacon illustrates well the confluence of interests among the Breton and Norman nobility – what Raymond Cazelles called 'la communauté des pays de l'ouest'.[45] Although the three were

[38] A.N., x2a 4, fol. 105r. I differ from Raymond Cazelles slightly on the chronology of what follows.

[39] A.N., x2a 4, fol. 100v.

[40] *Ibid.*, fol. 105v.

[41] Delisle, *Hist. de Saint-Sauveur-le-Vicomte*, *p.j.* lxx. Patri was pardoned in March 1347 (*ibid.*, *p.j.* lxxx).

[42] *Chron. normande*, pp. 50–1; *Chron. Reg. Franc.*, II. 208.

[43] Delisle, *Hist. de Saint-Sauveur-le-Vicomte*, *p.j.* lxxii. For grants on their confiscated property see A.N., JJ 68, no. 217; JJ 75, nos. 48, 241; JJ 81, no. 251; JJ 82, no. 55; Coll. Lenoir 18, fols. 81–2. Moranvillé, 'Rapports', pp. 388–9.

[44] *Grandes chron.* IX. 250–1; *Confessions et jugements*, p. 156.

[45] Cazelles, *La société politique*, pp. 143ff.

captured defending Quimper for Jean de Montfort, the *procès-verbal* of their execution did not, surprisingly, mention their Montfortist connection; it pointed rather to the treasonous relationship with Godefroi d'Harcourt, who, it was explicitly stated for the first time, had allied with the king of England against Philippe VI and Jean, duke of Normandy. The goal of the conspirators, the document elucidated, was to make Harcourt duke of Normandy.[46] If this was true, it must now have been clear to Philippe VI that the activities of Harcourt and his men in the previous year at Carentan, Montebourg and Saint-Sauveur-le-Vicomte had indeed been in preparation for a possible English invasion. On 15 July 1344 the Parlement declared Harcourt guilty of treason, banished him and pronounced his property forfeit to the crown. From Brabant, whither he had fled in 1343, Harcourt crossed the Channel to England and did homage to Edward III.[47]

Although Philippe VI had thus in one way or another eliminated some of his most troublesome opponents in the north-west, the political gains for the crown proved to be only temporary. The successful English invasion of Normandy in 1346, orchestrated by Godefroi d'Harcourt no less than by Edward III, was to make this clear. Indeed, one might argue that by his judicial repression in the early 1340s Philippe VI exacerbated an already fragile situation and made the invasion possible. In England, at the Parliament held in June 1344, Edward III referred to the executions of Clisson and the others as proof that Philippe VI could not be trusted to abide by the truce of Malestroit, which had been concluded on 19 January 1343.[48]

Godefroi d'Harcourt was no doubt urging Edward to invade Normandy immediately, but Edward apparently preferred to test safer waters first. A few months after the truce ended in 1345 the earl of Derby began what was to be a most successful campaign in Guyenne.[49] Many of the places that he captured fell to him by treason, but the guilty did not all go unpunished. The castellan of

[46] Delisle, *Hist. de Saint-Sauveur-le-Vicomte*, *p.j.* lxxii.

[47] Delisle, *Hist. de Saint-Sauveur-le-Vicomte*, *p.j.* lxxvi; E. Déprez, 'La double trahison de Godefroi d'Harcourt', *R.H.*, XCIX (1908), 32. For a grant on Harcourt's land see Delisle, *Hist. de Saint-Sauveur-le-Vicomte*, *p.j.* lxxviii.

[48] M. H. Keen, *England in the Later Middle Ages* (London, 1973), p. 134.

[49] Jean Le Bel, *Chronique*, II. 39–56, 121–3; see also Bertrandy, *Etude*; and K. Fowler, *The King's Lieutenant: Henry of Grosmont, First Duke of Lancaster 1310–1361* (London, 1969), pp. 53–74.

Bourg, who had sold that castle to the English, was captured by a party from Blaye and beheaded there.[50] Soon after Aiguillon was delivered by treason in December 1345, its captain, who was most probably Raymond de Montpezat, was hanged for his betrayal.[51] Derby captured Port-Sainte-Marie because of the treason of its inhabitants, but Jean, duke of Normandy, recaptured it in early 1346. Shortly afterwards Gaillard de la Motte and his accomplices took control of the town and tried to deliver it to the English, but they were murdered by several inhabitants who had remained loyal to the king and who subsequently received a pardon for their brave deed.[52] Port-Sainte-Marie itself did not obtain either a pardon or a confirmation of its privileges until December 1354.[53]

The example of Maillezais illustrates that civic leaders who were inclined to trim their sails to the prevailing political winds were also likely to be accused of treason. Maillezais was the most defensible place in all of Poitou, but when Derby, whose reputation no doubt preceded him, approached the vicinity of the town, the bishop, Jean de Marconnay, seems to have panicked. In opposition to the monks and other inhabitants he planned to submit to the earl. Derby abruptly changed course, however, and bypassed Maillezais. As soon as the town was safe the bishop was arrested for treason. His case came before the Parlement of Paris in 1349, but the outcome of it is not known.[54] Most likely the prosecution was suspended when the bishop was released later that year.

Encouraged by Derby's successes, Edward III prepared to invade France in the summer of 1346. Contrary winds made him decide against a descent in Guyenne, and so on 12 July 1346 the English landed at Saint-Vaast-la-Hougue in the Cotentin. Under the leadership of Godefroi d'Harcourt they marched through Normandy virtually unopposed by ill-prepared French forces. Within a week they took Valognes, Carentan and Saint-Lô.[55] It is not surprising that they captured Carentan, for the Norman knights Roland de Verdun and Nicolas de Grouchy, who were instrumental in betraying

50 *Chron. normande*, p. 65.

51 Bertrandy, *Etude*, p. 155.

52 A.N., JJ 76, no. 238.

53 A.N., JJ 84, no. 23.

54 *Actes du Parlement*, 2nd series, II. no. 8975; Guérin, *Arch. hist. Poitou*, XIII. pp. xxxi–v; A.N., X1a 12, fols. 343v–345r. The king's proctor charged that 'dictus episcopus contra nos et coronam francie crimen lese magestatis commiserat et contra nos et patriam proditionem fecerat' (fol. 343v).

55 Coville, *Les premiers Valois*, pp. 58–9.

the town to the English, had been put there in 1343 by Harcourt himself.[56] Not long after Edward III's departure a French force under Philippe le Despensier retook Carentan and arrested several traitors, Grouchy and Verdun among them. By order of the king they were summarily executed at Paris on 14 December 1346.[57] One Guillaume Varonne, who, after the English had landed in Normandy, incited the inhabitants of Saint-Clément to rebel against the king, also was executed at about that time.[58]

Sensing Philippe VI's weakness after the French defeat at Crécy in August 1346, Godefroi d'Harcourt returned to French obedience at the first opportunity, obtaining a pardon and restitution of his property in December. In July 1347, furthermore, he won for himself the title of *capitaine souverain* of the *bailliage* of Rouen.[59] But others, emboldened by Edward III's victories, continued to betray the king. At Saint-Quentin in November 1346 Morel de Fonsomes was beheaded and quartered 'for treason against the king'. In the county of Artois, Guillaume de Hez was executed sometime before December 1348. In March 1347 Philippe VI ordered the arrest of the priest Bertaut Jobelin of Valognes and Guillaume Poildor of Saint-Sauveur-le-Vicomte for 'treasons and conspiracies against us and our royal majesty'.[60] Between October 1345 and August 1350 there were at least thirty forfeitures.[61]

There is little information on the above incidents. More is known about the treason of Jean de Vervins, lord of Bosmont, and Gauvain de Bellemont, an advocate from Laon, who in March 1347 had conspired unsuccessfully to deliver Laon to the English. Bellemont was arrested in Reims on 1 April and was taken back to Laon, where he was stoned to death by an angry mob. His son was also executed as an accomplice. Jean de Vervins meanwhile had installed sixty English archers in his castle of Bosmont, whence they terrorized the countryside. When the *bailli* of Vermandois together with the count of Rouci and other troops besieged the castle, the defenders

[56] Cazelles, *La société politique*, p. 152.
[57] *Chron. normande*, pp. 75, 272 n. 4; Lescot, *Chronique*, p. 71 n. 4.
[58] A.N., JJ 81, no. 109.
[59] Delisle, *Hist. de Saint-Sauveur-le-Vicomte*, *p.j.* lxxix, lxxxii.
[60] *Arch. anciennes de Saint-Quentin*, II. 201 (Fonsomes); A.N., JJ 77, no. 422 (Hez); JJ 79A, no. 29 (Jobelin and Poildor).
[61] E.g., A.N., JJ 75, no. 283, JJ 76, nos. 169, 398; JJ 77, nos. 22, 162, 222; JJ 78, no. 38; JJ 81, no. 679.

surrendered. They were banished from the kingdom, and the castle was razed.[62] Vervin's land of Bosmont, worth 200 *livres* annually, was granted to the marshal, Jean de Clermont, while the denouncer of the plot, Colin de Vervins, possibly a relation of Jean, received a gift of 200 *l.p.*[63]

Even before the English invasion of Normandy in July 1346 Philippe VI's obsession with his legitimacy was patent. One will remember the fate of Simon Pouillet, who was brutally executed at Paris for having maintained that Edward III should be king of France.[64] In 1344 a Pierre Vital was imprisoned at Beaucaire because he had said that the king was a 'perjuror and a traitor [and] ought not to be king'. Edward's successes did not make Philippe VI any less sensitive. Jean de Lyons spent six years in prison at Les Andelys in Noımandy for having argued that Edward should be king of France because he cured scrofula. The esquire Guillaume Bronart or Brovart was imprisoned at Orléans because he had said that at Bouvines Philippe had not dared fight Edward, who was 'the most valiant of Christians', and that 'the devastation that [King Edward] has wrought in [France was] done in a good cause'.[65] There were several other cases of treason by words in the last years of Philippe VI's reign;[66] and it is most interesting to note that they were the first such cases since the trial of Bernard Saisset in 1301.

The reign of Philippe VI represents a perceptible break with the past. Not only the king but also his lieutenants and local officers – *baillis*, *sénéchaux* and *prévôts* – who surely took their lead from the king, punished treason quickly and severely. It was perhaps not unusual that men of little consequence were executed, but it is indeed significant that Philippe VI did not hesitate to exact the full penalties of the law against men like Olivier III de Clisson, Jean de la Roche-Tesson, Richard de Percy and Guillaume Bacon. Although

[62] Le Muisit, *Chronique*, pp. 172–5; *Grandes chron.*, IX. 293–4; H. Moranvillé, 'La trahison de Jean de Vervins', *B.E.C.*, LIII (1892), 605–11.

[63] A.N., JJ 82, no. 47 (Clermont); JJ 76, no. 387 (Colin de Vervins). One of Jean de Vervins's accomplices, Erard de Jouval, was pardoned in January 1351 (JJ 80, no. 396). On 24 June 1348 the *prévôt* of Laon seised Jeanne de Marle, Bellemont's widow, of the property 'lui revenant de la communaute du menage' (JJ 77, no. 183).

[64] *Supra*, p. 117. On 27 January 1347 Pouillet's children were allowed to recover their father's property. They had first to pay a *composition* of 2000 *l.t.*, however, and the moveables were to remain in royal possession (A.N., JJ 77, no. 77).

[65] A.N., JJ 75, no. 52 (Vital); JJ 82, no. 25 (Lyons); JJ 77, no. 145 (Bronart).

[66] E.g., A.N., JJ 78, no. 235; *Actes du Parlement*, 2nd series, II. no. 8054; no. 9049.

Godefroi d'Harcourt was reconciled with the crown – only temporarily, as we shall see – it is certainly possible that he, too, might have been executed had he, like the Normans, been captured.

The prosecution of traitors was also marked by its arbitrary character. Although the Parlement was not completely thrust aside in the case of the Bretons in 1343, it is clear that it was the king who decided their fate. In the cases of Clisson and the Normans, the court does not seem to have had any rôle at all. It was only in the prosecution of fugitive traitors like Jeanne de Belleville and Godefroi d'Harcourt that the Parlement exercised fully its judicial functions. Nor was Philippe VI's tendency in the last years of his reign to rush to judgement offset by an ability to pardon easily: only Godefroi d'Harcourt of his major political opponents was pardoned.

II

The reign of Jean II did not begin auspiciously. In mid-November 1350, when the constable Raoul de Brienne, count of Eu, came to Paris for the purpose of his ransom – he had been a prisoner of the English since his capture at Caen in July 1346 – the king had him arrested. On the night of 18–19 November he was summarily executed in the prison of the *hôtel* of Nesle. The reasons for his death are obscure. The official chronicler of Jean II and Charles V spoke only of his 'very great and evil treasons'; Jean Le Bel suggested that Eu had once had an affair with the queen; and Raymond Cazelles argued that Eu was executed because he had been acting as an intermediary between the Savoyards and the English.[67] It still seems most likely that Eu's treason was his intention to obtain his liberty from the English by selling to them the county and fortress of Guines that were strategically so important to them.[68] Whatever the reason, Eu's execution was cause for much grumbling, particularly in Normandy, where the count had held extensive property. This restiveness was certainly aggravated by the fact that Jean II chose to remain silent on the matter.[69]

[67] *Chron. de Jean II et Charles V*, I. 28–30; Jean Le Bel, *Chronique*, II. 198–200; Cazelles, *La société politique*, pp. 247–52. For grants on Eu's property see A.N., JJ 80, nos. 268, 368; Cazelles, *La société politique*, p. 370 n. 4; Anselme, *Hist. généalogique*, I. 388.

[68] Froissart, *Chroniques*, IV. p. xlviii n. 1.

[69] Cazelles, *La société politique*, p. 252.

Those members of the Norman nobility who were already disaffected, or who became so after the execution of Eu, found in Charles the Bad, king of Navarre, a leader around whom they could rally.[70] Eighteen years old in 1350, Charles, son of Philippe d'Evreux and Louis X's daughter Jeanne de Navarre, was the closest male descendant of the last Capetians. He had a stronger claim to the crown of France than did Edward III, and had he been born before 1328, he might well have been considered for the throne.

Apart from the kingdom of Navarre, which he inherited from his mother in 1349, Charles the Bad held the counties of Evreux and Mortain in Normandy, the former in peerage. In 1352 he married the king's daughter Jeanne, but good relations between Jean II and Charles the Bad did not last long. Jean II's favourite, the new constable Charles of Spain, was a rival of Navarre both in the Iberian peninsula and in France, for in the latter he held the county of Angoulême that Charles the Bad felt was his by right. In the presence of Jean II sometime in late 1353 the constable and Navarre's brother Philippe, count of Longueville, had a violent argument on this issue and almost came to dagger blows. A short time later, on 8 January 1354, Charles of Spain was assassinated at Laigle in Normandy.[71] Charles the Bad did not personally have a hand in the deed, but those who did were Philippe de Navarre; Jean V, count of Harcourt; Jean's brother Louis, *vicomte* of Châtellerault; Godefroi d'Harcourt; Jean Malet, lord of Graville; Guillaume de Mainemarès; Colin Doublel[72] – all persons we shall meet again – and about fifteen others.

Immediately after the assassination Charles the Bad went to Evreux, whence he issued a manifesto all but boasting of the murder. Realizing that he would need protection against the wrath of Jean II, he wrote on 10 January 1354 to Edward III, to the Prince of Wales and to Lancaster, asking for their help.[73] On 8 February Jean II, fearing just such an alliance, commissioned the cardinal Gui de

[70] It was only from the sixteenth century that Charles was called 'the Bad'; see S. Honoré-Duvergé, 'L'origine du surnom de Charles le Mauvais', *Mélanges Louis Halphen* (Paris, 1951), pp. 345–50. See also R. Cazelles, 'Le parti navarrais jusqu'à la mort d'Etienne Marcel', *Bull. philol. et hist. du comité des travaux historiques et scientifiques* (1960), 839–69.

[71] Delachenal, *Hist. de Charles V*, I. 82–3.

[72] *Chron. de Jean II et Charles V*, I. 37–8; A.N., JJ 82, nos. 469, 509, 511.

[73] Jean Froissart, *Oeuvres*, ed. Kervyn de Lettenhove (25 vols., Brussels, 1867–77), XVIII. 356–66; R. Delachenal, 'Premières négotiations de Charles le Mauvais avec les anglais (1354–1355)', *B.E.C.*, LXI (1900), 255.

Boulogne and Pierre, duke of Bourbon, to negotiate with Navarre.[74] They did not take long to reach an accord with Navarre, concluding the treaty of Mantes on 22 February. Jean II's desire to prevent an alliance between Navarre and the English is reflected in the terms of the treaty: Navarre obtained the county of Beaumont-le-Roger; the castellanies of Breteuil and Conches; the *vicomtés* of Coutances, Valognes and Carentan; the Clos du Cotentin; and pardons for himself, his brother and all those involved in the assassination.[75]

In November 1354 Navarre again broke with Jean II and went secretly to Avignon, where throughout the winter he tried to negotiate an alliance with the English that, had it been put into effect, would have dismembered France.[76] At about that time, perhaps a bit earlier, a member of the king's council, Robert de Lorris, lord of Ermenonville, fled the kingdom for reasons that remain obscure. It is suggested, though, that he was passing state secrets to Charles the Bad and that he was denounced by Jean and Louis d'Harcourt.[77] In September 1355 Navarre landed in Cherbourg, in anticipation of joining forces with the English, but he was again enticed away from them. By the treaty of Valognes, concluded on 10 September, Jean II again pardoned him and his allies.[78]

Let us leave Navarre for the moment to consider other evidence on the response to treason of Jean II and his officers – for the latter surely acted on express instructions from the king, or at least according to their understanding of his wishes – in the first five years of his reign. Immediately after a tax riot erupted at Rouen around 1350 Simon de Bucy was despatched to quell the disturbance: twenty-three of the most guilty were executed.[79] In January 1352 Hue de Beauconroy sold the castle of Guines, which had only recently been confiscated from the count of Eu, to the English for 34,000 *écus*; for his treason he was arrested, tortured and executed at Saint-Omer.[80] Sometime in 1353 two Frenchmen caught spying for the English

[74] A.N., J 615, no. 14 (printed in full in *Recueil*, ed. Secousse, pp. 31–2).
[75] *Recueil*, ed. Secousse, pp. 33–40. The pardons other than to Navarre and his brother are in A.N., JJ 82, nos. 183, 443, 445–6, 463–9, 474–7, 509–11.
[76] Delachenal, *Hist. de Charles V*, I. 88–90.
[77] *Chron. de Jean II et Charles V*, I. 46–7. Robert de Lorris was pardoned on 3 April 1355 (A.N., JJ 84, no. 173).
[78] Delachenal, 'Premières négotiations', p. 270.
[79] Cochon, *Chron. normande*, p. 75; A.N., JJ 81, nos. 309, 517; JJ 87, no. 92.
[80] Lescot, *Chronique*, p. 91; Jean Le Bel, *Chronique*, II. 203; *Chron. normande*, p. 292 n. 2.

were executed at Mirebeau in Poitou.[81] But such examples as these were few, a reflection of the fact that, except for local incidents, the truces with the English were in fact observed.

On the whole, the evidence for these first five years suggests that there was a clear intention to conciliate those who adhered to the king's enemies. In January 1351 the Bretons Tanneguy du Châtel and his son Bernard, for example, were pardoned their betrayal of the king in having supported Jean de Montfort.[82] In April of that year Bernard de Bailleul obtained a pardon after having defected to the English four years earlier at the siege of Calais.[83] Edward Balliol, sometime king of Scotland, whose ancestral lands in Picardy had been confiscated in 1330 because of his alliance with Edward III, was also pardoned in 1351.[84] Most of the evidence, however, pertains to the south-west. No retribution was taken against the inhabitants of Saint-Jean-d'Angély, which had been captured by the English in September 1346 and was recovered by the French in August 1351; a pardon issued that month forgave the townspeople their collaboration and confirmed the municipal charter.[85] Saint-Antonin received a similar pardon in March 1354.[86] Among the minor nobility who received pardons were Bernard de Conhac, lord of Bouillac; Amalvin, lord of Pestillac, and his brother Guillaume; Pierre de Mauveu, esquire; Hugues de Montfaucon, esquire; and Guillaume de Garlande, lord of Charlais.[87]

More than a pardon and restitution of property had to be offered to entice some of the greater Gascon nobility into the royal fold. Rudel, lord of Seyches, for example, demanded and received a rent of 500 *l.t.*, a grant of 1300 *écus* for himself, and one of 150 *écus* for his men.[88] To gain the submission of Arnaud-Raymond d'Aspremont, lord

81 A.N., JJ 82, no. 33.

82 A.N., JJ 80, nos. 193–4.

83 A.N., JJ 84, no. 237. A rent of 100 *livres* from his property of Bailleul-Sire-Bertoult in Artois had been granted at the time of his defection in April 1347 to André de Monche, a familiar of the count of Flanders (JJ 76, no. 133).

84 On Balliol see A.N., KK 2, fol. 149r; JJ 66, no. 1483; JJ 69, no. 59; JJ 80, no. 620; JJ 89, no. 684; X1a 10, fol. 75v; R. Nicholson, *Edward III and the Scots* (Oxford, 1965), pp. 64, 72 n. 2; J. P. Maitland, 'The Early Homes of the Balliols', *Trans. of the Dumfriesshire and Galloway Natural History and Antiquarian Society*, 3rd series, XVIII (1931–3), 235–42.

85 A.N., JJ 82, no. 233; *Chron. de Jean II et Charles V*, I. 32 n. 1.

86 A.N., JJ 82, no. 88.

87 A.N., JJ 84, no. 26 (Conhac; June 1353); no. 667 (Pestillac; September 1353); JJ 80, no. 777 (Mauveu; March 1351); JJ 82, no. 173 (Montfaucon; May 1354); JJ 80, no. 540 (Garlande; June 1351).

88 A.N., JJ 82, no. 597 (October 1353).

of Roquecor, Jean II granted him 5000 *écus* and a subvention for ten men-at-arms and twenty sergeants who were to serve as the garrison of Roquecor.[89] Arnaud de Caumont and his two sons were confirmed in their possession of the thirteen parishes – among them Miramont, Castillonès, Saint-Grégoire and Saint-Nazaire – that had been given to them by the duke of Lancaster; in addition they received 500 *l.t.* in rent, a grant of 3500 *écus*, a garrison to defend their castles, and all the forfeitures from rebels whose lands were in their jurisdiction.[90] Pons and Arnaud de Beauville, who jointly held the lordship of Beauville, drove a still harder bargain. In addition to pardons and restitutions for themselves and their followers, they obtained confirmation of all grants made to them by Edward III; a grant of 15,000 *écus*; and the place of Montjoie. Furthermore the king was to pay the wages of twenty-five men-at-arms, twenty-five mounted sergeants and twenty-five foot sergeants. He was also to arrange for the liberation of Pons's brother Gaubert, who was being held prisoner as a traitor by Aimery de Rochechouart; and Gaubert was then to be allowed to choose between French and English allegiance. Bernard de Rovignan, lord of Castelculier, a prisoner of the Beauvilles, was to be obliged to pay them a ransom of 4800 *écus*. Lastly, the king was to install at La Sauvetat-de-Savère a captain favourable to the Beauvilles.[91]

The Durforts were one of the most powerful families with whom Jean II had to deal. But we must go back to the reign of Philippe VI to follow the tergiversations of this house. As early as 1334 Ramfred de Durfort, lord of Bajamont, had forfeited his property for his rebellion against the crown. He was pardoned in 1336 but again went into rebellion not later than 1346, when he seized Bajamont and delivered it to Derby.[92] The brothers Aimeric and Bernard de Durfort were pardoned their rebellion in December 1338.[93] In January 1339 Philippe VI granted to Guilhem Amanieu de Madaillan, lord of Rauzan, all the confiscated lands of Arnaud de Durfort, lord of Frespech and his son; but Arnaud's property must have been restored to him almost immediately – he died in 1339 – for in 1343

[89] A.N., JJ 82, no. 656 (October 1353).
[90] A.N., JJ 82, no. 598 (October 1353).
[91] A.N., JJ 82, no. 655 (October 1353).
[92] *Documents sur la maison de Durfort (XIe–XVe siècle)*, ed. N. de Pena (2 vols., Bordeaux, 1977), I. no. 686; A.N., JJ 70, no. 3; JJ 77, no. 329.
[93] *Documents sur la maison de Durfort*, I. no. 811.

Philippe VI granted some of it to Arnaud de Beauville.[94] A Pierre de Durfort was implicated in the treason at Parcoul in 1337, and was pardoned in December 1342. A Cécile de Durfort was involved in some kind of treason in the 1340s, for in August 1345 some property of hers, worth 200 *livres* annually, was granted to Amanieu de Madaillan, lord of Cancon.[95] Another Arnaud de Durfort, lord of Bajamont, was pardoned in August 1351, and was still in French obedience in 1377. Pierre de Durfort, who had rebelled again, and about thirty-five others were pardoned with him.[96] Raymond Bernard de Durfort, lord of Fenouillet, who had been pardoned in June 1348 but who had evidently gone into rebellion again, was also pardoned in August 1351; thereafter and at least until 1356 he mustered along with Bernard de Durfort, lord of La Chapelle, under Jean, count of Armagnac. Bernard de Durfort was still in French obedience in 1359.[97]

Gaillard de Durfort, lord of Blanquefort and Duras, was the most influential member of the house. In 1345 he had made his submission to Derby, receiving from the English a pension of 2000 *écus*.[98] But in May 1352 he, Bertrand de Durfort, lord of Gaillac, and Bertrand Got, lord of Puyguilhem, returned to French obedience on the following conditions: they were to receive pardons; on the conclusion of peace they would recover their lands that were held by the English; they would be allowed to keep all prisoners that they might capture; together they would receive 14,000 *écus* for the maintenance of their places, and rents of 500 *l.t.* each; and Gaillard de Durfort alone was to receive a hereditary grant of 500 *l.t.*[99] With the submission of Gaillard de Durfort most of the members of his house who had not been pardoned by Philippe VI were won over to the crown under Jean II. The emphasis during Jean II's reign clearly was on conciliation. It was only in the last years of Charles V's reign that

94 *La Gascogne*, no. 543; *Documents sur la maison de Durfort*, I. no. 883; N. de Pena, 'Vassaux gascons au service du roi d'Angleterre dans la première moitié du XIVe siècle: fidélité ou esprit de profit?', *Ann. du Midi*, LXXXVIII (1976), 7.

95 A.N., JJ 74, no. 195 (Pierre de Durfort); JJ 76, no. 392 (Cécile de Durfort).

96 A.N., JJ 81, no. 658, and B.N., pièces originales 1043, dossier 23943, no. 56 for Arnaud de Durfort *et al.*; *Documents sur la maison de Durfort*, II. no. 1004.

97 *Documents sur la maison de Durfort*, II. nos. 955, 1000; B.N. pièces originales 1043, dossier 23943, nos. 14–22, 33.

98 Bertrandy, *Etude*, p. 158.

99 *Documents sur la maison de Durfort*, II. nos. 1012, 1030–44.

the Durforts definitively threw in their lot with the English.[100]

There is very little evidence on defections and treason during the Black Prince's campaigns of 1355–6, and thus very little on the crown's response. The only known example of any importance is that of Jean de Galard, lord of Limeuil. So incensed was Jean II with Galard, 'who recently has become our enemy and has gone over to the obedience of our adversary the king of England', that he specifically excluded him from the general pardon agreed upon in the treaty of Brétigny in 1360.[101]

In Normandy, however, events were moving quickly towards a crisis. The dauphin Charles, royal lieutenant in Normandy since March 1355, had been persuaded by Charles the Bad and Robert Le Coq, bishop of Laon, that Jean II hated him. A treasonous plot was hatched, but the details are obscure. It appears that Navarre was to lead a general uprising in Normandy at the same time that the dauphin, together with the emperor and imperial troops, would attack from the east. Ultimately they were to seize and kill the king. Among the conspirators, apart from Navarre and Le Coq, were the counts of Foix and Harcourt; Robert de Lorris; Jean Malet, lord of Graville; Pierre de Sacquenville; Guillaume de Mainemarès; Jean, baron of Clères; Navarre's chancellor Thomas de Ladit and several others. It was probably in November 1355 that the conspirators were discovered, for it seems likely that when Jean II invested the dauphin with the duchy of Normandy in appanage in December, he did so in order to convince him of his paternal affection. The others were pardoned in January.[102]

The pacification proved to be only temporary. Ever since the Estates-general of 1355 had voted an *aide* for the war, Navarre and Jean V d'Harcourt led the opposition to it in Normandy.[103] This treason, coming after the assassination of Charles of Spain, Navarre's traitorous negotiations with the English, and the plot of 1355, at last

[100] R. Boutruche, *La crise d'une société: seigneurs et paysans du Bordelais pendant la guerre de Cent ans* (Paris, 1963), p. 235.

[101] *Documents hist. sur la maison de Galard*, I. 522; *Les grands traités de la guerre de Cent ans*, ed. E. Cosneau (Paris, 1889), p. 56.

[102] *Recueil*, ed. Secousse, pp. 55f; B.N., ms. fr. 7598, fol. 137r; Delachenal, *Hist. de Charles V*, I. 115–19. Two pardons were issued, one on 6 January 1356 (*Recueil*, ed. Secousse, pp. 45–6) and the other on 23 January (La Roque de la Lontière, *Hist. de Harcourt*, III. 278–80).

[103] Chéruel, *Hist. de Rouen*, II. 170–5.

impelled Jean II to take drastic action. On 5 April 1356, having arrived unexpectedly from Mainville with his retinue, he burst into the hall of the castle of Rouen where the dauphin was dining with Navarre and other Norman barons and their followers. Immediately the king ordered the arrest of Navarre, Jean V d'Harcourt, Graville, Mainemarès, Jean de Bantelu, Friquet de Fricamps and Colin Doublel, the last for having drawn his dagger in a threat against him. Later that evening he had Harcourt, Graville, Mainemarès and Doublel summarily executed. According to Pierre Cochon, Harcourt, who was the first to be decapitated, was so fat that 'it seemed as if the executioner were striking a potful of butter: it took a good six blows before his head fell to the ground'. After the others were executed the four corpses were drawn to the gibbet of Rouen and hanged there. Except for Navarre, Friquet and Bantelu, the others were released.[104] Gaston Fébus, count of Foix, was also implicated in this affair, arrested and then imprisoned; but because Jean II feared a widespread defection of the nobility in Béarn, Foix was released in July 1356 at the latest.[105]

After the executions, rumours spread in Normandy that Jean II had ordered similar sentences against all partisans of Navarre, notwithstanding any pardons that they might have previously obtained. On 5 May, to allay such fears, the king confirmed earlier pardons and empowered the dauphin to issue new ones. But about two weeks later the continuing restiveness caused Jean II to have the *baillis* of Caux, Gisors, Caen and the Cotentin publish royal letters explaining why Harcourt and the others had been beheaded.[106] His efforts were in vain: although Louis d'Harcourt remained loyal to the king, Navarre's brothers Philippe and Louis, and Jean V d'Harcourt's brother Godefroi feverishly sought an English alliance. On 28 May, assured of support, they, Pierre de Sacquenville, Graville's son Jean and about twenty other Norman barons sent a formal letter of defiance to the king.[107] In retaliation Jean II immediately confiscated

104 Cochon, *Chron. normande*, pp. 81–6; *Chron. de Jean II et Charles V*, I. 62–5; Delachenal, *Hist. de Charles V*, I. 140–55.

105 P. Tucoo-Chala, *Gaston Fébus et la vicomté de Béarn 1343–1391* (Bordeaux, 1959), p. 71.

106 Delachenal, *Hist. de Charles V*, I. 160–1.

107 Froissart, *Chroniques*, IV. pp. lxv–lxvi, 180–4. Delachenal, *Hist. de Charles V*, I. 166–8. Godefroi d'Harcourt was in any case already in royal disfavour, having been banished on 7 May because of his private war against Nicolas de Chiffrevast (Delisle, *Hist. de Saint-Sauveur-le-Vicomte*, pp. 72ff).

their properties;[108] the time had long since passed since a *diffidatio* afforded legal protection.

In June the Normans joined forces with the duke of Lancaster. Jean II's counter-attack in Normandy was ineffectual and was in any case cut short when he withdrew to confront the formidable Black Prince, who had advanced north from Bordeaux. At Poitiers on 19 September 1356 the French army suffered a disastrous defeat, and Jean II was taken prisoner.[109]

At this point an assessment of Jean II's reign is in order. One distinguished historian, expressing a commonly held opinion, has written of Jean II that 'he struck without rhyme or reason at those whom he distrusted, and was incapable of letting these irrational hatreds subside'. Jean II's harsh justice, he added, 'was not balanced by pardons generously granted'.[110] With the possible exception of the execution of Raoul de Brienne, count of Eu, one must take Professor Perroy's remarks advisedly. If Jean II hated Charles the Bad and the count of Harcourt, one can hardly say that his bitterness was irrational, for the causes were certainly real enough. One must not lose sight of the fact that the arrest of Navarre and the executions of Harcourt and the others, arbitrary though these actions were, and disastrous as they proved to be for France, came after continued and unrepented treasons. Nor can one say that the king had not been generous in granting pardons. The four that he gave within the space of two years to Navarre and his intimates, not to mention the pardons issued to the Gascons and others, impel one to revise, if only slightly, the common judgement of Jean II's character.[111] For, focused largely on the arrest of Navarre and the executions of Eu, Harcourt and Graville, that judgement has been liable to distortion.

108 E.g., A.N., JJ 84, nos. 606, 640.

109 Coville, *Les premiers Valois*, pp. 104–6.

110 Perroy, *The Hundred Years War*, p. 125.

111 Froissart (*Chroniques*, II. 214) asserted that Jean II pardoned easily and was accessible to pity. For a general revision of Jean II's character see R. Cazelles, 'Jean II le Bon: quel homme? Quel roi?', *R.H.*, CCLI (1974), 5–26.

Chapter 7

TREASON AND THE CROWN

1356–1380

With Jean II in captivity France plunged into anarchy. In spite of the two-year truce signed at Bordeaux in March 1357,[1] the war continued, particularly against the Navarrese in Normandy. Free-booting soldiers devastated the countryside everywhere. A constitutional crisis threatened the very nature of the French monarchy. Politically weak, unsure of himself, in want of both troops and money, the eighteen-year-old dauphin Charles floundered in this sea of troubles. One indication of this was that in his first twenty-three months as royal lieutenant and then as regent, he took little action to stem the tide of treason.[2]

The dauphin's weakness at this time is exemplified by his relations with the king of Navarre. On the night of 8–9 November 1357 Navarre had been freed from his imprisonment in the castle of Arleux in Picardy by Jean de Picquigny. Immediately he made for Amiens, where he stayed with the canon Gui Quiéret.[3] On 29 November, having received a safe-conduct from the dauphin which was taken to him by Mathieu de Picquigny and Charles Toussac, Navarre entered Paris.[4] The strong support for Charles the Bad among the burgesses of Paris; the adverse course of the hostilities; and Navarre's virtual stranglehold on Paris forced the dauphin to yield. On 12 December 1357 he and Navarre reached an accord. Among the terms were provisions for Navarre and his adherents,

[1] Delachenal, *Hist. de Charles V*, I. 307.

[2] There were only two known executions: Guillaume Gryen (A.N., JJ 85, no. 145), and Guillaume Le Breton (JJ 84, no. 794); and only a few forfeitures, none from anybody of importance; see JJ 84, nos. 679, 797; JJ 85, nos. 26, 154; JJ 90, no. 458. Only five pardons are recorded: JJ 84, no. 627; JJ 89, nos. 11, 20; Guérin, *Arch. hist. Poitou*, XVII. 256–8; A.N., X2a 6, fols. 278v–279r.

[3] Delachenal, *Hist. de Charles V*, I. 325. Quiéret later fled the kingdom because of his known collaboration with the Navarrese. On the intercession of the king of Scotland – Quiéret was also archdeacon of Glasgow – he obtained a pardon in 1365 (A.N., JJ 98, no. 267 (partially printed in *Recueil*, ed. Secousse, p. 221)).

[4] *Chron. de Jean II et Charles V*, I. 118.

including Jean de Picquigny, to receive pardons and restitution of their property; for the remains of Harcourt and the others executed at Rouen in April 1356 to be taken down from the gibbet and given solemn burial; and for their property to be restored to their heirs.[5] On 8 January 1358 Navarre arrived in Rouen. Two days later the corpses of Graville, Mainemarès and Doublel were inhumed in a religious ceremony. Since Harcourt's corpse, however, had been removed secretly sometime before this, an empty coffin was buried along with the other three.[6]

The course of events convinced the dauphin, who had assumed the status of regent on 14 March 1358,[7] that he could no longer stay in Paris. Indeed, as if to confirm him in his decision, there was a plot to seize his person just before he did leave the capital. One of those implicated, an esquire named Filippo de Repenti, was beheaded at Les Halles on 19 March and then hanged.[8]

When the dauphin returned to Paris two days after the murder of Etienne Marcel on 31 July 1358 he acted with unwonted vigour and determination. On the day of his entry he appointed a ten-man commission[9] to punish the 'traitors, rebels and other malefactors' in Paris and the area around it. In those first days were executed the *échevin* Charles Toussac; Joceran Mâcon, the queen's treasurer;[10] Pierre Puisieux, an advocate in the Parlement of Paris;[11] Jean Godart, an advocate in the Châtelet; Gilles Caillart, castellan of the Louvre, whose tongue was cut out beforehand; the apothecary Pierre Gilles; the goldsmith Pierre Leblont; Jean Prévôt; Jean Bonvoisin; Gilles Marcel, Etienne's brother; Philippe Givart; Jean de l'Isle; and possibly Jean Porret the younger and Guillaume la Cate.[12] Thomas de Ladit, chancellor of Navarre and a cleric, was murdered by an angry mob on 12 September when he was being transferred from the Palais to the prison of the bishop of Paris.[13]

[5] *Recueil*, ed. Secousse, pp. 65–8. See A.N., JJ 89, nos. 215 and 330 for the restitutions to Mainemarès's brother Jean, and to Doublel's brother Jean. Friquet de Fricamps, having escaped from the Châtelet, was pardoned in March 1358 (JJ 89, no. 324).

[6] *Chron. de Jean II et Charles V*, I. 130–4.

[7] Perroy, *The Hundred Years War*, p. 135.

[8] *Chron. de Jean II et Charles V*, I. 162.

[9] *Recueil*, ed. Secousse, pp. 80–1.

[10] Mâcon had previously received a pardon in December 1357 (A.N., JJ 89, no. 11).

[11] See A.N., JJ 90, no. 210 for details on Puisieux.

[12] The first nine are mentioned in the dauphin's letter of 31 August to the count of Savoy (printed in Delachenal, *Hist. de Charles V*, II. 424–32. The other names were found in A.N., JJ 86, no. 295 (Marcel); no. 195 (Givart and Jean de l'Isle); JJ 90, no. 101(Porret); JJ 114, no. 65 (la Cate).

[13] *Chron. de Jean II et Charles V*, I. 215–16.

In a speech to the Parisians on 4 August, and in a letter of 31 August to his brother-in-law, Amadeus VI, count of Savoy, the regent recounted in detail the treason of Etienne Marcel and his adherents.[14] In addition to the general charges of usurpation of royal authority and rebellion in arms against the crown, Charles specifically pointed to the murders on 22 January 1358 of Robert de Clermont, marshal of Normandy, Jean de Conflans, marshal of Champagne, and Renaud d'Acy, king's advocate; the assault on the Marché of Meaux; the insults to himself; the naming of Navarre as captain of Paris on 14 June 1358; the accord between Marcel and Navarre for the English to enter Paris on 31 July; the obstruction of Jean II's deliverance from captivity; a plot to have the king and himself killed; and the use of magic to these ends by an 'heretical physician or astronomer of [Navarre] named Dominique'.

Charles liberally distributed the forfeited property of those who had been executed or who were in flight. To Aimery, lord of La Rochefoucauld, he granted a house in Paris confiscated from Jean Dionne, Charles Toussac's step-father. Aimar de Mullant, lord of Neubourg, acquired a house in Paris confiscated from Joceran Mâcon. Etienne Castel, a *valet de chambre* of the dauphin, received a rent of 40 *l.p.* from the property of the goldsmith Pierre des Barres. Lands worth 300 *l.p.* annually, and a manor worth 40 *livres* were assigned to Guillaume Brunel, *bailli* of Troyes and Meaux. Household officers like the royal secretary Julien des Murs and the chaplains Geoffroy Le Boutillier and Nicole Oiselet not surprisingly profited from the confiscations; and so too did the Parisian butchers Jean Givart and Raoul de Normandie, Jean de Sens, a shoemaker in the king's army, to whom a rent of 11½ *l.p.* was granted from the property of Etienne Marcel, and the book illuminators Jean Le Noir and his daughter Brigitte, who received a house confiscated from Charles Toussac and worth 400 *écus*.[15] Graciously he restored to the widows of Etienne and Gilles Marcel and Toussac, and to the wife of Pierre des Barres, some of their husbands' properties.[16] On 10 August he granted a

14 *Ibid.*, I. 212.

15 A.N., JJ 86, no. 474 (Rochefoucauld); no. 190 (Mullant); no. 537 (Castel); no. 279 (Brunel); JJ 90, no. 107 (Murs); JJ 86, no. 543 (chaplains); no. 200 (butchers); no. 201 (Sens); JJ 90, no. 4 (illuminators). Other grants, too numerous to cite, can be found in 'Pièces inédites relatives à Etienne Marcel et à quelques-uns de ses principaux adhérents', ed. S. Luce, *B.E.C.*, 5th series, I (1860), 76–92; and JJ 86–90, *passim*.

16 *Recueil*, ed. Secousse, pp. 115–17, 128–30 for the widows of Etienne Marcel and Toussac;

general pardon to the inhabitants of Paris who had not been party to 'the great treason'; and from August 1358 to February 1359 he issued thirty-two individual pardons to adherents of Etienne Marcel.[17]

One traitor whom the regent did not forgive was Robert Le Coq, bishop of Laon, a devoted partisan of Navarre, and, with Etienne Marcel, one of the leaders of the reform movement of 1356–8.[18] Although no judicial sentence was ever pronounced against Le Coq, there exists an anonymous document, most probably written in early 1358 – possibly by Simon de Bucy and the chancellor, Pierre de la Forêt – that was a most severe indictment of him. It was he, the document argued, who had incited Navarre to have the constable, Charles of Spain, assassinated; and, by convincing the dauphin that the king hated him, it was he who had instigated the plot of 1355. He had allegedly rejoiced over Jean II's capture, tried to impede his release, and said malicious things about the king: Jean II was 'rotten and of bad blood', for example; he was 'worthless', 'he governed badly', 'he was not worthy of being king', 'he did not have a right to the kingdom', even 'he was not worthy of living'. His intention in having wanted Navarre released from prison was to make him king of France. Le Coq's rôle in the Estates-general alone made him guilty of lese-majesty in the first degree.[19] The bishop could hardly have had any illusions about the attitude of the crown towards him.

After the fall of Etienne Marcel, all of Le Coq's property except for his library was given to the marshal Boucicaut.[20] Prudently he

A.N., JJ 86, no. 295 for the widow of Gilles Marcel; and no. 176 for the wife of Pierre des Barres.

17 *Ordonnances*, IV. 346–8 for the pardon to Paris. Those pardoned individually were Jean Marcel, Etienne's brother ('Pièces inédites', ed. Luce, pp. 81–3); Jean Morelet (A.N., JJ 86, no. 185); Pierre de Lagny (no. 206); Nicolas Le Flament (no. 209); Jacques du Châtel (no. 216); Nicolas de la Court (no. 220); Jean Fagnet (no. 253); Guillaume Lefèvre (no. 255); Geoffroy Le Flament (no. 272); Thomas Gascoigne (no. 273); Etienne de la Fontaine and his son Denisot (no. 278); Philippe de Juerre (no. 285); Jean Hasart (no. 287); Jean Pisdoe, who also paid a fine of 800 florins (no. 289); Martin Pisdoe, who paid a fine of 700 florins (no. 292); Laurent de Veullettes (no. 233); Pierre le Prêtre (no. 431); Jean de Saint-Leu and Jean Prévôt the younger (*Recueil*, ed. Secousse, pp. 101–2, 117–18); Jean de Saint-Benoît (JJ 90, no. 1); Thomas de Saint-Benoît (no. 2); Gérard and Jean Moret (no. 23); Pierre Moret (no. 25); Nicolas Pourret (no. 23); Jean Restable (no. 24); another Pierre le Prêtre (no. 26); Raoul Perrier (no. 27); Jean de la Court (no. 28); Guillaume Amé (no. 29); Jean de Castel (no. 30).

18 See E. Faral, 'Robert le Coq et les Etats généraux de 1356', *R.H.D.F.E.*, 4th series, XXIII (1945), 171–214; A. L. Funk, 'Robert Le Coq and Etienne Marcel', *Speculum*, XIX (1944), 470–87.

19 Douët-d'Arcq, 'Acte d'accusation', arts. 14–18, 20–3, 33–4, 37, 47–50, 56–60, 70.

20 Luce, 'Pièces inédites', p. 85 n. 1. For the fate of Le Coq's library, which numbered seventy-

withdrew to his episcopal city of Laon, but that was not the end of his treason, for in September he tried to deliver Laon to the Navarrese forces. The plot came to nought, however, and, according to Jean Le Bel, six of the wealthiest burgesses were executed for their part in it.[21] Le Coq again escaped, this time taking refuge in Mantes with the king of Navarre.[22]

The abortive plot at Laon coincided with a similar one at Amiens, where there were many partisans of Navarre, among them the mayor, Firmin de Cocquerel, and the captain, Jacques de Saint-Fuscien. Led by Jean and Robert de Picquigny – the wife of the latter and that of Robert d'Equennes, *vicomte* of Poix, had been arrested and held at Amiens in reprisal for the treason of their husbands – the Navarrese assaulted the city in mid-September, being stopped only at the foot of the ancient ramparts.[23] Firmin de Cocquerel and other burgesses who had supported the Navarrese from inside Amiens were executed for their treason.[24] Jacques de Saint-Fuscien, discovered a while later in hiding, was decapitated at the instigation of an angry mob.[25] Except for those executed, there was little confiscation of property.[26] Amiens itself received a pardon before the month was out.[27]

At Paris the repressive measures of August had not been enough to liquidate treasonable discontent. On 25 October about twenty-five people were arrested on suspicion of having made an alliance with the king of Navarre. But since the arrests were thought to have been

six volumes and was valued at 454 *l.* 4 *s.p.*, see R. Delachenal, 'La bibliothèque d'un avocat du XIVe siècle', *Nouv. rev. hist. du droit fr. et ét.*, XI (1887), 528.

21 Jean Le Bel, *Chronique*, II. 271.

22 Delachenal, 'La bibliothèque', p. 526.

23 Delachenal, *Hist. de Charles V*, II. 17–20.

24 Jean Le Bel (*Chronique*, II. 271) suggests that there were fourteen victims, while the *Chron. de Jean II et Charles V* (I. 217) says that there were only four.

25 Saint-Fuscien's wife brought suit against those who had illegally murdered her husband, but the regent forestalled her prosecution by pardoning the persons responsible, in January 1360 (A.N., JJ 90, no. 394).

26 For the distribution of Cocquerel's property see A.N., JJ 89, nos. 410, 565; JJ 90, nos. 44, 53; JJ 98, no. 94. For the property of the advocate Guillaume le Maréchal, who was also executed, see JJ 89, no. 686; JJ 90, no. 87. In September 1359 Jean and Jacques de Saint-Fuscien, sons of the captain of Amiens, were restored to their father's property (JJ 89, no. 165 (partially published in *Recueil*, ed. Secousse, pp. 156–7)). But in spite of this, further grants were made from Saint-Fuscien's property: to Robert de Fiennes, marshal of France, in September 1360 (JJ 90, no. 198); and to Enguerran de Hesdin, in October 1360 (JJ 88, no. 87/3).

27 *Recueil*, ed. Secousse, pp. 97–9.

tardy and vindictive, the dauphin made a concession to the burgesses and appointed a judicial commission. When no hard evidence could be produced to substantiate the charges, fourteen of the suspects were released on 23 November, the rest a few days later. In the cases of those who had been most guilty several months earlier at Paris, Amiens and Laon, there had been no opposition to the executions, confiscations and banishments; but the dauphin could now go only so far in prosecuting others without encountering political resistance from the burgesses. In effect he was constrained to act circumspectly in order not to alienate precisely those former partisans of Etienne Marcel whose support, and not just whose neutrality, he needed.[28]

The dauphin's principal enemy was, as ever, not the English but the king of Navarre, whose adherents had joined forces with demobbed English soldiers and were ravaging the countryside, particularly the area between the Somme and the Loire. On 3 August Navarre had formally defied the dauphin,[29] and it was from this time – as at Paris against the adherents of Etienne Marcel – that Charles began to act with great determination and authority against the Anglo-Navarrese forces and those who supported them. But he did not rely on military force alone. To weaken Navarre's power base he confiscated the properties of Charles the Bad's partisans, while at the same time he bolstered his own position by rewarding his supporters from the forfeitures.

In August 1358, for example, the knight Gui de Baveux was granted property in Normandy to the value of 400 *l.t.* that had been confiscated from Guillaume de Gauville, one of the more prominent of Navarre's partisans and the person chiefly responsible for the delivery of the castle of Evreux to the Navarrese.[30] Pierre de Sacquenville, one of the Normans who had defied Jean II in 1356, was again reputed a traitor and had his property confiscated. From that forfeiture Robert de Dreux, lord of Baigneux, received lands, including the lordship of Sacquenville, worth 1240 *l.p.* annually.[31] To Mouton de Blainville went all the property, worth some 500 *l.p.*, confiscated from the esquires Sauvage de Saint-Sanson and Perrin

[28] Delachenal, *Hist. de Charles V*, I. 468–70.

[29] *Chron. de Jean II et Charles V*, I. 211.

[30] A.N., JJ 86, no. 191; Froissart, *Chroniques*, v. 89–93. The knight Guillaume de Tronchevillier and the esquire Robert Boulart received rents of 100 *l.t.* each from the forfeited properties of Pierre du Bosc Renoult and Guillaume Houvet, who were accomplices of Gauville (*ibid.*, v. p. xxiii n. 2).

[31] A.N., JJ 86, nos. 179, 180.

Morel.[32] The lands of Jean de Bantelu, who had been implicated in the assassination of the constable in 1354, and who had been arrested in Rouen in April 1356, were confiscated and granted to the knight Martin de la Heuse.[33] The knight Robert Malet, a relation of the late lord of Graville, also lost his lands.[34]

The dauphin's policy had its effect on some of Navarre's supporters. The Tournebu family, for example, eventually submitted to the dauphin. Jean de Tournebu, lord of Marbeuf, had his lands confiscated not later than December 1358, but was pardoned in July 1359.[35] Both the knight Robert de Tournebu and the esquire Villart de Tournebu were rewarded for their support of the dauphin with rents of 200 *livres* from the forfeited property of Jean de Tilly and Jean de Gaillon respectively.[36]

All the above were Norman landholders.[37] But the king of Navarre also had strong support in Artois and Picardy, and this is reflected in the forfeitures decreed against his adherents there. In May and June 1359 Robert d'Equennes, *vicomte* of Poix, lost his lands partly to Gui de Châtillon, count of Saint-Pol, partly to Wales, lord of Quincampoix, and partly to Raoul de Renneval, lord of Pierrefont and *pannetier* of France. The value of this last grant alone, which included the *vicomté* of Poix, was 1000 *l.p.*[38] Jean de Picquigny's land of Fluy, worth about 700 *l.p.*, was given to Bernard de Paillart in May 1359; and Fossemanant, the lordship of Picquigny's late brother Mathieu, was granted to Fermin Audeluye, *prévôt* of Amiens.[39] Le Bègue de Créqui was another of Navarre's most staunch supporters from that region who forfeited his lands.[40]

The dauphin did not concern himself only with the wealthy nobles

[32] A.N., JJ 87, no. 82. [33] A.N., JJ 87, no. 81. [34] A.N., JJ 86, no. 531.

[35] A.N., JJ 90, no. 19 (grant to the esquire Pierre Behuchet of 150 *livres* in rent from Tournebu's lands of Musy and Etrignolles); *Recueil*, ed. Secousse, pp. 163–4 for the pardon.

[36] A.N., JJ 87, nos. 145, 149.

[37] Other Norman knights and esquires whose properties were confiscated before August 1359 and whom one can identify are Jean de Monceaux (A.N., JJ 86, no. 548); Jean de Graville (no. 558); Jean Avenel (no. 583); Jean de Tenray or Teuray (JJ 87, no. 106); Raoul de Beauchamps (no. 108); Pierre de Boscage (no. 119); Georges de Clère (no. 127); Robert de Bust (no. 126); Jean d'Auteuil (no. 140); Richard de Toulevast (no. 343); Robert de Covillartville (no. 355); Jean de Vaux, Jean de Bérangeville and the lord of Saint-Leu (JJ 90, no. 108 *bis*); Norman de Champeaux (Luce, *Bertrand du Guesclin*, *p.j.* xix).

[38] A.N., JJ 90, nos. 168, 175, 196.

[39] S. Honoré-Duvergé, 'Des partisans de Charles le Mauvais: les Picquigny', *B.E.C.*, CVII (1947), 85–6; A.N., JJ 86, no. 173; JJ 90, no. 256.

[40] A.N., JJ 90, nos. 120, 167, 181.

who adhered to the Navarrese party. For 1358–9 one can count at least forty-five forfeitures from the lowliest knights and esquires.[41] No traitor, in fact, was too insignificant. The potter Jean d'Agniaux forfeited his property because he lived voluntarily at Mantes, a Navarrese stronghold. The mercer Robin du Châtel forfeited his house in Rouen for having ridden in the company of Jean de Picquigny. Even common labourers like Jean Duchesne and Etienne Vint could lose their property for being supporters of Navarre.[42]

Until the fall of Etienne Marcel, the dauphin had been somewhat lack-lustre; though to be fair, his political feebleness at that time was due perhaps more to the situation in which he unexpectedly found himself than to defects in his own character: one must remember that in 1356 he was only a youth of eighteen. But the crisis of 1358 seems to have instilled in him the sense of purpose that he lacked before. For the rest of that year, as we have seen, and in the year following he showed the first signs of the political will that was to distinguish him thereafter and in his own reign.

The king of Navarre, abandoned as an ally by Edward III in the preliminary peace negotiations at London in 1358–9,[43] was ready to make his peace with the dauphin, who was no less eager because of an impending English invasion. At Pontoise on 21 August 1359 they came to an agreement, one of the terms of which provided for pardons to be granted to Navarre's adherents.[44] The regent then went to Paris to explain the peace settlement and to win the support of the civic leaders. In the Parlement Jean des Marès, king's advocate and spokesman for the burgesses, said that they would gladly receive Navarre in Paris, but that on no account would they suffer the presence of the traitors Robert Le Coq, Pierre des Barres, Geoffroy Le Flament, Vincent de Valrichier (one of the leaders of the Estates of 1356–7) and several others. And in fact, although Navarre requested pardons for them, the regent did not accept them into his grace.[45] He had learned his lesson in 1358: he would not unnecessarily antagonize the Parisians whose support he so desperately needed.

[41] A.N., JJ 86–90, *passim*.
[42] A.N., JJ 90, no. 195 (Agniaux); JJ 86, no. 502 (Châtel); JJ 87, no. 355 (labourers).
[43] Delachenal, *Hist. de Charles V*, II. 66ff.
[44] *Ibid.*, II. 125ff. For some individual pardons see A.N., JJ 87, nos. 184, 338; JJ 89, no. 476; JJ 90, nos. 270, 310, 336–44, 504; JJ 96, no. 319.
[45] *Chron. de Jean II et Charles V*, I. 244–6.

Navarre continued to intrigue in spite of the peace between himself and the regent. In early December 1359 the Parisian, Martin Pisdoe,[46] tried to recruit his fellow burgesses Denis Le Paumier and Jean Le Chanevacier into a conspiracy to kill the regent and his councillors, and then to seize the strategic points of Paris for the Navarrese. Le Paumier, however, revealed Pisdoe's plans to the regent, who instructed him to go along with the plot in order to learn more details about it. Perhaps upon the discovery of some written communication, Martin Pisdoe was then imprisoned in the Châtelet. Taken later to the regent and his council at the Louvre and confronted with Denis Le Paumier, he confessed all. In the last week of December he was beheaded and quartered at Les Halles. As a result of this plot the regent broke off all personal relations with Charles the Bad, but because he was preoccupied with the English at this time, he refrained from open hostilities.[47]

On 24 October 1360, when Jean II signed the treaty of Calais, he also concluded a separate agreement with the king of Navarre. The reason for this second accord is that Charles the Bad, unlike his brother Philippe, could not be included in the Anglo-French treaty because he was no longer a formal ally of the English, having already made his peace with the dauphin at Pontoise on 21 August 1359. The terms of his accord with Jean II were simple enough: he obtained pardons with restitution of property for himself and for three hundred of his adherents whom he was to name before Easter 1361. Among the most prominent were Jean VI d'Harcourt; Robert Le Coq; Robert Porte, bishop of Avranches; Robert d'Equennes, *vicomte* of Poix; Friquet de Fricamps; Pierre de Sacquenville, Jean Malet, lord of Graville; Le Bègue de Créqui; Robert de Corbie; Jean de Bantelu; Robert, Gérard and Philippe de Picquigny; and the Parisians Vincent de Valrichier, Jean de Sainte-Aude and Geoffroy Le Flament.[48] But not all of those named were able to obtain pardons. Robert Le Coq, for one, was never taken back into royal grace. Succeeded as bishop of Laon in 1363 by Geoffroy le Maingre,

[46] Pisdoe had received a pardon in 1358 (A.N., JJ 86, no. 292).

[47] Delachenal, *Hist. de Charles V*, II. 173–6. Jean Le Bel (*Chronique*, II. 303) mentions another plot at about that time to kill the dauphin. According to him the leader, Le Bascon de Mareuil, was executed on Christmas Eve. But Le Bascon died at the battle of Cocherel in 1364 (Jean de Venette, *Chronicle*, ed. R. Newhall and trans. J. Birdsall (New York, 1953), p. 122); what Jean Le Bel relates must surely be the Pisdoe plot. See also Chéruel, *Hist. de Rouen*. II. 207–8.

[48] *Recueil*, ed. Secousse, pp. 172–85.

Boucicaut's brother, he obtained the bishopric of Calahorra in Aragon 1367 through Navarre's patronage, and remained there until his death in 1372.[49]

For several years after the treaty of Calais the king of Navarre kept his peace with Jean II, who had returned from captivity in England. During Jean II's last years in France, before he returned to England, there was little known treasonable activity and little prosecution of it.[50] This, perhaps, can be taken in support of the argument presented in the previous chapter.

It was under Charles, first as regent and then as king, that conflict with the Navarrese began again. It is true that Navarre was preparing for hostilities after being cast aside from the succession to the duchy of Burgundy, but it was the regent who struck the first blow. On 7 April 1364, one day before Jean II died in England, French forces under Bertrand du Guesclin's cousin Olivier de Mauny captured Navarre's stronghold of Mantes. Twenty-eight men who had been defending the tower were taken to Paris and executed as traitors.[51] Renaud de Paris, *bailli* of Mantes; Jacques le Prestrel, Navarre's treasurer; and others escaped to Meulan, where they barricaded themselves in the keep. On 10 or 11 April du Guesclin captured Meulan, but the Navarrese in the keep continued to resist. When Charles, now king, passed through the town, they hurled stones as well as verbal abuse at him. Several days later, when they gave themselves up, they were taken to Paris and executed.[52] Then, after the decisive battle of Cocherel on 16 May, Pierre de Sacquenville, perhaps the most important prisoner apart from the Captal de Buch, was taken to Rouen, where, not later than 13 June he was beheaded and quartered as 'a traitor to us and the kingdom'. Indeed, it is very likely that Charles V personally ordered and witnessed the execution of Sacquenville, for the king was in Rouen from 11–15 June.[53]

[49] Delachenal, 'La bibliothèque', pp. 526–7.

[50] For some forfeitures, see A.N., JJ 91, no. 298; JJ 93, no. 121; JJ 95, no. 34. Very little is known about the rebellion of Thomas de La Marche; on this see M. Boudet, *Thomas de La Marche, bâtard de France 1318–1361* (Riom, 1900), pp. 184ff; A.N., JJ 89, no. 707; JJ 95, no. 155.

[51] Jean de Venette, *Chronicle*, p. 118.

[52] Delachenal, *Hist. de Charles V*, II. 359–60. Between 17 and 24 April du Guesclin and others received the confiscated property of some twenty inhabitants of Mantes (Luce, *Bertrand du Guesclin*, *p.j.* lv–lvii). For two pardons see A.N., JJ 94, no. 50 and JJ 95, no. 175.

[53] Luce, *Bertrand du Guesclin*, p. 455; Delachenal, *Hist. de Charles V*, III. 122–3. From Sacquenville's confiscated property his castles and manors of Sacquenville and Bérengeville-la-

On 1 June 1364, before Sacquenville's execution, Charles V issued a general pardon[54] and commissioned the knight Henri de Thieville, captain of Saint-Lô, *maître de l'hôtel du roi*, to pardon those Navarrese who wished to return to royal obedience, and to restore their property to them.[55] Meanwhile, in order to continue the pressure on the other Navarrese, the king declared forfeitures of their property. Philippe de Navarre's county of Longueville, for example, was granted to Bertrand du Guesclin. Jacques Blarrue, chamberlain of the king, obtained all the property of Guillaume de Gauville. Properties confiscated from Robert Guillet, Navarre's *vicomte* of Evreux, were granted to Jacques le Lieur, captain of Rouen, and to Pierre l'Aillerie, a *valet de chambre*. The esquire Hervé de Caume received lands worth some 70 *livres* that had been forfeited by Guillaume du Bois, Navarre's *bailli* of Pont-Audemer and Beaumont-le-Roger.[56] There were at least fourteen other confiscations.[57]

Thrown on the defensive, unable to turn to the English, Navarre concluded a peace accord with the king in the spring of 1365. By the terms of the agreement Navarre was to obtain the barony of Montpellier in compensation for Mantes, Meulan and Longueville; the Captal de Buch was to be released; and there was to be yet another general pardon, with restitution of property, to the adherents of Navarre for all their treasons since November 1357.[58] After the agreement Navarre turned his attention to his Pyrenean kingdom and was not to disturb the French scene again until 1369.

As in 1337 it was for treason that the duchy of Guyenne was formally declared confiscate on 30 November 1369 and again on 14 May 1370. Edward III, the Black Prince and their officers, it was stated, had obstructed and tried to obstruct the appeals of the Gascon lords and others, 'in magnum et grave prejudicium superioritatis et

Campagne, and all the land that he owned in Brie and Champagne, were granted to Pierre d'Omont, chamberlain of the king (A.N., JJ 96, no. 116). All the rest of his property was granted to Jean de Gaillon, lord of Grolay, himself a former partisan of Navarre (no. 118).

54 A.N., Coll. Lenoir 19, fols. 215–16.

55 A.N., JJ 98, no. 64. He is described as captain of Saint-Lô in no. 363, and as *maître d'hôtel* in JJ 99, no. 522. For some pardons see JJ 96, nos. 163, 199, 240, 311, 374.

56 *Recueil*, ed. Secousse, pp. 192–5 (Navarre); A.N., JJ 96, no. 124 (Gauville); nos. 67, 114 (Guillet); no. 358 (du Bois).

57 A.N., JJ 96, nos. 54, 71, 129, 175, 200, 201, 213, 234, 280, 333, 344, 355; JJ 98, no. 141; JJ 118, no. 223.

58 *Recueil*, ed. Secousse, pp. 222–31; see also *Mandements et actes diverses de Charles V (1364–1380)*, ed. L. Delisle (C.D.I.) (Paris, 1874), no. 225A; and see A.N., K 49, no. 11 for an individual pardon, to Jean le Moyne.

jurisdictionis nostre contemptum, et laesionem regiae majestatis'. Not only did they ignore the summonses for them to appear in the Parlement, but they also 'contra nos et coronam nostram praedictam evidenter et manifeste rebelles et inimicos nostros se reddiderant, nobisque et regno nostro guerram notorie et permanenter et apperte indixerant et fecerant'. All their French vassals were absolved from their oaths of allegiance to them, and those that continued to obey them would forfeit their properties for their treason.[59]

Charles V's threat was not an idle one; the lands of English adherents were being confiscated from at least June 1369, and until early 1373 one can count at least 250 forfeitures.[60] It seems obvious but it should be stated nevertheless: with few exceptions allegiance was dictated by the location of one's property. Those whose principal possessions were in a region of English obedience fought for the English; and *vice versa* for those with property in land of French obedience. In Poitou, for example, at the start of the hostilities only a very few lords and knights – Renaud de Pons, Raymond de Mareuil, and Renaud de Montléon, for example – remained loyal to Charles V.[61] But Louis d'Harcourt, who had supported Jean II and the dauphin in the 1350s, this time sided with the English because his *vicomté* of Châtellerault was in Poitou. His other properties were confiscated in November 1369 and were given to his nephew Jean VI d'Harcourt.[62]

Most of the forfeited properties lay in the provinces of Anjou and Touraine, and were granted to loyalists from those areas. But there were also a number of forfeitures from Berri,[63] Bourbonnais,[64] Maine,[65] Limousin,[66] Orléanais,[67] Guines,[68] Artois,[69] Picardy,[70] Boulogne,[71] and the *vicomté* of Caen.[72] Charles V's use of forfeitures

[59] Anselme, *Hist. généalogique*, III. 586–8. See Delachenal, *Hist. de Charles V*, IV. 71ff. for the background. See also A.N., X1a 1473, fol. 42r–v.

[60] A.N., JJ 100–6, *passim*; some of these have been published by Guérin, *Arch. hist. Poitou*, XVII, XIX. *passim*.

[61] Guérin, *Arch. hist. Poitou*, XIX. pp. x–xii. For his loyalty Raymond de Mareuil received an hereditary rent of 2000 *livres*, the castle of Courtenay and the revenues thereof (A.N., JJ 100, no. 223).

[62] Guérin, *Arch. hist. Poitou*, XIX. 18–20.

[63] *Ibid.*, XVII. 373–6; A.N., JJ 100, no. 91; JJ 102, no. 46.

[64] A.N., JJ 100, nos. 18, 19, 80, 106–8.

[65] A.N., JJ 100, no. 119.

[66] A.N., JJ 100, nos. 128, 419; JJ 103, no. 227; JJ 109, no. 64.

[67] A.N., JJ 100, no. 124.

[68] A.N., JJ 122, no. 338.

[69] A.N., JJ 100, no. 580; JJ 102, no. 231; JJ 103, no. 3.

[70] A.N., JJ 100, no. 257.

[71] A.N., JJ 100, no. 383.

[72] A.N., JJ 100, no. 101.

as reward and incentive – some of the grants were no doubt made on lands yet to be taken – must surely have served in large measure to help the French forces in their conquest of Poitou. But foreseeing an eventual peace, Charles V was prudently flexible in his policy: a great many of the grants specified that if and when there was a general settlement, with restitution of property, the crown would not be liable to recompense those to whom confiscated lands had been given.[73] At Loudun on 1 December 1372 the Poitevin lords, prelates and towns made their submission to the crown.[74] Apart from the general pardon, however, there are few individual pardons for treason recorded in the chancery registers.[75]

The renewal of hostilities between France and England in 1369 had given Charles the Bad another chance to intrigue in the French kingdom. On 13 August 1369 he landed at Cherbourg and began to negotiate with both the French and the English. On 2 December 1370 he concluded with the latter a preliminary treaty, supporting Edward III's claim to the French throne in return for Champagne, Brie, Burgundy and Maine. But since this accord was never ratified, Charles the Bad had to play his other card. On 25 March 1371 he signed the treaty of Vernon with Charles V. This time, however, he could prise little out of the king other than a reiteration of the terms agreed to in 1365. With that he returned to his kingdom of Navarre, never to reappear in France.[76]

Just as Charles the Bad was abandoning the English – or rather they him – Jean de Montfort was on the verge of embracing them openly. After he did cast off what semblance of neutrality he had managed to preserve, he lost his duchy in 1373.[77] Although there was no formal forfeiture of the duchy, nor any formal prosecution of him, Montfort was reputed a traitor and was referred to as 'nagueres duc de Bretagne';[78] and his own property in the duchy was confiscated. Olivier IV de Clisson, for example, received his lordship of Guillac, which was worth 400 *livres* annually. But as in

[73] E.g., A.N., JJ 100, nos. 18, 106, 143, 277, 328, 526. There is no perceptible reason – neither the status of the recipient nor the value of the lands granted – why some of the grants contained a non-obligation clause and others did not.

[74] Guérin, *Arch. hist. Poitou*, XIX. 176–90.

[75] See A.N., JJ 100, nos. 387–8; JJ 103, no. 7; JJ 104, nos. 90, 166, 186–7.

[76] Delachenal, *Hist. de Charles V*, IV. 365–75.

[77] Jones, *Ducal Brittany*, pp. 68ff.

[78] A.N., JJ 104, no. 321; see also B.-A. Pocquet du Haut-Jussé, 'La dernière phase de la vie de du Guesclin: l'affaire de Bretagne', *B.E.C.*, CXXV (1967), 152–3.

Poitou, it was clear that Charles V was holding out the prospect of a reconciliation, for in the letter of donation to Clisson he inserted a non-obligation clause in the event that Montfort returned to obedience and had his property restored to him.[79]

The events of Charles V's reign reached a climax in 1378. In the spring of that year the king learned 'from several great lords' – most probably Gaston de Foix among them[80] – that 'the king of Navarre had [planned] to have [him] poisoned and that . . . Jacques de Rue . . . knew these things and several others [too]'.[81] After Jacques de Rue was arrested and confessed that Navarre not only had planned to poison Charles V but also was trying to resurrect the 1370 accord with the English, the king acted immediately. On 29 March he wrote in his own hand to his brother Louis, duke of Anjou, denouncing Navarre's treason and instructing him to seize Montpellier. At about the same time a royal force under Philippe, duke of Burgundy, and the constable, Bertrand du Guesclin, was despatched to Normandy to effect the submission of the Navarrese strongholds.[82] In addition, the admiral Jean de Vienne was advised to take defensive measures against a possible invasion. On 4 April Vienne sent letters to all the sergeants in the *vicomté* of Auge and elsewhere explaining that 'it had come to his attention as much by letters of the king as by the relation of several notable persons that the enemies of the kingdom were ready to descend in very great number . . . at Harfleur and Honfleur'.[83]

The Norman campaign was a success.[84] After the state trial of Jacques de Rue and Pierre du Tertre in June, Robert Assire was commissioned to confiscate their property and that of other Navarrese adherents in Normandy and elsewhere.[85] But even before this, as early as March 1378, Charles V was making grants from forfeited properties in Normandy. To Jean de Vaudetar and Gilles Malet, for example, he granted a rent of 200 *l.p.* from the property of Pierre du Tertre. Grants on the properties of Jean Eude and Gillet Lohier, both of whom had been executed at Rouen, were made to Jean Auvart, marshal of the count of Harcourt; Robin d'Esneval, *échanson du roi*; and Hennequin Champenois, a royal sergeant-at-arms.

[79] A.N., JJ 104, no. 270. For another grant see no. 209.

[80] *Chron. Reg. Franc.*, II. 348.

[81] *Chron. de Jean II et Charles V*, II. 284–5.

[82] Delachenal, *Hist. de Charles V*, V. 185–95, 214.

[83] B.N., ms. fr. 26014, no. 2156.

[84] Delachenal, *Hist. de Charles V*, V. 199–205, 211–13.

[85] A.N., J 1050, no. 16.

Hennequin Suette, a *valet de chambre*; Audouin Chauveron, *bailli* of the Cotentin; Jean d'Estouteville; and Yon de Garencières also profited from the confiscations.[86]

The king showed, however, that he could also be magnanimous in victory. On 30 July 1378 he issued a general pardon for all crimes – treason or otherwise – committed by the Navarrese, provided that they swear on the Gospels henceforth to be loyal. The only persons excepted from this pardon were those who had already been punished or who had fled the kingdom.[87] Approximately seventy individual pardons were granted in the following year or so. Among those who returned to royal obedience were Martin Sens Durette, captain of Pont-Audemer; Ligier d'Orgessin, captain of Pacy; Alain de Frénal, *vicomte* of Mortain; Robert Vende, *vicomte* of Beaumont-le-Roger; Raoul Girard, *vicomte* of Breteuil; and Robert de Lettre, a former *vicomte* of Evreux.[88]

Like Jean II *vis-à-vis* Robert Le Coq, Charles V was not prepared to pardon Robert Porte, bishop of Avranches since 1359 and Navarre's chancellor, who at least since 1373 had been actively involved in Navarre's military affairs.[89] In 1378, when Charles V took the offensive in Normandy, he did not ignore the bishop's perfidy. In an undated letter of that year to the Parlement the king described the bishop's treasons: he had assembled troops in various towns and fortresses; and by words and written messages he had incited the people to sedition. He was thus 'false, a traitor and a perjuror', and he had committed 'the crime of lese-majesty and felony against us'. His present treason was all the more reprehensible, Charles V added, because Jean II had pardoned him a previous one.[90] 'We cannot and will not . . . let this go unpunished', the king wrote; 'by great and mature deliberation of all our council, we declare [him] a traitor, perjuror [and] conspirator.' Although the Parlement was thus thrust

[86] A.N., JJ 112, no. 197 (Vaudetar and Malet); no. 218 (Auvart); no. 331 (Esneval and Champenois); JJ 115, no. 5 (Suette); JJ 112, no. 378 (Chauveron); no. 247 (Estouteville); no. 193 (Garencières). For other grants to December 1378 see JJ 112, no. 343; JJ 113, nos. 12, 81, 84, 178, 275; JJ 114, no. 45.

[87] A.N., JJ 125, no. 197. About forty individual pardons had been granted before this (JJ 112–16, *passim*).

[88] *Recueil*, ed. Secousse, p. 442 (Durette); p. 445 (Orgessin, whose annual pension from the king of Navarre had been 120 francs (B.N., n.a. fr. 23634, no. 30); A.N., JJ 114, no. 350 (Frénal); no. 227 (Vende); no. 232 (Girard); no. 199 (Lettre).

[89] *Gallia Christiana*, XI. cols. 491–2; B.N., ms. fr. 26011, no. 1415.

[90] *Supra*, p. 171.

aside from the deliberative process, it was instructed to seize Porte's temporalities 'by all ways and means that justice and reason permit' and to apply them to the royal domain for the rest of the bishop's life.[91] That was not to be for long, as Robert Porte died in late summer 1379.[92]

After his successful campaign against Navarre, Charles V felt that the time was ripe for him to proceed to a formal confiscation of the duchy of Brittany.[93] Three days after the sentence of forfeiture on 18 December 1378 the king granted to Bertrand du Guesclin a rent of 600 *l.t.* from Montfort's castellany of La Guerche,[94] but this seems to have been the only donation. Charles had badly miscalculated, however, in confiscating the duchy. By also setting aside the Penthièvre claims to Brittany he aroused in the Breton nobility – to a man except for Olivier de Clisson – their spirit of independence, and he provoked them to seek the recall of Montfort from England. Once back in Brittany, Montfort shrewdly negotiated with both the English and the French. But it was not until Charles V died that Montfort made his peace with the crown, in the second treaty of Guerande, drafted in January 1381 and confirmed on 6 April.[95] In between those two dates a general pardon was issued, on 2 March, for all of Montfort's adherents.[96]

Normandy had not quite been pacified after the general pardon of July 1378. It came to the attention of Charles V that in spite of the oaths of fidelity which the adherents of Charles the Bad had sworn to the crown that summer, some of these Navarrese had recently taken up arms with the English. Consequently on 26 December he wrote to the *bailli* of Rouen, instructing him to publish an edict to the effect that, notwithstanding any previous pardons, all Navarrese must leave the kingdom, especially Normandy, within eight days of the document's publication, on penalty of being imprisoned as traitors, with confiscation of their property.[97]

From one case we learn that Charles V meant what he said. Barradaco de Barrante, a native of Navarre, had married the wealthy *dame* of Hondouville in the county of Evreux and was living peaceably in his *hôtel* when in the spring of 1378 the hostilities began. He

[91] *Thesaurus Novus Anecdotorum*, I. cols. 1529–31.
[92] *Gallia Christiana*, XI. col. 492.
[93] Jones, *Ducal Brittany*, pp. 84–5.
[94] A.N., JJ 114, no. 10.
[95] Jones, *Ducal Brittany*, pp. 85–91.
[96] A.N., JJ 118, no. 346.
[97] *Mandements de Charles V*, no. 1801.

then went to defend Navarre's castles, but since he wanted to continue living with his wife he advised the defenders of Evreux and Pacy to surrender to the crown. For this he received a pardon in June 1378.[98] When Charles V issued his decree of 26 December Barradaco chose to ignore it, assuming wrongly that it did not supersede his pardon. Shortly thereafter he was arrested and imprisoned in Valognes by Jean Le Mercier. Only in April 1382, after three years in prison, was he again pardoned and allowed to remain in Normandy.[99]

Although in general Charles V had dealt effectively with the Norman adherents of Navarre by 1379, Charles the Bad still commanded some support, as is clear from the confiscations that were still being decreed at least through 1383.[100] As for Navarre himself, Charles V thought of prosecuting him[101] but in the event did not do so, apparently remaining satisfied with the sequestration of Navarre's French possessions. Although Charles the Bad was still in disfavour during the first year of Charles VI's reign, on 6 February 1381 his sons Charles and Pierre were given the government and revenues of his former lands, principally the counties of Evreux, Beaumont-le-Roger and Mortain, the Cotentin, Conches, Breteuil, Orbec, Pont-Audemer, Nogent-le-Roi and the barony of Montpellier. In an amplification of this accord, Charles VI reserved to himself the regalia of Navarre's lands, and incorporated six minor fiefs into the royal domain.[102] This was not, however, the end of the Navarrese affair. Charles the Bad, though he remained in his own kingdom, was to be heard of yet again, as we shall see in the next chapter.

Just as the brutal prosecution of treason in the reign of Philippe VI was a clear departure from the practice of previous kings, so too in its own way, if perhaps less radically, did the prosecution of treason during the reign of Charles V differ from that of his predecessors. Although Charles V certainly did not shrink from sanctioning executions – as at Paris in 1358, after the battle of Cocherel in 1364, and in 1378 – we cannot isolate this as a remarkable feature of his reign, for such judicial action had surely come to be expected, or at

98 A.N., JJ 113, no. 18.

99 A.N., JJ 120, no. 145.

100 E.g., A.N., JJ 114, nos. 281, 286; JJ 115, nos. 101, 131; JJ 116, no. 21; JJ 117, nos. 23, 72; JJ 124, no. 78.

101 Delachenal, *Hist. de Charles V*, v. 216 n. 2.

102 *Recueil*, ed. Secousse, pp. 467–72, 479–80.

least accepted, by the mid fourteenth century. What does distinguish his regency and reign are two things. Firstly, one cannot help but notice that in the years of crisis – 1358–9, 1364, 1369–72, 1378 – he made the widest use of forfeitures as an instrument of policy, as a means of punishment, reward and incentive. Only a fraction of the evidence for this has been presented in this chapter and in chapter 5. Furthermore, and clearly, it was not only the nobility that was affected by confiscations. In chapter 2 it has been pointed out how even those non-combatants who gave support, if only by living voluntarily in enemy territory, could be reputed traitors and lose their property that was in control of the crown. By the most extensive application of forfeitures Charles V undermined the positions of Charles the Bad and Edward III. He struck at their supporters where it hurt these people the most: in their lands. This was of course all done in conjunction with military operations, and on the whole one must say that it was a most successful policy. One might add that Charles V's readiness to grant pardons accounts not insignificantly for his success in quelling the revolts of Navarre in particular.

The second noteworthy feature of Charles V's reign is his recourse to state trials in the latter part of his reign. Here, in keeping with his exalted view of the majesty of kingship, he resurrected a form of process at law that had not been used in the prosecution of treason since the trial of Robert de Béthune in 1315, and that had not been used at all in criminal cases since the affair of Robert d'Artois in 1331–2. One should, however, bear in mind that apart from these cases and those involving minor treasons such as private war or breach of safeguard, few others came before the courts. Far more, if less viciously, than his predecessors, Charles V prosecuted treason on his own record.

Chapter 8

TREASON AND THE CROWN

1380–1422

I

The last years of Charles V's reign and the first years of Charles VI's were marked by urban rebellions that were more often than not punished severely under the law of treason, and at considerable profit to the crown. In late 1379, after the imposition of a hearth tax of 12 francs, violence erupted at Nîmes, Le Puy, Alais, Montpellier, and other towns in the south. At Montpellier a contemporary source estimated that some eighty royal officers – surely an inflated figure – were murdered on 25 October.[1] Although Louis d'Anjou, the king's lieutenant, treated Nîmes leniently,[2] he was much more severe with Montpellier, where he arrived on 20 January 1380. On 24 January he pronounced a brutal sentence that was distinguished by its clear references to the Roman law of treason. 'Because there is no doubt that they have committed the crime of lese-majesty and have even committed a crime against the *ius gentium*,' his decree stated, 600 burgesses were to be executed, with confiscation of their property, 'as the *lex Julia maiestatis* provides'. Anjou's judicial sentence then quoted verbatim from the passage in the *lex Quisquis* on the disinheritance of traitors' children and their condemnation to a life of poverty and misery. The town as a whole was to pay a fine of 600,000 francs, and the commune was to be suppressed. On the following day, however, Anjou mitigated the sentence: only the ringleaders were to be executed and their property confiscated; the fine was revoked, but 130,000 francs still had to be paid to the duke 'for his expenses'. The political structure of the commune was left more or less as it was.[3]

1 *Le petit thalamus de Montpellier*, ed. Grassel, Desmazes and Saint-Paul (*Mém. de la soc. arch. de Montpellier*) (Montpellier, 1840), p. 398.

2 Ménard, *Hist. de Nismes*, III. 16–17. He had also treated it leniently on the occasion of an earlier revolt in 1378 (*ibid.*, III. 1–3; *preuves*, pp. 17–18).

3 The sentence and letter of pardon are printed in Germain, *Hist. de Montpellier*, II. 388–401.

One suspects that Anjou had intended all along to revise the sentence of 24 January so that his 'concessions' on the 25th would seem that much more generous. Undue severity, it is argued, would have jeopardized his position in Languedoc, compromising his candidacy for the crown of Naples. Whatever were Anjou's motives, the revolts at Montpellier and elsewhere did bring positive results for the inhabitants of those towns. Charles V recalled the rapacious Anjou from the south, and, later, on his death-bed, abolished the hearth tax.[4]

New taxes announced in January 1382 by Anjou, as president of Charles VI's council, precipitated new revolts not only in Languedoc, but also, and more seriously, in Normandy, Paris and the Ile-de-France, and in the north-east.[5] Alarmed by the extent of these urban rebellions the young king and his uncles suppressed them ruthlessly. At Paris in mid-March at least seventeen of the leaders of the Maillotins were executed, and there would have been yet more deaths but for the adverse reaction that the bloodshed was causing among even the uncompromised Parisians.[6] At Rouen, where the king arrived on 29 March, the leaders of that town's revolt were likewise executed, the commune was abolished, and a fine of 60,000 francs was imposed. Rouen received a pardon on 5 April, but the fine was not revoked, and the abolition of the commune remained in force. In August the Rouennais again revolted against the royal tax-collectors,[7] but for the moment the king was too busy preparing for an expedition against the rebellious towns of Flanders to return to punish them.

Two days after the battle of Roosebeke on 27 November 1382[8] Charles VI received the submission of Bruges. In return for a pardon he extracted from that town a fine of 120,000 francs and forced it to

[4] *Ibid.*, II. 198–9; Delachenal, *Hist. de Charles V*, v. 330ff.

[5] On the revolts in general see L. Mirot, 'Les insurrections urbaines en Normandie à la fin du XIVe siècle', *Rev. des ét. hist.* (1902), 558–82; Mirot, *Les insurrections urbaines*; C. Radding, 'The Estates of Normandy and the Revolts in the Towns at the Beginning of the Reign of Charles VI', *Speculum*, XLVII (1972), 79–90.

[6] Coville, *Les premiers Valois*, p. 275.

[7] Radding, 'The Estates of Normandy', pp. 81–2; Chéruel, *Hist. de Rouen*, II. 446–9; the pardon is printed at pp. 547–9.

[8] Guillaume Coquel, who had deserted the royal army just before the battle, had his property confiscated; a rent of 100 *l.p.* from it was granted to the esquire Gilles de Vengin (A.N., JJ 121, no. 295). The *attornés* of Senlis were accused of treason for having recalled their contingent of six *arbalétriers* before the end of the campaign (*Choix de pièces*, ed. Douët-d'Arcq, I. 42–3).

abandon its alliances with the enemies of the crown.[9] If not before the battle of Roosebeke, certainly after it the Flemish rebels were considered traitors. On 14 December 1382, in granting a rent of 200 *livres* to the count of Dammartin from the lands of Jean Boude and Aubert Le Boux, Charles VI declared that 'all the property of those who have adhered or still adhere to the party of Ghent . . . is confiscated to us . . . for the crime of lese-majesty'.[10]

Returning victorious from the Flemish campaign, Charles VI entered Paris on 11 January 1383.[11] He, Burgundy, Berri and Bourbon were determined to punish the burgesses responsible for both the disturbances the previous March and the resistance thereafter to the new taxation. Over 300 people were arrested immediately, among them the king's advocate Jean des Marès and Guillaume de Sens, a president of the Parlement.[12] On 12 January two drapers, Aubert de Dampierre and Guillaume Rousseau, and the goldsmith Henri de Pons were beheaded.[13] Another draper, Jean de la Carrière, was also executed at about that time.[14] More arrests were made during all of the next week. Nicolas Le Flament, who had been implicated in Etienne Marcel's treason in 1358, was beheaded on 19 January. Eight more executions occurred on 24 January. On the 27th Charles VI abolished the privileges of the Parisians and placed the *prévôté des marchands* under his own control. On 31 January Jean Maillart and six others were beheaded.[15] It was estimated that more than 100 persons in all were executed for their parts in the disturbances.[16]

Certainly the most prominent of the victims was the septuagenarian Jean des Marès. He was accused of having spoken too freely on behalf of the Parisians, of having gained their submission in March 1382 by unnecessary appeasement, even of having advised them to defend Paris against the king; and it was thought by some that his worst offence was having supported the duke of Anjou against the dukes of Berri and Burgundy. With Anjou now off in Italy pursuing his dynastic claims, Jean des Marès, left without a protector, was

[9] *Chron. de Jean II et Charles V*, III. 31–2.

[10] A.N., JJ 121, no. 285 *bis*; see also JJ 122, no. 142; JJ 124, no. 107. Apart from these examples I have not found further evidence on forfeitures from the Flemish rebels. It is most likely that the duke of Burgundy profited the most from whatever confiscations there were.

[11] Froissart, *Chroniques*, XI. p. xviii.

[12] Coville, *Les premiers Valois*, p. 282.

[13] *Chron. de Jean II et Charles V*, III. 41.

[14] A.N., JJ 123, no. 203.

[15] *Chron. de Jean II et Charles V*, III. 43–6.

[16] *Chron. de Saint-Denys*, I. 244.

arrested. The bishop of Paris claimed him as a cleric, but Berri and Burgundy, feeling that an ecclesiastical trial not only would take too long but would not punish des Marès severely enough, brushed aside the bishop's motion and ordered the *prévôt* of Paris to execute him. On 28 February des Marès was beheaded along with fourteen others.[17]

On 1 March 1383, the anniversary of the Maillotin uprising, Charles VI pardoned the inhabitants of Paris except for the fugitives, who, if they did not return to Paris by 8 March, would be banished with forfeiture of their property. One who did have his property confiscated was Maître Jean de Romilly, two of whose *hôtels*, worth 24 *l.p.* annually, were granted to Nicolas Braque and Pierre de Chevreuse, *maîtres de l'hôtel du roi*.[18] Elsewhere, in the north-east of France, around the diocese of Reims, and in Normandy, reformers-general were commissioned to punish traitors.[19] Substantial fines were imposed on towns in those regions and elsewhere in France. Caen, for example, had to pay 22,000 francs, Laon 25,000, Orléans 30,000.[20] In the south the inhabitants of the *sénéchaussées* of Beaucaire and Nîmes bought a pardon for their 'conspiracies . . . disobediences, rebellions, crimes under the *lex Julia maiestatis*' for 80,000 francs, while the whole of Languedoc was fined the enormous sum of 800,000 francs.[21]

The tax revolts of the 1380s brought the full weight of the monarchy to bear against the malcontents, who were indeed punished as traitors. The crown not only filled its coffers as a result of the revolts, but had so intimidated the inhabitants of the kingdom that it was now able to collect the taxes that had precipitated the rebellions. Never again would there be such general resistance to the crown's fiscal policies.

17 *Chron. de Jean II et Charles V*, III. 47; Froissart, *Chroniques*, XI. 80–1; Guérin, *Arch. hist. Poitou*, XXI. 213 n. 2; M. Félibien, *Histoire de la ville de Paris* (5 vols., Paris, 1725), II. 697–8. Two of des Marès's houses were given to Gui de La Trémoïlle (Guérin, *Arch. hist. Poitou*, XXI. 213).

18 *Chron. de Jean II et Charles V*, III. 48–53; Froissart, *Chroniques*, XI. p. xix n. 4. For the forfeiture from Romilly see A.N., JJ 122, no. 278; for another forfeiture see no. 300.

19 Mirot, *Les insurrections urbaines*, pp. 198–9 n. 1; Chéruel, *Hist. de Rouen*, II. 450–1.

20 A.N., JJ 125, no. 244 (Caen); JJ 123, no. 85 (Laon); J. Calmette and E. Déprez, *La France et l'Angleterre en conflit* (vol. VII (1) of *Histoire générale*, published under the direction of G. Glotz) (Paris, 1937), p. 24 (Orléans).

21 Ménard, *Hist. de Nismes*, III. *preuves*, pp. 55–8 (Beaucaire and Nîmes); Calmette and Déprez, *La France et l'Angleterre*, p. 26 (Languedoc).

Apart from the urban disturbances and the unrest in the south there was no serious treasonable activity before 1385. There were several executions about which little is known,[22] two instances of treason by words,[23] and at least fifteen or so forfeitures,[24] but all these incidents were minor and isolated ones. The only case worth mentioning is that of Waleran de Luxembourg, count of Saint-Pol, who in the first months of Charles VI's rule was accused of treason; but this affair, too, though it involved a great personage, does not appear to have been very serious. A prisoner of the English since 1374, Saint-Pol had agreed on 11 July 1379 to deliver all his fortresses to them in exchange for his freedom. When Charles V learned of this accord he seized all of Saint-Pol's places and transferred them to Waleran's brother, Jean de Luxembourg, count of Ligny. Waleran then returned to England, where he married the half-sister of Richard II. When Charles V died Waleran came back to France 'ut staret in judicio coram rege', for, as he had no doubt anticipated, the youthful Charles VI was inclined to mercy. In spite of the accusations by the royal uncles, the king pardoned Saint-Pol in November 1380, just after his coronation.[25]

The last known attempt of Charles the Bad to disrupt the affairs of France came in 1385, when he recruited one Robert Wourdreton [Worthington?], an English varlet of a travelling minstrel, to try and poison not only the king of France, but also the royal dukes and other great French lords. Worthington was discovered, however, and was arrested at Paris in mid-March 1385 in possession of a rather large piece of arsenic. Navarre's plot was clearly taken very seriously, for among the commissioners appointed to try Worthington were the chancellor, the constable, the admiral, the chancellor of Dauphiné, two presidents of the Parlement of Paris, and the *prévôt* of Paris. At the Châtelet on 20 March Worthington confessed to his treason; he was most probably executed the following day.[26]

The reaction against Charles the Bad was swift and sure. On the

[22] A.N., JJ 122, no. 121 *bis*; no. 302; JJ 133, no. 95; B.N., ms. fr. 26018, no. 246.

[23] A.N., X2a 11, fols. 34r–v, 39r–v.

[24] In addition to the documents cited *supra*, see e.g., A.N., JJ 118, no. 304; JJ 120, nos. 64, 73; JJ 121, nos. 293, 309; JJ 124, nos. 26, 78; Guérin, *Arch. hist. Poitou*, XXI. 263–4; Boutruche, *La crise d'une société*, p.j. xvii; A.N., Coll. Lenoir 20, fol. 3.

[25] *Chron. de Jean II et Charles V*, II. 370–1 and nn.; *Chron. de Saint-Denys*, I. 36.

[26] *Recueil*, ed. Secousse, pp. 493–503; Anselme (*Hist. généalogique*, I. 285) gives a date of March 1386 for the execution but this must be incorrect.

same day on which the trial started, 20 March, Charles VI announced the sequestration of Navarre's French lands, which until then had been administered by Charles the Bad's sons.[27] It was most surely because of this affair that on 5 June 1385 Navarre wrote to Jean, count of Armagnac, asking him to act as an intermediary between himself and the king. He wanted a safe-conduct, he explained, so that he could appear before the king in order to defend himself against 'certain great and defamatory words'.[28] The measures that the king had taken had obviously struck home. It is not clear, however, why there was no prosecution of Navarre between the time of the Worthington affair and his death in January 1387, after which he was tried posthumously in the Parlement.[29] One can hazard a guess and suggest that the king and his uncles did not want anything to distract them from their preparations for the projected invasion of England, since the trial of Navarre would have required their presence in the Parlement then as it did in March 1387.

The dominant theme of the late 1380s and early 1390s is to be found in the conflicts between the constable Olivier IV de Clisson and Jean de Montfort; and between Clisson and the royal uncles, who resented his influence with the king.[30] In June 1387, partly to curry favour with the dukes of Berri, Bourbon and Burgundy, partly to strike a decisive blow at the Penthièvre party – of which Clisson was now the standard-bearer – and partly to appease the English, Montfort seized Clisson at Vannes when the latter was in Brittany preparing for an invasion of England. The attack on the constable, largely because it completely disrupted French military plans, brought down charges of treason on Montfort's head. He quickly realized that he had placed himself in an untenable position, for neither Berri nor Burgundy would swim against the tide of public opinion that was swelling in support of Clisson. Faced with the threat of invasion, Montfort came to an accommodation with the king in December 1387, and with his domestic enemies in July 1388.[31]

[27] A.N., J 619, no. 12; see also *Recueil*, ed. Secousse, p. 493.

[28] B.N., Coll. Doat 202, fols. 203r–205v.

[29] *Supra*, pp. 99–100.

[30] On this in general see Jones, *Ducal Brittany*, pp. 54, 86, 94–5, 105–13, 119–26; A. de La Borderie, *Histoire de Bretagne*, completed by B.-A. Pocquet du Haut-Jussé (6 vols., Rennes, 1896–1914), IV. 71–82.

[31] In addition to the references cited in the previous note, see J. J. N. Palmer, *England, France and Christendom 1377–99* (London, 1972), pp. 99–102; Juvenal des Ursins, *Hist. de Charles VI*, pp. 61–6.

But Clisson and Montfort had only papered over their differences. One cannot discount the possibilities that Montfort had prior knowledge of or indeed was the instigator of his cousin Pierre de Craon's attempted assassination of Clisson in Paris on the night of 13–14 June 1392.[32] Whatever the truth of the matter, Montfort certainly appeared to be an accomplice after the fact. Informed that Craon had taken refuge with the duke of Brittany, Charles VI decided to lead a punitive expedition against Montfort, in spite of the opposition of Berri and Burgundy. It was at Le Mans on 5 August, on his way to Brittany, that Charles VI suffered that fateful, first fit of insanity. The campaign was of course cancelled.[33] Berri and Burgundy seized the reins of government, but the outcry over the attack on Clisson was so great that they could not impede the prosecution of Craon, however much they might have secretly disapproved of it. On 26 August the *prévôt* of Paris declared him guilty of lese-majesty.[34]

With Charles VI *non compos mentis* the dukes of Berri and Burgundy resolved to destroy Clisson, who wisely had retired to Brittany. Under the guise of prosecuting Clisson for maladministration, the dukes had the Parlement begin proceedings against him. After the formalities of pronouncing several summonses, the Parlement convicted Clisson of treason, stripping him of his office of constable, fining him 100,000 silver marks, and banishing him from the kingdom.[35] Other royal officers – Jean Le Mercier, Bureau de la Rivière, Le Bègue de Villaines, Jean de Montagu – were also disgraced,[36] but they do not seem to have been prosecuted as traitors.

When Charles VI recovered his sanity in 1394 he annulled the sentence against Clisson, who, through the mediation of Burgundy, was reconciled with Montfort in 1395.[37] The fate of Craon, on the other hand, was not a happy one. Although the king granted him a pardon in March 1396, he could not obtain enregistration of it, and

[32] Immediately after the attack on Clisson three of the assailants were captured and beheaded at Paris. All of their property and that of the others was confiscated, while Craon's houses in Paris and his magnificent castle of Porchefontaine twelve miles away were razed to the ground (*Chron. de Saint-Denys*, II. 6).

[33] Jones, *Ducal Brittany*, pp. 128–9.

[34] A.N., K 54, no. 20, published in Juvenal des Ursins, *Hist. de Charles VI*, pp. 574–5. For the confiscation of Craon's property see A.N., J 359, no. 20; JJ 144, no. 17; M. Nordberg, *Les ducs et la royauté. Etude sur la rivalité des ducs d'Orléans et de Bourgogne 1392–1407* (Studia Historica Upsaliensia) (Stockholm, 1964), p. 13.

[35] Froissart, *Oeuvres*, ed. Kervyn de Lettenhove, XV. 56–62, 71–3.

[36] Perroy, *The Hundred Years War*, p. 195.

[37] La Borderie, *Hist. de Bretagne*, IV. 87; Jones, *Ducal Brittany*, p. 133.

the Parlement condemned him again in June 1399. Though he did live at court for some time under the personal protection of Charles VI, he nonetheless remained legally convicted in the eyes of the Parlement. None of his confiscated property, most of which went to Louis, duke of Orléans, was left in his possession when he died in 1409.[38]

The period of relative calm inaugurated by the truce of 1389 enabled the crown to prosecute with more vigour such disturbers of the peace as the *routier* Mérigot Marchès and Jean de Beaufort, lord of Limeuil.[39] The most important trials in the late fourteenth century, however, were those instituted against the last two counts of Périgord because of their private war against the town of Périgueux since 1382. The first summons for Archambaud V to appear in the Parlement was issued on 15 July 1391.[40] At the same time as the wheels of justice were turning, the king, when he was lucid, tried by gentle diplomacy to restore order to the region.[41] Charles VI's relapses, on the other hand, only encouraged Archambaud V to persist in his rebellion; and in 1394 the count began to communicate with Richard II to ensure for himself the control of his lands.[42]

Archambaud V's *démarche* was quite possibly precipitated by two related events: Richard II's grant of Guyenne in perpetuity to John of Gaunt in 1393; and a secret Anglo-French peace treaty whereby *inter alia* Périgord would have become part of the duchy of Guyenne.[43] If this was so, then Archambaud no doubt feared the same thing that provoked the Gascon revolt in 1394; being under the political sway of a powerful, hereditary duke whose ties to France would grow stronger over the years. If Périgord was to be absorbed in Guyenne, Archambaud no doubt preferred to have his political masters in England rather than on his own door-step.

The prosecution of Archambaud V remained in limbo for several

[38] On Craon's adventures after his attempted assassination of Clisson see H. Courteault, 'La fuite et les aventures de Pierre de Craon en Espagne, d'après des documents inédits des Archives d'Aragon (1392)', *B.E.C.*, LII (1891), 431–48. On his failure to have his pardon enregistered see the references cited *supra*, p. 136 n. 125. On the last years of his life see Bertrand de Broussillon, *La maison de Craon*, II. 230–1, 260.

[39] Keen, *Laws of War*, pp. 97–9; A.N., x2a 16, fols. 221v–223v.

[40] Dessalles, *Périgueux*, p. 112; and *preuves*, pp. 8–10. A warrant for his arrest was issued in September (B.N., Coll. Périgord 55, nos. 105, 109).

[41] B.N., Coll. Périgord 55, no. 120.

[42] Dessalles, *Périgueux*, pp. 193–4.

[43] On the grant of Guyenne to John of Gaunt, the secret treaty and the revolt of 1394, see Palmer, *England, France and Christendom*, pp. 146–63.

years until, on 3 February 1397, the Parlement convicted him *in absentia* and pronounced the confiscation of his county.[44] Jean d'Arpedonne, *sénéchal* of Périgord, and Guillaume Le Bouteiller, *sénéchal* of the Limousin, were then instructed to publish the *arrêt* at Auberoche and to seize Périgord for the crown.[45] When Archambaud V died in March 1397 his son Archambaud VI ignored the *arrêt*, installed himself as count and pursued his father's war against Périgueux, this time with the active help of English soldiers.[46] The prosecution of Archambaud VI was swifter than that against his father. But even before the Parlement convicted him of treason on 19 July 1399,[47] a royal army of 1200 men-at-arms and 300 *arbalétriers* under Boucicaut had conquered the county in 1398.[48] As for Archambaud, he managed to reach Bordeaux and eventually England. Thereafter he remained in obscurity until his death in 1430. His confiscated county of Périgord was granted on 23 January 1400 to Louis, duke of Orléans.[49]

Whereas arbitrary punishment had marked the unsettled first years of Charles VI's reign, there was a noticeable shift in the last fifteen years of the fourteenth century towards prosecution of treason in the Parlement and the Châtelet, that is to say, in the courts. This was surely due in large measure to the absence of a serious military threat from the English: without that sense of danger there was not as great an urgency to repress the crimes of treason.

II

The assassination in November 1407 of Louis, duke of Orléans, ushered in a period of civil strife that saw the reversal of the recent tendency to impartial prosecution in the courts. And much treason – treason, at least, as viewed by the party in power – went unprosecuted and unpunished altogether. John the Fearless, for example,

[44] A.N., x2a 13, fols. 171v–178r (published in Dessalles, *Périgueux, preuves*, pp. 8–30).

[45] B.N., Coll. Périgord 55, no. 142.

[46] G. Lavergne, 'La guerre d'Archambaud fils contre Périgueux (1397–1398)', *Bull. soc. hist. et arch. du Périgord*, LXVI (1939), 279–96.

[47] A.N., x2a 13, fols. 292r–297v (printed in Dessalles, *Périgueux, preuves*, pp. 77–93). The contention of the *Chron. de Saint-Denys* (II. 648), repeated by E. Jarry (*La vie politique de Louis de France, duc d'Orléans 1372–1407*) (Paris, 1889), pp. 218–19), that Archambaud was brought before the Parlement is incorrect.

[48] *Chron. de Saint-Denys*, II. 644ff.

[49] Dessalles, *Périgueux*, pp. 276–9; 306–8, 317; *preuves*, pp. 93–6; Vale, *English Gascony*, p. 44.

far from being prosecuted for his assassination of Louis d'Orléans, received a pardon in March 1408,[50] the same month in which Jean Petit delivered his *Justification*.

After the reconciliation at Chartres in March 1409, Burgundy regained his influential position at the French court and he quickly set about to eliminate those like Jean de Montagu, *grand maître de l'hôtel*, who were hindering him in the full exercise of power. On 7 October 1409 Montagu was arrested by Pierre des Essarts, *prévôt* of Paris, on charges of maladministration and embezzlement. Two days later commissioners from the Parlement were appointed to conduct his trial. When Montagu denied the charges, Burgundy's determination to have him convicted led to a new accusation: that Montagu had been an accomplice of Orléans in sorcery directed against the king and the dauphin. Tortured several times, he confessed, but later retracted his avowal and appealed to the Parlement on the grounds that it had been extracted from him by force. Unsure how to proceed, Pierre des Essarts turned to Burgundy and the other lords who had ordered Montagu's arrest. According to Monstrelet they convoked the Parlement, which then voided the appeal; but whether this is true or not, the appeal was indeed rejected. By order of John the Fearless Pierre des Essarts had Montagu executed for treason on 17 October.[51] Though a purge of other royal officials followed the execution of Montagu, it does not seem as if charges of treason were brought against any of them.[52]

Once firmly in power the duke of Burgundy used his influence to have Charles VI proscribe the Armagnacs on several occasions,[53] but this legal and propaganda offensive was rather feckless. Burgundy was more effective in interfering in the case of one of his own allies, Charles, duke of Lorraine. Charles and his father before him had been involved in a private war against the town of Neufchâtel, which, though in Lorraine – an imperial duchy – was juridically attached to the county of Champagne, and was under the express safeguard of

[50] R. Vaughan, *John the Fearless* (London, 1966), p. 72.

[51] L. Merlet, 'Biographie de Jean de Montagu', *B.E.C.*, 3rd series, III (1852), 274–7; Vaughan, *John the Fearless*, pp. 79–80. The *procès-verbal* of the execution is in A.N., J 369, no. 5. See nos. 6, 7, 7c, 8, 13; JJ 164, nos. 9, 74, 140 for the forfeiture, which was reversed in favour of his heirs in September 1412.

[52] Vaughan, *John the Fearless*, p. 80.

[53] E.g., *Chron. de Saint-Denys*, IV. 328ff, 460ff; Monstrelet, *Chronique*, II. 190–1; *Ordonnances*, IX. 635–7, 640–2.

the king. In 1406 Charles VI had sent Jean de Montagu and the admiral, Clignet de Brabant, to negotiate a settlement with him. In spite of his subsequent agreement to keep the peace, the duke later continued his outrages against the town of Neufchâtel. On 12 March 1410 the *bailli* of Chaumont had him summonsed to the Parlement. Charles de Lorraine defaulted on that and three other summonses before the Parlement convicted him of treason on 1 August 1412.[54]

The fact that his patron was John the Fearless emboldened the duke of Lorraine to take his case directly to the king. When the Parlement heard that Lorraine had come to Paris, it sent its advocates and proctors to the king to implore him either to punish the duke or to turn him over to the Parlement. There was a vivid exchange on this matter in the presence of the king between Burgundy and Juvenal des Ursins, king's advocate. Lorraine himself broke the tension, however, supplicated for a pardon and promised to serve the king loyally. Charles VI assented and the formal pardon was granted in February 1413.[55]

This was not the first nor the last time that the Parlement manifested an independent will in the prosecution of traitors. On other occasions, however, it was more successful. Pierre de Craon, it will be remembered, never succeeded in obtaining enregistration of his pardons in the 1390s. In the 1360s the Parlement had similarly rejected the validity of a pardon granted to Guillaume de Cardaillac, and judged against him.[56] But the Parlement could also prefer leniency where the king was inclined to harshness. In the 1340s, when Philippe VI was so viciously punishing his enemies, the court appeared to be quite willing to drop charges against their accomplices.[57] Although Charles VII did not have any problems with the Parlement in his prosecution of traitors, Louis XI did not always find the court so tractable.[58]

For the several years that John the Fearless was master of France, until the Cabochien episode at Paris in 1413, the evidence, apart from the case of Jean de Montagu, does not indicate that he abused his position to punish his enemies under the law of treason. Confiscations

[54] Luce, *Jeanne d'Arc, preuve*, xx, pp. 30–72.
[55] Juvenal des Ursins, *Hist. de Charles VI*, p. 247. For the pardon see A.N., JJ 167, no. 23.
[56] A.N., X2a 8, fols. 24v–29v; JJ 97, no. 192.
[57] Cazelles, *La société politique*, pp. 153–5.
[58] *Supra*, pp. 108, 110–12; *infra*, p. 228.

were few,[59] executions fewer. Besides Jean de Montagu, the only person worthy of note was Simon de Clermont, whose confiscated property was granted to Jean de Menou in January 1413.[60] It was enough, it seems, for Burgundy to rid himself of his enemies, like Montagu, within the government.

His influence in Paris weakened by the zeal of the Cabochiens, outmanoeuvred politically after the peace of Pontoise that he concluded at the end of July 1413, John the Fearless fled Paris on 23 August.[61] On 29 August Charles VI pardoned the inhabitants of Paris, except for Simon Caboche and over sixty of those most compromised with him, among them Hélion de Jacqueville, Jean de Troyes and Denis de Chaumont. Now under the influence of the Armagnacs, Charles VI by two separate letters of 5 and 12 September revoked the proscription of them that had been published on 3 October 1411.[62]

Meanwhile, executions, banishments and confiscations continued through 1414. At least 107 persons were banished between 12 December 1413 and 28 July 1414.[63] After the fall of Soissons in May 1414, Jean de Menou; his son Pierre; Raoul, lord of Le Plessis, and at least three others were executed as traitors along with Enguerran de Bournonville for having appeared in arms against Charles VI, who had led the royal forces in person.[64] But Guillaume de Crannes was called back from the dead, one could say. When Soissons was captured he was found hiding in the church of Notre-Dame. Taken to Laon, he was condemned to death and was actually handed over to the executioner. Fortunately for him, however, the count of Alençon made a successful intervention literally at the last minute, and the execution was delayed. Crannes then managed to obtain a pardon and partial restitution of his property.[65]

The rather desultory Armagnac campaign of 1414 ended in a

[59] For some of these see A.N., JJ 165, nos. 100, 102; J 369, nos. 16, 17; JJ 168, no. 86.

[60] B.N., ms. fr. 6539, fol. 43r.

[61] Vaughan, *John the Fearless*, pp. 100–1.

[62] *Ordonnances*, x. 163–5, 167–70, 173–7.

[63] Coville, *Les premiers Valois*, p. 351. See also *Chron. de Saint-Denys*, v. 171–83, 246–70; Monstrelet, *Chronique*, VI. 152ff; Vaughan, *John the Fearless*, p. 196.

[64] *Chron. de Saint-Denys*, v. 328; J.-L. Chalmel, *Histoire de Touraine* (4 vols., Paris and Tours, 1828), II. 171. Pierre de Menou's property was granted in June 1414 to the duke of Bourbon (A.N., JJ 167, no. 336); but on 9 September 1420 it was re-granted to the duke of Orléans, who was still a prisoner in England (A.N., K 59, no. 30). The widow and children of Raoul du Plessis were restored to his confiscated property on 26 July 1415 (A.N., JJ 168, no. 334).

[65] *Choix de pièces*, ed. Douët-d'Arcq, II. 116–17.

preliminary peace at Arras in September that was only sworn to definitely by John the Fearless in July 1415.[66] Although the peace included a general pardon, about 500 Cabochiens and other Burgundian partisans remained proscribed.[67] A month later, however, Burgundy managed to obtain a pardon for most of the 500, the exceptions being Simon Caboche, Hélion de Jacqueville, Jean de Troyes, Denis de Chaumont and about forty others whom the Armagnacs were determined not to forgive.[68] In August 1416 Hélion de Jacqueville was again proscribed for treason for breaking the peace, specifically for assaults on Paris, Orléans, Nesle, Beaumont and Chablis.[69]

Ever since his flight from Paris in 1413 John the Fearless had been seeking to recover the capital city and with it political mastery over France. For their several attempts to deliver Paris to him, a number of his adherents were executed as traitors. Although in March 1416 Nicolas d'Orgemont escaped a death sentence by virtue of his clerical status, Renaud Maillot, also a cleric, did not; and several others were executed as well.[70] There were more executions in November 1417 as a result of a similar attempt to deliver Paris which was again discovered by the *prévôt* of Paris, Tanneguy du Châtel, at the very last moment.[71]

Towards the end of 1417, in a move that was no doubt calculated to rally support against the English, who had invaded France that summer, Charles VI declared a general pardon for the Burgundians, and at the same time he established a commission to handle the expected requests for individual pardons. Towns that supported the Burgundian party were offered similar pardons provided that they return to royal obedience before 6 January 1418. All these measures, however, produced only the most negligible results.[72]

On the night of 28–9 May 1418 Paris finally fell to the Burgundians. In the weeks that followed hundreds of Armagnacs, including the constable Bernard, count of Armagnac, and the chancellor Henri

[66] Vaughan, *John the Fearless*, pp. 199–204.

[67] Monstrelet, *Chronique*, VI. 167.

[68] A.N., X1a 8603, fol. 1r.

[69] Monstrelet, *Chronique*, III. 152–60.

[70] *Journal d'un bourgeois*, pp. 71–2; *supra*, pp. 72–3. Some of Orgemont's property was sold to the benefit of the crown, and some was granted away (A.N., JJ 170, no. 43; Mirot, 'Le procès d'Orgemont', pp. 402–8). The property of the fugitive traitors was also confiscated (*Choix de pièces*, ed. Douët-d'Arcq, I. 393–4; Mirot, 'Le procès d'Orgemont', p. 383 n. 2).

[71] Vaughan, *John the Fearless*, pp. 220–1.

[72] Beaucourt, *Hist. de Charles VII*, II. 29.

de Marle, were savagely murdered.[73] Their properties and those of other Armagnacs were confiscated, and an air of legality was given to these political murders and forfeitures with the justification that the Armagnacs were 'crimineulx de lese-majeste'.[74] In all, the revenues from forfeitures between 1418–20 amounted to 13,477 *livres*.[75] The duke of Burgundy also had the king issue letters patent on 9 June 1418 annulling all condemnations and forfeitures since 1413 against his own supporters.[76] For his part the future Charles VII let it be known that he considered Burgundy's seizure of power as nothing but treason.[77]

After the assassination of John the Fearless on the bridge of Montereau in September 1419, Charles VI, now under Anglo-Burgundian influence, branded his own son a traitor.[78] Then by the treaty of Troyes (21 May 1420) he disinherited Charles in favour of Henry V and declared that all who opposed the treaty would be punished as traitors.[79] Summonsed to appeared at the Table de Marbre, the dauphin refused to comply and was legally banished in the first week of January 1421.[80]

Generally speaking, first because of Charles VI's youth and then because of his chronic incapacity, the prosecution of treason during his forty-two year reign reflected above all else the political *desiderata* of the magnates who for most of that time controlled the machinery of government. With rare exception, both sides in the French civil war not surprisingly preferred arbitrary means of prosecuting their enemies. But however much the prosecution of treason accompanied the political vicissitudes of the early fifteenth century – and one can argue that in fact there was not all that much – its effect on the political fortunes and behaviour of the contending parties seems to have been minimal, if not non-existent. The one exception was the fate of the dauphin Charles.

[73] Monstrelet, *Chronique*, III. 259ff.

[74] For some of the confiscations see A.N., JJ 170, no. 152 (grant to Marguerite d'Harcourt, dame d'Estouteville, of a house in Paris forfeited by Martin Gouge, bishop of Clermont); no. 185 (grant to Jean de Belloy, esquire, *pannetier* of the duke of Burgundy and son of the Robert de Belloy executed in 1416, of 200 *l.p.* in rent from the property of Perrin Pilot); JJ 171, no. 185 (grant to Pierre Leclerc of property worth 200 *l.p.* annually from the forfeiture of Henri de Marle); nos. 186–95, and *supra*, p. 127.

[75] B.-A. Pocquet du Haut-Jussé, 'Le compte de Pierre Gorremont, receveur-général du royaume (1418–1420)', *B.E.C.*, XCVIII (1937), 247–8.

[76] *Ordonnances*, X. 453–5.

[77] Beaucourt, *Hist. de Charles VII*, I. 94–5, 98–100.

[78] *Ordonnances*, XII. 273ff.

[79] *Chron. de Saint-Denys*, VI. 436ff.

[80] Chastellain, *Oeuvres*, I. 218–19; Beaucourt, *Hist. de Charles VII*, II. 48, 218.

Chapter 9

TREASON AND THE CROWN 1422–1461

Little is known about the prosecution of treason during the first fifteen years of Charles VII's reign. A few minor cases only came before the Parlement of Poitiers.[1] Struggling to consolidate his position against the Anglo-Burgundians, Charles VII appears to have tacitly approved of, even to have subtly encouraged, court intrigues.[2] But when political machinations went beyond certain limits, as was the case with Louis d'Amboise, *vicomte* of Thouars, André de Beaumont, baron of La Haye, and Antoine de Vivonne, Charles VII did not hesitate to act with the full authority at his disposal.

During the winter of 1429–30 Amboise, Beaumont and Vivonne plotted not only to seize Georges de La Trémoïlle, the most powerful lord at court, and to kill him if necessary, but also to take the king into custody. Amboise was one of Artur de Richemont's staunchest allies, and one does not have to look very hard to see the hand of the constable, then fallen from grace, in this conspiracy to take control of the government. Amboise, Beaumont and Vivonne were arrested in mid-November 1430, but it seems that not all the details of their treason were known to the king at that time. When Charles VII decided to take Amboise with him from Loches to Saint-Aignan, Amboise managed to send word to his intimates and advised them to ambush the royal party in order to free him. It was the king's discovery of this communication that sealed Amboise's fate.

He, Vivonne and Beaumont were subsequently imprisoned at Poitiers. Charles VII then commissioned the presidents and lay councillors of the Parlement there, along with several members of the *grand conseil*, to conduct their trial. On the advice of his commissioners Charles VII himself then condemned the three traitors to

[1] E.g., A.N., x2a 18, fols. 179r–184r, 308r–309r; x2a 20, fols. 46v–47r; x2a 21, fols. 171v, 179r; Lanhers, 'Deux affaires de trahison'.

[2] Beaucourt, *Hist. de Charles VII*, II. 132–8, 150–68; Vale, *Charles VII*, pp. 38–42.

death, with confiscation of their property. This procedure was a compromise between the king's personal act of justice and condemnation by a court, and was to be a regular feature of the prosecution of treason in the reigns of Charles VII and Louis XI.

On 31 May 1431 Beaumont and Vivonne were executed, but Charles VII commuted Amboise's death sentence to a term of imprisonment 'at our good pleasure'; and Amboise's children were spared the penalty of complete disinheritance that would ordinarily have ensued.[3] In not having Amboise executed Charles VII demonstrated for the first time the clemency towards members of the higher nobility that was a distinct characteristic of his rule. In September 1434, at the intercession of Yolande d'Aragon and Charles d'Anjou – La Trémoïlle had since fallen from power and the Angevins were now in the ascendant at court – Charles VII released Amboise from prison and restored to him all of his property except for the castellanies of Chaumont, Château-Gontier and Amboise.[4]

Charles VII again demonstrated a firmness of purpose, tempered by leniency towards the higher nobility, in meeting the challenge to his authority posed by the princes in the late 1430s and in the Praguerie.[5] Perhaps the most important immediate cause that precipitated the Praguerie, which broke out in February 1440, was the reforming, military *ordonnance* of 2 November 1439.[6] The leader of the revolt, as in the 1430s, was Charles, duke of Bourbon. Among those allied with him were Jean d'Alençon; the dauphin Louis; Jean, count of Dunois; the count of Vendôme; the marshal Lafayette; the two bastards of Bourbon; Antoine and Jacques de Chabannes; Georges de La Trémoïlle; Pierre d'Amboise; and Jean de La Roche.[7] But Charles VII's decisive action in arms brought the rebel princes to the negotiating table in May 1440 to sue for peace.[8]

Although it was within his powers to punish them, Charles

[3] A.N., J 366, nos. 1–3; Beaucourt, *Hist. de Charles VII*, II. 269–70. La Trémoïlle not surprisingly was the principal beneficiary of Amboise's confiscated property (Cosneau, *Le connétable de Richemont*, pp. 181–2).

[4] A.N., P 2298, fols. 689–95.

[5] A. Leguai, *Les ducs de Bourbon pendant la crise monarchique du XVe siècle* (Paris, 1962), pp. 155–8; Beaucourt, *Hist. de Charles VII*, III. 44–50; R. Favreau, 'La Praguerie en Poitou', *B.E.C.*, CXXIX (1971), 277–301.

[6] *Ordonnances*, XIII. 306–13; see Beaucourt's commentary (*Hist. de Charles VII*, III. 384–416).

[7] Escouchy, *Chronique*, III. 4.

[8] Leguai, *Les ducs*, pp. 166–72; Beaucourt, *Hist. de Charles VII*, III. 121–33; Vale, *Charles VII*, pp. 78–81.

declared, he was prepared to exercise his right of pardon, but they first had to disband their troops, 'for all warfare in the said kingdom belongs to the king and to his officers, and to no other . . . and whoever acts to the contrary should, according to the laws, forfeit his life and property'. Although the princes acquiesced in this demand and in the king's request that they hand over the dauphin, they refused to deliver to the king La Trémoïlle, Pierre d'Amboise, the lords of Montjean and Prie, La Roche and others who had broken their oaths to abide by the *ordonnance* of 2 November 1439.[9] But that did not prove to be a stumbling block: Bourbon and the other leaders of the Praguerie were pardoned on 15 July 1440,[10] and two weeks later Louis was invested with the Dauphiné.[11] Jean de La Roche and several others who had held Niort against the king were pardoned on 14 September.[12] La Trémoïlle, Amboise and Prie, however, were refused pardons and remained banished from the court;[13] but this political disgrace seems to have been their only punishment, for there is no evidence that judicial action was taken against them.

The Praguerie only delayed and did not derail Charles VII's plans to extirpate the *routier* bands. At the peace talks at Montferrand in 1440 the princes gave the king a free hand to deal with the anarchic soldiery.[14] Within a year, as Charles VII was about to embark on a campaign against the English, he profited from the occasion to move against the *routiers*. In Champagne in 1441 he had an example made of Alexandre, bastard of Bourbon, who had been involved in the revolts of his brother the duke in 1437 and 1440. Tried by summary court martial on the king's orders, he was tied in a sack and drowned in the Aube. That and twenty other executions got the message across, for leaders of *routier* bands in the region lost no time in making their submission.[15]

In January 1442, before the campaign to relieve the siege of Tartas, Charles VII turned his attention to Poitou and the south-west, where the *routiers* had been particularly ill-controlled. From Niort on 24

[9] Escouchy, *Chronique*, III. 18–27.

[10] A.N., P 1372/2, no. 2099.

[11] Vale, *Charles VII*, p. 81.

[12] Guérin, *Arch. hist. Poitou*, XXIX. 364. Jean Marsillac, a member of La Roche's company at Niort, received his pardon only in August 1445 (A.N., JJ 177, no. 182).

[13] Vale, *Charles VII*, p. 82.

[14] Escouchy, *Chronique*, III. 20–1, 25.

[15] Guillaume Gruel, *Chronique d'Arthur de Richemont*, ed. A. Le Vavasseur (S.H.F.) (Paris, 1890), p. 162; Beaucourt, *Hist. de Charles VII*, III. 170.

January Charles VII issued a proclamation that reiterated the principle of the *ordonnance* of 2 November 1439. 'No one', he declared, 'can or ought to assemble men and take to arms, nor maintain men-at-arms . . . without our authority . . . and if anyone does the contrary, he becomes a traitor . . . and an enemy of the public weal.' In spite of this and other prohibitions dating from 1439, Jacques de Pons, Maurice de Ploesquellec, Guiot de La Roche, Brimet de Saint-Cire, Pierre de Saint-Gelais, Jean Raymond, Jacques and Olivier Percival and Pierre Bechet remained in arms in Poitou and Saintonge, 'making war on our said lands and against our subjects . . . as enemies are accustomed to do', in complete disregard of previous pardons by the king and of promises by themselves. Charles VII now banished them and declared their property forfeit, but 'wishing always to prefer mercy to the rigours of law and justice', he would pardon any who came before him within ten days of this decree's publication.[16]

Fortunately there is enough evidence on this episode and its *dénouement* to illustrate Charles VII's method of dealing with such problems. Let us concentrate on Ploesquellec and Pons. Maurice de Ploesquellec, lord of Bourbe in Brittany,[17] came from a Breton family that had long served the crown and royal princes.[18] In 1424 his uncle, Henri de Ploesquellec, was given the strategically important lordship of Taillebourg in compensation for a loan of 14,000 *écus* that he had made to the king. Being childless, Henri later willed Taillebourg to Tanneguy du Châtel on condition that Tanneguy execute his testament and liquidate his debts and obligations.[19] In early 1441, when Henri died, Maurice illegally took possession of Taillebourg. Immediately, in April, Olivier de Coëtivy, to whom Tanneguy du Châtel was to transfer his rights formally in June, obtained royal letters ordering the *sénéchal* of Saintonge to recover Taillebourg. By July the land of Taillebourg had been seized, but Maurice still was holding out in the castle.[20]

16 A. Tuetey, *Les écorcheurs sous Charles VII* (2 vols., Montbéliard, 1874), I. 126–9. Guiot de La Roche, Pierre de Saint-Gelais and the Percivals had already been pardoned once for their participation in the Praguerie (A.N., JJ 178, no. 95).

17 C. Fouché, *Taillebourg et ses seigneurs* (Chef-Boutonne, 1911), p. 183.

18 B.N., pièces originales 2305, dossier 52077, nos. 2–19; Coll. Clairambault 86, nos. 158, 160–2; *idem* 87, nos. 1–3.

19 *Répertoire des titres du comté de Taillebourg*, ed. G. Tortat, *Arch. hist. de la Saintonge et de l'Aunis*, XXIX (1900), 11–14. Fouché, *Taillebourg*, p. 184.

20 A.N., X2a 24, fols. 73r, 84r, 98r; *Arch. hist. de la Saintonge et de l'Aunis*, XXIX. 15.

Maurice and his brothers Guillaume and Charles had taken part in the Praguerie in 1440; and afterwards they had continued their depredations on land and sea, from the Seine to the Garonne.[21] When Charles VII came to Poitou after the French victory at Pointoise in September 1441, he summoned Maurice to appear before him, but Ploesquellec refused to go. Charles VII then issued the declaration of 24 January 1442. Several days after that the king despatched a force of 200 men-at-arms to take possession of Taillebourg. After undergoing siege Maurice reached an agreement with Olivier de Coëtivy whereby he and his companions could leave Taillebourg alive and with their personal property. But the admiral Prégent de Coëtivy, who arrived at Taillebourg a few days after Olivier, vetoed the agreement, and the siege continued under the expert direction of Gaspard Bureau. The castle fell shortly thereafter and at least five of the defenders were hanged by the provost-marshal Tristan l'Hermite. For the moment nothing was done with Maurice de Ploesquellec and his brothers; later they were taken to La Rochelle and were kept in prison there.[22] On 24 September 1442 Charles formally granted Taillebourg to Prégent de Coëtivy.[23] That the king was later inclined to clemency towards the Ploesquellec brothers is borne out by the fact that he allowed them to have their case taken up in the Parlement of Paris in 1445. They never did obtain a reversal of the forfeiture, however, and only Maurice's refusal to admit to any wrong-doing prevented him from obtaining a pardon. Eventually in 1453 the Ploesquellec brothers were released and faded into obscurity.[24]

Much more is known about Jacques, lord of Pons, *vicomte* of Turenne. A son-in-law of Gaston de Foix and a nephew of Georges de La Trémoïlle, Pons was one of the most powerful lords in Saintonge,[25] and he was certainly the most important of those named in the declaration of 24 January 1442. On 8 March, after Charles VII arrived in Saintes to enforce that decree against him, Pons made his

[21] L. Delayant, 'Procès des frères Plusqualec', *Arch. hist. Poitou*, II (1873), 220.

[22] A.N., X2a 24, fols. 73v–74r, 83v–84r; Delayant, 'Procès des frères Plusqualec', pp. 223–49.

[23] A.N., P 2298, fols. 1213–23.

[24] A.N., X2a 23, fols. 250r–v, 358r–361v; X2a 24, fols. 73r–v, 83r–84v, 97r–98r, 100v–101r, 221 *bis* r–v, 223r–226v; X2a 25, fols. 4r, 5r, 6r–v, 93r–v, X2a 26, fols. 116v, 316v–317r.

[25] For this and other biographical details on Pons see B.N., pièces originales 2329, dossier 52504, fol. 282; dossiers bleus 534, nos. 13995, 13998–9; Coll. Clairambault 188, nos. 109, 130; Denis d'Aussy, 'La tour de Broue 1115–1789'. *Arch. hist. de la Saintonge et de l'Aunis*, XIX (1891), 344–5; C. Dangibeaud, 'La maison de Rabaine en Saintonge', *ibid.*, XIX (1891), 107–10; *Chartrier de Pons*, ed. G. Musset, *ibid.*, XXI (1892), 242–307.

submission to the king.[26] He took up arms against the English that summer,[27] but his loyalty to the crown did not last long. Charles VII's plans to capture Blaye in the autumn of 1442 came to nothing when Pons divulged the details to the English. Furthermore, Pons tried – unsuccessfully as it turned out – to seize the town of Pons from its royal garrison and deliver it to the English. On 29 June 1443, after the Parlement of Paris made an investigation, Charles VII instructed that he be summonsed to appear in court on penalty of being convicted *in absentia* of treason.[28]

Pons ignored the summons and captured from their royal garrisons the places of Plassac, Nieul-le-Virouil, Pérignac, Perguillac, Villars, Jemozac, Royan and others in the region of Pons. When royal forces under Jean Bureau, *maître d'artillerie*, laid siege to Royan, Pons realized that he could not resist the might of the crown, and he hastened to Tours again to make his submission to the king. This was approximately in the spring of 1444, when the French were negotiating a truce with the English. On condition that Pons surrender his places Charles VII pardoned him all his crimes except his treason, for which Pons was required to justify himself before either the *grand conseil* or the Parlement of Paris.[29]

Pons chose to appear before the *grand conseil*. But when he came to Paris for that purpose, the Parlement had him arrested and imprisoned in the Conciergerie because he had not had his pardon enregistered first. Fearing torture, fearing even more his enemies in the king's council, Pons managed to escape on 28 February 1445 and fled to Périgord, where he and his band of followers lived off the countryside.[30]

In early 1446, while the Parlement continued its proceedings against him, Pons wrote several conciliatory letters to the king and the *grand conseil*, imploring them for mercy.[31] Charles VII pardoned

[26] A.N., J 389, no. 10.
[27] Thomas Bekynton, *Official Correspondence*, ed. G. Williams (Rolls Series) (2 vols., London, 1872), II. 187; H. Ribadieu, *Histoire de la conquête de la Guyenne* (Bordeaux, 1866), p. 145.
[28] B.N., pièces originales 2328, dossier 52504, no. 13.
[29] A.N., JJ 177, no. 238; see also Denis d'Aussy, *La Saintonge pendant la guerre de Cent ans (1372–1453)* (La Rochelle, 1894), pp. 46–7.
[30] A.N., JJ 177, no. 238. For the evidence on his imprisonment see B.N., ms. fr. 20494, fols. 81r–93v; A.N., JJ 177, no. 189.
[31] B.N., ms. fr. 2811, fols. 20–2, printed with some errors in *Arch. hist. de la Saintonge et de l'Aunis*, XXX (1902), pp. 209–13.

him and over 100 of his men in April 1446, but again he excepted the 'principal case of the crime of lese-majesty'. This crime he evoked to the *grand conseil*, suspending the Parlement's prosecution of it.[32] But since Pons refused to appear even before the *grand conseil*, the king sent the case back to the Parlement in April 1448. On 28 June 1449, after nine defaults, the court convicted Pons of treason and banished him from the kingdom.[33]

Pons withdrew into Spain, where he remained in exile, but he made at least one appearance north of the border during Charles VII's lifetime: in 1454 he was reported to have attended the duke of Burgundy's Feast of the Pheasant.[34] In November 1461, shortly after Louis XI acceded to the throne, Pons obtained a pardon[35] and passed the last twelve years of his life in docile obscurity.

As for the others mentioned in the proclamation of 24 January 1442, Guiot de La Roche, Pierre de Saint-Gelais, the Percivals, Brimet de Saint-Cire, Jean Raymond *et alii* did not immediately make their peace with the king. They withdrew to Angoulême, and from that region they continued to pillage, murder and take ransoms. But when they learned from the examples of Maurice de Ploesquellec and Jacques de Pons that Charles VII was determined to suppress free-booting, they sought and were granted a pardon, which was confirmed in June 1446.[36]

After his adroit handling of the magnate coalitions of the late 1430s and early 1440s, and following on his successes against the *routiers* and the English in 1442, Charles VII turned his attention to that fractious southern lord, Jean IV, count of Armagnac. The king's *gravamina* against him were many. In general, Armagnac's claim to be 'count by the grace of God' certainly rankled with Charles VII. For at least fifteen years, without royal authority, he had coined money, 'even money similar in form to ours, and [which] was of lesser weight and more feeble alloy'. He negotiated truces in his lands with the English (another treasonable usurpation of royal authority), he impeded royal officers from exercising the king's rights in his lands, and he did nothing to stop his own men from desecrating the king's arms. For the previous twenty years Armagnac had employed

32 A.N., JJ 177, no. 238; the pardon was published at Saint-Jean-d'Angély on 19 and 20 August (K 68, no. 26).

33 A.N., X2a 26, fols. 41v–43v.

34 Escouchy, *Chronique*, II. 140, 166.

35 A.N., JJ 198, no. 513.

36 Guérin, *Arch. hist. Poitou*, XXIX. 364–79.

the services and tolerated the abuses of mercenary captains – men like André de Ribes and Amanieu de Madaillon – who were in the avowal of the English. Since early 1441 Armagnac had been involved in a private war against the town of Millau, and the king's proctor had accused him of treason for this. More seriously, in 1442 he was trying to arrange a marriage alliance with Henry VI, but this was perhaps not yet known to Charles VII. Last in his series of crimes was his illegal seizure of the county of Comminges and his refusal to allow his subjects to contribute to an *aide* for the war.[37] On any of these charges Charles VII had good reason to prosecute the count.

In December 1443, after the dauphin's successful campaign in Normandy, Charles VII sent him to subdue Armagnac. Louis took Jean IV into custody in February 1444.[38] During the count's captivity several of his men were permitted to plead on his behalf at Châlons before the king and royal council. One of the envoys complained that in spite of Armagnac's requests either that he be heard in his own defence, or at least 'that justice be done in his case', no response had been forthcoming. After Armagnac's envoy finished his argument in favour of the count, Jean Barbin, king's advocate in the Parlement, asked for and was granted leave to reply on another day. Within a week he presented the case for the crown. After summarizing what was said on Armagnac's behalf he described the count's crimes in detail, finishing with the request that the king let justice run its course.[39]

Armagnac's envoys, though given the chance to re-state their case for the count, were advised by 'several lords and others of great authority' to seek mercy from the king. They followed this advice, which was just as well, for Charles VII was intending to have Armagnac prosecuted in the Parlement of Paris.[40] Not only the envoys but also the king of Castille, the dukes of Savoy, Orléans, Bourbon and Alençon, and the counts of Maine, Richemont, Foix, Dunois, Vendôme and La Marche requested a pardon for Armagnac. On 26 August 1445 Charles VII enumerated for the count the conditions that had to be agreed to before a pardon would be granted.

[37] Escouchy, *Chronique*, III. 125–32; Bekynton, *Correspondence*, II. 181–4, 198ff; Artières, *Récits de la ville de Millau*, pp. 95–9; Samaran, *La maison d'Armagnac*, pp. 62, 79ff.

[38] Samaran, *La maison d'Armagnac*, pp. 90–2.

[39] For this paragraph and the first sentence of the following one, see Escouchy, *Chronique*, I. 61–5.

[40] *Ibid.*, III. 132–3.

Essentially, Armagnac had to swear to be loyal and not to impede royal officers from exercising the king's rights. He had to renounce his alliances with the English and abandon the title 'count by the grace of God'. And Charles VII would retain Lectoure, Séverac, Capdenac, Chaudesaigues, Gourdon, the county of Comminges, the four castellanies of Rouergue and all his other properties 'deça la rivière de Garonne'.

Although Armagnac accepted the conditions and received his pardon that same month,[41] he was still in prison in February 1446. In March, however, he was in Toulouse to have his pardon enregistered by the Parlement there. After this, reduced to impotence, he retired to his castle of Isle-Jourdain, where he remained until his death in 1450.[42]

In the later 1440s Charles VII had to be as much on his guard against court intrigues as against his greater vassals. In the summer of 1446 the dauphin Louis, anxious to gain for himself a larger measure of power, inspired a plot to put the king under tutelage. Richemont, Maine, Saint-Pol, René d'Anjou, Jean de Bueil and Antoine de Chabannes were counted on for support, since the plan seems also to have called for the removal of Pierre de Brézé from his position of influence. But Chabannes had second thoughts about the conspiracy and disclosed it to the king. Death sentences were meted out, but only to several archers of the king's Scots guard who had been suborned by the dauphin.[43] No formal action was taken against the dauphin's other fellow conspirators, who easily obtained pardons.[44]

In 1448 Charles VII again made an example of the most insignificant person in a court intrigue while showing indulgence to the person most responsible. Pierre de Brézé had concocted with Guillaume Mariette a subtle scheme of disinformation intended to exacerbate the already tense relationship between the king and the dauphin. Since Mariette was a *maître des requêtes* in the dauphin's household, Charles VII was presumably to be taken in by Mariette's 'revelations' of Louis's plans to seize power from him. In the event,

41 *Ibid.*, III. 116–39. Apparently there was a separate act in which Armagnac named twenty-five persons who were to be included in his pardon; see A.N., JJ 178, no. 220; JJ 179, no. 33.

42 Samaran, *La maison d'Armagnac*, pp. 97–9.

43 This was not the last time that the king's most trusted servants were involved in a plot against him; see *supra*, p. 30.

44 Jean de Bueil, *Le jouvencel*, ed. C. Favre and L. Lecestre (S.H.F.) (2 vols., Paris, 1887 and 1889), I. pp. cxxix–cxlvii; II. *p.j.* xvii; Vale, *Charles VII*, pp. 100–4.

if Charles VII was not entirely convinced, his suspicions about his son were certainly further aroused.

It was only by accident that this intrigue came to light. Mariette had been arrested by royal officers at Bourges in October 1447 on charges of counterfeiting the king's seal for purposes unrelated to the conspiracy. In February 1448, his treason as yet undiscovered, he escaped to the Dauphiné. In March, under torture by the dauphin's commissioners, he confessed to his crimes of counterfeiting and to his part in Brézé's ruse as well. Delivered immediately to the king's justice, he was beheaded and quartered at Tours.[45] At about that time the dauphin denounced Brézé, accusing him of 'moult de crimes et grans mallefices', as Mathieu d'Escouchy put it. Brézé appeared before the king and offered to stand trial in order to clear himself. His case came before the Parlement of Paris that year, but there is unfortunately no record of it. Whatever the outcome, Brézé was soon reconciled with the king, and was pardoned in the first months of 1449.[46]

From 1449 court intrigues receded into the background as efforts were focused on the expulsion of the English from France. The conquests of Normandy in 1449–50 and Guyenne in 1451 clearly illustrate Charles VII's inclination not to retard the process of pacification by employing vindictive measures.

The English hold on Normandy and Guyenne had been due in no small part to the support given them by the towns, or at least to the towns' acquiescence in English rule. After the successful French campaigns the civic leaders, fearing with reason that they might be punished for treason, supplicated for pardons and confirmations of their privileges. Charles VII readily granted such pardons to Rouen, Caen, Avranches, Bayeux, Verneuil, Domfront and several other towns in Normandy; and to Bordeaux, Bourg, Bayonne, Dax, Libourne, Saint-Macaire, Bergerac, Blaye and a few other places in Guyenne.[47]

[45] Mariette's *procès* is printed in Escouchy, *Chronique*, III. 264–341; Dr Vale skilfully untangles this complicated affair (Vale, *Charles VII*, pp. 106–11).

[46] Escouchy, *Chronique*, I. 135–6. The undated pardon is printed in *Recueil de pièces pour servir de suite à l'histoire de Louis XI*, ed. C. Duclos (Paris, 1746), pp. 74–82.

[47] For Normandy see *Ordonnances*, XIV. 59–66, 71–8, 91–8; A.N., JJ 180, no. 4; JJ 185, nos. 1, 90. For Gascony see *Ordonnances*, XIV. 109–11, 158–63, 176–7, 262–4, 270–5; A.N., JJ 181, no. 143; JJ 182, no. 13; JJ 185, nos. 125–6, 140. See also Allmand, 'The Aftermath of War', 347.

Individual pardons were not that numerous.[48] Several were given to parish priests in Normandy who feared prosecution for having remained in their prebends.[49] One can hardly doubt that in general there must have been some formal prosecutions and executions, but at least in the Archives Nationales no evidence for this has survived. There were indeed confiscations from former adherents of the English,[50] but it is difficult to estimate how numerous these forfeitures were.

If Charles VII was lenient towards the Gascons after the first conquest of Guyenne in 1451 – perhaps he had bowed to the argument that the Gascons were ancient enemies but not traitors, since they had never sworn an oath of allegiance to him[51] – he was certainly less so after the re-conquest in 1453. Even then, however, he did not indulge in large-scale retribution. Pardons were distributed – to Bertrand de Montferrand; to Charles de Chazau, lord of Lamothe-Saint-André; to Mondot de Lansac, captain of Cognac; to several merchants; to the town of Langoiran, for example.[52] But not all the pardons were complete amnesties. At Saint-Macaire Pierre Froment and his wife, Guillaume Raymond and his son, and Antoine Pasqual were excepted from the king's grace.[53] In October 1453 Bordeaux received a pardon but was fined 100,000 *écus*. The fine was rescinded in a confirmation of the pardon in April 1454, but one clause that remained in force decreed the banishment of twenty traitors most closely associated with the town.[54] Among the proscribed were Gaillard de Durfort, lord of Duras, Pierre de Montferrand and François de Montferrand.[55]

Pierre de Montferrand continued his intrigues just one year after his exile to England. Having obtained a safe-conduct he returned from London on the pretext of finishing some business, but he

48 For Normandy see e.g., A.N., JJ 179, no. 379; JJ 180, nos. 33, 61, 106, 117, 147, 155; JJ 185, no. 56. For Gascony see e.g., A.N., JJ 181, no. 153; JJ 186, no. 81.

49 E.g., A.N., JJ 179, no. 377; JJ 180, no. 1; see also Allmand, 'The Aftermath of War', p. 348.

50 E.g., A.N., PP 118, fols. 43–55; JJ 187, no. 84; Coll. Lenoir 25, fols. 99–100; *ibid.*, 75, fol. 57; Vale, *Charles VII*, pp. 120–1, 152–3.

51 Vale, *English Gascony*, p. 223.

52 A.N., JJ 182, no. 101 (Montferrand); no. 62 (Lansac); nos. 34–5 (merchants); no. 143 (Langoiran); Boutruche, *La crise d'une société*, *p.j.* XX (Chazau).

53 A.N., JJ 191, no. 7.

54 *Ordonnances*, XIV. 270–5.

55 *Recueil des privilèges accordés à la ville de Bordeaux par Charles VII et Louis XI*, ed. M. Gouron (Bordeaux, 1937), pp. 84–5; see A. Peyrègne, 'Les émigrés gascons en Angleterre 1453–1485', *Ann. du Midi*, LXVI (1954), 113–28.

secretly plotted with Jean Dalhayre, a jurist from Bordeaux, to capture Bayonne. The French had not been deceived, however, and Montferrand was arrested and taken to Poitiers, where he was tried by a commission that included the provost-marshal Tristan l'Hermite. In July 1454 he was beheaded and quartered, possibly by order of Charles VII himself; and his severed limbs were hanged in divers places.[56] Apart from the executions of André de Beaumont and Antoine de Vivonne in 1431, and that of the bastard of Bourbon in 1441, this was the only other known execution of a noble for treason in the reign of Charles VII.

Géraud d'Albret, lord of Puypardin, received Montferrand's confiscated property in February 1455.[57] Other forfeitures, some of them repetitions of grants made in 1451, followed the re-conquest of 1453. In spite of the pardon to Bertrand de Montferrand, his lordship of Lesparre was granted to Arnaud-Amanieu, lord of Orval. Antoine d'Aubusson received the property of the lord of Anglade, and Louis de Beaumont, *sénéchal* of Poitou, obtained La Brède from the lord of Lalande. Antoine de Chabannes acquired the lordship of Blanquefort from the confiscated property of Gaillard de Durfort, and Antoine du Lau was given the lordship of Duras.[58] There seems to have been little other re-distribution of forfeited property.

A number of those who had betrayed Charles VII by rallying to Talbot in 1452 waited many years before being pardoned. The count of Foix-Candale was released from prison in 1459, but the lord of Anglade had to wait until Louis XI became king to be freed from captivity. Louis d'Aspremont, *vicomte* of Orthe, was pardoned only in 1463, Gaillard de Durfort and his bastard brother, Bertrand, only in 1476. Some Gascons were never pardoned: Bertrand d'Agès, lord of Saint-Magne, was perhaps not the only one who died in prison.[59]

One means by which Charles VII financed the campaign of 1453 and lightened his debts from the previous ones was by confiscating, on charges of treason, the property of two of his principal financial

[56] Ribadieu, *Hist. de la conquête de la Guyenne*, pp. 379–80; Vale, 'The Last Years of English Gascony', *T.R.H.S.*, 5th series, XIX (1969), 130–1; Chartier, *Chronique*, III. 49–50.

[57] Beaucourt, *Hist. de Charles VII*, VI. 348.

[58] *Bordeaux de 1453 à 1715*, ed. R. Boutruche (vol. IV of *Histoire de Bordeaux*) (Bordeaux, 1966), p. 14.

[59] Boutruche, *La crise d'une société*, pp. 413 n. 9 and 414 (Foix-Candale); *La Gascogne*, no. 1410 (Aspremont); A.N., JJ 201, no. 89 (Bertrand de Durfort); X1a 8607, fol. 67r (Gaillard de Durfort). See also B.N., ms. fr. 6968, fols. 64v–68v.

officers: Jean Barillet, lord of Saincoins, *receveur-général des finances* and a member of the *grand conseil*; and Jacques Coeur. In 1450–1 Saincoins was tried by a commission on the grounds that 'he had ... badly employed the money from his receipt to such an extent that the king, in his great need, could not find the money to pay his soldiers ... for the war ... in Guyenne'. Convicted of treason, but spared the death penalty, Saincoins was fined 60,000 *écus d'or* and sentenced to imprisonment.[60] The simplicity and effectiveness of this procedure must surely have given the king thoughts about his *argentier*, Jacques Coeur, from whom he had borrowed 70,680 *l.t.* in the spring and summer of 1451 alone.[61]

Shortly before Jacques Coeur was arrested on 31 July 1451 the king ordered a preliminary investigation to be made concerning his activities. The results of this were presented to Charles VII and his *grand conseil* at Taillebourg, just as the king was about to embark on his conquest of Guyenne. On the advice of the council and other royal officers Charles VII instructed that Coeur be arrested and that his property be sequestered. Before this directive could be put into effect, Coeur himself appeared before the king and the council and requested that Charles VII 'luy tenir termes de raison et justice'.[62] May we not see in this last encounter between Charles VII and the man to whom he owed so much – literally and metaphorically – the reason why the trial lasted almost a full two years?

On one most important point the *arrêt* of 29 May 1453[63] and the *procès*[64] are silent. Only from the revision of the trial in 1462 do we learn that Jacques Coeur was arrested on just two charges: of 'conspiracy against the person of the king and of poisoning [Agnès Sorel, Charles VII's mistress, who had died in 1450]'.[65] What the conspiracy charge was we do not know, for nothing more was said of it. Perhaps Coeur was accused of having given the dauphin financial support in his intrigues against the king.

The original commission to try Jacques Coeur – on the two charges only – included Antoine de Chabannes, count of Dammartin; Jean Barbin, king's advocate in the Parlement of Paris; Elie de Tourrettes, lieutenant of the *sénéchal* of Saintonge; and two others.

60 Chartier, *Chronique*, II. 244–5; Beaucourt, *Hist. de Charles VII*, V. 88–91.
61 Vale, *Charles VII*, p. 129 for this sum; Guillot, *Jacques Coeur*, p. 27.
62 Clément, *Jacques Coeur*, *p.j.* xii. pp. 293–4.
63 *Ibid.*, *p.j.* xii. pp. 293–309.
64 B.N., ms. fr. 16541, fols. 313–1202.
65 A.N., X2a 32, fol. 81v.

Coeur was held incommunicado from the time of his arrest until 10 September, the date of his first interrogation;[66] but by then the number of commissioners had swollen to twenty.[67] Still, according to François Hallé, proctor for Coeur's sons in 1462, Jacques Coeur was to be acquitted 'if he was not found guilty of the charges concerning the person of the king and the poisons'.[68] Perhaps this is what Charles VII told Jacques Coeur at their last meeting in July 1451. If so, then it seems that only after no positive proof was adduced against Coeur on the two charges did the king empower the commission to enquire into his alleged financial malpractices and other crimes, which singly or taken together could be construed as being treasonable: selling military supplies to the Turks and otherwise doing commerce with them; coining money of weak alloy; peculation in Languedoc; illicitly exporting bullion; counterfeiting the king's seal; returning a Christian slave to the Turks.[69]

The first phase of Jacques Coeur's trial extended from September 1451 until June 1452, during which time the commissioners collected evidence against him.[70] On 14 June, after convoking the princes of the blood, the *grand conseil*, the commissioners and members of the Parlement – an unusual step in the trial of a commoner – Charles VII declared that the process was not yet in a state to be judged. A delay was granted so that the problem of Coeur's claim to clerical privilege could be resolved, and so that Coeur could present written evidence on his own behalf. He was not, however, allowed to produce witnesses.[71]

The second phase of the trial began in January 1453 with the naming of a new commission, even though the question of Coeur's clericature had yet to be decided. In March he was tortured; and under this duress he made a confession. On 2 May 1453 Charles VII examined the transcript of the trial, after he had again assembled his *grand conseil*, the princes of the blood, members of the Parlement and others, numbering in all some thirty or forty persons.[72] The claims of the church to have cognizance of the case were thoroughly brushed aside.[73] Then, having had 'great and mature deliberation on

66 A.N., x2a 32, fol. 81v.

67 Guillot, *Jacques Coeur*, pp. 30–1.

68 A.N., x2a 32, fol. 84v.

69 Clément, *Jacques Coeur*, *p.j.* xii, pp. 295–308.

70 B.N., ms. fr. 16541, fols. 325–451; Guillot, *Jacques Coeur*, p. 28.

71 Guillot, *Jacques Coeur*, p. 28.

72 *Ibid.*, pp. 28–54.

73 A.N., x2a 32, fols. 83v–84r.

this matter', the king approved the conviction of Jacques Coeur. At Lusignan on 29 May 1453 the chancellor Guillaume Jouvenel des Ursins pronounced the sentence against the former *argentier*. Although Coeur was convicted of treason, no mention was made of the conspiracy charge, and the king declined to judge on the charge of poisoning. Coeur was not in fact condemned to death, but his property was confiscated – it took Jean Dauvet until 1457 to liquidate it all[74] – and he was fined a total of 400,000 *écus*. Towards the end of December 1454 Jacques Coeur escaped from prison at Poitiers, arriving at the court of Pope Nicholas V by early March 1455. He was later named captain-general of a flotilla sent against the Turks, and he died on the island of Chios in November 1456.[75]

Neither Jean de Saincoins nor Jacques Coeur had posed any political threat to the king. They were simply royal financial officers whose wealth made them victims of the king's cupidity in his time of need. That they were corrupt, perhaps more so than their colleagues, was a convenient pretext and not the real cause of their downfall. Trial by commission, out of the public eye, was the best way to conduct the prosecution of their cases. But Charles VII preferred different procedures to impress upon unruly magnates, like Jean V d'Armagnac and Jean, duke of Alençon, both his political power and the legal authority of the crown.

Since succeeding his father as count of Armagnac in 1450 Jean V had renewed the exercise of regalian rights in spite of royal prohibitions. The count further angered the king by forcibly replacing Philippe de Lévis as archbishop of Auch with his own client, Jean de Lescun. Armagnac's relations with the king's rebellious son Louis were also suspect, but it was apparently the count's refusal to end his scandalous incestuous liaison with his sister that provoked Charles VII to take action against him. In May 1455 an army under Jean de Bourbon, count of Clermont, and Antoine de Chabannes invaded Armagnac's lands, capturing Rodez and Lectoure by June, and forcing Jean V to flee with his sister to Spain.[76]

Armagnac's exile did not, however, afford him judicial immunity, for Charles VII had the Parlement initiate proceedings against

[74] *Les affaires de Jacques Coeur.*
[75] A. Thomas, 'L'évasion et la mort de Jaques Cuer', *R.H.*, XCVIII (1908), 72–86.
[76] Samaran, *La maison d'Armagnac*, pp. 114–24. The account of the capture of Rodez on 9 June 1455 is contained in A.N., J 854, no. 6/3.

him. After defaulting on two summonses, Armagnac surprisingly appeared in court on 8 December 1457 and was interrogated immediately afterwards.[77] The count, who was granted the unusual privilege in a treason trial of having a counsel, put forward a claim of peerage. After it was rejected in December 1458 he asserted that he was a cleric and should be tried in an ecclesiastical court. This pretension, too, was rebuffed.[78] By the spring of 1459 his legal defences had been systematically stripped away; and the conviction of Jean, duke of Alençon, in October 1458 could not have inspired him with much confidence about his own fate. In November 1459 he escaped from Paris, fleeing to Flanders, and thence to Italy and Spain.[79] After several more defaults the Parlement convicted him of treason on 13 May 1460.[80]

Although Jean d'Alençon, who had been captured at Verneuil in 1424, had sworn to John, duke of Bedford, that 'I am unshakeable in my purpose never in all my life to take an oath against my rightful sovereign lord Charles, king of France',[81] he in fact became one of the leaders of the Praguerie, and, throughout the 1440s and early 1450s, was in treasonable communication with the English.[82] Alençon was not unaware that Charles VII suspected him,[83] but he nevertheless felt secure enough in 1455 to begin planning in detail with the English for an invasion of Normandy. Both Richard, duke of York, and Henry VI did indeed seem willing,[84] though for the moment the civil strife in England was absorbing their energies. Even so they must have made some kind of preparations, for in April 1456 rumours of an imminent invasion reached Charles VII.[85] At about that time, whatever the truth of those reports, one of Alençon's messengers, Pierre Fortin, disclosed incriminating details of the duke's treason to Louis d'Harcourt, archbishop of Narbonne, and to Guillaume Cousinot, *bailli* of Rouen.[86] Cousinot went immediately to Charles VII, who was then at Le Chastelier in Bourbonnais, and

77 A.N., x2a 29, fols. 107v–108r.
78 A.N., x2a 28, fols. 202r–205r, 233v; x2a 29, fol. 35r–v.
79 Samaran, *La maison d'Armagnac*, pp. 129, 133.
80 A.N., x2a 29, fols. 107v–118v (printed in Lancelot, *Mémoires concernant les pairs, preuves*, pp. 780–805).
81 Quoted in Lewis, *Later Medieval France*, p. 228.
82 Escouchy, *Chronique*, III. 2; Beaucourt, *Hist. de Charles VII*, VI. 41.
83 B.N., ms. fr. 18441, fols. 44r, 45v.
84 *Ibid.*, fols. 47r–v, 63r–65v, 111r–114r.
85 *Ibid.*, fol. 67r.
86 *Ibid.*, fols. 22v–25r.

was followed a while later by Pierre de Brézé after Fortin had made a second report. As soon as Brézé arrived with the corroborative report Charles VII assembled his council; it was decided to arrest Alençon without delay.[87] On 27 May 1456 Dunois took the duke into custody in Paris, where Alençon had gone to give his deposition in the rehabilitation of Jeanne d'Arc.[88]

Immediately after Charles VII was informed of Alençon's arrest he wrote to Pierre I, duke of Brittany – and no doubt to other magnates – to explain the circumstances and implicitly to seek his support.[89] The king also took measures to bury rumours that Philippe, duke of Burgundy, was implicated in this affair;[90] at least for the moment he did not wish to worsen his relations with Burgundy. Alençon meanwhile had been taken to Melun, but, claiming the privilege of peerage, refused to answer the questions put to him by his interrogators. After several days he was taken before the king at Nonnette in Bourbonnais, and was told that he would be put on trial. Charles VII then had the duke transferred to the prison in the castle of Aigues-Mortes, where Alençon remained until he was taken to Vendôme in August 1458.[91]

The impending trial of Alençon caused a minor crisis in Franco-Burgundian relations in the summer of 1458. In mid-April[92] Charles VII had sent a summons to the duke of Burgundy, requesting him to appear on 1 June at Montargis, where the trial was then scheduled to take place. Burgundy, however, felt that the king was acting 'more by malice than by necessity', since, by virtue of the treaty of Arras, he was exempt from all personal summonses during Charles's lifetime. Furthermore, the opening of the trial was so near at hand that 'it seemed as if [Charles VII] wanted to catch him out on the hop and make him hurry as one would do to a man of little weight'.[93] On 2 May[94] the duke sent Toison d'Or to notify the king that he would not attend the trial; if Charles VII still persisted, Toison d'Or was instructed to reply with the veiled threat that to 'honour' the king, Burgundy would come at the head of 40,000 troops. Although Charles VII accepted Burgundy's excuses and asked that he at least send a delegation, he also responded to the duke's threat by convoking

[87] Beaucourt, *Hist. de Charles VII*, VI. 60–1.
[88] Escouchy, *Chronique*, II. 320–1.
[89] B.N., n.a. fr. 6525, no. 4 (2 June 1456).
[90] Duclercq, *Mémoires*, II. 184.
[91] Beaucourt, *Hist. de Charles VII*, VI. 62–3.
[92] *Ibid.*, VI. 181–2.
[93] Chastellain, *Oeuvres*, III. 417–18.
[94] Beaucourt, *Hist. de Charles VII*, VI. 182 n. 2.

the *ban* and the *arrière-ban*. Rumours that Charles had intentions of putting the duke on trial for treason along with Alençon did not help matters at all, and the threat of war was a real one during the summer of 1458.[95]

The trial of Alençon and the juridical problems associated with it have already been discussed in chapter 4. Here, however, some general comments would be appropriate. The punctilious procedure was made possible because of the real political power and authority that Charles VII had acquired in growing measure since the early 1440s. No chicanery, subterfuge or tinkering with the legal machinery was necessary to achieve his ends. For after all, from the viewpoint of the crown and those who supported it, Alençon was a manifest traitor. After more than 100 years of almost continuous warfare against the English – recently concluded so successfully – there had evolved amongst influential Frenchmen enough of a national sentiment for them to look most uncharitably on Alençon's treasonous flirtations with the English; from the speech of Juvenal des Ursins on 8 October it is clear that many were in favour of the death penalty for the duke. There is no indication, however, that Charles VII himself really wanted to have Alençon executed. Indeed, the message of this most impressively managed trial – the confident, unyielding assertion of royal authority, without vindictiveness – would most assuredly have been vitiated by a death sentence. The prosecution of Jean V d'Armagnac struck much the same theme, though less forcefully.

[95] Chastellain, *Oeuvres*, III. 420–3.

Chapter 10

TREASON AND THE CROWN

1461–1494

Within months of ascending the throne in 1461 Louis XI pardoned Alençon, Armagnac[1] and Jacques de Pons,[2] prosecuted some of his Dauphinois subjects on charges of treason for their disloyalty to him when he was dauphin,[3] purged some of his father's officers and councillors,[4] and prosecuted at least one of them – Antoine de Chabannes, count of Dammartin – as a traitor. Louis XI's grudge against the count went back at least fifteen years to 1446: it was Chabannes who had betrayed to Charles VII his planned *coup d'état*, and it was Chabannes, furthermore, who in 1456 had led the royal army against him in the Dauphiné.

On 5 September 1461 Louis XI instructed his proctor-general to begin proceedings in the Parlement against Chabannes. After three defaults the count thought better of remaining in exile, gave himself up, and was imprisoned first in the Conciergerie, then in the Louvre. During his trial pressure was exerted on the Parlement by both Louis XI and Charles de Melun, *bailli* of Sens, to whom the king had promised Chabannes's property. Either unable or unwilling to thwart Louis XI, the court convicted Chabannes of treason on 20 August 1463.[5]

Louis XI's motive in this case had not been solely one of revenge. Surely the one reason why he had Chabannes tried in the Parlement

[1] A.N., JJ 198, no. 36; see also J 776, nos. 13–15; J 779, nos. 6–7 (pardon to Alençon dated 11 October; his acceptance of it dated 12 October; amplification dated 1462); these documents are published in Commynes, *Mémoires*, ed. Lenglet-Dufresnoy, II. 347–52. For the pardon to Armagnac and the reiteration of it, dated 11 and 21 October, see A.N., JJ 198, no. 1; X2a 30, fol. 92r.

[2] A.N., JJ 198, no. 513 (pardon dated 3 November). But in spite of the pardon Pons was still having difficulty as late as 1467 in obtaining the full restitution of his property (A.N., K 68, no. 2 *bis*; X1a 4808, fol. 16v; B.N., ms. fr. 25713, no. 38; n.a. fr. 2840, no. 11).

[3] *Supra*, pp. 49–50.

[4] Basin, *Hist. de Louis XI*, I. 38ff.

[5] H. de Chabannes, *Histoire de la maison de Chabannes* (4 vols., Dijon, 1892–9, and supplement, published in 1901), II. 73–82. The *arrêt* is printed in *Preuves de la maison de Chabannes*, II. no. 55. For other evidence on the trial see A.N., X2a 32, fols. 4v, 34v, 64r, 102v, 103r, 110v–111r, 130r, 212r–v, 216v–217r.

rather than by commission was to have himself publicly exonerated of the accusations levied against him when he was dauphin. For if Chabannes had truly been guilty, if Louis had truly been innocent of plotting against Charles VII in 1446, it is most unlikely that, as king, Louis XI would have commuted the death sentence to a term of imprisonment, as in fact he did.

Chabannes did not remain long in prison, for on 10 March 1465 he escaped from the Bastille and fled to Moulins to join the duke of Bourbon. Also in early March the king's brother, Charles de France, stole away to Brittany.[6] Chabannes, Bourbon, Charles de France and the other magnates who were to form the League of the Public Weal had now unmasked themselves. Louis XI's political response was not long in coming. On 16 March he sought to weaken the position of the magnates by offering a pardon to all who would abandon those 'seducteurs, traistres, rebelles'.[7] But if the lack of evidence in the chancery registers, where pardons were normally recorded, is any indication, that appeal was singularly unsuccessful.

The threat from the south was particularly strong. In May, in a letter to the *sénéchaux* of Toulouse, Carcassonne, Périgord, Rouergue and the Agenais, Louis XI instructed them to make it known that any followers of Armagnac, Bourbon or Albret would be considered traitors. Again he offered pardons to all who would leave the service of those lords, and again the lack of evidence suggests that there were few defections at that stage.[8] Charles d'Anjou, count of Maine, and Jean, duke of Alençon, were the only princes of the blood who remained loyal to the king, if only superficially. Louis XI had, in fact, resorted to bribery to keep Alençon's loyalty. On 24 April he had instructed Antoine Raguier, *trésorier de guerre*, to pay the duke 1500 *l.t.* 'to come presently with us and in our company'; and on 10 October Alençon received from Jean le Rabinel, *receveur des aides* in the duchy of Alençon, 3820 *l.t.* for the upkeep of his places.[9] But Maine, who had been in charge of negotiations with the Leaguers, secretly signed an agreement with them in September for which

[6] Jean Maupoint, *Journal parisien (1437–1469)*, ed. G. Fagniez (*Mém. soc. de l'hist. de Paris et de l'Ile de France*, IV (1878)), p. 51 for Chabannes's escape. Basin, *Hist. de Louis XI*, I. 160ff; Stein, *Charles de France*, p. 57.

[7] Commynes, *Mémoires*, ed. Lenglet-Dufresnoy, II. 434ff.

[8] B.N., Coll. Doat 221, fols. 242r–245r.

[9] B.N., ms. fr. 20496, fol. 16r; ms. fr. 20371, fol. 83r.

Louis XI later accused him of treason. Maine was then deprived of his *gens d'armes*, his pension and the government of Languedoc; and he remained in disgrace until 1468, at which time he was again allowed to receive his pension.[10]

As for the Leaguers, Louis could do little else but pardon them and grant them virtually everything that they asked for.[11] But if he was in no position to avenge himself on the magnates, he could at least exercise his wrath against some of the lesser figures who had betrayed him. Foremost among these was Pierre d'Amboise, lord of Chaumont, who, along with his son, Charles, and Jean Daillon, lord of Le Lude, had led the anti-royal party in Rouen.[12] Louis XI did try or at least wanted to prosecute him formally, but Amboise had fled the kingdom. The king then did what he could: he razed Amboise's castle of Chaumont and in May 1465 granted the lordship of Amboise together with some other properties to the duchess of Orléans.[13] In a general pardon published on 24 August 1466 Pierre and Charles d'Amboise and Jean Daillon alone were excepted from it.[14] Louis XI did pardon the Amboises eventually, in April 1467, but he restored to them only a portion of their property.[15] Jean Daillon soon afterwards returned to the service of the king.[16]

One royal officer who felt the king's wrath was Jacques de Canlers, comptroller of the *argenterie*. During the summer of 1465 he was imprisoned at Lyon on charges of having been in treasonous correspondence with the Leaguers. By 4 October Louis XI had seen written proof of Canlers's treason. In a letter sent to his commissioners on that day he emphasized how much 'we take this matter

10 *Documents historiques inédits*, ed. J.-J. Champollion-Figeac (C.D.I.) (4 vols., Paris, 1841–8), II. 384–5; G. Duboscq, 'Charles d'Anjou, premier comte du Maine (1414–1473)', *Positions des thèses soutenues à l'Ecole National des Chartes* (1933), 27–8; B.N., ms. fr. 6963, fol. 61r.

11 Commynes, *Mémoires*, ed. Lenglet-Dufresnoy, II. 512–17. Further pardons were given in the spring and summer of 1466 (*ibid.*, II. 600–4; B.N., Coll. Doat 221, fols. 265r–267r; A.N., JJ 202, no. 71). See Stein, *Charles de France*, *p.j.* xxii and xxxvi for pardons to Lisieux and the Cotentin, Mortain, Caen, Vire and Avranches; A.N., JJ 194, nos. 113, 116, 124 for pardons to Dieppe, Louviers and Caudebec; nos. 117, 118, 141 for pardons to Jeanne Crispin, countess of Maulevrier, Louis d'Harcourt, patriarch of Jerusalem, and Michel Basin, Thomas's brother.

12 Maupoint, *Journal*, p. 99.

13 A.N., P 2299, fols. 557r–558v; K 70, no. 36; Roye, *Chron. scan.*, I. 154.

14 A.N., JJ 194, no. 191.

15 A.N., X1a 8607, fol. 44r–v. In October 1472 Louis XI granted to Commynes the lordships of Talmont, Olonne, Curzon, La Chaume, Château-Gontier and several other properties in Poitou (X1a 8606, fols. 286r–288r). Earlier, in February 1472, Louis XI granted 2000 *l.t.* to Charles d'Amboise to help rebuild the castle of Chaumont (B.N., ms. fr. 20497, fols. 22r–23r).

16 Roye, *Chron. scan.*, I. 320 n. 5.

to heart... Therefore on your life, and as greatly as you desire us never to be discontented with you, take care that as soon as you have read this letter, and without waiting any further, you have him punished as he deserves... in such a manner that all others will have this as an example.'[17] No more is heard of Jacques de Canlers.

Antoine de Castelnau, lord of Le Lau, had been Louis XI's lieutenant-general in Forez and Lyonnais during the War of the Public Weal. He, too, apparently had had intelligence with the Leaguers, Burgundy in particular. In May 1466, after this became known, he was imprisoned for his treason.[18] Louis XI confiscated his property,[19] but even though Castelnau was at his mercy, the king does not seem to have proceeded further. Castelnau escaped from prison in early summer 1468,[20] and he was one of those whose presence at Péronne in October 1468 no doubt caused Louis XI some uneasy moments.[21] By early 1472, however, Castelnau had returned to the king's favour. He recovered his property on 27 February and was named governor of Roussillon shortly thereafter.[22]

Although Louis XI had been constrained in October 1465 to restore Antoine de Chabannes's property to him, he did not have the sentence of August 1463 reversed. Perhaps he let it stand as a subtle means of maintaining Chabannes's loyalty. By 1467, however, Chabannes had won the king's full favour: on 23 February he replaced his rival Charles de Melun as *grand maître*,[23] and he now felt that the time was ripe to press for a reversal of his conviction.

On 21 September 1467 Louis XI ordered the Parlement to review Chabannes's case.[24] Since the Parlement was clearly reluctant to do so, Louis XI had to renew his directive on 30 June 1468. Sending

[17] *Docs. hist. inédits*, ed. Champollion-Figeac, II. 380–3; *Lettres de Louis XI*, II. 364–6.

[18] Roye, *Chron. scan.*, I. 157; *Docs. hist. inédits*, ed. Champollion-Figeac, II. 209 n. I. Jean de Bos Redon, captain of Châtillon-sur-Indre, was paid 100 *l.t.* for the expenses of guarding du Lau (B.N., ms. fr. 20685, fol. 388).

[19] The king granted du Lau's lordship of Blanquefort in Médoc to Jean Aubin, lord of Malicorne, in April 1471 (A.N., XIa 8606, fols. 247v–248v).

[20] Several persons responsible for engineering his escape were executed; see Maupoint, *Journal*, p. 106; Roye, *Chron. scan.*, I. 207; *Lettres de Louis XI*, III. 281–3; A.N., J 950, nos. 5–6.

[21] Philippe de Commynes, *Mémoires*, ed. J. Calmette and G. Durville (Classiques de l'hist. de France au moyen âge) (3 vols., Paris, 1964–5), I. 127. Poncet de Rivière and Pierre d'Urfé were also present at Péronne. They were pardoned in August 1470 (Guérin, *Arch. hist. Poitou*, XXXVIII, 264–9).

[22] *Docs. hist. inédits*, ed. Champollion-Figeac, II. 209 n. 1; *Lettres de Louis XI*, V. 73 n. 3.

[23] *Preuves de la maison de Chabannes*, II. no. 71.

[24] Chabannes, *Hist. de la maison de Chabannes*, II. 119.

Jean Balue, cardinal of Angers, to the Parlement to ensure its compliance, Louis XI now instructed the court to annul the sentence, not just review it, 'because my conscience will never be at ease until his case is cleared up'. The verdict reversing the judgement of 1463 was handed down on 13 August 1468.[25] Thus, just as Louis XI had manipulated the Parlement in 1463 to have it condemn Chabannes, in 1468 he again interfered directly, but this time to have it do the opposite, to annul that very same sentence.

The return of Chabannes to royal favour augured the end of Charles de Melun, who had also incurred the enmity of the powerful cardinal of Angers.[26] On 2 July 1468 Louis XI appointed a commission headed by the provost-marshal, Tristan l'Hermite, to arrest Melun for his treason against 'our person, kingdom, lordship . . . crown, majesty and the public weal', and to try him at Château-Gaillard in Normandy.[27] On the following day the king notified the commission that the chancellor, Pierre de Morvilliers, would be advising them on the case. 'Be diligent in this matter,' the king added, 'and take care that there is no slip-up.'[28]

Melun's treason ostensibly dated back to the War of the Public Weal in 1465, when he was the king's lieutenant-general at Paris and in the Ile-de-France. Among the charges adduced to prove his collusion with the Leaguers were that he had prevented the marshal, Joachim Rouault, from making a sortie from Paris; that without the king's knowledge he had sent gifts and messages to some of the princes, and had received the same from them; that he had even met secretly with the Leaguers at Saint-Maur-des-Fossés and elsewhere; that he had left the Saint-Antoine gate open so that they could gain entry to Paris; that he knew of Maine's secret accord with the Leaguers.[29]

There had certainly been no suspicion of Melun in 1465,[30] but Melun himself admitted enough during his interrogation in 1468 – and without any physical constraint – to give substance to at least the second and third charges.[31] Still, the commissioners were willing to let him prove otherwise.[32] On 6 August and the days following,

[25] *Preuves de la maison de Chabannes*, II. nos. 81–3, 85.
[26] In addition to the references cited below, see Anchier, 'Charles de Melun', pp. 87, 106–10 for what follows.
[27] B.N., ms. fr. 2921, fols. 56r–58v.
[28] *Lettres de Louis XI*, III. 234–5.
[29] B.N., ms. fr. 2921, fols. 19r–28r.
[30] Maupoint, *Journal*, pp. 55–83; Roye, *Chron. scan.*, I. 40–120.
[31] B.N., ms. fr. 2921, fols. 49r–110r.
[32] *Ibid.*, fol. 112r.

all of them except for Tristan l'Hermite, who remained at Château-Gaillard, went to Evreux and other places in Normandy in search of the letters and papers that Melun said would exculpate him. On 16 August they consulted with the chancellor who, after having read the *procès*, suggested on the 17th that they should speak personally to the king.[33]

On 19 August the commissioners were granted an audience with Louis XI at Senlis. On 21 August, in a most unusual occurrence in a treason trial, the king testified through his notary-secretary, Baude Meurin, on the articles of the indictment. Never, he asserted, had he given Melun permission to speak to the Leaguers; and when Melun informed him that he had done so nonetheless, he had been greatly displeased.[34] Meanwhile, in the absence of the commissioners, and at the behest of Louis XI, who perhaps thought that the commissioners with whom he spoke were inclined to be lenient with Melun, Tristan l'Hermite put Melun to the torture. Having confessed to the satisfaction of Tristan l'Hermite, Melun was sentenced to death and decapitated between 9 and 10 a.m. on the morning of 22 August 1468.[35]

It has already been stated that Melun was ostensibly tried for his treason during the War of the Public Weal. The charges did indeed have a measure of truth in them, but if one posits that Louis XI prosecuted Melun solely on the basis of the indictment, one is hard put to explain why he waited until 1468 to do so, for the evidence on which the charges were founded was known to the king in 1465. It is more logical to look upon Melun as a victim of court intrigue, as a sacrificial lamb thrown by Louis XI to the wolves Antoine de Chabannes and Jean Balue.

Balue, who had risen so dramatically to a position of power, began to lose his influence after Louis XI's disastrous meeting with Charles the Bold at Péronne in 1468. As a consequence he turned to treasonable intrigue with the bishop of Verdun, the duke of Burgundy, the count of Armagnac and the duke of Nemours. Their primary aims were to convince Charles de France not to accept Guyenne in appanage instead of Champagne and Brie, and to revive the coalition of 1465. Louis XI acted quickly against the prelates

[33] *Ibid.*, fols. 112v–113v. [34] *Ibid.*, fols. 114r–116r.

[35] *Ibid.*, fols. 116v–122v; see also Roye, *Chron. scan.*, I. 209–10; Maupoint, *Journal*, p. 107.

when he discovered their plot in late April 1469, arresting them on the 23rd.[36] By taking Balue and Haraucourt into custody Louis XI dealt a severe blow to the opposition centred around Charles de France, indeed to Charles himself, who in the last days of April 1469 accepted Guyenne in appanage.[37] In May, in accordance with the terms of the settlement, Louis XI granted a full pardon to the adherents of his brother.[38] But the accord with Charles de France did not altogether pacify the south-west, for the count of Armagnac, the duke of Nemours and their partisans remained in rebellion. The king's main grievances against them, apart from their support of Charles de France, were that without royal authority they maintained men-at-arms whom they could not control and that in general they impeded the exercise of royal authority. Furthermore, certain people were said to have conspired to deliver Bordeaux to the English. On 26 January 1469 Louis XI empowered Antoine de Chabannes to punish as traitors those who would not make their submission to the crown.[39]

By late 1469, after decreeing some executions and forfeitures, Chabannes came to a peaceful settlement with the duke of Nemours, granting provisional pardons to him,[40] to some of his followers and to the town of Saint-Flour.[41] Bertrand, count of Boulogne and Auvergne, seems to have gone straight to the king for his pardon in November 1469.[42] Armagnac, however, was recalcitrant. When he did not respond to a summons for him to appear before the *grand conseil* on 28 September 1469, Louis XI issued a warrant for his arrest on 3 October.[43]

On 11 November, one day before Armagnac defaulted on another summons to appear in the Parlement, Louis XI ordered Antoine de Chabannes to seize Armagnac's lands. Four days later a delegation sent by Jean V was told by the *grand conseil* that the army would not be recalled unless Armagnac presented himself before the Parlement. By early December 1469 Chabannes had conquered Armagnac's lands. Though the count fled to Spain,[44] the Parlement continued its prosecution in order to make the confiscation legal. After allowing

[36] Forgeot, *Jean Balue*, pp. 70–80.
[37] Basin, *Hist. de Louis XI*, I. pp. 342ff.
[38] *Ordonnances*, XVII. 214–16.
[39] *Preuves de la maison de Chabannes*, II. no. 92.
[40] Anselme, *Hist. généalogique*, III. 398–407.
[41] *Preuves de la maison de Chabannes*, II. nos. 109–10. See also A.N., JJ 196, no. 74.
[42] A.N., K 70, no. 56.
[43] A.N., J 854, no. 612.
[44] Samaran, *La maison d'Armagnac*, pp. 173–6; *Lettres de Louis XI*, IV. 59–60.

Armagnac four more defaults,[45] it convicted him *in absentia* on 7 September 1470 of 'lese-majesty, sedition, treason, conspiracy, machination, perjury, [and] infidelity'.[46]

The hostilities between France and Burgundy in the winter of 1470–1 and in the summer and autumn of 1472 were not accompanied by much prosecution under the law of treason. Though it was clear that Louis XI considered Charles the Bold a traitor,[47] he did not initiate any formal process at law against him. Nor were there any other known trials. As for confiscations, the evidence is rather slender. After the battle of Buxy (14 March 1471), for example, the only person known to have forfeited his property was Charles de Montagu, lord of Couches, who had died in the fray.[48]

Although Louis XI could not proceed with a strong hand against the Burgundians because of the protection afforded them by the duke, the power of the crown was less easily resisted in the south, as Jean V d'Armagnac discovered in 1469. In 1471 it was the turn of Jean V's brother Charles, *vicomte* of Fezansaguet, who was arrested in January as much for his criminal excesses and exercise of regalian rights as for his support of his brother. After being tried and convicted in 1472, he was kept prisoner in the Bastille for the duration of Louis XI's reign. Worthy of note is the fact that apart from Jean Balue and the bishop of Verdun he was the only traitor who was kept in prison for such a long time. On 16 November 1483 Charles VIII had him released; and in April 1484, the king had Charles d'Armagnac's property, which was, however, to remain 'soubz la main du roi', restored to him.[49]

In November 1471 Jean V d'Armagnac was received back into his lands by Charles de France, now duke of Guyenne. When Charles

[45] A.N., X2a 35, fols. 214r–v (24 November 1469), 262r–v (19 February 1470), 300v (27 April 1470), 348v–349r (6 August 1470).

[46] A.N., X2a 36, fols. 308r–309v (printed in Commynes, *Mémoires*, ed. Lenglet-Dufresnoy, III. 141–5). For grants from his lands, see Samaran, *La maison d'Armagnac*, pp. 223–6.

[47] *Preuves de la maison de Chabannes*, II. no. 120; see also J. Rouvier, 'Louis XI et la déclaration d'Amboise du 3 décembre 1470', *R.H.D.F.E.*, 4th series, XLI (1963), 196–237.

[48] A.N., X1a 8606, fols. 256v–257r (grant of his lordship of La Ferté in Nivernais, and other properties, to Jean de Vienne, lord of Listenois; September 1471). For some other confiscations see A.N., JJ 211, no. 78 (grant to Jean de Norigier of some property forfeited by Louis d'Enghien; September 1472); J 808, no. 64 (grant to Joachim Rouault of all the property in Picardy, Ponthieu, Vimeu and Normandy forfeited by Jacques de Cambron, lord of Rambures; August 1472); B.N., ms. fr. 5909, fols. 115r–v, 132r, 155v; n.a. fr. 2611, fols. 1r–8r.

[49] C. Samaran, *Charles d'Armagnac, vicomte de Fezansaguet* (Auch, 1902), pp. 34ff; Samaran, *La maison d'Armagnac*, pp. 210–33, 236–60.

died in May 1472 Louis XI reclaimed the duchy and sent a force against Armagnac, who was preparing to defend himself in Lectoure.[50] To win over the former adherents of Charles de France Louis XI published a general pardon, with full restitution of forfeited property, on 14 June and again on 20 June.[51] Armagnac, fighting virtually alone, could not hold out against Beaujeu and capitulated on 17 June. The pressing problems faced by Louis XI in the north were no doubt the reason for the lenient terms agreed to by Beaujeu: Armagnac was given a safe-conduct and six months within which to present himself before the king.[52]

Taking advantage of Louis XI's preoccupation in the north, Armagnac captured Lectoure on 19 October 1472; Beaujeu was taken prisoner in the process. Furious, Louis XI gave orders on 31 October that all those who had helped Armagnac should be arrested, and their houses destroyed.[53] One who paid with his life for his treason was Jean Desmier, governor of Pardiac for the duke of Nemours.[54] Soon after the king concluded a truce with Burgundy, royal forces were sent in January 1473 to besiege Lectoure.[55] By early March Armagnac had agreed to surrender the town in exchange for a pardon. On 6 March, the day on which Lectoure was to be taken over by Ruffet de Balsac, Armagnac was killed, though the circumstances leave it unclear whether his death happened by royal order or simply as a result of frayed tempers.[56]

Of the traitors brought to trial, the most notable was Jean V's cousin Charles d'Albret, lord of Sainte-Bazeille, alias the Cadet d'Albret. Feigning loyalty to Louis XI, he had remained with Beaujeu at Lectoure after June 1472, all the while secretly helping Armagnac to capture the town. Even after 19 October 1472 he pretended that he had no allegiance to Armagnac, but clearly he had played his rôle

[50] Mandrot, 'Louis XI, Jean V d'Armagnac et le drame de Lectoure', *R.H.*, XXXVIII (1888), 261–3.

[51] Commynes, *Mémoires*, ed. Lenglet-Dufresnoy, III. 195–8.

[52] Mandrot, 'Louis XI, Jean V', pp. 262–5, and for the first sentence of the following paragraph, pp. 277–8. See also A.N., JJ 197, no. 216.

[53] Samaran, *La maison d'Armagnac*, *p.j.* xlvii.

[54] Roye, *Chron. scan.*, I. 288; B.N., ms. fr. 20428, fol. 68r.

[55] During the month of January pardons were issued to Guillaume de Soupplainville and Odet d'Aydie (A.N., JJ 197, nos. 240, 241).

[56] Mandrot, 'Louis XI, Jean V', pp. 284–98. For the distribution of the properties confiscated from Armagnac see Samaran, *La maison d'Armagnac*, pp. 223–5. See also A.N., JJ 197, nos. 312, 372, 420 for pardons to Jean de Fases, Jacques de Beaufort and Carbon de Montpezat.

badly: he was arrested immediately on 6 March when Lectoure was delivered to the royal forces.[57]

A royal commission was empowered to try Albret, and the interrogations commenced on 20 March 1473 at Lusignan in Poitou. On 21 March Albret's deposition, together with his plea for mercy, was sent to Louis XI. Further interrogations of Albret and other witnesses were made at Poitiers on 25 and 26 March.[58] On 7 April the chancellor Pierre d'Oriole, Guillaume Cousinot and several members of the Parlement of Paris – all of whom had recently been added to the original commission – condemned Albret to be executed, and the sentence was carried out on the same day. Albret's nephew, the covetous Alain d'Albret, obtained all of his property in a grant from Louis XI made in June 1473.[59]

While his soldiers were besieging Armagnac in Lectoure in the first months of 1473, Louis XI was putting an end to the intrigues of that tireless conspirator, Jean, duke of Alençon. Although the duke had remained loyal to the king during the War of the Public Weal, he had done so only for a price.[60] In December 1466 he had sworn fidelity to Louis XI,[61] but on 1 October 1467, in spite of that oath, he contracted an alliance with the duke of Burgundy against the king,[62] and on 11 October he delivered his place of Alençon to the Bretons.[63] On the orders of Louis XI the Parlement issued a warrant for his arrest on 5 December 1467,[64] but the prosecution of the duke was halted when Louis XI concluded an agreement with René d'Alençon, who had been left in command of Alençon.[65] Then, in the early 1470s, Jean d'Alençon plotted with the duke of Brittany and Edward IV for an invasion of France by the English. His treason discovered, he was arrested at Brezolles in Le Perche by Tristan l'Hermite in February 1473.[66]

[57] Mandrot, 'Louis XI, Jean V', pp. 267, 301.

[58] B.N., ms. fr. 18442, fols. 3r–91v; Mandrot, 'Louis XI, Jean V', pp. 266–82 for a summary of the depositions.

[59] Roye, *Chron. scan.*, I. 294–5; Mandrot 'Louis XI, Jean V', p. 303. For the grant to Alain d'Albret see *Archives historiques de la Gironde*, VI (1864), 193–5.

[60] *Supra*, p. 214.

[61] B.N., ms. fr. 15538, fol. 9r.

[62] B.N., ms. fr. 5041, fol. 186r.

[63] Roye, *Chron. scan.*, I. 187 n. 1; Maupoint, *Journal*, p. 105.

[64] A.N., x2a 36, fol. 56r–v.

[65] Roye, *Chron. scan.*, I. 198. The texts of the agreement are to be found in *Ordonnances*, XVII. 53–4, 58–66; B.N., ms. fr. 20430, fol. 12r.

[66] Roye, *Chron. scan.*, I. 290; Anselme, *Hist. généalogique*, III. 274ff. Louis XI had also ordered the arrest of several of his accomplices (*Lettres de Louis XI*, V. 106–8).

After being interrogated at the castle of Rochecorbon near Tours by Pierre d'Oriole, Jean de Dunois, Guillaume Cousinot, Jean Le Boulanger, first president in the Parlement, and other members of the Parlement and the *grand conseil*, Alençon was transferred in June to the Louvre, where more interrogations took place. On 4 January Louis XI, having consulted the princes of the blood and the *grand conseil*, gave the Parlement jurisdiction in the case. The Parlement, however, was not to be *garnie de pairs*, for Alençon had forfeited his privileges as a peer; indeed, a trial in the Parlement was not necessary at all, and Louis XI would no doubt have preferred to have the commission that conducted the interrogations finish the prosecution. Yet although he bowed to the wishes and sensibilities of the princes and his other advisers, he did, nevertheless, second the commissioners to the case, ostensibly because of their knowledge of the details,[67] but more likely as an instrument of pressure on the court.

Alençon appeared in court several times, but always without a lawyer. Interrogated on each occasion, he was also confronted with witnesses, accomplices and evidence written in his own hand, in the face of which he could not help but confess to his treason. The *dictum* of the condemnation was pronounced on 2 July 1474, and the *arrêt* was read by the chancellor, Pierre d'Oriole, on the 18th. On neither occasion was Alençon present.[68] As in 1458 he was spared the death penalty, but remained a prisoner until his death in 1476 at the age of seventy-two.[69]

The treasons of Balue, Armagnac, Albret and Alençon in the late 1460s and early 1470s hardened even more Louis XI's policy on prosecuting treason. On 31 March 1474, for example, the Burgundian agent, Jean Hardi, suffered exemplary punishment after being tried by a commission and convicted by the Parlement of having attempted to poison the king.[70] Also in the spring of 1474 a royal

[67] Anselme, *Hist. généalogique*, III. 274.

[68] The *arrêt*, from which most of the information on the trial is taken, is printed in Anselme, *Hist. généalogique*, III. 274–9 from A.N., X2a 40, fols. 28r–31v. See also B.N., ms. fr. 5908, fols. 142r, 144r–v. The trial cost the crown 1223 *l.* 11 *s.t.* (B.N., ms. fr. 5908, fol. 145r). For two donations from his confiscated property see A.N., JJ 195, no. 1311 (grant to Pierre de Saint-Aubin, lord of Préaux, of the lands of Saint-Silvain and Le Tuit); and *supra*, p. 137.

[69] Roye, *Chron. scan.*, II. 4.

[70] A.N., Z1h 16, fols. 128r, 141r, 143r; B.N., ms. fr. 5908, fols. 142v–143r; Jean de Roye, *Chron. scan.*, I. 303–9. For the execution see *supra*, pp. 117–18. A Jean Nivet and his wife were accused of complicity but were acquitted (A.N., X2a 40, fol. 140v). Poncet de Rivière, Ythier Marchand and one Alexandre Larget were also implicated, and warrants for their

commission led by Ymbert de Batarnay, lord of Le Bouchage, and Pierre de Rohan, lord of Gié, repressed most severely, at Louis XI's direction, a tax revolt at Bourges that the king perhaps thought might spark a general uprising.[71] But it was the way in which Louis XI reacted to the great conspiracy of the mid-1470s that set the stamp on his policy towards treason and that differed so markedly from his humiliating political surrender to the demands of the princes in 1465.

Louis de Luxembourg, count of Saint-Pol, constable of France,[72] was the driving force of this conspiracy of 1474–5, the aims of which were nothing less than the deposition, possibly the murder, of Louis XI, and the division of France among the dukes of Burgundy, Bourbon, Brittany and Nemours, the count of Maine, Edward IV and Saint-Pol himself.[73] But Burgundy's honour and stubbornness would not let him leave Neuss until it was too late for concerted action with the other conspirators; Nemours would not act without Bourbon; while Bourbon, whose nerve failed him, went over to Louis XI in May 1475.[74] Saint-Pol's own hesitations[75] were to prove fatal to him.

Edward IV, having concluded the treaty of Picquigny with Louis XI on 29 August 1475, turned over to the king written evidence of Saint-Pol's treason.[76] And when Burgundy and Louis XI agreed to the nine-year truce of Soleuvre on 13 September, he and the king drew up a separate accord that sealed the constable's fate: if the duke apprehended Saint-Pol he would punish him within eight days 'as one ought to do with traitors', or would hand him over to the king within the four days following; for his part Louis XI granted to Burgundy Saint-Pol's places of Ham, Bohain and Beaurevoir, together with his moveables and all other property that he held from

arrest were issued on 4 May (fol. 147r–v). They were later banished and their property confiscated. Poncet de Rivière was pardoned in November 1475 (B.N., ms. fr. 10187, fol. 94r) and again on 31 October 1477 (A.N., K 72, no. 10 *bis*).

[71] Full references to this revolt are given *supra*, p. 50 n. 98.

[72] A biography of Louis de Luxembourg is a *desideratum*. The thesis of C. Cagé ('Louis de Luxembourg, comte de Saint-Pol, connétable de France (1418–1475)'), submitted to the Ecole National des Chartes in 1885, is not available in that institution's library. There remains only a summary of it in the *Positions des thèses* (1885), 29–41.

[73] B.N., ms. fr. 3869, fols. 22v–25v.

[74] R. Vaughan, *Charles the Bold* (London, 1973), pp. 328–51; Mandrot 'Jacques d'Armagnac', *R.H.*, XLIV (1890), 267; H. de Surirey de Saint-Rémy, *Jean II de Bourbon, duc de Bourbonnais et d'Auvergne* (Paris, 1944), pp. 160–9.

[75] Commynes, *Mémoires*, ed. Calmette, II. 33ff.

[76] *Ibid.*, II. 47, 75; Roye, *Chron. scan.*, I. 346–7; Molinet, *Chroniques*, I. 110–11, 130–1.

the duke.[77] Contrary to what Commynes has suggested, the grant did not include Saint-Quentin, which was seized by a royal force on 14 September.[78]

In the first days of September, before the truce of Soleuvre, Saint-Pol had gone to Le Quesnoy, Binche and finally to Mons in Hainault, hoping somehow to regain the favour of the duke. To this end he no doubt hoped to enlist the support of his friend Antoine Rolin, sire d'Aimeries and *grand bailli* of Hainault. But by order of Charles the Bold and with the consent of Rolin, Saint-Pol was placed under house arrest in late September.[79] Though still able to receive visits from his intimates, Saint-Pol was understandably becoming increasingly desperate, speaking morosely of a 'prognostication of his birth that indicated that he was to die a dishonourable death'.[80]

Throughout September, October and early November, Charles the Bold neither prosecuted Saint-Pol nor delivered him to royal justice, for he intended to exact one further concession from the king: a free hand in his campaign against René of Lorraine. Eager to have Saint-Pol prosecuted, Louis XI acquiesced on 12 November.[81] On 14 November Saint-Pol made a final plea to the duke, but Burgundy ignored it.[82] On 18 November, following ducal orders, Philippe de Croy, count of Chimay, informed the *échevins* of Mons that Saint-Pol was to be delivered to the king's officers. He and Antoine Rolin escorted Saint-Pol under heavy guard to Valenciennes on the following day, and then, on the 20th, to Péronne, where the admiral Louis de Bourbon, Jean Blosset, lord of Saint-Pierre, Ymbert de Batarnay and others took custody of him for the king.[83] When news of the arrest reached Paris it was said that 'there had been a war in Paradise and that Saint-Pierre had captured Saint-Pol'.[84] Even Louis XI was said to have exercised his formidable wit on the occasion, reportedly jesting that the duke of Burgundy 'had done with the constable what one does with the fox: like a clever man he

[77] Commynes, *Mémoires*, ed. Lenglet-Dufresnoy, III. 422–4.
[78] Commynes, *Mémoires*, ed. Calmette, II. 83–5; Molinet, *Chroniques*, I. 131.
[79] 'Documents relatifs à l'arrestation de Louis de Luxembourg à Mons en 1475', ed. L. Devillers, *Bull. comm. roy. d'hist.*, 4th series, XVII (1890), 304–10.
[80] Bibl. Ste-Geneviève, ms. 2000, fol. 236v.
[81] Commynes, *Mémoires*, ed. Lenglet-Dufresnoy, III. 443–4.
[82] Roye, *Chron. scan.*, II. 347–9.
[83] Poncelet, 'L'exécution de Louis de Luxembourg', pp. 181–2.
[84] Roye, *Chron. scan.*, II. 350.

had kept the pelt while he [the king] had only the carcass which was hardly worth anything'.[85]

During the time of Saint-Pol's detention at Mons others involved in the conspiracy were being prosecuted by royal justice. Charles d'Anjou, count of Maine, whom Louis XI had so unnerved over the years that 'he did not know on which foot to dance', received a pardon in October after disclosing full details about his own rôle.[86] Pierre d'Urfé, François II's intermediary between himself and Edward IV, and Poncet de Rivière, who played the same rôle *vis-à-vis* the count of Maine, were both pardoned on 5 November following the truce concluded on 29 September by Louis XI and the duke of Brittany.[87] But Renaud de Velourt, captain of Maine's archers, who had been the count's chief contact with Saint-Pol and Nemours, met a different fate. Tried by a commission that included the chancellor d'Oriole and Philippe de Commynes, and condemned formally by the Parlement, he was beheaded and quartered on 20 November.[88]

Arriving in Paris on 27 November, Saint-Pol's escort delivered him at the Bastille to d'Oriole; Jean Le Boulanger, first president in the Parlement; Charles de Gaucourt, king's lieutenant-general in Paris and the Ile-de-France; Philippe Luillier, captain of the Bastille; and several others. The admiral then told the chancellor that 'by express command and ordinance of the king', Saint-Pol was to be tried by the Parlement.[89] An incomplete minute of a royal letter empowering the Parlement to prosecute the constable and instructing it to call upon Saint-Pierre, Gaucourt and Luillier for assistance can probably be dated to that same 27 November.[90]

Saint-Pol was not actually tried in the Parlement itself but rather by a commission of the court, together with the king's appointees. On 28 November the commission, led by the chancellor, went to the Bastille to interrogate Saint-Pol, who was examined on that day and

85 Molinet, *Chroniques*, I. 132.

86 A.N., JJ 204, no. 65; copy in d'Oriole's register (B.N., ms. fr. 10187, fols. 68v–71r); B.N., ms. fr. 3869, fols. 8v–10v.

87 B.N., ms. fr. 10187, fols. 14r, 93r–95v; B.-A. Pocquet du Haut-Jussé, *François II, duc de Bretagne, et l'Angleterre (1458–1488)* (Paris, 1929), p. 197.

88 B.N., ms. fr. 5908, fol. 146v; ms. fr. 18442, fols. 130r–141v; n.a. fr. 1001, fols. 116r–121v; Roye, *Chron. scan.*, I. 348–9.

89 B.N., ms. fr. 3869, fol. 3r.

90 B.N., ms. fr. 10238, fols. 1r–3r.

again on 4 December.[91] On 11 December a plenary session of the Parlement decided that Saint-Pol's testimony thus far would be read back to him, so that he could confirm it on oath. This done, the interrogation continued on 12 December. On 13 and 14 December the *procès* was read in open court. On 15 December, after the withdrawal of the *présidents des enquêtes* and the clerical councillors to the *chambre des enquêtes*, the Parlement and the commissioners considered the case. Judgement was deferred, however, until Saint-Pol could be interrogated one more time. That same day he was confronted with a most damning piece of evidence: the letter, affixed with his seal, in which he promised without reservation to serve the duke of Burgundy.[92]

On 16 December the full Parlement pronounced its *dictum* condemning Saint-Pol to death for treason, but the court spared him the ignominy of being quartered, stipulating execution by decapitation only.[93] On the morning of Tuesday 19 December Robert d'Estouteville, *prévôt* of Paris, and Jean Blosset, lord of Saint-Pierre, escorted the constable from the Bastille to the Parlement. There in the *tournelle criminelle*, behind closed doors, the chancellor removed from Saint-Pol's neck the collar of the Order of Saint-Michel; received symbolically the constable's sword, of which Saint-Pol had long ago been deprived; and pronounced the *arrêt* in his presence. Saint-Pol was then taken to the chapel of the Conciergerie to contemplate on his soul. Later that morning d'Oriole read out the *arrêt* in a public session of the Parlement.[94] At approximately three o'clock that afternoon Saint-Pol was decapitated in the Place de Grève. Jean Cousin, the executioner, struck so hard that '[Saint-Pol's] body hit the ground before his head'.[95]

The only other major conspirator to be executed was Jacques d'Armagnac, duke of Nemours, who was gravely compromised by

[91] B.N., ms. fr. 3869, fols. 3v–30v. There is no evidence to substantiate Molinet's assertion (*Chroniques*, I. 132) that Saint-Pol claimed privilege of peerage.

[92] B.N., ms. fr. 3869, fols. 30v–37r.

[93] *Ibid.*, fols. 37r–38r (printed in Roye, *Chron. scan.*, II. 351–2).

[94] Périnelle, 'Un texte officiel sur l'exécution du connetable de Saint-Pol', pp. 428–32; Roye, *Chron. scan.*, I. 355–8.

[95] Roye, *Chron. scan.*, I. 358–61; Poncelet, 'L'exécution de Louis de Luxembourg', pp. 188–94. Saint-Pol's execution was occasion for much versifying; see Roye, *Chron. scan.*, I. 366; Commynes, *Mémoires*, ed. Lenglet-Dufresnoy, III. 458–9; B.N., ms. fr. 1707, fols. 43v–44r; Molinet, *Les faictz et dictz* (Paris, 1537), fol. 212v.

the information that came out in the trial of Saint-Pol and its aftermath. Nemours was arrested at Carlat in March 1476 and underwent preliminary interrogation by June at the latest,[96] though Louis XI did not appoint a commission to try him until 22 September.[97] One of the commissioners, Jean Blosset, wrote immediately to the king for precise instructions. 'My lord of Saint-Pierre', Louis XI replied on 1 October,

> it seems to me that you have to do only one thing, and that is to find out what guarantee the duke of Nemours gave to the constable to join with him in order to make the duke of Burgundy regent, to have me killed, to take custody of the dauphin, and to seize the authority and government of the kingdom.[98]

Louis XI had no scruples about voicing his suspicions of his chancellor, Pierre d'Oriole, 'who wanted the Parlement to have cognizance of the trial of the duke of Nemours in order to find a way to have him escape'. Indeed, Louis XI even suspected that d'Oriole and Antoine de Chabannes might have been involved in the conspiracy, and that Saint-Pol had been tried so quickly for fear that he might implicate them. But this suspicion must have been a whimsical one, for both d'Oriole and Chabannes remained in the king's good graces.

The course of Nemours's trial and his claims to benefit of clergy and to the privilege of peerage have already been discussed.[99] It is, however, worth emphasizing again how closely involved Louis XI was in the trial, how he manipulated it. For the sake of appearances, and in spite of his reservations, he allowed the Parlement to pass judgement, but he made sure that his commissioners controlled the prosecution itself. We know, too, that he was in constant communication with them. It can be reasonably assumed that the king was responsible for the court's rejection of Nemours's claim of clericature. Furthermore, in July 1477, Louis XI all but ordered the Parlement, which in any case was packed with his chosen officers, to condemn the duke of Nemours. Some members of the Parlement resented Louis XI's interference in the trial, his haste to have it concluded, and the death sentence against the duke.[100] In retribution the

96 Mandrot, 'Jacques d'Armagnac', *R.H.*, XLIV (1890), 273–9.

97 Bibl. Ste-Geneviève, ms. 2000, fols. 105r–107r; see also C. Samaran and L. Favier, 'Louis XI et Jacques d'Armagnac, duc de Nemours: les instructions secrètes du roi au chancelier Pierre Doriole pour la conduite du procès', *Journal des savants* (1966), 65–77.

98 For this and the next paragraph see *Lettres de Louis XI*, VI. 88–91.

99 *Supra*, pp. 82, 106–9.

100 B.N., Coll. Duchesne 108, fols. 63r–64r.

king removed at least three of them – Guillaume Leduc, Etienne Dubois and Guillaume Gougnon – from their offices, and he refused to reinstate them. In fact, Louis XI threatened to purge the whole Parlement.[101]

The marshal, Joachim Rouault, had also been implicated in the conspiracy of 1474–5. The royal commission that had been given jurisdiction in his case considered the charge of peculation as well as that of treason. Regrettably there is little information either on his rôle in the conspiracy or on his trial. Convicted on 17 May 1476, he was stripped of all his offices, fined 20,000 *l.t.* and sentenced to incarceration. He died in 1480,[102] presumably while still in prison.

Of the minor characters in the plot there were but two known executions: Renaud de Velourt in November 1475; and Miquelot Fauvel, Nemours's principal messenger, who was tried and convicted summarily by David Collesson, lieutenant of the provost-marshal, in June 1476.[103] Those who are known to have been formally pardoned after rallying to the king were Hector de l'Escluse, lord of Le Mas in Bourbonnais, who had been Saint-Pol's principal agent;[104] Jean de Hangest, lord of Genlis and *bailli* of Evreux; Louis de Sainville and Jean Richier, intimates of Saint-Pol; Jean Gaudet, a *valet de chambre* of the count of Maine; Pierre de Dercé, a man-at-arms under the command of the marshal Rouault; Henri de Pompignac, *sénéchal* of Castres for the duke of Nemours; Pardiac Herald; and Louis de Marrasin, captain of La Charité.[105]

Louis XI's use of the law of treason as a political weapon is well illustrated by the case of René d'Anjou, king of Sicily, who had been incriminated in the conspiracy of 1474–5 and was suspected as well of negotiating the cession of his county of Provence to the duke of Burgundy. On 6 March 1476 Louis XI instructed the Parlement to indict and try him. One month later, after its investigations confirmed

101 *Lettres de Louis XI*, VIII. 25–6 (11 June 1479).

102 B.N., ms. fr. 6983, fols. 1r–2r; Coll. Dupuy 751, fols. 66r–67v; Roye, *Chron. scan.*, II. 144 n. 2.

103 For the execution of Fauvel see Bibl. Ste-Geneviève, ms. 2000, fols. 75r–86r, 159v–178v; Mandrot, 'Jacques d'Armagnac', *R.H.*, XLIV (1890), 267 n. 1.

104 A.N., JJ 204, no. 38. In April 1477 Louis XI granted to him La Bove in Laonnais, and some other properties confiscated from Philippe de Croy (X1a 8607, fols. 82v–84v).

105 A.N., X1a 8607, fols. 50v–51v (Hangest); JJ 204, no. 140 (Sainville); no. 163 (Richier); no. 28 (Gaudet); B.N., Coll. Dupuy 634, fols. 99r–101v (Dercé); ms. fr. 2895, fol. 17r (Pompignac and Pardiac); ms. fr. 21498, no. 235 and *Ordonnances*, XVIII. 194–5 (Marrasin).

that Anjou had committed 'great crimes of lese-majesty against the king and the public weal of the kingdom', the Parlement issued a summons for him to appear in court. At the same time, however, Louis XI made an overture to Anjou, sending a three-man embassy to induce him to sign an accord. The implication was clear: if he refused to assent to the king's terms, he would be prosecuted for treason before the Parlement. Consequently René agreed on 11 April not to have any intelligence with the king's enemies, particularly Burgundy;[106] and most probably he also promised at that time to cede Provence to the crown on his death.

The ruthless prosecutions that followed in the wake of the conspiracy of 1474–5 caused some nervous nobles to seek pardons for treasons committed many years before. In February 1476, for example, Robert de Beaufort, lord of Valéry, was pardoned for having borne arms with the princes in the War of the Public Weal. François de Beaujeu, lord of Ligniers, received his pardon for the same in March 1477. Jean de Bourbon, count of Vendôme, likewise sought and received a pardon in April 1477 for having given assistance to the Leaguers. In February 1478 both Gui d'Arpajon, *vicomte* of Lautrec, and Jean, lord of Roquefeuil, were also pardoned for having made common cause with Nemours in 1465.[107]

On 16 January 1477, less than two weeks after Charles the Bold died at Nancy, Louis XI published a general pardon for all adherents of the late duke.[108] But throughout that year and in the following one the king confiscated the properties of those who would not make their submission, and of those who had already died in rebellion. Louis XI's policy in the two Burgundies was an astute, if natural one: there he redistributed forfeited properties to Burgundians loyal to him, thus serving his two-fold purpose of rewarding his supporters and keeping that region divided and weak.[109]

In the spring of 1478, at the same time as he mounted a military

[106] A. Lecoy de La Marche, *Le roi René* (2 vols. in 1, Paris, 1875), I. 400–4; B.N., ms. fr. 6964, fols. 57r–60r; ms. fr. 18429, fols. 36r–37r; Coll. Dupuy 339, fols. 205r–206v.

[107] A.N., X1a 8607, fols. 52v–53r, 64r–v (Beaufort and Beaujeu); *Docs. hist. inédits*, ed. Champollion-Figeac, II. 359ff (Vendôme); *La Gascogne*, no. 65 (Arpajon); no. 69 (Roquefeuil).

[108] Commynes, *Mémoires*, ed. Lenglet-Dufresnoy, III. 498. On 19 January Louis XI published a pardon specifically for the two Burgundies (B.N., ms. fr. 5042, fol. 35r–v).

[109] E.g., A.N., JJ 201, nos. 31–3, 40, 211; J 808, no. 65; K 72, no. 9; Rossignol, *Hist. de la Bourgogne*, pp. 163–6. See also A. Leguai, 'La conquête de la Bourgogne par Louis XI', *Ann. de Bourgogne*, XLIX (1977), 87–92.

campaign against Mary of Burgundy, Louis XI had the Parlement of Paris initiate proceedings against Charles the Bold.[110] Mary, too, 'nova infidelitatis, rebellionis et inobedientiae crimina veteribus sui patris criminibus accumulans', was to be included in that prosecution. But after the diplomatic intervention of the emperor, Frederick III, Louis XI seems not to have carried the prosecution to a conclusion.[111] It was in any case an act of political pressure and propaganda rather than a legal necessity. From the strictly legal point of view Louis XI's declaration of Charles the Bold as a traitor was sufficient for the confiscation of his property.

In the late 1470s Louis XI felt most betrayed by Jean de Chalon, prince of Orange. After the death of Charles the Bold, Orange had rallied to the king in the hopes of becoming governor of the two Burgundies and of being restored to the property that the late duke had confiscated from him in 1470. The king passed over Jean de Chalon, however, appointing Georges de La Trémoïlle as his governor on 1 February 1477. Even this might have been acceptable to Orange, who was named as La Trémoïlle's lieutenant, had La Trémoïlle not obstructed the restitution of his property. Orange wasted no time in returning to Mary of Burgundy, who immediately appointed him as her lieutenant in the two Burgundies.

In spite of his earlier defection to Louis XI, Jean de Chalon was much respected by the Burgundian nobility, and his leadership gave a fillip to their resistance. The reverses that followed for the royal army infuriated Louis XI, who then instructed the Parlement of Grenoble to prosecute the prince of Orange. On 13 April he urged Pierre Gruel, president in that court, to hasten the matter. Within three weeks, on 5 May 1477, Orange was condemned to death, with confiscation of his property.[112] Since, however, he could not be captured, he was executed in effigy in June at Dijon, Mâcon, Paris, Caen and elsewhere in the kingdom, and his *hôtel* at Dijon was razed.[113]

In the next year Orange, still out of reach, was accused of a more specific treason – an attempt to have the king poisoned. On 8 May

[110] *Ordonnances*, XVIII. 399–402.

[111] Plancher, *Hist. de Bourgogne*, IV. 493 and *preuve* CCXC.

[112] U. Legeay, *Histoire de Louis XI* (2 vols., Paris, 1874), II. 270–1; Plancher, *Hist. de Bourgogne*, IV. 486–9; Rossignol, *Hist. de la Bourgogne*, pp. 70–1; Roye, *Chron. scan.*, I. 246; II. 52–3.

[113] *Supra*, pp. 118–19.

1478 Louis XI wrote to La Trémoïlle, urging him to 'capture [Orange] and burn him, or . . . have his head cut off and his corpse burned'. Then on 6 June the king instructed the Parlement of Paris to read out publicly the details of the treason of 'the prince of Thirty Pennies'. On 19 June the councillors of Lyon published the letters of Louis XI that put a price of 20,000 *écus* on Jean de Chalon's head.[114] But for all of Louis XI's fulminations against Orange, he could not bring him to justice. There were indeed limits to his ability to enforce the law. Orange was pardoned by Charles VIII in 1483.[115]

The law of treason existed so that the enemies of the crown could be punished; sometimes it could be used actively as a means of political pressure; and, with few exceptions, by its very existence it acted as a constraint on the political activity of the nobility and other members of later medieval French society. But none of this applied in the case of Charles de Martigny, bishop of Elne, in 1480, for his trial was a political ploy intended purely for foreign consumption. Martigny, Louis XI's permanent ambassador to England since 1477, had been given full powers on 13 July 1478 to negotiate a treaty with the English; significantly Louis XI promised in advance to ratify whatever would be concluded. In February 1479, faced with the undesirable prospect of an alliance between Edward IV and Maximilian, Martigny reluctantly signed a truce on terms demanded by the English. Louis XI showed no displeasure with the bishop at the time; indeed he even entrusted him with another mission. Yet in the summer of 1480 Martigny was accused of treason, of having exceeded his powers and of having thereby compromised the interests of the kingdom, and was brought to trial in the Parlement. The outcome of the trial is not known, but Martigny did keep his bishopric and was not at all harassed afterwards. The whole point of this episode, which was scripted, it is suggested, by Louis XI and Martigny together, was to provide the king with a legal cover for his non-ratification of the truce, and to give him time to strengthen his position *vis-à-vis* Maximilian and Mary.[116]

[114] *Lettres de Louis XI*, VII. 90–1, 317, *p.j.* vi.

[115] J. S. C. Bridge, *A History of France from the Death of Louis XI* (5 vols., London, 1921–36), I. 36.

[116] J. Calmette, 'Une manoeuvre politique de Louis XI: l'aventure de l'évêque d'Elne, Charles de Martigny, ambassadeur de France à Londres', *Rev. d'hist. mod.*, IV. (1929), 117–21; J. Calmette and G. Périnelle, *Louis XI et l'Angleterre (1461–1483)* (Paris, 1930), Appendix II.

The trial of René d'Alençon, the final one in the reign of Louis XI, lasted from August 1481 to March 1483.[117] Ever since the mid-1470s Alençon had gradually been losing what little favour he had with the king;[118] therefore, as he claimed, he decided to withdraw into Brittany because then 'the king would have a greater desire to recall him, and, in recalling him, be more responsive to his needs'.[119] Louis XI had him arrested in mid-August 1481 just as Alençon was about to leave for Brittany. Because Louis XI believed that the duke of Brittany would not have risked provoking him by openly receiving Alençon, he thought that Alençon's true intention was to go ultimately to England or to Maximilian.[120]

As explained in chapter 4 Alençon's trial followed the pattern established by the second trial of Jean d'Alençon and that of the duke of Nemours. At first Louis XI entrusted the prosecution to a royal commission, and then he permitted the Parlement to have jurisdiction, but the commissioners nonetheless maintained a vital rôle in the prosecution. Perhaps because of the nebulous nature of the charge against Alençon, the Parlement was not particularly enthusiastic about prosecuting him. The threats that Louis XI had made in the wake of the Nemours trial and the pressure that he had exerted during René d'Alençon's trial clearly had not intimidated the court.

There was little prosecution of treason during the reign of Charles VIII. The case of Jean de Jaucourt was the only one not connected with the Breton revolt of 1486–8. Jaucourt, lord of Villarnoul, had served as captain of 100 lances under Charles the Bold. Immediately after the duke's death he, like Jean de Chalon, rallied to the crown, and Louis XI appointed him governor of Auxerre. In April 1478, using his influence with the king, he obtained a pardon for his cousin Philbert de Digoine. But Jaucourt, like Jean de Chalon, soon changed sides again, becoming Maximilian's lieutenant-general in Burgundy.[121]

In December 1484 Jaucourt and several of his accomplices were arrested for having recruited subjects for Maximilian, and also for having stolen state papers from the *chambre des comptes* at Dijon.

[117] A.N., J 949, no. 6.
[118] B.N., ms. fr. 18442, fols. 98r–108r; A.N., J 949, no. 6, fols. 60v–61r.
[119] A.N., J 949, no. 6, fol. 18v.
[120] *Lettres de Louis XI*, IX. 70–2; A.N., J 949, no. 6, fol. 53v.
[121] Guérin, 'Pierre d'Urfé', pp. 114–15. For the pardon to Digoine see A.N., JJ 205, no. 474.

Apprised of his arrest, the regency council on 5 January 1485 empowered the Parlement to try his case.[122] On 21 August, after Jaucourt had been tortured and had signed a confession, the king instructed the Parlement to proceed without delay to judgement.[123] On the 27th the court condemned Jaucourt to be drawn, beheaded and quartered.[124] The sentence was not carried out, however, because Maximilian had arrested Pierre d'Urfé, who had been sent to Bruges on a diplomatic mission, and was holding him hostage: whatever was done to Jaucourt, he warned, would be done to Pierre d'Urfé. The regency council, with little choice, released Jaucourt on 10 September.[125]

The formation of a new feudal league in mid-December 1486 and the consequent flight of Louis d'Orléans to Brittany in early January 1487 precipitated the last flurry of prosecution under the law of treason in the later middle ages. On 18 January the property of François de Dunois, Orléans's cousin and co-conspirator, was confiscated.[126] Before the end of the month it was discovered that a number of influential persons at court – Philippe de Commynes, the bishops of Périgueux and Montauban, and the lord of Bucy – had been informing the rebel princes of all that transpired there. They were arrested immediately. With Commynes and the others languishing in prison, and with the princes caught off balance, the Beaujeus decided to strike against the rebels at their weakest point, in the Midi, and to have the young Charles VIII lead the royal army in person. By March 1487 Guyenne had capitulated and Charles VIII entered Bordeaux in triumph.[127] The county of Comminges, confiscated from Jean de Lescun, was incorporated into the royal domain.[128]

On 22–3 April 1487 Charles VIII gave instructions for the houses of Orléans's chancellor, Denis Le Mercier, and those of other adherents of the duke to be razed for their treason. Ten days earlier

[122] *Procès-verbaux du conseil de régence*, pp. 230–7.
[123] *Lettres de Charles VIII*, ed. P. Pélicier and B. de Mandrot (S.H.F.) (5 vols., Paris, 1898–1905), I. 84; A.N., X2a 48, unpaginated; Guérin, 'Pierre d'Urfé', pp. 122–3.
[124] A.N., X2a 48, unpaginated (printed in Guérin, 'Pierre d'Urfé', pp. 124–5).
[125] Guérin, 'Pierre d'Urfé', pp. 172–3.
[126] J. Dufournet, *La vie de Philippe de Commynes* (Paris, 1969), p. 170.
[127] Jaligny, *Hist. de Charles VIII*, pp. 14–15, 19–22.
[128] P. Pélicier, *Essai sur le gouvernement de la dame de Beaujeu (1483–1491)* (Chartes, 1882), p. 129.

Le Mercier had been summonsed to appear in the Parlement.[129] Throughout the rest of 1487 and the first months of 1488, while the royal army under Louis de La Trémoïlle was campaigning against the rebels in Brittany, the Parlement continued its proceedings against Le Mercier and others. On 7 June 1487 it issued a warrant for the arrest of Jean de Chalon, prince of Orange,[130] and on 23 July Commynes appeared in court after previously having been interrogated by commissioners from the Parlement.[131] That same day Orléans was summonsed to present himself for judgement in the Parlement 'suffisament garny de pairs'. The summons was repeated on 12 August,[132] at which time Guillaume de Soupplainville, now *bailli* of Montargis, and Guillaume Charnier, lord of Chêne-Artoult, were also summonsed.[133]

Charles VIII, meanwhile, had decided to prosecute the duke of Brittany as well as the duke of Orléans. Having sought advice from the Parlement in the autumn, he summonsed the two dukes on 22 January 1488 for 14 April,[134] but he quickly and inexplicably changed the date to 20 February; perhaps this explains why the trial of Orléans and Brittany was such a half-hearted affair. Of the lay peers and princes of the blood the only ones present were Beaujeu, Alençon, Laval, the count of Vendôme, the count of Guise and Louis de Luxembourg. Bourbon, Nevers, Angoulême and several ecclesiastical peers were absent. After Jean Magistri, the king's advocate, presented the case for the crown, and after the dukes failed to appear, the court adjudged a default and adjourned to an indefinite date.[135] As far as is known the *cour garnie* never re-assembled for the prosecution of the dukes, though it did continue its proceedings against the others. On 23 May 1488 Dunois, Le Mercier, Soupplainville, Charnier, Lescun, Olivier de Coëtmen and Odet d'Aydie were convicted *in absentia* of treason and were banished from the kingdom, with confiscation of their property.[136]

[129] Maulde La Clavière, *Hist. de Louis XII*, II. 181–2; A.N., x2a 56, fol. 85r for the summons to Le Mercier.

[130] A.N., x2a 51, unpaginated.

[131] Commynes, *Mémoires*, ed. Dupont, III. 140–1; A.N., x2a 51, unpaginated.

[132] B.N., ms. fr. 2832, fols. 119r–120r.

[133] A.N., x2a 56, fols. 90v, 105v.

[134] *Lettres de Charles VIII*, I. 248–9; B.N., ms. fr. 2832, fols. 120r–121r for the summons.

[135] Godefroy, *Le ceremonial françois*, II. 450–1; Jaligny, *Hist. de Charles VIII*, pp. 43–5; Maulde La Clavière, *Hist. de Louis XII*, II. 207–9.

[136] A.N., x2a 56, fols. 85r–v, 90v–93r, 105v–108r; J. de Jaurgain, *Deux comtes de Comminges*

The Breton revolt came to an end with the defeat of the rebels and the capture of Orange and Orléans at Saint-Aubin-le-Cormier on 27 July 1488.[137] On 20 August François II signed the peace of Sablé, and in September Charles VIII pardoned Albret, Dunois, Lescun and the intimates of Orléans and Orange.[138] In spite of the earlier prosecution in the Parlement, however, Charles VIII now made no effort to try either Orléans or Orange, both of whom were kept in prison. In September 1489 the bishops of Montauban and Périgueux and the lord of Bucy were released from detention.[139] In early October of that year Charles VIII instructed the Parlement to conclude the case against Commynes. On 24 March 1490 the court sentenced him to ten years' house arrest and fined him 10,000 *écus*.[140] Orange was set free in 1489, Orléans in 1491.[141] When, in 1491, Charles VIII married Anne of Brittany and assured for himself the succession to the duchy, he removed at a stroke the single greatest cause of magnate opposition. Supported now by a loyal Louis d'Orléans, heir presumptive to the throne, Charles VIII could devote his energies to his plans for Italian conquests.

Important as were the reigns of Charles VII and Charles VIII with regard to the prosecution of treason, the reign of Louis XI was by far the most striking of the three. Much more so than either his father or his son and the Beaujeus, Louis XI used royal commissions to great effect. Tristan l'Hermite, provost-marshal, played a prominent rôle in these commissions, though it should be said that his services were similarly, if less frequently, employed by Charles VII. Furthermore, whereas Charles VII scrupulously adhered to procedural formalities in the case of Jean d'Alençon – and even, one might add, in the case of Jean V d'Armagnac – and was reluctant generally to exact the full penalties of the law, Louis XI determinedly rid himself of Louis de Luxembourg and Jacques d'Armagnac. Nor did Louis hesitate to prosecute even those like Antoine de Chabannes, Charles de Melun and René d'Alençon, who had lost his favour. In general, it might be said that for Charles VII the treason trial, though

béarnais du XVe siècle: Jean de Lescun, bâtard d'Armagnac, et Odet d'Aydie, seigneur de Lescun (Paris, 1919), p. 149.

137 Jaligny, *Hist. de Charles VIII*, pp. 48–53.

138 *Ordonnances*, xx. 95–8; A.N., JJ 219, no. 196.

139 Jaligny, *Hist. de Charles VIII*, p. 69; B.N., n.a. fr. 2398, fol. 24v.

140 Commynes, *Mémoires*, ed. Dupont, III. 145–6.

141 Bridge, *A History of France*, I. 206 (Orange); *Procédures politiques*, pp. 673–5 Orléans).

inevitably a political event, was primarily a legal remedy; while for Louis XI the treason trial, though always a legal remedy, was, as exemplified by the cases of René d'Anjou and Charles de Martigny, much more of a political instrument that he used dexterously to achieve his ends.

CONCLUSION

From the beginning of the period under review in this study, the interrelated notions of sovereignty and obedience had become integral parts of the law of treason. However imprecisely defined, that law thus expressed the nature of political authority. Since the king was sovereign, all the inhabitants of France were his subjects and owed him absolute obedience; furthermore, since he embodied public majesty, any treason against him was treason against the realm, and conversely any treason against the realm was treason against him. One need not belabour the fact that injured majesty was the central, all-encompassing aspect of treason in later medieval France; and that betrayal, though primordial, was but a subordinate one. *Trahison* could be committed against anybody, whereas *lèse-majesté* could be committed only against the king, the crown or the kingdom.

The wide scope of the law of treason developed naturally from this concept of lese-majesty. Given the poor state of public order and the frequent political crises – conditions that were aggravated, if not caused, by the English threat to the crown – one might argue that such a development of the law was also inevitable. The kings, though theoretically *legibus absoluti*, were nevertheless expected to rule by law, and consequently the law of treason provided for the monarchy a most important legal justification with which to anticipate charges of arbitrary repression or personal vengeance.

There were other dimensions of such a far-reaching law of treason. More severe than those for other crimes, the penalties for treason were intended to deter, control and influence as much as to punish effectively. A related aspect came within what one might call the domain of public relations: since royal authority was justified by the king's ability to defend the realm and to maintain public order, it was politically important that the monarchy should actually be seen to be fulfilling those functions. The wide scope of the law of treason also permitted the crown, which determinedly claimed sole cognizance of crimes of treason, to make inroads against municipal, seigneurial and above all ecclesiastical jurisdictions. It was not lost on crown officers that the administration of justice was a manifestation of power and authority. The crown generally succeeded against the towns and the lords in this matter; but it is a measure of the church's great power that, in cases of treason committed by clerics, ecclesiastical tribunals managed on most occasions to maintain, if only in appearance, control of the prosecution.

With respect to legal administration, the prosecution of treason was not channelled into any one court, though the Parlement of Paris, as the offshoot of the *curia regis*, was inevitably the most important jurisdiction. The rôle of this court was emphasized when the king, with the peers of France, sat there in judgement of another peer. Important as was the Parlement of Paris, other courts – the provincial Parlements in the fifteenth century, the Châtelet from the mid fourteenth century, indeed virtually the whole spectrum of civil and military tribunals – were competent to try treason. Royal commissions were also a significant part of the administration of justice, though the uses to which they were put varied considerably from the fourteenth to the fifteenth centuries. In the earlier century commissions were appointed generally to suppress local or urban revolts, or to punish persons of low standing. In the fifteenth century those functions did of course continue, but Charles VII and especially Louis XI could also employ commissions to try such traitors as Louis d'Amboise, Jacques Coeur, Charles de Melun and Charles d'Albret. The cases of Jacques d'Armagnac and René d'Alençon, too, it should be remembered, had begun as trials by commission.

Just as there was no court with exclusive jurisdiction over crimes of treason, there was no special procedure either. One short-lived procedure was trial by battle, which, at least for treason, fell into desuetude by the mid fourteenth century. In the various courts the procedures were essentially the same as for other aggravated felonies. Thus in the Parlement of Paris the *procédure ordinaire* as well as the *procédure extraordinaire* could be followed. State trials, few though there were, are notable for their jurisdictional aspects, the extreme formalities of procedure, and for the actual composition of the court in such cases. In general what is most noticeable about the actual prosecution of treason is that judgement by notoriety and the personal justice of the king, exemplified by the trials of Olivier III de Clisson in 1343 and the count of Eu in 1350, gave way, though admittedly not entirely, to institutionalized procedures. A comparison of the reigns of Philippe VI, Jean II and even Charles V with those of Charles VII, Louis XI and Charles VIII is a telling one.

Particularly in the fourteenth century, forfeiture played a greater rôle than has hitherto been realized. What is most striking is the use of confiscated property primarily as a source of political patronage rather than as a source of wealth for the crown itself. Louis XI was generous in his distribution of forfeitures, but it was Charles V who was most politically dexterous in this respect. A forfeiture and any subsequent donation could of course always be annulled in a pardon. Sometimes, however, only partial restitution was made: the property that the crown kept was both the price of the pardon, and, because it could at some future time be restored, an incentive for the person pardoned to prove his loyalty. In forfeiture and restitution the crown thus had a valuable means of political control.

Although the principal features of the law of treason had taken form by the early fourteenth century, the prosecution of the crime did not begin in earnest until the beginning of the Hundred Years War. Philippe VI in the late 1320s had provided an indication of his future policy in his prosecution of Guillaume de Deken, his chastisement of the Flemish towns and his prosecution of those, whether dead or still alive, who had fought at Cassel. His stern measures at that time in Flanders and again in the late 1330s did not, however, deter the Flemings from seeking an English alliance. And indeed one can argue that his vengeance in 1343–4 against Olivier III de Clisson, Godefroi d'Harcourt and other Norman and Breton lords sowed the seeds of future misfortune for both himself and his son.

Jean II's execution of Raoul de Brienne, count of Eu, in 1350 did, it is true, exacerbate the disaffection of the Norman nobility; and the arrest of Navarre at Rouen in April 1356 did have grave consequences for Jean II personally and for France. But one should bear in mind that the situation in Normandy, at least during his first year on the throne, was as much of Philippe VI's as of Jean II's own making. Furthermore, it has been argued in this study that Jean II took action against Navarre, Jean V d'Harcourt, Graville and the others only after multiple treasons by them and fruitless attempts on his part at pacification, if not reconciliation. Evidence from the south of France indicates that there, too, Jean II's efforts had been towards pacification rather than towards punishment.

During the regency and reign of Charles V the prosecution of treason became a more prominent feature of royal policy. The extensive confiscation of property was as much a means of weakening the power base of, for example, Navarre, Edward III and the Black Prince as of punishing the persons who owned the property. Charles V cast his net far and wide in the prosecution of treason; those caught were only slightly less likely to be potters, mercers or common labourers than knights and esquires. Charles V could also be quite strict in matters of loyalty: one could forfeit one's property merely for living voluntarily in land under enemy control. Yet although Charles V was not loath to exact the full penalties of the law when necessary, he was not loath, either, to grant pardons. The most significant legal development of his reign was his revival of the state trial, but one should not lose sight of the fact that judgement on the king's record was the dominant theme of Charles V's prosecution of treason.

Charles VI, first because of his youth and then because of his chronic insanity, did not take a particularly active part in the prosecution of treason. For this reason, until 1413, there was a considerably more important rôle for the Parlement of Paris and for the Châtelet than during the preceding reigns; the duke of Burgundy, virtual master of France from 1409 to 1413, seemed to favour this trend. Between 1413 and 1422, however, there was, in general, a reversion to arbitrary prosecution – summary executions, decrees of banishment and confiscations – as first one party, then the other, used its influence over the king to proscribe its enemies.

The juridical emphasis on royal power during the reign of Charles VII came many years after his coronation at Reims in 1429. It was only after the Praguerie that Charles VII, now firmly in control of the affairs of state, prosecuted treason with the full authority of the law. The most important event of this latter part of his reign was the trial of Jean, duke of Alençon, in 1458. In that prosecution were exemplified Charles VII's adherence to the formalities of procedure, his emphasis on royal majesty, and, a most important feature generally of his policy in the prosecution of treason, his clemency.

In the hands of Louis XI the law of treason was a devastating weapon. He could use it to take vengeance on those who had betrayed him when he was dauphin, to give legal cover to court intrigue, to justify a declaration of war against the duke of Burgundy in 1470, to have urban revolts suppressed, to put political pressure on such as René d'Anjou and Mary of Burgundy, to justify the non-ratification of a truce, but above all, to prosecute with great effect those who most seriously plotted against him, particularly in the last years of his reign. If Louis XI was the most feared of the later medieval French kings, it was for good cause.

From the late fifteenth century to the mid seventeenth century the law of treason was made more precise on points of detail, but departed little from medieval precedents. An edict of François I issued in July 1534, for example, specifically stated that whoever received messages from a foreign prince with whom the king was at war would be guilty of lese-majesty if he did not reveal this fact. More precise on this subject was an edict of 16 August 1563, which declared that it would be treason to communicate about state affairs in any way with foreign princes or their subjects. The Ordonnance of Blois in May 1579 repeated this prohibition, and added that levying troops without royal permission was also treasonable. By edicts of 29 November 1565 and 14 February 1621 it was declared that raising taxes without royal authority was a crime of lese-majesty. A famine of the mid-1590s precipitated an edict of 12 March 1595 that condemned as treason the exporting of corn. After numerous prohibitions during the sixteenth century, the *porte d'armes* and illicit assemblies were declared treasonable on 27 May 1610.[1] By ordinances of December 1567 and January 1580 seditious words were to be punished as for treason. Thus François Le Breton, a Parisian lawyer, was executed on 2 November 1586 for having said that Henry III was 'one of the greatest hypocrites that ever was'. In December 1621 the Parlement of Bordeaux condemned Jean-Pierre de Leseur, a *conseiller* in the *conseil souverain* of Pau, as guilty of lese-

1 'Crimes contre l'état', *Répertoire méthodique et alphabétique de législation, de doctrine et de jurisprudence*, ed. D. Dalloz *et al.* (vol. XIV, Paris, 1853), 526 (edict of 1534); *Recueil général des anciennes lois*, XIV. 145–6 (edict of 1563); 424 (Ord. of Blois); 183 (edict of 1565); XV. 98 (edict of 1595); XVI. 7 (edict of 1610); 140 (edict of 1621).

majesty for having published *La persécution des églises réformes à Béarn* as well as for having presided at the assembly of La Rochelle.[2] After Richelieu's belabouring of the Assembly of Notables in 1626–7, the writing, publication or dissemination of defamatory libel was again declared punishable as lese-majesty. This was specified in the Code Michaud, which was promulgated in 1629, and which declared the following offences as treasonable, too, if done without royal permission: communicating with foreign ambassadors; raising troops, casting cannon, accumulating war matériel, or maintaining more arms than were necessary for protection; fortifying strategic places; convoking assemblies, entering into leagues, or even leaving the realm.[3]

As in the later middle ages the crown pressed to have the knowledge of treason punished as for the crime itself. Thus in January 1524 Jean de Poitiers, lord of Saint-Vallier, was condemned to death for lese-majesty because he had not revealed his knowledge of Charles de Bourbon's treason. Saint-Vallier was pardoned just as he was about to be executed, but de Thou in 1642 suffered the full force of Richelieu's wrath for his complicity in and non-revelation of the treason of Cinq-Mars.[4] One jurist in the seventeenth century argued that one's guilt dated not from the day one committed treason, but rather from the day that one conceived treasonous thoughts.[5] Following this logic, another royal lawyer concluded that one was guilty for one's thoughts alone, and that no overt acts need follow;[6] proving such guilt was, of course, another matter altogether. The posthumous prosecution of traitors continued into the seventeenth century and no doubt beyond. Nicolas l'Hôte, *commis* of a *secrétaire d'état*, had divulged to the king of Spain the deliberations of the *conseil d'état* of Henry IV. When he learned that his treason had been discovered, he drowned himself in the Marne in order to avoid prosecution. His corpse was nevertheless taken to Paris, and a trial

[2] 'Crimes contre l'état', p. 526; G.-A. Guyot, *Répertoire universel et raisonné de jurisprudence civile, criminelle, canonique et bénéficiale*, vol. XXXVI (Paris, 1778), 199; J. H. Mariéjol, *La réforme et la Ligue – l'Edit de Nantes (1559–1598)* (vol. VI (1) of *Histoire de France*, ed. Lavisse) (Paris, 1911), pp. 263–4; *Recueil général des anciennes lois*, XVI. 142.

[3] W. F. Church, *Richelieu and Reason of State* (Princeton, 1972), pp. 185–6.

[4] *Procès criminel de Jehan de Poytiers, seigneur de Saint-Vallier*, ed. G. Guiffrey (Paris, 1868), pp. 130–1, 146–7, 155–71; Church, *Richelieu*, p. 332.

[5] B.N., ms. fr. 17318, fol. 71r.

[6] B.N., ms. fr. 10977, fols. 1–24.

ensued. He was convicted of lese-majesty on 15 May 1604; after being drawn on a hurdle, his corpse was then quartered.[7]

The prosecution for lese-majesty reached its historical climax in France during the ministry of Cardinal Richelieu, whose versatile use of the law of treason to control the fractious nobility can only be compared with that of Louis XI. Like that monarch, Richelieu was most adept at empanelling *ad hoc* tribunals to conduct the prosecutions of accused traitors such as the marquis de Chalais in 1626 or Cinq-Mars and de Thou in 1642. Nor was he concerned about the privileges of peers: the duke of Montmorency was tried in 1632 before the Parlement of Toulouse; and in 1639 Bernard de Nogaret, duke of La Valette, was prosecuted before an enlarged *conseil d'état*. Richelieu's influence on the treason legislation in the Code Michaud of 1629 has been alluded to above. One can hardly doubt that the cardinal's knowledge of historical and legal precedents was thorough: the extensive and systematic manuscript collections of material pertaining to treason from the early middle ages right up to the time of Richelieu himself were compiled by the royal *bibliothécaires*, Pierre Dupuy and Théodore Godefroy, at his behest. Even more so than Louis XI, Richelieu expended much of his energy in setting forth, in opposition to the nobles' concept of personal allegiance to the monarchy, his notion of unconditional loyalty to the state.[8]

In its evolution the law of treason was an expression of political authority and a response to the exigencies of power. Richelieu used the law of treason very effectively as an instrument with which to enforce obedience and to advance his concept of *raison d'état*; detailed research will show how much he owed in this regard to the medieval law and to its application by Louis XI in particular.

[7] 'Crimes contre l'état', p. 527.

[8] Church, *Richelieu*, pp. 179, 181, 183–4, 235–6, 324–8, 328–32; and generally see his index *sub* '*lèse-majesté*'.

BIBLIOGRAPHY

MANUSCRIPT SOURCES

Archives Municipales de Lyon

AA 98, no. 18

Archives Nationales de France

Série J (trésor des chartes): 187A, 187B, 335, 336, 359, 366, 369, 389, 615, 619, 776, 777, 779, 794, 808, 854, 860, 949, 950, 954, 1021, 1047, 1050

Série JJ (chancery registers): In this series I have gone exhaustively through vols. 61–225 for the years 1321–1492. Since virtually every volume contains some evidence on treason – in the form of letters of pardon or letters granting confiscated property – it would be misleading to list here only those volumes cited in the footnotes.

Série K (cartons des rois): 49, 54, 59, 68, 70–2

Série KK: 2, 893

Série P: 943, 1372/2, 2298–9

Série PP: 118

Série Q1: 1020

Série X1a (civil registers of the Parlement of Paris): 6, 8, 10, 12, 1469, 1471, 1473, 1484, 1487, 4784, 4793, 4794, 4808, 8603, 8606–8, 9317, 9319

Série X2a (criminal registers of the Parlement of Paris): Again I have gone exhaustively through vols. 1–56 for the years 1309–1492.

Série Z1b (cour des monnaies): 60

Série Z1h (hôtel de ville): 16

Collection Lenoir: 1, 3–5, 8, 10, 13, 14, 16, 18–20, 22, 24–9, 75

Bibliothèque Nationale de France

Collection Baluze: 272

Collection Clairambault: 86, 87, 188

Collection Doat: 2, 8, 202, 221

Collection Duchesne: 108

Collection Dupuy: 38, 339, 480, 634, 751, 762

Collection Périgord: 55

Dossiers bleus: 534

Manuscrits français: 1707, 2811, 2832, 2895, 2896, 2897, 2907, 2912, 2913, 2914, 2921, 3869, 3876, 4487, 4773, 5040, 5041, 5042, 5738, 5908, 5909, 5943, 6539,

6750, 6963, 6964, 6983, 7593, 7598, 7645, 10187, 10238, 10971, 10977, 11221, 15538, 16536, 16541, 17318, 18425, 18429, 18441, 18442, 20371, 20428, 20430, 20494, 20496, 20497, 20685, 21498, 22469, 23838, 25698, 25713, 25996, 25997, 25998, 26011, 26014, 26015, 26018, 26080, 26081, 26091, 26095

Nouvelles acquisitions françaises: 1001, 2398, 2611, 2840, 3360, 6525, 23634

Pièces originales: 1043, 2305, 2328–9

Bibliothèque Sainte-Geneviève: ms. 2000

College of Arms: MS Arundel 48

PRINTED PRIMARY SOURCES

Legal Texts

L'ancienne coutume de Normandie, ed. W. L. de Gruchy. Jersey, 1881.

Andreas, Joannes. *In Sex Decretalium Libros Novella Commentaria.* 3 vols. Venice, 1581.

Bartolus of Sassoferrato. *Glosa in Extravagantes.* Venice, 1489.

Beaumanoir, Philippe de. *Coutumes de Beauvaisis*, ed. A. Salmon. 2 vols. Paris, 1899 and 1900.

Blanosco, Joannes de. *Commentaria super Titulum de Actionibus in Institutis.* Mayence, 1539.

Boutillier, Jean. *Somme rural*, ed. L. Charondas Le Caron. Paris, 1603.

Breuil, Guillaume de. *Stilus Curie Parlamenti*, ed. F. Aubert. Paris, 1909.

Capitularia Regum Francorum, ed. A. Boretius and V. Krause (Monumenta Germaniae Historica). 2 vols. Hanover, 1883–97.

Caramanico, Marinus de. *Proemium in Constitutiones Regni Siciliae*, in *Utriusque Siciliae Constitutiones.* Venice, 1590.

Codex Justinianus, ed. P. Krueger. Berlin, 1877.

Codex Theodosianus, ed. G. Haenel. 2 vols. Bonn, 1840–2.

Coutumes et institutions de l'Anjou et du Maine antérieures au XVIe siècle, ed. C.-J. Beautemps-Beaupré. 4 vols. in 8. Paris, 1877–97.

Digesta Justiniani Augusti, ed. T. Mommsen. 2 vols. Berlin, 1870.

Durandus, Gulielmus. *Speculum Juris.* Frankfurt, 1592.

Etablissements de Saint Louis, ed. P. Viollet (S.H.F.). 4 vols. Paris, 1881–6.

Le grand coutumier de France, ed. E. Laboulaye and R. Dareste. Paris, 1868.

Imperatoris Justiniani Institutionum Libri Quattuor, ed. J. B. Moyle. Oxford, 1903.

Jacobi, Petrus. *Aurea Practica Libellorum.* Cologne, 1575.

Le livre des droiz et des commandemens d'office de justice, ed. C.-J. Beautemps-Beaupré. 2 vols. Paris, 1865.

Li livres de jostice et de plet, ed. Rapetti (C.D.I.). Paris, 1850.

Masuer, Jean. *Practica Forensis.* Lyon, 1577.

Pape, Gui. *Decisiones.* Lyon, 1613.

Questiones Johannis Galli, ed. M. Boulet [-Sautel]. Paris, 1944.

Songe du verger, in P. Dupuy, *Traitez des droits et libertez de l'église gallicane*, edn J.-L. Brunet (4 vols. Paris, 1731–51), vol. II.

Summa de Legibus Normannie, ed. E.-J. Tardif (Soc. de l'hist. de Normandie). Rouen and Paris, 1896.

Terra-Rubea, Joannes de. *Contra Rebelles Suorum Regum*, ed. J. Bonaud. Lyon, 1526.

Published and calendared documents

Actes de la chancellerie d'Henri VI concernant la Normandie sous la domination anglaise (1422–1435). Extraits des registres du Trésor des Chartes aux Archives Nationales, ed. P. Le Cacheux (Soc. de l'hist. de Normandie). 2 vols. Rouen, 1907 and 1908.

Actes du Parlement de Paris (1254–1328). 1st series, ed. E. Boutaric. 2 vols. Paris, 1863 and 1867.

Actes du Parlement de Paris (1328–1350). 2nd series, ed. H. Forgeot. 2 vols. Paris, 1920 and 1960.

Additions aux recherches d'Alençon et du Perche, ed. G. Bry de la Clergerie. Paris, 1621.

Les affaires de Jacques Coeur. Journal du procureur Dauvet, ed. M. Mollat. 2 vols. in 1. Paris, 1952–3.

Archives anciennes de la ville de Saint-Quentin, ed. E. Lemaire. 2 vols. Saint-Quentin, 1888–1910.

Archives d'un serviteur de Louis XI, ed. L. de la Trémoïlle. Nantes, 1888.

Archives historiques de la Gironde, VI (1864), 193–5.

Arrest de la cour de Parlement contre le tres-meschant parricide François Ravaillac. Paris, 1610.

Bekynton, Thomas. *Official Correspondence*, ed. G. Williams (Rolls Series). 2 vols. London, 1872.

Chartrier de Pons, ed. G. Musset. *Arch. hist. de la Saintonge et de l'Aunis*, XXI (1892).

'Choix de pièces inédites', ed. H. Duplès-Agier *et al. B.E.C.*, 4th series, III (1857), 246–72.

Choix de pièces inédites relatives au règne de Charles VI, ed. L. Douët-d'Arcq (S.H.F.). 2 vols. Paris, 1863 and 1864.

'Compte de Jean Le Muet, vicomte d'Orbec, pour la Saint-Michel 1444', ed. H. de Frondeville, *Etudes lexoviennes*, IV (1936), 117–327.

Confessions et jugements de criminels au Parlement de Paris (1319–1350), ed. M. Langlois and Y. Lanhers. Paris, 1971.

Documents historiques inédits, ed. J.-J. Champollion-Figeac (C.D.I.). 4 vols. Paris, 1841–8.

Documents historiques sur la maison de Galard, ed. J. Noulens. 5 vols. in 4. Paris, 1871–6.

Documents inédits pour servir à l'histoire du Maine au XIVe siècle, ed. A. Bertrand de Broussillon. *Arch. hist. du Maine*, V (1905).

Documents parisiens du règne de Philippe VI de Valois (1328–1350), ed. J. Viard. 2 vols. Paris, 1899 and 1900.

'Documents relatifs à l'arrestation de Louis de Luxembourg à Mons en 1475', ed. L. Devillers. *Bull. comm. roy. d'hist.*, 4th series, XVII (1890), 302–18.

Documents sur la maison de Durfort (XIe–XVe siècle), ed. N. de Pena. 2 vols. Bordeaux, 1977.

'Exécution en effigie de Jean de Chalons, prince d'Orange', *Le cabinet historique*, IX (1) (1863), 46–8.

La Gascogne dans les registres du Trésor des Chartes, ed. C. Samaran (C.D.I.). Paris, 1966.

Les grands traités de la guerre de Cent ans, ed. E. Cosneau. Paris, 1889.

Innocentii III Romani Pontificis Opera Omnia, ed. J.-P. Migne (Patrologia Latina). 4 vols. Paris, 1855.

Inventaire analytique des ordonnances enregistrées au Parlement de Paris jusqu'à la mort de Louis XII, ed. H. Stein. Paris, 1908.

Letters and Papers Illustrative of the Wars of the English in France, ed. J. Stevenson (Rolls Series). 2 vols. in 3. London, 1861–4.

Lettres de Charles VIII, ed. P. Pélicier and B. de Mandrot (S.H.F.). 5 vols. Paris, 1898–1905.

Lettres de Louis XI, ed. E. Charavay, J. Vaesen and B. de Mandrot (S.H.F.). 11 vols. Paris, 1883–1909.

Lettres reçues et envoyées par le Parlement de Paris (1376–1591), ed. S. Clemencet and M. François. Paris, 1961.

Mandements et actes diverses de Charles V (1364–1380), ed. L. Delisle (C.D.I.). Paris, 1874.

Les Olim, ed. le comte Beugnot (C.D.I.). 3 vols. in 4. Paris, 1839–48.

Ordonnances des roys de France de la troisième race. 21 vols. Paris, 1723–1849.

Paris pendant la domination anglaise (1420–1436), ed. A. Longnon. Paris, 1878.

Le petit thalamus de Montpellier, ed. Grassel, Desmazes and Saint-Paul (*Mém. de la soc. arch. de Montpellier*). Montpellier, 1840.

'Pièces inédites relatives à Etienne Marcel et à quelques-uns de ses principaux adhérents', ed. S. Luce. *B.E.C.*, 5th series, I (1860), 73–92.

Preuves généalogiques et historiques de la maison de Harcourt, ed. (Dom.) P. J.-L. Le Noir and published by the marquis d'Harcourt. Paris, 1907.

Preuves pour servir à l'histoire de la maison de Chabannes, ed. H. de Chabannes. 4 vols. Dijon, 1892–7.

Procédures politiques du règne de Louis XII, ed. R. de Maulde La Clavière (C.D.I.). Paris, 1885.

Procès criminel de Jehan de Poytiers, seigneur de Saint-Vallier, ed. G. Guiffrey. Paris, 1868.

Procès-verbaux des séances du conseil de régence du roi Charles VIII, ed. A. Bernier (C.D.I.). Paris, 1836.

'Rapports à Philippe VI sur l'état de ses finances', ed. H. Moranvillé. *B.E.C.*, XLVIII (1887), 380–95.

Recueil de pièces imprimées sous le règne de Louis XI, ed. E. Picot and H. Stein. Paris, 1923.

Recueil de pièces pour servir de suite à l'histoire de Louis XI, ed. C. Duclos. Paris, 1746.

Recueil de pièces servant de preuves aux mémoires sur les troubles excités en France par Charles II, dit le Mauvais, roi de Navarre et comte d'Evreux, ed. Secousse. Paris, 1755.

Recueil des documents concernant le Poitou contenus dans les registres de la chancellerie de France, ed. P. Guérin (vols. XI, XIII, XVII, XIX, XXI, XXIV, XXVI, XXIX, XXXII, XXXVIII, XLI, XLIV, L, LVI of *Arch. hist. Poitou*).

Recueil des privilèges accordés à la ville de Bordeaux par Charles VII et Louis XI, ed. M. Gouron. Bordeaux, 1937.

Recueil général des anciennes lois françaises, ed. Isambert, Jourdain and Decrusy. 29 vols. Paris, 1822–33.

Registre criminel du Châtelet de Paris, ed. H. Duplès-Agier. 2 vols. Paris, 1861 and 1864.

Registres du Trésor des Chartes, ed. R. Fawtier *et al.* 3 vols. Paris, 1958–78.

Répertoire des titres du comté de Taillebourg, ed. G. Tortat. *Arch. hist. de la Saintonge et de l'Aunis*, XXIX (1900).

'Rôles normands et français et autres pièces tirées des archives de Londres par Bréquigny', *Mém. soc. des antiquaires de Normandie*, XXIII (1858), 1–306.

Rotuli Normanniae, ed. T. D. Hardy. London, 1835.

Rouen au temps de Jeanne d'Arc et pendant l'occupation anglaise (1419–1449), ed. P. Le Cacheux (Soc. de l'hist. de Normandie). Rouen and Paris, 1931.

Seine-Maritime. *Inventaire sommaire des archives départementales*, ed. Ch. de Robillard de Beaurepaire. vol. II. Paris, 1874.

Le soulèvement de la Flandre maritime de 1323–8 (documents inédits), ed. H. Pirenne. Brussels, 1900.

Thesaurus Novus Anecdotorum, ed. E. Martène and U. Durand. 5 vols. Paris, 1717.

Titres de la maison ducale de Bourbon, ed. A. Huillard-Bréholles and A. Lecoy de La Marche. 2 vols. Paris, 1867–74.

Ville de Toulouse. *Inventaire des archives communales antérieures à 1790*, ed. E. Roschach. vol. I. Toulouse, 1891.

The War of Saint-Sardos, ed. P. Chaplais. *Camden Miscellany*, 3rd series, LXXXVII (1954).

Chronicles

Basin, Thomas. *Histoire de Louis XI*, ed. and trans. C. Samaran and M.-C. Garand (Classiques de l'hist. de France au moyen âge). 3 vols. Paris, 1963–72.

Baye, Nicholas de. *Journal*, ed. A. Tuetey (S.H.F.). 2 vols. Paris, 1885 and 1888.

Bueil, Jean de, *Le jouvencel*, ed. C. Favre and L. Lecestre (S.H.F.). 2 vols. Paris, 1887 and 1889.

Chartier, Jean. *Chronique de Charles VII*, ed. A. Vallet de Viriville. 3 vols. Paris, 1858.

Chastellain, Georges. *Oeuvres*, ed. Kervyn de Lettenhove. 8 vols. Brussels, 1863–6.

Chronique des règnes de Jean II et de Charles V, ed. R. Delachenal (S.H.F.). 4 vols. Paris, 1910–20.

Chronique du Mont-Saint-Michel (1343–1468), ed. S. Luce. 2 vols. Paris, 1879–83.

Chronique du religieux de Saint-Denys, ed. L. Bellaguet (C.D.I.). 6 vols. Paris, 1839–52.
Chronique normande du XIVe siècle, ed. A. and E. Molinier (S.H.F.). Paris, 1882.
Chronique parisienne anonyme de 1316–1339, ed. A. Hellot. *Mém. soc. hist. de Paris et de l'Ile de France*, XI (1885).
Chronographia Regum Francorum, ed. H. Moranvillé (S.H.F.). 3 vols. Paris, 1891–7.
Cochon, Pierre. *Chronique normande*, ed. Ch. de Robillard de Beaurepaire (Soc. de l'hist. de Normandie). Rouen, 1870.
Commynes, Philippe de. *Mémoires*, ed. J. Calmette and G. Durville (Classiques de l'hist. de France au moyen âge). 3 vols. Paris, 1964–5.
Commynes, Philippe de. *Mémoires*, ed. Mlle Dupont (S.H.F.). 3 vols. Paris, 1840–7.
Commynes, Philippe de. *Mémoires*, ed. Lenglet-Dufresnoy. 4 vols. Paris, 1747.
Les cronicques de Normandie (1223–1453), ed. A. Hellot. Rouen, 1881.
Duclercq, Jacques. *Mémoires*, ed. Fr. Baron de Reiffenberg. 4 vols. Paris, 1826–7.
Escouchy, Mathieu d'. *Chronique*, ed. G. du Fresne de Beaucourt (S.H.F.). 3 vols. Paris, 1863–4.
Fauquembergue, Clément de. *Journal*, ed. A. Tuetey and H. Lacaille (S.H.F.). 3 vols. Paris, 1903–15.
Froissart, Jean. *Chroniques*, ed. S. Luce *et al.* (S.H.F.). 15 vols. published. Paris, 1869–1975.
Froissart, Jean. *Oeuvres*, ed. Kervyn de Lettenhove. 25 vols. Brussels, 1867–77.
Les grandes chroniques de France, ed. J. Viard (S.H.F.). 10 vols. Paris, 1920–53.
Gregory of Tours. *Histoire ecclésiastique des Francs*, ed. and trans. J. Guadet and N. Taranne (S.H.F.). 4 vols. Paris, 1836–8.
Gruel, Guillaume. *Chronique d'Arthur de Richemont*, ed. A. Le Vavasseur (S.H.F.). Paris, 1890.
Jaligny, Guillaume de. *Histoire de Charles VIII*, in *Histoire de Charles VIII*, ed. D. Godefroy. Paris, 1684.
Journal d'un bourgeois de Paris (1405–1449), ed. A. Tuetey. Paris, 1881.
Juvenal des Ursins, Jean. *Ecrits politiques*, ed. P. S. Lewis (S.H.F.). 1 vol. published. Paris, 1978.
Juvenal des Ursins, Jean. *Histoire de Charles VI*, ed. D. Godefroy. Paris, 1653.
Le Bel, Jean. *Chronique*, ed. J. Viard and E. Déprez (S.H.F.). 2 vols. Paris, 1904 and 1905.
Le Fèvre, Jean. *Chronique*, ed. F. Morand (S.H.F.). 2 vols. Paris, 1876 and 1881.
Le Muisit, Gilles. *Chronique et annales*, ed. H. Lemaître (S.H.F.). Paris, 1905.
Lescot, Richard. *Chronique*, ed. J. Lemoine (S.H.F.). Paris, 1896.
Masselin, Jean. *Journal des Etats généraux de France tenus à Tours en 1484*, ed. A. Bernier (C.D.I.). Paris, 1835.
Maupoint, Jean. *Journal parisien (1437–1469)*, ed. G. Fagniez. *Mém. soc. de l'hist. de Paris et de l'Ile de France*, IV (1878).
Molinet, Jean. *Chroniques*, ed. G. Doutrepont and O. Jodogne. 3 vols. Brussels, 1935–7.
Molinet, Jean. *Les faictz et dictz*. Paris, 1537.

Monstrelet, Enguerran de. *Chronique*, ed. L. Douët-d'Arcq (S.H.F.). 6 vols. Paris, 1857–62.
Nangis, Guillaume de. *Chronique de Guillaume de Nangis et de ses continuateurs*, ed. H. Géraud (S.H.F.). 2 vols. Paris, 1843.
Recueil des historiens des Gaules et de la France, ed. M. Bouquet *et al.* 24 vols. Paris, 1738–1904.
Richer, *Histoire*, ed. and trans. J. Guadet (S.H.F.). 2 vols. Paris, 1845.
Roye, Jean de. *Journal, connu sous le nom de Chronique scandaleuse (1460–1483)*, ed. B. de Mandrot (S.H.F.). 2 vols. Paris, 1894 and 1896.
Venette, Jean de. *Chronicle*, ed. R. Newhall and trans. J. Birdsall. New York, 1953.

SECONDARY WORKS

Acher, J. 'Notes sur le droit savant au moyen âge', *Nouv. rev. hist. de droit fr. et ét.*, xxx (1906), 125–78.
Allison, J. E. and J. D. Cloud. 'The lex Julia Maiestatis', *Latomus*, xxi (1962), 711–31.
Allmand, C. T. 'The Aftermath of War in Fifteenth-Century France', *History*, lxi (1976), 344–57.
Allmand, C. T. 'The Collection of Dom Lenoir and the English Occupation of Normandy in the Fifteenth Century', *Archives*, vi (1964), 202–10.
Allmand, C. T. 'The Lancastrian Land Settlement in Normandy 1417–50', *Econ. Hist. Rev.*, 2nd series, xxi (1968), 461–79.
Allmand, C. T. 'The Relations between the English Government, the Higher Clergy and the Papacy in Normandy 1417–1450', unpublished Oxford D.Phil. thesis. 1962.
Anchier, C. 'Charles Ier de Melun, grand maître de France et lieutenant-général du roi Louis XI à Paris et dans l'Ile de France', *M.A.*, v (1892), 80–7, 106–10.
Andrieu, J. *Histoire de l'Agenais*. 2 vols. Agen, 1893.
Anselme de Sainte-Marie (le Père). *Histoire généalogique et chronologique de la maison royale de France*, continued by M. du Fourny. 9 vols. Paris, 1726–33.
Armstrong, C. A. J. 'Politics and the Battle of Saint-Albans', *B.I.H.R.*, xxxiii (1960), 1–72.
Armstrong, C. A. J. 'La Toison d'Or et la loi des armes', *Publication du centre européen des études burgundo-médianes*, v (1963), 71–7.
Artières, J. *Récits, documents et études sur l'histoire de la ville de Millau. Ière partie: Annales de Millau depuis les origines jusqu'à nos jours*. Millau, 1894–9.
Artonne, A. *Le mouvement de 1314 et les chartes provinciales de 1315*. Paris, 1912.
Aubert, F. *Histoire du Parlement de Paris de l'origine à François I*. 2 vols. Paris, 1894.
Aubert, F. *Le Parlement de Paris de Philippe-le-Bel à Charles VII (1314–1422): sa compétence, ses attributions*. Paris, 1890.
Aubert, F. *Le Parlement de Paris de Philippe-le-Bel à Charles VII (1314–1422): son organisation*. Paris, 1887.
Aussy, Denis d'. *La Saintonge pendant la guerre de Cent ans (1372–1453)*. La Rochelle, 1894.

Aussy, Denis d'. 'La tour de Broue 1115–1789', *Arch. hist. de la Saintonge et de l'Aunis*, XIX (1891), 333–79.

Bar, C. L. von, *et al. A History of Continental Criminal Law*, trans. T. S. Bell *et al.* London, 1916.

Bardoux, A. *Les légistes: leur influence sur la société française.* Paris, 1877.

Batiffol, L. 'Le Châtelet de Paris vers 1400', *R.H.*, LXI (1896), 225–64; LXII (1896), 225–35; LXIII (1897), 42–55, 266–83.

Bauman, R. *The Crimen Maiestatis in the Roman* Republic *and Augustan Principate.* Johannesburg, 1970.

Beaucourt, G. du Fresne de. 'La conspiration du duc d'Alençon (1455–1456)', *Rev. des quest. hist.*, XLIX (1891), 410–33.

Beaucourt, G. du Fresne de. *Histoire de Charles VII.* 6 vols. Paris, 1881–91.

Beauvillé, V. de. *Histoire de la ville de Montdidier.* 3 vols. Paris, 1875.

Bellamy, J. G. *The Law of Treason in England in the Later Middle Ages.* Cambridge, 1970.

Bellamy, J. G. *The Tudor Law of Treason: an Introduction.* London, Toronto and Buffalo, 1979.

Bertrand de Broussillon, A. *La maison de Craon 1050–1480.* 2 vols. Paris, 1893.

Bertrandy, M. *Etude sur les chroniques de Froissart.* Bordeaux, 1870.

Bloch, M. *Les rois thaumaturges.* Paris, 1924.

Bonamy, M. 'Mémoire sur les suites du procès de Jacques Coeur', in Duclercq, *Mémoires*, II. 391–409.

Bossuat, A. 'La formule "Le roi est empereur en son royaume", Son emploi au XVe siècle devant le Parlement de Paris', *R.H.D.F.E.*, 4th series, XXXIX (1961), 371–81.

Bossuat, A. 'Le rétablissement de la paix sociale sous le règne de Charles VII', *M.A.*, LX (1954), 137–62.

Boudet, M. *La Jacquerie des Tuchins 1363–1384.* Riom, 1895.

Boudet, M. *Thomas de La Marche, bâtard de France 1318–1361.* Riom, 1900.

Boulet-Sautel, M. 'Le concept de souveraineté chez Jacques de Révigny', *Actes du congrès sur l'ancienne Université d'Orléans* (Orléans, 1962), 15–27.

Boulet-Sautel, M. 'Jean de Blanot et la conception du pouvoir royal au temps de Louis IX', *Septième centenaire de la mort de Saint Louis: actes des colloques de Royaumont et de Paris*, ed. L. Carolus-Barré (Paris, 1976), 57–68.

Boulet-Sautel, M. 'Le *Princeps* de Guillaume Durand', *Etudes d'histoire du droit canonique dédiées à Gabriel Le Bras* (2 vols., Paris, 1965), II. 803–13.

Boulet-Sautel, M. 'Le rôle juridictionnel de la cour des pairs aux XIIIe et XIVe siècles', *Recueil de travaux offert à M. Clovis Brunel* (2 vols., Paris, 1955), II. 507–20.

Boutaric, E. *La France sous Philippe le Bel.* Paris, 1861.

Boutruche, R. *La crise d'une société: seigneurs et paysans du Bordelais pendant la guerre de Cent ans.* Paris, 1963.

Boutruche, R. (ed.) *Bordeaux de 1453 à 1715* (vol. IV of *Histoire de Bordeaux*). Bordeaux, 1966.

Bridge, J. S. C. *A History of France from the Death of Louis XI*. 5 vols. London, 1921–36.
Bristow, A. 'Fourteenth-Century Rodez', unpublished Oxford D.Phil. thesis. 1976.
Burney, E. 'The English Rule in Normandy 1435–1450', unpublished Oxford B.Litt. thesis. 1958.
Cagé, C. 'Louis de Luxembourg, comte de Saint-Pol, connétable de France (1418–1475)', *Positions des thèses soutenues à l'Ecole Nationale des Chartes* (1885), 29–41.
Caillemer, R. 'Jean de Blanot', *Mélanges Ch. Appleton* (Lyon and Paris, 1903), 51–101.
Calasso, F. *I glossatori e la teoria della sovranità*. 3rd edn. Milan, 1957.
Calasso, F. 'Origini italiane della formola "rex in regno suo est imperator"', *Rivista di storia del diritto italiano*, III (1930), 213–59.
Callies, G. 'Le procès civil et criminel de Robert III d'Artois', *Positions des thèses soutenues à l'Ecole Nationale des Chartes* (1932), 35–41.
Calmette, J. 'Une manoeuvre politique de Louis XI: l'aventure de l'évêque d'Elne, Charles de Martigny, ambassadeur de France à Londres', *Rev. d'hist. mod.*, IV (1929), 117–22.
Calmette, J. and E. Déprez. *La France et l'Angleterre en conflit*. vol. VII (1) of *Histoire générale*, published under the direction of G. Glotz. Paris, 1937.
Calmette, J. and G. Périnelle. *Louis XI et l'Angleterre (1461–1483)*. Paris, 1930.
Carel, P. *Histoire de la ville de Caen depuis Philippe-Auguste jusqu'à Charles IX*. Paris, 1886.
Carlyle, A. J. and R. W. *A History of Medieval Political Theory in the West*. 6 vols. London, 1903–36.
Cazelles, R. 'Jean II le Bon: quel homme? Quel roi?', *R.H.*, CCLI (1974), 5–26.
Cazelles, R. 'Le parti navarrais jusqu'à la mort d'Etienne Marcel', *Bull. philol. et hist. du comité des travaux historiques et scientifiques* (1960), 839–69.
Cazelles, R. 'La réglementation royale de la guerre privée de St-Louis à Charles V et la précarité des ordonnances', *R.H.D.F.E.*, 4th series, XXXVIII (1960), 530–48.
Cazelles, R. 'La saisie de la Bourgogne en 1334', *Ann. de Bourgogne*, XXXII (1960), 169–82.
Cazelles, R. *La société politique et la crise de la royauté sous Philippe de Valois*. Paris, 1958.
Chabannes, H. de. *Histoire de la maison de Chabannes*. 4 vols. Dijon, 1892–9, and supplement, published in 1901.
Chalmel, J.-L. *Histoire de Touraine*. 4 vols. Paris and Tours, 1828.
Chaplais, P. 'Règlement des conflits internationaux franco-anglais au XIVe siècle (1297–1327)', *M.A.*, LVII (1951), 269–301.
Chaplais, P. 'La souveraineté du roi de France et le pouvoir législatif en Guyenne au début du XIVe siècle', *M.A.*, LXIX (1963), 449–69.
Chénon, E. 'Le droit romain à la *curia regis* de Philippe-Auguste à Philippe le Bel', *Mélanges Fitting* (2 vols., Montpellier, 1907 and 1908), I. 195–212.

Chérest, A. *L'archiprêtre: épisodes de la guerre de Cent ans au quatorzième siècle*. Paris, 1879.
Chéruel, P. *Histoire de Rouen pendant l'époque communale 1150–1382*. 2 vols. Rouen, 1843–4.
Church, W. F. *Richelieu and Reason of State*. Princeton, 1972.
Clément, P. *Jacques Coeur et Charles VII*. 2 vols. Paris, 1853.
Cloud, J. D. 'The Text of Digest XLVIII, 4 Ad Legem Iuliam Maiestatis', *Zeitschrift der Savigny-Stiflung für Rechtsgeschichte, romanistische Abteilung*, LXXX (1963), 206–32.
Cloud, J. D. and J. E. Allison. See under Allison.
Combet, J. *Louis XI et le Saint-Siège (1461–1483)*. Paris, 1903.
Contamine, P. *Guerre, état et société à la fin du moyen âge*. Paris and The Hague, 1972.
Contamine, P. 'L'idée de guerre à la fin du moyen âge: aspects juridiques et éthiques', *Comptes rendus de l'Académie des Inscriptions* (1979), 70–86.
Cosneau, E. *Le connétable de Richemont (Artur de Bretagne) (1393–1458)*. Paris, 1886.
Courteault, H. 'La fuite et les aventures de Pierre de Craon en Espagne, d'après des documents inédits des Archives d'Aragon (1392)', *B.E.C.*, LII (1891), 431–48.
Coville, A. *Jean Petit: la question du tyrannicide au commencement du XVe siècle*. Paris, 1932.
Coville, A. 'Le véritable texte de la Justification du duc de Bourgogne par Jean Petit (8 mars 1408)', *B.E.C.*, LXXII (1911), 57–91.
Coville, A. *Les premiers Valois et la guerre de Cent ans (1328–1422)*. vol. IV (1) of *Histoire de France*, ed. Lavisse. Paris, 1911.
'Crimes contre l'état', *Répertoire méthodique et alphabétique de législation, de doctrine, et de jurisprudence*, ed. D. Dalloz *et al.*, vol. XIV (Paris, 1853), 526–7.
Dangibeaud, C. 'La maison de Rabaine en Saintonge', *Arch. hist. de la Saintonge et de l'Aunis*, XIX (1891), 44–219.
Daniel, E. *Le procès de Jacques Coeur. Du crime de lèse-majesté et des juridictions séculière et ecclésiastique au XVe siècle*. Bourges, 1889.
David, M. *La souveraineté et les limites juridiques du pouvoir monarchique du IXe au XVe siècle*. Paris, 1954.
Delachenal, R. 'La bibliothèque d'un avocat du XIVe siècle', *Nouv. rev. hist. du droit fr. et ét.*, XI (1887), 524–37.
Delachenal, R. *Histoire de Charles V*. 5 vols. Paris, 1909–31.
Delachenal, R. 'Premières négotiations de Charles le Mauvais avec les anglais (1354–1355)', *B.E.C.*, LXI (1900), 253–82.
Delayant, L. 'Procès des frères Plusqualec', *Arch. hist. Poitou*, II (1873), 217–51.
Delisle, L. 'L'auteur du Grand coutumier de France', *Mém. soc. hist. de Paris et de l'Ile de France*, VIII (1881), 140–60.
Delisle, L. *Histoire du château et des sires de Saint-Sauveur-le-Vicomte*. Valognes, 1867.
Déprez, E. 'La double trahison de Godefroi d'Harcourt', *R.H.*, XCIX (1908), 32–4.
Déprez, E. and J. Calmette. See under Calmette.
Dessalles, L. *Périgueux et les deux derniers comtes de Périgord*. Paris, 1847.
Devic, C. See under Vaissete.

Digard, G. *Philippe le Bel et le Saint-Siège de 1285 à 1304.* 2 vols. Paris, 1936.
Douët-d'Arcq, L. 'Acte d'accusation contre Robert Le Coq', *B.E.C.*, II (1840), 350–87.
Duboscq, G. 'Charles d'Anjou, premier comte du Maine (1414–1473)', *Positions des thèses soutenues à l'Ecole National des Chartes* (1933), 21–35.
Ducoudray, G. *Les origines du Parlement de Paris et la justice aux XIIIe et XIVe siècles.* Paris, 1902.
Dufayard, C. 'La réaction féodale sous les fils de Philippe le Bel', *R.H.*, LIV (1894), 241–72; LV (1895), 241–90.
Dufournet, J. *La vie de Philippe de Commynes.* Paris, 1969.
Duparc, P. *Origines de la grace dans le droit pénal romain et français du Bas-Empire à la Renaissance.* Paris, 1942.
Dupont-Ferrier, G. *Gallia regia, ou état des officiers royaux des bailliages et des sénéchaussées de 1328 à 1515.* 7 vols. Paris, 1942–65.
Dupont-Ferrier, G. *Les officiers royaux des bailliages et sénéchaussées et les institutions monarchiques locales en France à la fin du moyen âge* (Bibl. de l'Ec. des Hautes Et: 145). Paris, 1902.
Dupont-Ferrier, G. 'Le rôle des commissaires royaux dans le gouvernement de la France spécialement du XIVe au XVIe siècle', *Mélanges Paul Fournier* (Paris, 1929), 171–84.
Dupont-Ferrier, G. 'Le sens des mots "patria" et "patrie" en France au moyen âge et jusqu'au début du XVIIe siècle', *R.H.*, CLXXXVIII (1940), 89–104.
Dupuy, P. *Histoire du differend d'entre le pape Boniface VIII et Philippes le Bel roy de France.* Paris, 1655.
Ercole, F. 'L'origine francese di una nota formola bartoliana', *Archivio storico italiano*, LXXIII (1915), 241–94.
Ercole, F. 'Sulla origine francese e le vicende in Italia della formola "rex superiorem non recognoscens est princeps in regno suo" ', *Archivio storico italiano*, LXXXIX (1931), 197–238.
Esmein, A. *Cours élémentaire d'histoire du droit français.* 14th edn. Paris, 1921.
Esmein, A. *A History of Continental Criminal Procedure*, trans. J. Simpson. London, 1914.
Faral, E. 'Robert le Coq et les Etats généraux de 1356', *R.H.D.F.E.*, 4th series, XXIII (1945), 171–214.
Faussemagne, J. *L'apanage ducal de Bourgogne dans ses rapports avec la monarchie française (1363–1477).* Lyon, 1937.
Favier, J. *Un conseiller de Philippe le Bel: Enguerran de Marigny.* Paris, 1963.
Favier, L. See under Samaran.
Favreau, R. 'La Praguerie en Poitou', *B.E.C.*, CXXIX (1971), 277–301.
Fawtier, R. See under Lot.
Fédou, R. 'Fidélité lyonnaise et propagande bourguignonne au temps de Louis XI', *Mélanges Fugier* (Lyon, 1968), 71–80.
Feenstra, R. 'Jean de Blanot et la formule "Rex Franciae in regno suo princeps est" ', *Etudes d'histoire du droit canonique dédiées à Gabriel Le Bras* (2 vols., Paris, 1965), II. 885–95.

Feenstra, R. 'Quaestiones de materia feudorum de Jacques de Revigny', *Studi Senesi*, LXXXIV (1972), 379–401.
Félibien, M. *Histoire de la ville de Paris*. 5 vols. Paris, 1725.
Fontaine de Resbecq, F. de. 'Les rapports du gouvernement anglais et de la noblesse normande dans la vicomté de Valognes pendant l'occupation 1418–1450', *Mém. soc. archéol. artist., litt., et sc. de l'arrondissement de Valognes*, IX (1907–12), 17–42.
Forgeot, H. *Jean Balue, cardinal d'Angers (1421?–1491)* (Bibl. de l'Ec. des Hautes Et.: 106). Paris, 1895.
Fouché, C. *Taillebourg et ses seigneurs*. Chef-Boutonne, 1911.
Fournier, M. *Histoire de la science du droit en France*. Paris, 1892.
Fournier, P. 'Les conflits de juridiction entre l'église et le pouvoir séculier de 1080 à 1328', *Rev. des quest. hist.*, XXVII (1880), 432–64.
Foviaux, J. *La rémission des peines et des condamnations*. Paris, 1970.
Fowler, K. *The King's Lieutenant: Henry of Grosmont, First Duke of Lancaster 1310–1361*. London, 1969.
Frondeville, H. de. 'La vicomté d'Orbec pendant l'occupation anglaise (1417–1449)', *Etudes lexoviennes*, IV (1936), 1–115.
Funck-Brentano, F. *Les origines de la guerre de Cent ans: Philippe le Bel en Flandre*. Paris, 1896.
Funck-Brentano, F. 'Les pairs de France à la fin du XIIIe siècle', *Etudes d'histoire du moyen âge dédiées à Gabriel Monod* (Paris, 1896), 351–60.
Funk, A. L. 'Robert Le Coq and Etienne Marcel', *Speculum*, XIX (1944), 470–87.
Gallia Christiana, ed. D. Sammarthan *et al.* 16 vols. Paris, 1715–1865.
Ganshof, F. L. *Feudalism*, trans. P. Grierson. New York, 1964.
Gaudemet, J. 'Maiestas Populi Romani', *Synteleia Vincenzo Arangio-Ruiz* (2 vols., Naples, 1964), II. 699–709.
Genestal, R. *Les origines de l'appel comme d'abus*. Paris, 1951.
Genestal, R. *Le Privilegium Fori en France du Décret de Gratien à la fin du XIVe siècle*. 2 vols. Paris, 1921 and 1924.
Germain, A. *Histoire de la commune de Montpellier*. 3 vols. Montpellier, 1851.
Godefroy, D. and T. *Le ceremonial françois*. 2 vols. Paris, 1649.
Gothofredus, Jacobus. *Discursus Historicus ad Legem Quisquis Cod. ad L. Iuliam Maiestatis*. Geneva, 1654.
Gouron, A. 'Les juristes de l'école de Montpellier', *Ius Romanum Medii Aevi*, part iv, fasc. IIIa. Milan, 1970.
Gransden, A. 'The Alleged Rape by Edward III of the Countess of Salisbury', *E.H.R.*, LXXXVII (1972), 333–44.
Guérin, P. 'Pierre d'Urfé, grand écuyer de France, et Jean de Jaucourt', *Le cabinet historique*, XXVI (1) (1880), 113–26, 172–80.
Guillot, R. *Le procès de Jacques Coeur*. Paris, 1975.
Guyot, G.-A. *Répertoire universel et raisonné de jurisprudence civile, criminelle, canonique et bénéficiale*. vol. XXXVI. Paris, 1778.
Harcourt, L. W. Vernon. *His Grace the Steward and the Trial of Peers*. London, 1907.

Hauréau, J. B. *Bernard Délicieux et l'inquisition albigeoise*. Paris, 1877.
Hellegouarc'h. J. *Le vocabulaire latin des relations et des partis politiques sous la république*. Paris, 1963.
Honoré-Duvergé, S. 'Des partisans de Charles le Mauvais: les Picquigny', *B.E.C.*, CVII (1947), 82–92.
Honoré-Duvergé, S. 'L'origine du surnom de Charles le Mauvais', *Mélanges Louis Halphen* (Paris, 1951), 345–50.
Jackson, R. 'Peers of France and Princes of the Blood', *French Historical Studies*, VII (1971), 27–46.
Jarry, E. *La vie politique de Louis de France, duc d'Orléans (1372–1407)*. Paris, 1889.
Jaurgain, J. de. *Deux comtes de Comminges béarnais du XVe siècle: Jean de Lescun, bâtard d'Armagnac, et Odet d'Aydie, seigneur de Lescun*. Paris, 1919.
Jones, M. *Ducal Brittany 1364–1399*. Oxford, 1970.
Jouet, R. *La résistance à l'occupation anglaise en Basse-Normandie (1418–1450)* (Cahiers des Annales de Normandie: 5). Caen, 1969.
Kantorowicz, E. *The King's Two Bodies: a Study in Medieval Political Theology*. Princeton, 1957.
Keen, M. H. *England in the Later Middle Ages*. London, 1973.
Keen, M. H. *The Laws of War in the Late Middle Ages*. London and Toronto, 1965.
Keen, M. H. 'Treason Trials under the Law of Arms', *T.R.H.S.*, 5th series, XII (1962), 85–103.
La Borderie, A. de, and B.-A. Pocquet du Haut-Jussé. *Histoire de Bretagne*. 6 vols. Rennes, 1896–1914.
Lagarde, G. de. *La naissance de l'esprit laïque au déclin du moyen âge*. 5 vols. New edn. Louvain, 1956–70.
Lancelot, A. *Mémoires concernant les pairs de France*. 2 vols. in 1. Paris, 1720.
Lander, J. R. 'Attainder and Forfeiture 1453–1509', *Historical Journal*, IV (1961), 120–51.
Langlois, C.-V. *Le règne de Philippe III le Hardi*. Paris, 1887.
Lanhers, Y. 'Deux affaires de trahison défendues par Jean Jouvenel des Ursins (1423–1427)', *Mélanges Pierre Tisset* (Montpellier, 1970), 317–28.
La Roque de La Lontière, G.-A. de. *Histoire généalogique de la maison de Harcourt*. 4 vols. Paris, 1762.
Lavergne, G. 'La guerre d'Archambaud fils contre Périgueux (1397–1398)', *Bull. soc. hist. et arch. du Périgord*, LXVI (1939), 279–96.
Lear, F. S. *Treason in Roman and Germanic Law*. Austin, Texas, 1965.
Le Barrois d'Orgeval, G. *La justice militaire sous l'Ancien Régime. Le tribunal de la connétablie de France du XIVe siècle à 1790*. Paris, 1918.
Lecoy de La Marche, A. *Le roi René*. 2 vols. in 1. Paris, 1875.
Lefèvre-Pontalis, G. 'La guerre des partisans dans la Haute-Normandie (1424–1429)', *B.E.C.*, LIV (1893), 475–521; LV (1894), 239–305; LVI (1895), 433–508; LVII (1896), 5–54; XCVII (1936), 102–30.
Lefranc, A. *Olivier de Clisson, connétable de France*. Paris, 1898.
Legeay, U. *Histoire de Louis XI*. 2 vols. Paris, 1874.

Leguai, A. 'La conquête de la Bourgogne par Louis XI', *Ann. de Bourgogne*, XLIX (1977), 87–92.

Leguai, A. *Les ducs de Bourbon pendant la crise monarchique du XVe siècle*. Paris, 1962.

Leguai, A. 'Emeutes et troubles d'origine fiscale pendant le règne de Louis XI', *M.A.*, LXXIII (1967), 447–87.

Lehugeur, P. *Histoire de Philippe le Long, roi de France (1316–1322)*. 2 vols. Paris, 1897 and 1931.

Lemarignier, J.-F. 'A propos de deux textes sur l'histoire du droit romain au moyen âge', *B.E.C.*, CI (1940), 157–68.

Lemosse, M. 'La lèse-majesté dans la monarchie franque', *Rev. du moyen âge latin*, II (1946), 5–24.

Lettenhove, Kervyn de. 'Procès de Robert d'Artois', *Bull. de l'acad. roy. de Belgique*, 2nd series, X (1860), 641–69; XI (1861), 107–25.

Lewis, P. S. 'Jean Juvenal des Ursins and the Common Literary Attitude towards Tyranny in Fifteenth-Century France', *Medium Aevum*, XXXIV (1965), 103–21.

Lewis, P. S. *Later Medieval France*. London, 1968.

Lot, F. and R. Fawtier. *Histoire des institutions françaises au moyen âge*, vol. II (*Institutions royales*). Paris, 1958.

Luce, S. *Histoire de Bertrand du Guesclin et de son époque*. Paris, 1876.

Luce, S. *Jeanne d'Arc à Domremy*. Paris, 1886.

Luchaire, A. *Alain le grand, sire d'Albret*. Paris, 1877.

Luchaire, A. *Histoire des institutions monarchiques de la France sous les premiers capétiens*. 2 vols. Paris, 1891.

Maitland, J. P. 'The Early Homes of the Balliols', *Trans. of the Dumfriesshire and Galloway Natural History and Antiquarian Society*, 3rd series, XVIII (1931–3), 235–42.

Mandrot, B. de. 'Jacques d'Armagnac, duc de Nemours', *R.H.*, XLIII (1890), 274–316; XLIV (1890), 241–312.

Mandrot, B. de. 'Louis XI, Jean V d'Armagnac et le drame de Lectoure', *R.H.*, XXXVIII (1888), 241–304.

Mandrot, B. de. *Ymbert de Batarnay, seigneur du Bouchage*. Paris, 1886.

Mariéjol, J. H. *La réforme et la Ligue – l'Edit de Nantes (1559–1598)*. vol. VI (1) of *Histoire de France*, ed. Lavisse. Paris, 1911.

Maugis, E. *Histoire du Parlement de Paris de l'avènement des rois Valois à la mort d'Henri IV*. 3 vols. Paris, 1913–16.

Maulde La Clavière, R. de. *Histoire de Louis XII*. 6 vols. Paris, 1889–93.

Meijers, E. M. *Etudes d'histoire du droit*, ed. R. Feenstra. 4 vols. Leyden, 1956–73.

Ménard, L. *Histoire civile, ecclésiastique et littéraire de la ville de Nismes*. 7 vols. Paris, 1750–68.

Merlet, L. 'Biographie de Jean de Montagu', *B.E.C.*, 3rd series, III (1852), 248–84.

Mirot, L. *Les insurrections urbaines au début du règne de Charles VI (1380–1383)*. Paris, 1905.

Mirot, L. 'Les insurrections urbaines en Normandie à la fin du XIVe siècle', *Rev. des ét. hist.* (1902), 558–82.

Mirot, L. 'Le procès de Maître Jean Fusoris', *Mém. soc. hist. de Paris et de l'Ile de France*, XXVII (1900), 137–279.

Mirot, L. 'Le procès du Boiteux d'Orgemont', 4th part, *M.A.*, XXV (1912), 353–410.

Mitchell, J. H. *The Court of the Connétable*. New Haven, Connecticut, 1947.

Mommsen. T. *Le droit pénal romain*, trans. J. Duquesne. 3 vols. Paris, 1907.

Moranvillé, H. 'La trahison de Jean de Vervins', *B.E.C.*, LIII (1892), 605–11.

Morice, (Dom.) P.-H. *Histoire ecclésiastique et civile de Bretagne*. 2 vols. Paris, 1750 and 1756.

Neuville, D. 'Le Parlement royal à Poitiers 1418–1436', *R.H.*, VI (1878), 1–28, 272–314.

Newhall, R. 'Henry V's Policy of Conciliation in Normandy 1417–1422', *Anniversary Essays in Medieval History by Students of Charles Homer Haskins*, ed. C. H. Taylor and J. L. LaMonte (Boston and New York, 1929), pp. 205–29.

Nicholson, R. *Edward III and the Scots*. Oxford, 1965.

Nordberg, M. *Les ducs et la royauté. Etude sur la rivalité des ducs d'Orléans et de Bourgogne 1392–1407* (Studia Historica Upsaliensia). Stockholm, 1964.

Odolant-Desnos, P. *Mémoires historiques sur la ville d'Alençon et sur ses seigneurs*. 2 vols. Alençon, 1787.

Ourliac, P. 'The Concordat of 1472: an Essay on the Relations between Louis XI and Sixtus IV', *The Recovery of France in the Fifteenth Century*, ed. P. S. Lewis (London, 1971), 102–84.

Palmer, J. J. N. *England, France and Christendom 1377–99*. London, 1972.

Pegues, F. J. *The Lawyers of the Last Capetians*. Princeton, 1962.

Pélicier, P. *Essai sur le gouvernement de la dame de Beaujeu 1483–1491*. Chartres, 1882.

Pena, N. de. 'Vassaux gascons au service du roi d'Angleterre dans la première moitié du XIVe siècle: fidélité ou esprit de profit?', *Ann. du Midi*, LXXXVIII (1976), 5–21.

Périnelle, G. 'Un texte officiel sur l'exécution du connétable de Saint-Pol', *Mélanges d'archéol. et d'hist. de l'Ecole française de Rome*, XXIII (1903), 427–32.

Périnelle, G. and J. Calmette. See under Calmette.

Perol, J.-F. 'Six siècles avant nous: la tragédie briviste de 1374', *Lemouzi*, 5th series, LIII (1975), 52–9.

Perret, P.-M. 'Boffile de Juge, comte de Castres, et la république de Venise', *Ann. du Midi*, III (1891), 159–231.

Perrot, E. *Les cas royaux*. Paris, 1910.

Perroy, E. *The Hundred Years War*, trans. W. B. Wells. London, 1965.

Pesant, M. le. 'Les manuscrits de Dom Lenoir sur l'histoire de Normandie', *Bull. soc. des antiquaires de Normandie*, L (1946–8), 125–51.

Petit, J. *Charles de Valois (1270–1325)*. Paris, 1900.

Peyrègne, A. 'Les émigrés gascons en Angleterre 1453–1485', *Ann. du Midi*, LXVI (1954), 113–28.

Pfister, C. *Etudes sur le règne de Robert le Pieux 996–1031*. Paris, 1885.

Pirenne, H. *Histoire de Belgique*, 5 vols. Brussels, 1972–5.

Plancher, U. *Histoire générale et particulière de Bourgogne.* 4 vols. Dijon, 1739–81.

Pocquet du Haut-Jussé, B.-A. 'Le compte de Pierre Gorremont, receveur-général du royaume (1418–1420)', *B.E.C.*, XCVIII (1937), 66–98, 234–82.

Pocquet du Haut-Jussé, B.-A. 'La dernière phase de la vie de du Guesclin: l'affaire de Bretagne', *B.E.C.*, CXXV (1967), 142–89.

Pocquet du Haut-Jussé, B.-A. *François II, duc de Bretagne, et l'Angleterre (1458–1488).* Paris, 1929.

Pocquet du Haut-Jussé, B.-A. 'Une idée politique de Louis XI: la sujétion éclipse la vassalité', *R.H.*, CCXXVI (1961), 383–98.

Pocquet du Haut-Jussé, B.-A. and A. de La Borderie. See under La Borderie.

Poncelet, E. 'L'exécution de Louis de Luxembourg, comte de Saint-Pol, en 1475', *Bull. comm. roy. d'hist.*, XCIX (1927), 181–98.

Portal, C. 'Les insurrections de Tuchins dans les pays de langue d'oc, vers 1382–1384', *Ann. du Midi*, IV (1892), 433–74.

Post, G. *Studies in Medieval Legal Thought.* Princeton, 1964.

Puiseux, L. *L'émigration normande et la colonisation anglaise au XVe siècle.* Caen, 1866.

Quaritsch, H. *Staat und Souveränitat*, vol. I. Frankfurt, 1970.

Quillet, J. *La philosophie politique du Songe du Vergier (1378).* Paris, 1977.

Radding, C. 'The Estates of Normandy and the Revolts in the Towns at the Beginning of the Reign of Charles VI', *Speculum*, XLVII (1972), 79–90.

Raynal, L. *Histoire du Berry.* 4 vols. Bourges, 1844–7.

Reiffenberg, Fr. baron de. *Histoire de l'Ordre de la Toison d'Or.* Brussels, 1830.

Rezneck, S. 'Constructive Treason by Words in the Fifteenth Century', *American Hist. Rev.*, XXXIII (1928), 544–52.

Ribadieu, H. *Histoire de la conquête de la Guyenne.* Bordeaux, 1866.

Riesenberg, P. *Inalienability of Sovereignty in Medieval Political Thought.* New York, 1956.

Rigault, A. *Le procès de Guichard, évêque de Troyes (1308–1313).* Paris, 1896.

Rivière, J. *Le problème de l'église et de l'état au temps de Philippe le Bel.* Louvain and Paris, 1926.

Ross, C. D. 'Forfeiture for Treason in the Reign of Richard II', *E.H.R.*, LXXI (1956), 560–75.

Rossignol, C. *Histoire de la Bourgogne pendant la période monarchique (1476–1483).* Dijon, 1853.

Rouvier, J. 'Louis XI et la déclaration d'Amboise du 3 décembre 1470', *R.H.D.F.E.*, 4th series, XLI (1963), 196–237.

Rowe, B. J. 'John, duke of Bedford, and the Norman "Brigands"', *E.H.R.*, XLVII (1932), 583–99.

Russell, F. H. *The Just War in the Middle Ages.* Cambridge, 1975.

Saenger, P. 'Burgundy and the Inalienability of Appanages in the Reign of Louis XI', *French Historical Studies*, X (1977), 1–26.

Samaran, C. *Charles d'Armagnac, vicomte de Fezansaguet.* Auch, 1902.

Samaran, C. 'Les frais du procès et de l'exécution de Jacques d'Armagnac, duc de Nemours', *Mém. soc. hist. de Paris et de l'Ile de France*, XLIX (1927), 142–54.

Samaran, C. *La maison d'Armagnac au XVe siècle et les dernières luttes de la féodalité dans le Midi de la France.* Paris, 1908.
Samaran, C. and L. Favier, 'Louis XI et Jacques d'Armagnac, duc de Nemours: les instructions secrètes du roi au chancelier Pierre Doriole pour la conduite du procès', *Journal des savants* (1966), 65–77.
Sauval, H. *Histoire et recherches des antiquités de la ville de Paris.* 3 vols. Paris, 1724.
Schisas, P. M. *Offences against the State in Roman Law.* London, 1926.
Sée, H. *Louis XI et les villes.* Paris, 1891.
Shennan, J. H. *The Parlement of Paris.* London. 1968.
Smith, C. E. *Tiberius and the Roman Empire.* London, 1972.
Stein, H. *Charles de France, frère de Louis XI.* Paris, 1921.
Stein, H. 'Les conséquences de la bataille de Cassel pour la ville de Bruges et la mort de Guillaume de Deken, son ancien bourgmestre (1328)', *Bull. comm. roy. d'hist.*, 5th series, IX (1899), 647–64.
Strayer, J. R. 'Defense of the Realm and Royal Power in France', *Studi in onore di Gino Luzzatto* (4 vols., Milan, 1949–50), I. 289–96.
Strayer, J. R. 'The Laicization of French and English Society in the Thirteenth Century', *Speculum*, XV (1940), 76–86.
Surirey de Saint-Rémy, H. de. *Jean II de Bourbon, duc de Bourbonnais et d'Auvergne.* Paris, 1944.
Tardif, A. *La procédure civile et criminelle aux XIIIe et XIVe siècles.* Paris, 1885.
Thibault, M. *La jeunesse de Louis XI.* Paris, 1907.
Thomas, A. 'L'évasion et la mort de Jaques Cuer', *R.H.*, XCVIII (1908), 72–86.
Thornley, D. 'Treason by Words in the Fifteenth Century', *E.H.R.*, XXXII (1917), 556–61.
Timbal, P.-C. 'La confiscation dans le droit français des XIIIe et XIVe siècles'. *R.H.D.F.E.*, 4th series, XXII (1943), 44–79; (1944), 35–60.
Tourtoulon, P. *Les oeuvres de Jacques de Révigny (Jacobus de Ravanis) d'après deux mss. de la B.N.* Paris, 1899.
Tucoo-Chala, P. *Gaston Fébus et la vicomté de Béarn 1343–1391.* Bordeaux, 1959.
Tuetey, A. *Les écorcheurs sous Charles VII.* 2 vols. Montbéliard, 1874.
Ullmann, W. 'Arthur's Homage to King John', *E.H.R.*, XCIV (1979), 356–64.
Ullmann, W. 'The Development of the Medieval Idea of Sovereignty', *E.H.R.*, LXIV (1949), 1–33.
Ullmann, W. *The Individual and Society in the Middle Ages*, London, 1967.
Ullmann, W. *Law and Politics in the Middle Ages.* London, 1975.
Ullmann, W. *Principles of Government and Politics in the Middle Ages.* 4th edn. London, 1978.
Ullmann, W. 'This Realm of England is an Empire'. *Journ. Ecc. Hist.*, XXX (1979), 175–203.
Vaissete, (Dom.) J. and Dom. C. Devic. *Histoire générale de Languedoc*, ed. and annotated by A. Molinier *et al.* 16 vols. Toulouse, 1872–1905.
Vale, M. G. A. *Charles VII.* London, 1974.
Vale, M. G. A. *English Gascony 1399–1453.* Oxford, 1970.

Vale, M. G. A. 'A Fifteenth-Century Interrogation of a Political Prisoner', *B.I.H.R.*, XLIII (1970), 78–85.

Vale, M. G. A. 'The Last Years of English Gascony', *T.R.H.S.*, 5th series, XIX (1969), 119–38.

Valois, N. *Le conseil du roi aux XIVe, XVe et XVIe siècles*. Paris, 1888.

Vaughan, R. *Charles the Bold*. London, 1973.

Vaughan, R. *John the Fearless*. London, 1966.

Viala, A. *Le Parlement de Toulouse et l'administration royale laïque 1420–1525 environ*. 2 vols. Albi, 1953.

Viard, J. 'Les domaines de Vaux de Pierre de Remi', *Annuaire Bull. de la soc. de l'hist. de France* (1921), 139–49.

Vidal, J.-M. *Bernard Saisset (1232–1311)*. Paris and Toulouse, 1926.

Vignier, N. *Histoire des comtes et ducs de Luxembourg*. Paris, 1619.

Viollet, P. *Histoire des institutions politiques et administratives de la France*. 3 vols. Paris, 1890–1903.

Wright, N. 'The *Tree of Battles* of Honoré Bouvet and the Laws of War', *War, Literature and Politics in the late Middle Ages: Essays in Honour of G. W. Coopland*, ed. C. T. Allmand (Liverpool, 1976), 12–31.

INDEX

Ableiges, Jacques d', 69
Agès, Bertrand d', lord of Saint-Magne, 206
Aiguillon, 151
Alais, 181
Albret, Alain, lord of, 140, 214, 222, 236
Charles d', lord of Sainte-Bazeille, 35, 63, 90 n. 32, 221–2, 223, 239
Géraud d', lord of Puypardin, 206
Alençon, Charles d', 140
Jean II, duke of, 1, 44, 100–1, 103–6, 108, 109, 110, 111, 114, 117, 118, 121, 128, 135, 137, 196, 202, 210–12, 213, 214, 222–3, 233, 236, 241
René d', 63, 90 n. 28, 91 nn. 35, 36; 105, 106, 109–12, 115, 135, 222, 233, 236, 239
allegiance, divided, 10, 11, 15–16
Amboise, Charles, lord of, 129, 137, 215
Georges d', bishop of Montauban, 77–8, 234, 236
Louis d', *vicomte* of Thouars, 30, 63, 118, 195–6, 239
Pierre d', lord of Chaumont, 86, 126, 137, 196, 197, 215
Amiens, 167
Anglade, lord of, 206
Anjou, Charles I d', count of Maine, 196, 202, 214–15, 217
Charles II d', count of Maine, 224, 226
Louis, duke of, 176, 181, 182, 183
René, king of Sicily and duke of, 203, 229–30, 237, 242
appeal of Gascon lords, 45–6
appeal of treason, *see* procedure
Aragon, Yolande d', 196
Arc, Jeanne d', 211
Armagnac, Charles d', *vicomte* of Fezansaguet, 45, 140, 220
Armagnac, counts of, 142
Bernard VI, 87
Bernard VII, 25, 127, 193
Jean IV, 33, 44, 45, 47, 51, 56, 93, 201–3
Jean V, 35, 45, 81–2, 90 n. 25, 101–3, 126, 128, 129, 130, 135, 137, 140, 209–10, 212, 213, 214, 218, 219–20, 220–1, 223, 236
Armagnac, Jacques d', *see* Nemours
Armagnac, Jean, bastard of, 146
Jean d', bishop of Castres, 77
see also La Marche; Lescun
Armagnacs, 24, 60, 66, 127, 190, 192, 193, 194
Arpajon, Gui d', *vicomte* of Lautrec, 230
Arras, 85
Artois, 143, 169, 174
Robert III d', 96–7, 101, 102, 143, 180
Aspremont, Arnaud-Raymond d', lord of Roquecor, 157–8
Louis d', *vicomte* of Orthe, 206
Aubigny, Jacques de Bourbon, lord of, 135
Aubusson, Antoine d', 206
Aulnay, Gauthier and Philippe, 29–30, 54
Avaugour, Henri d', 148
Avranches, 204
Aydie, Odet d', lord of Lescun, 128, 137, 221 n. 55, 235

Bacon, Guillaume, 56, 93, 148, 149, 153
Bailleul, Bernard de, 157
Baldus, 14
Balliol, Edward, King of Scotland, 157
Balsac, Ruffet de, 221
Balue, Jean, cardinal of Angers, 22 n. 65, 64, 75–7, 126, 128–9, 217, 218–19, 223
banners, display of, 31, 98
Bantelu, Jean de, 161, 169, 171
Barbin, Jean, king's advocate, 48, 202, 207
Bardi, 39
Barrante, Barradaco de, 178–9
Barres, Pierre des, 165, 170
Bartolus, 14, 24, 76
Batarnay, Ymbert de, lord of Le Bouchage, 49, 64, 129–30, 224, 225
Bayeux, 204
Bayonne, 204
Beaucaire, 184

Beauconroy, Hue de, 156
Beaufort, Jean de, lord of Limeuil, 37, 188
Robert de, lord of Valéry, 230
Beaujeu, Anne de, 234, 236
François de, lord of Ligniers, 230
Pierre de, 109, 110, 111, 221, 234, 236
Beaumanoir, Philippe de, 4, 5, 8
Beaumont, André de, baron of La Haye, 195–6, 206
Louis de, *sénéchal* of Poitou, 206
Beauvais, Vincent de, 24
Beauville, Arnaud de, 158, 159
Gaubert de, 158
Pons de, 158
Bechet, Pierre, 198, 201
Bellemont, Gauvain de, 152, 153 n. 63
Belleville, Jeanne de, 125, 147 and n. 28, 154
lordship of, 125
Belloc, Pierre de, 146
Belon, Jean de, 36
Bergerac, 204
Berri, 174
Jean, duke of, 125, 183, 184, 186, 187
Bigars, Raoul de, 148
Blanot, Jean de, 10–11, 12, 13, 15, 16, 26
Blaye, 146, 200, 204
Blois, Charles de, 148, 149
Blosset, Jean, lord of Saint-Pierre, 129, 225, 227
Bon, Jean, 29
Bonvoisin, Jean, 164
Bordeaux, 136 n. 121, 204, 205
Bos, Hennequin du, 38, 60
Boulogne, 174
Bertrand, count of Auvergne and, 219
Jeanne, countess of, 52
Bourbon, Alexandre, bastard of, 197
Charles I, duke of, 196, 197, 202
Charles II, duke of, constable of France, 114, 243
Jean, duke of, 126, 214, 224
Louis, duke of, 123
Louis de, admiral of France, 225, 226
see also Aubigny; Carency; Clermont; Vendôme
Bourbonnais, 174
Bourg, 204
Bourg, castellan of, 150–1
Bourges, 50, 63, 224
Bournonville, Enguerran de, 56, 192
Boutillier, Jean, 21–2, 23, 26, 52
Bovet, Honoré, 19
Bracton, 8, 52
Breuil, Guillaume de, 20, 68
Brézé, Pierre de, 26, 127, 203, 204, 211
brigandage, 42–3
Brimeu, David, lord of Humbercourt, 127
Brittany, 32, 37, 69, 97, 98, 146, 148, 149, 178, 186, 187, 214, 233, 234, 235
claims to jurisdiction by dukes of, *see* jurisdiction
François II, duke of, 111, 114, 222, 224, 226, 233, 235, 236
Jean III de Montfort, duke of, 146–7, 148, 149, 157
Jean IV de Montfort, duke of, 1, 21, 31, 37, 89, 97–8, 99, 101, 113, 114, 175, 176, 178, 186, 187
Pierre I, duke of, 100
Britton, 52
Brive, 36
Bruges, 182–3
Bueil, Jean de, admiral of France, 203
Bureau, Gaspard, 199
Jean, 200
Burgundians, 24, 58, 60, 192, 193, 220
Burgundy, Antoine, grand bastard of, 114, 129
Burgundy, 37, 112, 121, 172, 230, 231
Charles the Bold, duke of, 31, 32, 37, 45, 94, 112–14, 121, 218, 220, 222, 224, 225, 227, 228, 229, 230, 231, 242
claims to jurisdiction by dukes of, *see* jurisdiction
John the Fearless, duke of, 22, 24, 49, 72, 127, 189, 190, 191, 192, 193, 194, 241
Mary of, 85, 112, 139, 231, 242
Philip the Bold, duke of, 183, 184, 186, 187
Philip the Good, duke of, 211, 216; as count of Charolais, 127

Cabochiens, 191, 192, 193
Cadillac, Alain de, 148
Caen, 184, 204
vicomté of, 174
Caillart, Gilles, 164
Cambron, *see* Rambures
Campbell, John and Robin, 30, 117
Canlers, Jacques de, 63, 215–16
Capdenac, 51
Caramanico, Marinus de, 13
Carcassonne, 119, 135, 142
Cardaillac, Guillaume de, 89, 191
Carency, Pierre de Bourbon, lord of, 135
cas royaux, 18–19
Cassane, Guillaume de, 146
Cassel, battle of, 50, 122, 145
Castillon, Pons de, lord of Bruch, 58
Caumont, Arnaud de, 158
Cazans, Guillaume, 146

Chabannes, Antoine de, count of Dammartin, 49, 64, 106, 121, 128, 129, 138, 139, 196, 203, 206, 207, 209, 213–14, 216–17, 219, 228, 236
Jacques de, 196
Chalais, marquis of, 244
Champagne, 143
Charles de France, 126, 128, 137, 214, 218, 219, 220
Charles IV, King of France, 116, 144, 145
Charles V, King of France, 17, 24, 34, 35, 49, 66, 86, 92, 97, 98, 123, 124, 126, 130–1, 135, 159, 172–82 *passim*, 240, 241
as dauphin, 17, 29, 47, 49, 60, 67, 87, 123, 126, 130, 137, 160, 161, 163–72 *passim*
Charles VI, King of France, 29, 44, 56, 60, 66, 73, 78, 99, 120, 125, 127, 179, 181–94 *passim*, 241
Charles VII, King of France, 30, 34, 36, 48, 49, 52, 63, 80, 93, 100, 103, 104, 105, 108, 120, 121, 123, 127, 128, 195–212 *passim*, 213, 214, 236, 239, 240, 241
as dauphin, 58, 190, 194
Charles VIII, King of France, 3, 78, 112, 139, 140, 220, 233–6 *passim*, 240
as dauphin, 29, 228
Charnier, Guillaume, lord of Chêne-Arnoult, 235
Châtel, Tanneguy du, governor of Roussillon, 128
Chazau, Charles de, lord of Lamothe-Saint-André, 205
Cinq-Mars, Henri Coiffier de Ruzé, marquis of, 243, 244
Clères, Jean, baron of, 160
clergy, rejection of benefit of, 69, 73, 74, 76–7, 79–82, 184
clerics, prosecution of, 44, 45, 163 n. 3, 164, 184, 205
degradation of, 71, 74, 76, 78–9
ecclesiastical jurisdiction after conviction by crown, 72–3
ecclesiastical jurisdiction after preliminary royal procedure, 69–70, 75
exclusive ecclesiastical jurisdiction, 69
exclusive royal jurisdiction, 45, 57, 79–80, 184
mixed jurisdiction, 71, 74, 78
papal participation in royal prosecution, 77–8
participation by crown in ecclesiastical procedure, 69, 70–1, 71–2, 76
preference by king for papal prosecution, 75, 76, 77
punishment of, 71, 72, 73, 78–9, 118
separate royal and ecclesiastical jurisdictions, 75, 76
see also Amboise, Georges d'; Armagnac, Jean d'; Balue; Guichard; Haraucourt; Latilly; Marconnay; Martigny; Poitiers, Guillaume de; Pompadour; Porte; Saisset
Clermont, Jean de Bourbon, count of, 209
Simon de, 192
Clisson, Olivier III de, 55, 125, 147, 148, 150, 153, 240
Olivier IV de, 46, 97, 135, 175, 178, 186–7
Cocquerel, Firmin de, mayor of Amiens, 167
Code Michaud, 243
Codex Justinianus, 7
Codex Theodosianus, 7
Coëtivy, Olivier de, 198, 199
Prégent de, 127, 199
Coëtmen, Olivier de, 235
Coeur, Jacques, 1, 52, 56, 63, 64, 81, 90 n. 28, 91 n. 33, 93, 118, 119, 121, 128, 135, 137–8, 141, 207–9, 239
Commynes, Philippe de, 118 n. 16, 215 n. 15, 226, 234, 236
Conhac, Bernard de, lord of Bouillac, 157
Corbie, Robert de, 171
Courcelles, Louis de, lord of Breuil, 46, 117
Courtrai, Sohier de, 145–6
Cousinot, Guillaume, lord of Montreuil, 64, 75, 76, 210, 222, 223
coutumiers, 2, 4, 5, 9, 20
Crannes, Guillaume de, 192
Craon, Pierre de, 46, 125, 136, 187, 188, 191
Créqui, Le Bègue de, 169, 171
crimen maiestatis, 6–7
crown, concept of, 16–17, 26
Croy, Philippe de, lord of Chimay, 225, 229 n. 104
Crussol, Louis de, 128
Crusy, Hugues de, 52
customary law, 4–5, 9, 20

Daillon, Jean, lord of Le Lude, 129, 215
Dauphiné, 25–6, 49–50, 213
Dauvet, Jean, king's proctor, 52, 100, 122, 138, 209
Dax, 204
defensio regni, 18, 238
Deken, Guillaume de, 145, 240
Délicieux, Bernard, 71
Derby, Henry of Grosmont, earl of, 150, 151
Desmier, Jean, 221
Dieppe, 35
diffidatio, 5, 21, 31, 161
Digest, 7, 76

Dionne, Jean, 165
Domfront, 204
Doublel, Colin, 155, 161, 164
Dubois, Etienne, 229
du Bois, Guillaume, 173
Dunois, François de, 234, 235
  Jean, count of, 196, 202, 211, 223
Durand, Guillaume, 12, 13, 14, 15, 16
Durette, Martin Sens, captain of Pont-Audemer, 177
Durfort, house of, 158–60
  Bertrand de, 206
  Gaillard de, lord of Duras, 205, 206

Edward III, King of England, 20, 49, 59, 96, 97, 117, 147, 149, 150, 151, 152, 153, 155, 157, 170, 173, 175, 241
Enghien, Louis d', 220 n. 48
England
  Statute of Treasons, 28
  treason by clerics, 82
  treason in, 1–2, 8, 32, 33, 35, 38, 47, 52, 53, 54, 57, 61, 62–3, 82, 88, 94, 116, 118, 120, 137
Equennes, Robert d', *vicomte* of Poix, 167, 169, 171
Escluse, Hector de l', 137, 229
Essarts, Pierre des, 60, 135, 190
Estouteville, Robert d', *prévôt* of Paris, 227
Etablissements de Saint Louis, 5, 9, 11
Eu, Raoul de Brienne, count of, 55, 154, 162, 240
Evreux, Charles d', count of Etampes, 125
  Louis d', 125

false witness, 4
Fauvel, Miquelot, 91, 229
Flanders, 143, 145
  Gui de Dampierre, count of, 31, 95
  rebellion of 1320s, 50, 122–3, 240
  rebellion of 1380s, 50, 182–3
  Robert de Béthune, count of, 31, 92, 95–6, 114, 142, 143, 180
Fleta, 52
Floquet, Robert de, *bailli* of Evreux, 127
Foix, counts of, 142
  Gaston Fébus, 160, 161
  Gaston IV, 199, 202
  Roger Bernard III, 87
Foix-Candale, count of, 206
forfeitures, 3, 22, 37, 39, 40, 50, 56, 64, 79, 86, 87, 89, 97, 98, 100, 105, 112, 113, 143 n. 10, 146, 147 n. 33, 149 n. 43, 150, 154, 157, 158, 163 n. 2, 167, 169, 172 n. 50, 173, 174, 176, 179, 180, 181, 183 n. 10, 185, 187 nn. 32, 34; 190 n. 51, 192, 193 n. 70, 194, 198, 205, 206, 209, 216, 219, 220, 221 n. 56, 224, 230, 231, 234, 235, 240, 241
  debts owed to a traitor, 122
  French lands of Englishmen, 40
  grants to greater nobility, 34, 86, 166, 167 n. 26, 169, 172 n. 52, 173, 174, 175, 178, 196 n. 3, 199, 206, 215, 222
  grants to king's relatives, 123, 125–6, 130, 188, 189, 192 n. 64
  grants to lesser nobility, 86, 124, 130–1, 146, 158, 159, 165, 169, 173, 174 n. 61, 176–7, 182 n. 8, 184, 206, 216 n. 19, 220 n. 48, 223 n. 68, 229 n. 104
  grants to principal crown officers and favourites, 124, 126–30, 165, 172 n. 53, 173, 176–7, 194 n. 74, 205, 215 n. 15, 220 n. 48
  miscellaneous grants, 130, 153, 157 n. 83, 165, 194 n. 74
  opposition to restitution, 137–40, 213 n. 2, 231
  partial restitution, 137, 196, 215
  property of a traitor's wife, 120–1
  restitution, 136, 157, 164, 171, 173, 175, 220
  restitution to member of traitor's family, 109, 134–5, 137–40, 153 nn. 63, 64; 164, 165, 167 n. 26, 192 n. 64
  royal commissions, 122–5
François I, King of France, 140, 242
Frénal, Alain de, *vicomte* of Mortain, 177
Fricamps, Friquet de, 161, 171
Fusoris, Jean, 71–2

Gaillon, Jean de, 169, 173 n. 53
Gaius, 6
Galard, Jean de, lord of Limeuil, 86, 160
Ganelon, 116
Garencières, Yon de, 124, 126–7, 177
Garlande, Guillaume de, lord of Charlais, 157
Gaucourt, Charles de, 226
Gauville, Guillaume de, 168, 173
Gerson, Jean, 24
Ghent, 145, 183
Giac, Pierre de, chancellor of Berri, 127
Gié, *see* Rohan
Gilles, Pierre, 164
Girard, Raoul, *vicomte* of Breteuil, 177
Givart, Philippe, 164
Glanville, 8, 52
Godart, Jean, 164
Got, Bertrand, lord of Puyguilhem, 159

Gouge, Martin, bishop of Clermont, 194 n. 74
Gougnon, Guillaume, 229
Graville, Jean Malet, lord of, 55, 137, 155, 160, 161, 164, 241
Grouchy, Nicolas de, 151–2
Guesclin, Bertrand du, 97, 126, 172, 173, 176, 178
Guichard, bishop of Troyes, 29, 75
Guillet, Robert, *vicomte* of Evreux, 173
Guines, 156, 174
Guyenne, 20, 37, 45, 51, 58, 97, 117, 128, 142, 146, 150, 157–60, 173, 188, 204, 205, 206, 218, 219
  treason by English duke of, 45, 97, 173–4

Hangest, Jean de, lord of Genlis, 139
Haraucourt, Guillaume de, bishop of Verdun, 75–7, 218, 219, 220
Harcourt, Godefroy d', 1, 57, 148–9, 150, 151, 152, 154, 155, 161, 240
  Jean V, count of, 55, 137, 155, 156, 160, 161, 162, 241
  Jean VI, count of, 134, 171, 174
  Louis d', archbishop of Rouen, later patriarch of Jerusalem, 210, 215 n. 11
  Louis d', *vicomte* of Châtellerault, 134, 155, 156, 161, 174
Hardi, Jean, 29, 62, 117, 223
Henri III, King of France, 242
Henri IV, King of France, 116, 243
Hermite, Tristan l', 64, 85, 199, 206, 217, 218, 222, 236
Hôte, Nicolas l', 243

Ile-de-France, 50, 182
Innocent III, Pope, 9, 10
Isernia, Andreas de, 13–14
Isle, Jean de l', 164
Isle-Jourdain, 126
  Jourdain de l', 46, 57, 88, 116, 144–5
ius resistendi, 11

Jame, Pierre, 12–13, 19
James II, King of Scotland, 30
Jaucourt, Jean de, 90 n. 31, 233–4
Jean II, King of France, 29, 47, 55, 65 n. 78, 69, 86, 87, 154–63 *passim*, 165, 166, 171, 172, 240, 241
  as duke of Normandy, 49, 125, 150, 151
Jews, 62
John XXII, Pope, 144
Juge, Boffile de, 108, 111, 112, 129, 140
jurisdiction, 2, 239
  baillis, *sénéchaux* and *prévôts*, 58–9, 66, 68, 70, 80, 84, 153
  cession to towns, 66
  Châtelet, 34, 38, 39, 52, 53, 59–61, 84, 187, 189, 190
  claims to jurisdiction by dukes of Brittany, 68
  claims to jurisdiction by dukes of Burgundy, 68
  cour du roi, 94, 95–6
  grand conseil, 48, 84, 200, 219
  Grands Jours, 58, 84
  king alone, 29, 55–6, 84, 85, 147, 154, 161
  king and council, 56–7, 73, 84, 92–3, 97, 144, 149, 171, 185, 202
  king's lieutenant, 181, 219
  military officers, 61–2, 67, 84, 85, 197, 229, 239
  municipal claims to, 2, 65, 84, 239
  Parlement of Bordeaux, 242
  Parlement of Grenoble, 58, 84, 231
  Parlement of Paris, 17, 29, 30, 31, 32, 37, 40, 47, 48, 49, 52, 57, 60–1, 66, 77, 79, 84, 88, 89, 93, 116, 117, 136, 144–5, 147, 148, 149, 150, 151, 154, 187, 188, 189, 191, 199, 200, 201, 209–10, 213, 217, 219–20, 222–3, 227, 228, 229, 230, 231, 232, 233, 234, 235, 236, 239, 240
  Parlement of Paris in trial of peers, 96–115, 235
  Parlement of Poitiers, 48, 58, 84, 195
  Parlement of Toulouse, 58, 68, 84, 244
  prévôt de l'hôtel, 62
  prévôt des marchands and *échevins* of Paris, 62
  prévôt of Paris, *see supra* Châtelet
  royal commissions, 48, 49, 63–4, 67, 71, 75, 78, 79, 80, 84, 85, 156, 168, 184, 195, 204, 206, 207, 208, 215, 217, 222, 223, 224, 226, 228, 233, 239, 244
  seigneurial claims to, 2, 66–8, 84, 239
  see also clerics
Jouvenel des Ursins, Guillaume, 105, 127, 209
Juvenal des Ursins, Jean, 25, 105, 117, 212

kingship, theocratic view of, 5

La Chapelle, Pierre de, 17, 67
Ladit, Thomas de, chancellor of Navarre, 160, 164
Lalande, lord of, 206
La Marche, Bernard d'Armagnac, count of, 202
  Charles de, 125
  Thomas de, 172 n. 50

Lancastrian France
forfeitures, 131–4
jurisdictional conflict between church and crown, 82–4
law of treason, 40–4
Langoiran, 205
Languedoc, 184
Lansac, Mondot de, captain of Cognac, 205
Laon, 36, 167, 184
La Roche, Guiot de, 198, 201
Jean de, 196, 197
La Roche-Tesson, Jean de, 56, 93, 120, 149, 153
Latilly, Pierre de, bishop of Châlons, 28, 69
La Trémoïlle, Georges I de, 195, 196, 197, 199
Georges II de, lord of Craon, 129, 231, 232
Gui de, 127
Louis de, 235
Lau, Antoine du, *sénéchal* of Beaucaire, 53, 128, 206, 216
Laval, Fulk de, 148
La Vallette, Bernard de Nogaret, duke of, 244
Leblont, Pierre, 164
Le Boulanger, Jean, 64, 223, 226
Le Breton, François, 242
Le Coq, Robert, bishop of Laon, 44, 49, 79, 160, 166–7, 170, 171–2, 177
Leduc, Guillaume, 229
Le Flament, Geoffroy, 166 n. 17, 170, 171
Nicolas, 166 n. 17, 183
Le Mans, 36
Le Mercier, Denis, 234, 235
Lens, Charles de, admiral of France, 127
lepers, 52–3, 62
Le Plessis, Raoul, lord of, 192
Le Puy, 181
Lescun, Jean de, bastard of Armagnac, count of Comminges, 234, 235
lese-majesty, 2, 8, 9, 10, 11, 12, 13, 14, 15, 18, 20, 21, 22, 24, 25, 26, 27, 31, 32, 33, 37, 38. 40, 44, 46, 47, 48, 49, 50, 51, 52, 53, 60, 62, 68, 73, 76, 82, 86, 98, 99, 113, 117, 147, 151, 152, 166, 174, 177, 181, 183, 184, 194, 201, 217, 220, 230, 238, 242, 243, 244
in first degree, 18, 22, 25, 44, 47, 48, 166
in second degree, 22, 25
in third degree, 22, 76
Leseur, Jean-Pierre de, 242
Lettre, Robert de, *vicomte* of Evreux, 177
lex Falcidia, 8
lex Julia maiestatis, 2, 7, 10, 20, 21, 25, 28, 181, 184
lex Quisquis, 2, 7–8, 20, 22, 25, 28, 46, 120, 181
Libourne, 204
Limousin, 174
Limoux, 142
Lisieux, 51
lit de justice, 98, 99, 103, 235
Le livre des droiz et des commandemens d'office de justice, 68
Li livres de jostice et de plet, 5
Lorraine, Charles duke of, 33, 47, 89, 190–1
René, duke of, 225
Lorris, Robert de, lord of Hermenonville, 156, 160
Louis IX, King of France, 8
Louis X, King of France, 18, 19, 69, 95, 125, 143
Louis XI, King of France, 17, 29, 31, 45, 49, 62, 63, 66, 70, 75, 77, 82, 86, 91, 94, 106–13 *passim*, 115, 117, 121, 122, 126, 128, 129, 130, 135, 137, 138, 139, 140, 191, 196, 201, 206, 213–33 *passim*, 236, 237, 239, 240, 242, 244
as dauphin, 35, 49, 51, 196, 197, 202, 203, 204, 207, 209, 213, 214, 242
Luillier, Philippe, captain of the Bastille, 226
Luxembourg, Jacques de, lord of Richebourg, 129
Jean de, count of Marle, 93, 129
see also Saint-Pol

Mâcon, Joceran, 164, 165
Madaillon, Amanieu de, 202
Maillotins, 182, 184
Maine, 174
see also Anjou
Mainemarès, Guillaume de, 155, 160, 161, 164
Malestroit, Geoffroy de, father and son, 148
Henri de, 69–70, 149
Malet, Robert, 169
Mantes, 172
Marcel, Etienne, 17, 47, 67, 123, 164, 165, 168, 170
Gilles, 164, 165
Marchès, Mérigot, 33–4, 37, 60, 117, 125, 188
Marconnay, Jean de, bishop of Maillezais, 57, 79, 151
Marès, Jean des, 127, 170, 183–4
Mareuil, Le Bascon de, 171 n. 47
Mariette, Guillaume, 203–4
Marigny, Enguerran de, 56, 93, 116 n. 2, 125
Marmande, Arnaud de, captain of Parcoul, 146
Marrasin, Louis de, captain of La Charité, 229

Martigny, Charles de, bishop of Elne, 79, 232, 237
Masuer, Jean, 25
Maulevrier, Jeanne Crispin, countess of, 215 n. 11
Mauveu, Pierre de, 157
Maximilian, archduke of Austria, 35, 232, 233, 234
Melun, Charles de, 36, 63, 90 n. 28, 91, 128, 135, 137, 138, 139, 213, 217–18, 236, 239
Menou, Jean de, 192
  Pierre de, 192
Mercoeur, Béraud de, 56, 93, 143–4
Millau, 33, 202
Montagu, Charles de, lord of Couches, 220
  Jean de, 1, 60, 187, 190, 191, 192
Montaubon, Jean de, 148
Montdidier, 51
Montespedon, Jean de, *bailli* of Rouen, 128
Montfaucon, Hugues de, 157
Montferrand, Bertrand de, 205, 206
  François de, 205
  Pierre de, 205–6
Montfort, *see* Brittany
Montjean, lord of, 197
Montmirat, Raymond de, 146
Montmorency, Henri II duke of, 244
Montpellier, 50, 136 n. 121, 181, 182
Montpezat, Raymond de, 151
Morvilliers, Pierre de, 217, 218
Motte, Gaillard de la, 151
Murat, *vicomté* of, 89

Narbonne, *vicomte* of, 142
Navarre, Charles the Bad, King of, 17, 29, 30, 37, 39, 55, 56, 67, 68, 79, 92, 96, 97, 99–100, 101, 123, 124, 126, 134, 137, 155, 156, 160–76 *passim*, 179, 180, 185, 186, 240, 241
  Louis de, 161
  Philippe de, count of Longueville, 31, 126, 155, 161, 171, 173
Navarrese, 56, 97, 123, 124, 126, 130, 135, 163, 167, 168, 169, 170, 171, 172, 173, 176, 177, 178, 179
Nemours, Jacques d'Armagnac, duke of, 1, 17, 63, 64, 82, 91, 106–9, 115, 129, 130, 135, 137, 140, 218, 219, 221, 224, 226, 227–8, 229, 233, 236, 239
Neufchâtel, 33, 191
Nîmes, 50, 181
Normandy, 37, 49, 50, 51, 56, 63, 97, 123, 124, 130, 137, 143, 146, 148, 149, 150, 151, 152, 154, 155, 160–2, 163, 168, 169, 176, 177, 178, 182, 184, 202, 204, 205, 210, 240
  see also Lancastrian France

Orange, Jean de Chalon, prince of, 26–7, 29, 32, 35, 53, 58, 118–19, 129, 130, 231–2, 233, 235, 236
Orgemont, Nicolas d', 56, 72–3, 93, 193
Orgessin, Ligier d', captain of Pacy, 177
Oriole, Pierre d', 64, 106, 107, 109, 128–9, 222, 223, 226, 227, 228
Orléans, 184
  duchy of, 174
  Charles, duke of, 104, 202
  Louis I, duke of, 22, 44, 125–6, 188, 189, 190
  Louis II, duke of (King Louis XII), 78, 114, 234, 235, 236
Orval, Arnaud-Amanieu, lord of, 206

Pape, Gui, 25–6, 49–50, 53, 63
Parcoul, 146
pardons, 3, 29, 33, 38, 39, 45, 51, 52, 65, 67, 69, 70 n. 101, 80, 86, 106, 111, 135–7, 146, 149 n. 41, 153 n. 63, 156, 157, 158, 159, 160, 163, 164, 166, 167, 170, 171, 173, 175, 177, 178, 179, 180, 182, 184, 185, 187, 190, 191, 192, 193, 196, 197, 198, 199, 200, 201, 202, 203, 204, 205, 206, 214, 215, 216 n. 21, 219, 221, 224 n. 70, 226, 229, 230, 236, 240
Paris, 36, 63, 64, 72, 123, 136 n. 121, 163, 164, 165, 166, 167, 168, 171, 182, 183, 184, 192, 193
Parlement of Paris, 24, 46, 59
  procedure, 88–92
  see also jurisdiction
Patri, Raoul, 149
peers, trial of, 57, 94–115, 239–40
  see also Alençon, Jean II, duke of; Alençon, René d'; Artois, Robert d'; Bourbon, Charles II, duke of; Brittany, François II, duke of; Brittany, Jean IV de Montfort, duke of; Burgundy, Charles the Bold, duke of; Flanders, Robert de Béthune, count of; La Vallette; Montmorency; Navarre, Charles the Bad, King of; Nemours; Orléans, Louis II, duke of
Penthièvre, Jeanne de, 98
Percival, Jacques, 198, 201
  Olivier, 198, 201
Percy, Richard de, 56, 93, 126, 149, 153
perduellio, 6–7

Périgord, 188–9
  Archambaud V, count of, 33, 188
  Archambaud VI, count of, 33, 126, 189
Périgueux, 33, 188–9
Peruzzi, 39
Pestillac, Amalvin, lord of, 157
Petit, Jean, 22–3, 53, 104, 190
petty treason, 4
Philippe III, King of France, 31
Philippe IV, King of France, 18, 28, 29, 31, 69, 74, 75, 87, 88, 95, 118, 142, 143
Philippe V, King of France, 52, 62, 143, 144
Philippe VI, King of France, 39, 50, 55, 65, 69, 80, 86, 96, 97, 117, 120, 121, 122, 125, 145–54 *passim*, 158, 159, 240
  as count of Valois, 125, 144
Picardy, 143, 169, 174
Picquigny, Ferri de, 88, 143
  Gérard de, 171
  Jean de, 163, 164, 167, 169
  Mathieu de, 163, 169
  Philippe de, 171
  Robert de, 123, 167, 171
Pierrelongue, Raymond de, 146
Pisan, Christine de, 19
Pisdoe, Martin, 56, 93, 166 n. 17, 171
Ploesquellec, Maurice de, 36, 81, 127, 198–9
Poitiers, Guillaume de, bishop of Langres, 57
  Jean de, lord of Saint-Vallier, 243
  Louis de, count of Valentinois and Diois, 125
Poitou, 39, 130, 174, 175, 198, 199
Pompadour, Geoffroi de, bishop of Périgueux, 77–8, 234, 236
Pompignac, Henri de, *sénéchal* of Castres, 229
Pons, Jacques de, *vicomte* of Turenne, 90, 127–8, 198, 199–201, 213
  Renaud de, lord of Ribérac, 146
  Renaud VI de, *vicomte* of Turenne, 37, 174
Porte, Robert, bishop of Avranches, 49, 79, 171, 177–8
Port-Sainte-Marie, 51, 151
Pot, Guiot, *bailli* of Vermandois, 129, 139
Pouillet, Simon, 48, 117, 153
Praguerie, 31, 49, 196, 197, 199, 241
Préaux, Pierre de, 149
Presles, Raoul de, 28, 56
Prévôt, Jean, 164
Prie, Antoine de, 197
procedure, 3, 239–40
  appeal of treason, 85, 86, 87, 89, 143, 203; false appeal, 53
  before king and council, 85, 92–3
  defaults for contumacy, 89–90
  determinants of, 85
  judgement by king's record, 56, 79, 86, 147, 148, 152, 161, 168, 172, 180
  judgement by notoriety, 86–7, 98, 99–100, 174, 240
  posthumous, 93–4, 99–100, 112–14, 243–4
  procédure extraordinaire, 85, 88, 90–2, 106, 107, 108, 239
  procédure ordinaire, 85, 88–90, 107, 114, 239
  state trials other than trials of peers, 85, 92
  summary execution, 55, 56, 85, 152, 154, 197, 199, 229, 240
  torture, 91, 145, 156, 218
  see also peers, trial of; trial by battle
proditio, 24, 74
public good, 15–16
Puisieux, Pierre, 17, 126, 164
punishment, 3, 6, 19, 21–2, 23, 54, 93, 105, 109, 145, 154, 189, 191, 238
  abscission of hands, 116, 145
  abscission of tongue, 164
  banishment, 50, 118, 149, 150, 153, 184, 187, 192, 197, 201, 205
  boiling alive, 118
  burning of corpse, 22, 116, 118
  castration, 118
  decapitation, 30, 38, 55, 56, 116, 117, 118, 146, 147, 148, 151, 152, 161, 164, 171, 172, 183, 184, 204, 206, 218, 226, 227, 234
  drawing, 30, 38, 116, 117, 118, 145, 147, 148, 244
  drowning, 118, 197
  execution in effigy, 26–7, 118–19
  fines, 51, 119, 181, 182, 184, 187, 205, 207, 209, 229, 236
  flaying alive, 22, 118
  gouging out of eyes, 29, 118
  hanging, 116, 117, 118, 145, 146, 147, 148, 151, 164, 199, 206
  imprisonment, 105, 118, 143, 153, 196, 206, 207, 209, 216, 220, 223, 229, 236
  pillory, 54, 118, 145
  quartering, 30, 116, 117, 152, 171, 172, 204, 206, 226, 234
  razing of castles and houses, 215, 221, 234
  wheel, 118, 145
  see also clerics
Puyanne, lord of, 34

Quiéret, Gui, 163

raison d'état, 18, 244
Rambures, Jacques de Cambron, lord of, 220 n. 48
Ravaillac, François, 116

Raymond, Guillaume, lord of Caumont, 146
Jean, 198, 201
Reims, 184
Remi, Pierre, 116–17, 125
Repenti, Filippo, 164
Révigny, Jacques de, 11, 12, 13, 15, 16, 19
Ribes, André de, 202
Richard II, King of England, 88, 188
Richelieu, Cardinal de, 243, 244
Richemont, Artur de, 104, 195, 202, 203
Richier, Jean, 229
Rivière, Poncet de, 224 n. 70, 226
Rohan, Pierre de, lord of Gié, marshal of France, 58, 94, 129, 224
Rolin, Antoine, lord of Aimeries, 225
Roman law, revival of in France, 8–9
Roman law of treason, 2, 6–9, 15, 20, 21, 22, 23, 24, 25, 26, 93
Roquefeuil, Jean, lord of, 230
Rouault, Joachim, marshal of France, 119, 217, 220 n. 48, 229
Rouen, 50, 63, 136 n. 121, 156, 182, 204
routiers, 33–4, 194–201
Rue, Jacques de, 57, 92, 123, 176

Sacquenville, Isabelle de, 124
Marguerite de, 126
Pierre de, 123, 126, 161, 168, 171, 172
sacrilege, treason as, 17, 21, 23, 45, 99
Saincoins, Jean Barillet, lord of, 52, 63, 119, 207, 209
Saint-Antonin, 51, 157
Saint-Cire, Brimet de, 198, 201
Saint-Flour, 219
Saint-Fuscien, Jacques de, 167
Saint-Gelais, Pierre de, 198, 201
Saint-Jean-d'Angély, 51, 136 n. 121, 157
Saint-Macaire, 51, 204, 205
Saint-Maixent, 34
Saint-Pol, Louis de Luxembourg, count of, constable of France, 1, 2, 64, 90 n. 32, 91, 106, 113, 117, 129, 135, 137, 139, 203, 224–7, 228, 229, 236
Waleran de Luxembourg, count of, 56, 93, 185
Sainte-Aude, Jean de, 171
Sainville, Louis de, 229
Saisset, Bernard, bishop of Pamiers, 1, 56, 73–5, 92, 93, 142, 153
Salisbury, William Montagu, earl of, 147
Savoy, Amadeus VI, count of, 29, 165
Amadeus VIII, duke of, 202
Seyches, Rudel, lord of, 157
Simon, Jean, king's advocate, 81, 82, 100, 101, 102
Songe du verger, 20, 21, 22
Sorel, Agnès, 207
Soupplainville, Guillaume de, 137, 221 n. 55, 235
sovereignty, 2, 5, 6, 9–14, 19, 20, 21, 25, 26, 31, 32, 37, 44, 45, 47, 58, 102, 113, 142, 238
Spain, Charles of, 155, 160
Sully, Henri de, 144

Taillebourg, lordship of, 127, 198, 199
Terre-Vermeille, Jean de, 14, 23–5, 69
Tertre, Pierre du, 57, 92, 123, 124, 125, 176
Tesson, Jean, 124
Thibouville, Robert de, 148, 149
Thou, Jacques-Auguste de, 243, 244
Tilly, Jean de, 169
torture, *see* procedure
Tournebu, Jean de, lord of Marbeuf, 169
Robert de, 169
Villart de, 169
Toussac, Charles, 163, 164, 165
trahison, 2, 21, 238
treason
accepting bribes, 52
adhering to enemy, 20, 25, 35, 38, 67, 69, 70, 86, 89, 95, 98, 113, 150, 157, 167, 170, 174, 178, 231
against army, 30
against crown, 17, 21, 26, 51, 60, 76, 80, 87, 94, 119, 147, 151 n. 54, 165, 174, 217
against dauphin, 164, 190
against king, 4, 17, 18, 20, 21, 22, 24, 25, 26, 34, 38, 39, 47, 60, 74, 87, 94, 116, 147, 152, 172, 190, 195, 207, 208, 217, 230
against kingdom, 4, 20, 24, 25, 26, 33, 34, 35, 39, 51, 53, 74, 116, 119, 172, 217
against public weal, 16, 20, 22, 24, 30, 52, 80, 94, 112, 147, 198, 217, 230
against royal councillors, 20
against royal relatives, 22, 23 n. 65, 29, 53, 185
appealing to Roman Curia, 46
assaulting royal officers, 25, 46, 47, 66–7, 144, 155, 165, 186, 187
attempted *coup d'état*, 30, 195, 203, 224, 228
bearing arms against king, 34, 56
betrayal of strategic places, 25, 35, 146, 151–2, 168, 221, 222; unsuccessful, 36, 67, 72, 152, 154, 171, 185
betrayal of state secrets, 25, 70, 143
breach of loyalty, 5, 21, 26, 34, 37, 112, 205
by towns for adhering to enemy, 51, 157, 193, 204, 205
by words, 47–8, 59, 74, 153, 164, 165, 166, 177, 185, 242, 243

treason—*cont.*
communicating with enemy, 45, 71, 78, 210, 215, 216, 217, 242, 243
concealment of, 21, 53–4, 217, 243
conspiring with enemy, 100, 106, 210, 222
counterfeiting coin, 18, 52
counterfeiting royal seal, 18, 52, 204, 208
crimes on public highways, 53, 66
desecrating royal insignia, 47, 201
desertion, 25, 35
encompassing death of dauphin, 29, 165 171
encompassing death of king, 11, 17, 20, 21, 23, 28, 29, 48–9, 52, 53, 70, 113, 165, 176, 185, 223, 224, 228, 231
engaging in commerce with enemy, 38, 80, 208
espionage, 38–9, 65, 156
exporting corn in time of famine, 242
felony, 1, 4, 27, 98
free-booting, 33–4, 197–201
giving counsel, comfort and aid to enemy, 21, 23, 25, 39
going absent without leave, 35
helping convicted traitor escape from prison, 23, 26, 53, 216 n. 20
illicit convocation of assemblies, 25, 44, 242
inciting to sedition, 48–9, 70, 112, 152
infidelity, 5, 12, 20, 24, 26, 27, 74, 220, 231
in natural law, 99
levying taxes without royal permission, 242
levying troops without royal permission, 25, 177, 197, 242, 243
levying war against king, 10, 11, 12, 14, 19, 21, 31–2, 51, 86, 95, 98, 112, 174
living voluntarily in enemy territory, 39–40, 170, 180, 241
Maitland's definition of, 1
necromancy, 23, 53, 71, 78, 165, 190
negotiating with enemy, 44, 145, 147, 165, 185, 201
obstructing appeals to king's courts, 45–6, 173
obstructing military operations against enemy, 23, 25, 217
peculation, 52, 116, 119, 190, 207, 208, 229
perjury, 5, 27, 37, 98, 153, 177, 220
poisoning wells, 52–3, 62
porte d'armes, 26, 242
private war, 18, 19, 32–3, 119
rebellion, 31, 32, 49, 51, 61, 86, 87, 106, 142, 143, 147, 165, 184, 219, 231, 234
refusing entry to royal troops, 36
regicide, 28, 116
resisting royal officers, 18, 47
rural rebellions, 50
sedition, 21, 32, 220
selling military equipment to enemy, 38, 71, 208
selling military places, 151, 154, 156, 185
sowing dissension between king and army, 49
sowing dissension between king and dauphin, 49–50, 203–4
stealing state papers, 233
surrendering stronghold without undergoing siege, 35–6
unauthorized maintenance of troops, 198, 219
unauthorized occupation of stronghold, 25, 36
unauthorized waging of war, 25
under law of arms, 34–7, 56, 85
urban revolts, 50–1, 181–4
usurpation of sovereignty, 20, 25, 45, 113, 165, 201–2, 209, 220
violation of safe-conduct, 4, 18
violation of safeguard, 18, 45, 89, 119
violation of truce, 4, 33, 37, 89, 119
trial by battle, 85, 87–8, 143, 239
Tuchins, 50
Tudert, Jean, 100, 101–2

Ulpian, 6
Urfé, Pierre d', 226, 234
Usage d'Orlenois, 5, 9

Valois, Charles de, 125, 143, 144
Valrichier, Vincent de, 170, 171
vassalage, 5–6
Velourt, Renaud de, 226, 229
Vende, Robert, *vicomte* of Beaumont-le-Roger, 177
Vendôme, Jean de Bourbon, count of, 196, 202, 230
Verdun, Roland de, 151, 152
Verneuil, 204
Vervins, Jean de, lord of Bosmont, 152–3
Vivonne, Antoine de, 195–6, 206

War of the Public Weal, 25, 31, 214–15, 216, 217, 218, 222, 230
war, public (just), 2, 5, 10, 11, 12, 14, 19, 31
women
punishment of, 22, 118
treason by, 8, 22, 39, 40, 45, 52, 59, 79, 86, 124, 125, 126, 135, 147, 159
Worthington, Robert, 185.

Lightning Source UK Ltd.
Milton Keynes UK
09 December 2010

164137UK00001B/15/A